Strategic Management
in the 21st Century

Strategic Management in the 21st Century

Volume 1:
The Operational Environment

Timothy J. Wilkinson, Editor

 PRAEGER

AN IMPRINT OF ABC-CLIO, LLC
Santa Barbara, California • Denver, Colorado • Oxford, England

Copyright 2013 by ABC-CLIO, LLC

Library of Congress Cataloging-in-Publication Data

Wilkinson, Timothy J.
  Strategic management in the 21st century / Timothy J. Wilkinson and Vijay R. Kannan, editors.
     v. cm.
  v. 1. The Operational environment — v. 2. Corporate strategy — v. 3. Theories of strategic management.
  Includes index.
  ISBN 978-0-313-39741-7 (hbk. : 3 vol. set : alk. paper) — ISBN 978-0-313-39742-4 (ebook)   1. Strategic planning.   2. Strategic alliances (Business).
3. Management.   I. Title.
  HD30.28.W524   2013
  658.4'012—dc23   2012041185

ISBN: 978-0-313-39741-7
EISBN: 978-0-313-39742-4

17   16   15   14   13   1   2   3   4   5

This book is also available on the World Wide Web as an eBook.
Visit www.abc-clio.com for details.

Praeger
An Imprint of ABC-CLIO, LLC

ABC-CLIO, LLC
130 Cremona Drive, P.O. Box 1911
Santa Barbara, California 93116-1911

This book is printed on acid-free paper ∞

Manufactured in the United States of America

Contents

commercial landscapes. The origin of modern strategy and its evolution over time can be found in the writings mentioned above, and more
demonstrably in military history's battles and wars. Moreover, the distinctions between strategy and tactics contribute to the military's great and
unmistakable impact upon the development of the concept of strategy.[7]

STRATEGY—FROM MARTIAL ART TO MARKETS—THE WHO

Historically, one of the first acknowledged uses of strategy in business
happened when Socrates counseled the Greek militarist, Nichomachides, after he had lost an election for the position of general to the Greek
businessman, Antisthenes. Comparing the duties of a general with that
of a businessman, Socrates demonstrated to Nichomachides that both instances required planning how to use one's resources to meet objectives.
Unfortunately, this viewpoint was apparently lost with the fall of the
Greek city-state and was not resurrected until after the beginnings of the
Industrial Revolution.[8]

Table 1.1 portrays the development of modern strategic thought. The
first vestiges of what would become modern strategy resulted as an outcome from the then newly emerging vertically integrated, multidivisional
corporations of the late 1800s and early 1900s. These corporations made
large investments in manufacturing and marketing and in managerial
hierarchies to coordinate those functions. Over time, the largest of these
companies managed to alter the competitive environment within their industries and to even cross industry lines.[9] The need for a more formal
approach to corporate strategy was first brought to the forefront by top
executives of these large, vertically integrated and multidivisional corporations. Among the most notable were Alfred Sloan, chief executive of
General Motors from 1923 to 1946, who devised a strategy explicitly based
upon the perceived strengths and weaknesses of its competitor, Ford
Motor Company.[10] Chester Barnard, a top executive with AT&T, argued in
the 1930s that managers need to pay especially close attention to "strategic
factors," which depend on "personal or organizational action."[11,12]

It wasn't until after World War II that the concept of strategy, as related to business, began to move to the forefront. It was at this time that
business moved from a relatively stable, if not static, environment into
one comprising increasingly rapid change and competition. Igor Ansoff,
considered by some as the father of modern strategic thought, has attributed this evolution to two significant factors: first, the marked increase in
the rate of change within and between firms, and second, the accelerated
application of science and technology to the process of management.[13]
This acceleration in the rate of change places a premium on the ability
to anticipate change, take advantage on new opportunities, and to proactively avoid threats to the firm. New technologies spawned interest in,

which literally translates as "tricks of war." The Romans are also credited with introducing the terms *stragia* in referring to the territories under the control of a military commander, and *strategus*, referring to a member of the council of war.[5]

Strategy as applied to the art of war was revolutionized at the time of the French Revolution and the subsequent Napoleonic wars. Napoleon capitalized upon the advancements in armament technology and the lessening of the costs associated with the tools of war. He employed a brutally effective "strategy of annihilation" (read scorched earth) that placed little value on the mathematical perfection of geometric strategy. His goal was to achieve victory in the battlefield. His sole aim was the utter and total destruction of his opponent, usually achieving this success through the deployment of superior maneuvers.

The 19th century marked the beginning of a new era in warfare and by extension in the development of strategy. The most notable contributors of the time are Carl von Clausewitz (1780–1831) and Antoine Jomini (1779–1869). Clausewitz's seminal work, *On War*,[6] stressed the close relationship between war and national policy. He emphasized the importance of the principles of mass, economy of force, and the destruction of enemy forces. In contrast, Jomini focused on the occupation of enemy territory through a combination of carefully planned, rapid, and precise geometric maneuvers.

The 19th century was an era of far-reaching technological changes that radically altered the breadth and scope of both tactics and strategy. Railroads and steamships extended the volume, reach, and speed of mobilization. Telegraphic communications linked widening theaters of operations and by extension made large-scale strategy and tactics both possible and necessary. The impact of technology has only increased since the late 20th century, and will continue to increase as we proceed the 21st century.

Ultimately, the development of a strategy requires the ability to accept uncertainty. Strategists must come to accept that they will not have all of the information they need and will not be able to see the full spectrum of events. Yet they must be committed to creating and implementing strategy. Uncertainties exist, not only from incomplete information, but also as the result of the actions of a dynamic and thinking opponent. The design of a strategy with a specific opponent in mind and undetermined actions is what requires a strategist to accept, if not embrace, uncertainty. The inherent uncertainty associated with strategy is one of the key reasons why so many military and business leaders cling to the tangible world of tactics and options.

Strategy's roots in the military have had a significant impact upon their adoption and adaption in the world of business. Going as far back as the works of Sun Tzu in the period of 400 BC, one sees that strategy has been an important force in the shaping of political, sociological, and entity needed to develop "something," a feature, survival mechanism, approach, or other means of differentiation, that provided it with a unique advantage. In the realm of human existence, competition first exhibited itself in the need to protect and preserve—to protect oneself and the other members of the clan from the elements and nature, and later from those who needed or coveted what they had. As the nature of man continued to change, there became an increased desire to use or possess what belonged to others. This often manifested itself in the form of forays into the territory, or raids on the possessions, of others. At first, these ventures were most likely conducted in a manner that was random and disorganized. As the powers of perception and cognitive abilities of human beings improved, the search for a "better way" began to emerge. This better way entailed the achievement of the desired result in a more efficient and effective manner. This desire for a better way was the very foundation of what was to become strategy.

The unique combination of acquired wisdom, craft, and later science, has led to the creation of strategy and its use as a much sought after skill. The utilization of strategy has changed the map of the world. Long before its application to commerce, it was responsible for the rise and fall of nations and their people. The "tap root" of what we know as strategy can be found in the history of the military arts. Looking back at this beginning provides the foundation for a more thorough understanding of the genesis of the discipline.

STRATEGY—A MARTIAL ART

The beginning of organized forms of strategy sprang from the need for people either to defend themselves or to defeat their enemies. In keeping with the earlier extrapolation of Gause's principle, this is really a manifestation of competition between similar entities requiring the same resources. At the extreme, competition presents itself as warfare. Among the earliest acknowledged writings discussing the concepts of strategy is the Taoist Sun Tzu's *The Art of War* written around 400 BC. The title of the work is somewhat misleading in as much as the text addresses the concepts of strategy in a much broader fashion by also referencing public administration and planning. Although the text does outline theories of battle, it also delves into the area of diplomacy and the need to cultivate relationships with other nations as being essential to the overall well-being of a state.[2]

The word strategy is derived from the Greek word *strategos,* which actually translates as "general." As such, it was originally viewed in the more narrow confines as the "art of the general," or the "the art of arrangement" of troops.[3,4] The term *strategamata* is the title of an early Latin work attributed to Frontius. It describes a collection of *strategema*, or stratagems,

Chapter 1

The Origins of Strategy and Strategic Thought

Marc D. Sollosy

COMPETITION LEADS TO STRATEGY

In 1934, Professor Gause of Moscow University published the results of a series of experiments that led to Gause's principle of competitive exclusion. This principle contends that no two species can coexist when they make their living in the identical way. When any pair, or more, of species compete for essential resources, sooner or later one will overcome the other. Without some form of intervening factor that helps to maintain equilibrium by providing each species an advantage in its own territory, only one of them will survive. For millions of years, this natural competition required no strategy. Survival was based upon the laws of probability. Strategy was not involved; rather, adaptation and survival of the fittest was the modus operandi. This pattern of survival exists for all living organisms.[1]

Gause's principle—that competitors making their living in the same way cannot coexist—explains the phenomenon of competition. Similar entities often required the same resources in order to exist. As competition among entities for these common resources became more intense, ways to achieve an advantage became increasingly important. Each

Part I

The Basics of Strategy

place for "settled" theories. At the same time, insights from older strategic management theories can remain just as relevant today as when they appeared decades ago, as demonstrated by Tom Hinthorne's SWOT analysis of the Northrop Grumman Corporation.

Strategic Management in the 21st Century is divided into three volumes. *Volume 1: The Operational Environment* sets the stage upon which businesses make their strategic decisions. The volume begins with a section on the history of strategy, which is followed by chapters explaining the societal context that forms, and is formed, by the strategic decisions of firms. Ron Hrebenar's chapter on political strategy is a reminder (as well as a primer) on how politics can be used to further the goals of businesses. Given the resurgence of federal government statism, understanding lobbying is more important now than it ever has been. Corporate social responsibility, entrepreneurship, gathering firm resources, and strategic alliances are also discussed in volume 1.

Volume 2: Corporate Strategy focuses on the practical implications of strategic management for firms. The volume examines many of the nuts-and-bolts issues that face managers as they endeavor to implement firm strategy. Understanding competitors, mergers and acquisitions, human resource management, and corporate financial strategies are among the topics explored. Robert Winsor's chapter on marketing is a primer on the trade-offs that necessarily take place as managers prefer one strategy over another. Amitava Mitra's explanation of how quality became a major strategic objective in the 20th century and how firms must embrace it if they are to be successful in the 21st century provides a link between strategic objectives and the quality initiatives of firms. Other topics covered include innovation, corporate culture, and outsourcing.

Volume 3: Theories of Strategic Management departs from the applied focus of the volume set, and takes a thorough look at the frameworks that have shaped strategic management ever since Ansfoff initiated the field with his product-market growth matrix in 1957. The volume begins with a history of strategic management, including an overview of the discipline's roots in military strategy. After covering the basic theoretical trajectory of the field—structure, conduct, performance, the resource-based view, transaction cost economics, hypercompetition, and the like—the volume diverges into an exploration of related topics. These include excurses into areas such as trust, entrepreneurship, and corporate social responsibility.

My fellow editor, Vijay R. Kannan, and I believe that this set is a comprehensive and in-depth examination of the field of strategic management. Because it ranges from rich presentations of theory, to their practical applications, it should prove to be a valuable resource to scholars, students, and business strategists. We are pleased to present to you *Strategic Management in the 21st Century.*

Set Introduction

Timothy J. Wilkinson

For such a new field of inquiry, strategic management exhibits a breadth of ideas and robustness of thought that places it at the forefront of business disciplines. Unlike academic marketing, where "A" level journal articles seem to apply ever-greater levels of statistical sophistication to increasingly trivial questions, strategy is theoretically rich and eminently practical. Years ago I heard the CEO of Barco—the Belgian projection systems company—explain the firm's strategy with the use of terms such as "price premium," "quality focus," and not wanting to get "stuck in the middle." After his presentation I asked if he had ever hired Michael Porter as a consultant. He said that he hadn't, but that his management team had read Porter and it was through Porter's lens that they viewed company strategy. Newer ideas from the strategy domain are also being embraced as analytical tools by firms. The resource-based view, the dynamic capabilities perspective, and real options theory have each yielded insights that have helped companies become more effective competitors. At the same time, the conscious application of many strategic management theories to real-world situations remains limited for most business enterprises.

The most evident contribution of strategy theory may be its ability to help us understand what has already happened in the past. The digital overthrow of the analog world's rigid industrial boundaries upended the neat categories of Porter's static analysis. Robert R. Wiggins and Frances H. Fabian's chapter on hypercompetition clearly explains this phenomenon, and demonstrates why theorizing in strategy is likely to remain a work in progress. A world driven by constant change is not a comfortable

Table 1.1
Development of Modern Strategic Thought

Who	What	When
Alfred Chandler	Strategy and Structure	1952
Igor Arcoff	Corporate Strategy	1955
Peter Drucker	The Age of Discontinuity	1959
Michael Porter	Competitive Strategy	1980
Kenichi Ohmae	The Mind Of the Strategist	1982
Peter Senge	The Fifth Discipline	1990
Hammer & Chempy	Reengineering The Corporation	1993
Henry Mintzberg	The Rise And Fall of Strategic Planning	1994
Hamel & Prahalad	Competing For the Future	1994

and ultimately acceptance of, analytical and explicit approaches to decision making. This resulted in the increasing ability of management to deal with the expanding uncertainties of the future.[14]

Viewing the development of strategic thought in a loose chronological order brings us to Von Neumann and Morgenstern, who were among the first modern writers to relate the concepts of strategy to business in their opus, *Theory of Games and Economic Behavior.*[15] In that work, they defined strategy as a series of actions by the firm decided upon according to the particular situation facing the firm. Since the release of *Theory of Games and Economic Behavior,* numerous other writers have developed subsequent concepts and theories of strategy.

In his work, *The Practice of Management,* Peter Drucker argued that rather than being passive and adaptive, management is about taking action to achieve desirable results. He noted that prevalent economic theory had long viewed markets as impersonal forces, beyond the control of the individual entrepreneur and organization. With the emergence of the vertically integrated, multidivisional corporation, managing "implies responsibility for attempting to shape the economic environment, for planning, initiating, and carrying through changes in that economic environment, for constantly pushing back the limitations of economic circumstances on the enterprise's freedom of action."[16] In Drucker's view, strategy is about analyzing the present situation and changing it if necessary. Underlying this view is the need for finding out what one's resources are or what they should be.[17]

Philip Selznick first introduced the concept of matching the organization's internal factors with the external environment in 1957 with the publication of *Leadership in Administration: A Sociological View.*[18] This core idea would later be developed by E. P. Learned, K. R. Andrews and others at the Harvard Business School General Management Group into what has more commonly become known as SWOT (strengths, weaknesses, opportunities, and threats).[19]

Alfred Chandler expressed the importance, for the first time, of coordinating the various and often disparate aspects of management under one all-encompassing strategic umbrella. Prior to Chandler's work, the various functions of management were often separated with little, or no, overall coordination or strategy. What interactions existed between functions or departments were typically handled by a boundary position wherein one or two managers relayed information back and forth between the departments. Chandler further emphasized the importance of taking a long-term perspective when looking to the future. His work *Strategy and Structure*[20] posited that a long-term coordinated strategy was required in order to give a company structure, direction, and focus. Chandler viewed strategy as the determiner of the basic long-term goals of an organization, and the adoption of courses of action and the allocation of resources necessary for carrying out those goals.

Igor Ansoff built upon the work of Chandler and others to develop the keystone approach to the emerging field of corporate strategy through a framework of theories, techniques, and models. In his book *Corporate Strategy: An Analytical Approach to Business Policy for Growth and Expansion*,[21] Ansoff presents a grid of elements that compare market penetration, product development, market development, and integration and diversification. By understanding and using these strategic elements, he felt management could systematically prepare for future opportunities and challenges. In this work, he developed "Gap" analysis, which posits that management must try to understand the gap between where they currently are and where they would like to be, and then develop what he described as "gap reduction actions."

Prior to Ansoff, there was little in the way of guidance for companies on how to plan for, or make decisions about, the future. Planning was traditionally based upon existing budgeting systems, used for annual budgets, and was intended for just a few years into the future. This approach largely ignored strategic issues. However, as competition increased, along with greater interest in acquisitions, mergers and diversification, and higher turbulence in the business environment, strategic issues could no longer be overlooked. According to Ansoff, strategy development was essential and required the company to systematically anticipate future environmental challenges, and to develop plans to appropriately respond to those challenges. To Ansoff, strategy is a rule for making decisions determined by product/market scope, growth direction, competitive advantage, and synergy.[22]

If Igor Ansoff is considered the father of modern strategic thought, then Michael Porter is its "rock star." An economist by training, Porter made his mark in the area of strategy with the publication of "How Competitive Forces Shape Strategy."[23] His principal and enduring contribution to the field of strategy is the concept of the five forces analysis, where he identifies the forces that shape a firm's strategic environment. The five forces analysis is similar to Selznick's SWOT analysis with the structure and purpose focusing on the external forces that shape a company's strategic environment. This approach portends to provide an approach for a company to obtain a sustainable competitive advantage. Where Chandler presented the concept of structure following strategy, Porter extended it by introducing a second level; organizational structure follows strategy, which in turn follows industry structure.

In addition to the five forces, Porter contributed to the strategic knowledge base by writing about the generic strategies, the value chain, strategic groups, and clusters. Porter's work on generic strategies focuses on the interactions between cost-minimization strategies, product-differentiation strategies, and market-focus strategies. Although he did not conceive these terms or concepts, his work does highlight the importance of choosing one over another rather than trying to position the company between them. Porter proposes that a firm will only be successful to the extent that it contributes to the industry's value chain. As such, management must look at the operations of their companies from the viewpoint of the customer. Every operational facet of the company needs to be examined in light of the value it adds in the eyes of the customer. This view is grounded in Porter's economic training of supply and demand, where the buyer will purchase a given quantity at a given price, where the price differential is equal to the perceived incremental added value of the product or service.

A principal criticism of Porter's view of the firm is that it is based on a rather static perception of the world, with the size of markets being fixed. In essence, companies compete in a zero-sum game where one company's gain in market share comes at the loss of another company's.[24]

As the nature of the economy and its technological underpinnings began to change so did perceptions of strategy and strategic activities. One of the earliest thinkers who reexamined the paradigm of strategy was Kenichi Ohmae. Ohmae's view was that successful strategy stems from creative minds, not from some rote formula. In his seminal work, *The Mind of the Strategist,* published in 1982, Ohmae wrote that successful strategy comes from a thought process that is creative and intuitive rather than simply from step-by-step analysis. He defines strategy as the way a corporation attempts to differentiate itself positively from its competitors, using its relative strengths to better satisfy customer needs. He goes on to assert that strategy is really no more than a plan of action for maximizing one's strengths against the forces at work in the environment.[25] Ohmae focuses on how organizations allocate and utilize resources. To be effective, a company's strategy should be difficult to imitate, and to achieve this, the company must either develop a completely new product or make use of a position of relative superiority. Jay Barney, a strong proponent of the criticality of the organization's internal resources, would later extend this view and suggest strategy as assembling the optimum mix of resources, including technological, human, and supplier relations, and then configuring them in unique and sustainable ways.[26] This is what is known as the resource-based view.

The delineation between strategy and strategic planning is exemplified by the works of Henry Mintzberg. In *Crafting Strategy,*[27] Mintzberg likens the strategic process to a craft. He presents the position that strategies are not necessarily deliberate acts, but that they can also emerge through circumstances; and that they can form as much as they are formulated. He also goes on to expand upon the old adage "those who cannot remember the past are condemned to repeat it,"[28] with his assertion that organizations must make sense out of the past if they hope to manage the future. He asserts that only by understanding the patterns of past behavior does an organization come to know its capabilities and potential.

To Mintzberg, strategy provides a vehicle for organizations and individuals to examine their internal and external worlds.[29] Finally, Mintzberg's contention that because analysis is not synthesis—implying that strategic planning is not strategy formulation—has been the source of much intellectual discourse, particularly by Ansoff.[30]

Continuing along the line of thought started by Ohmae and Mintzberg, Gary Hamel and C.K. Prahalad question the more traditional approach to strategy development. In "Competing for the Future,"[31] they suggest that companies need to spend less time talking about strategy and planning and more time thinking about strategizing, which entails the concepts of "strategic intent," "strategic architecture," "industry foresight," and "core competencies." The last of these may be the best known and most important concept to come from their work.[32] Core competencies are those one or two key things a company does better than any of its competitors.

Around the same time that Hamel and Prahalad were writing about core competencies, Michael Hammer and James Champy published *Reengineering the Corporation*,[33] where they proposed that the internal resources of the company need to be restructured around whole processes rather than just tasks. They asserted the benefits of having a team of people see a project through, from inception to completion. They posited that this approach avoids functional silos where isolated departments seldom communicate with each other, as is so often found in organizations. They felt that this approach had the benefit of eliminating waste due to functional overlap.

The next logical step in the evolution of strategic thought was presented by Peter Senge. He examined the impact of the Information Age upon a company's performance. In "The Fifth Discipline,"[34] Senge presents the theory that a company's ability to gather, analyze, and use information is necessary for success in the Information Age. In what is an extension of the work of his predecessors, Senge proposes that an organization needs a structure through which people can continuously expand their capacity to learn and be productive—new patterns of thinking are nurtured, collective aspirations are encouraged, and people are encourage to see the "whole picture" together. Thinking strategically starts with reflection on the deepest nature of the undertaking and on the central challenge that it possesses.[35] The most commonly cited barrier to the implementation of what Senge proposes is that few organizations come close to having the characteristics that he identifies with a learning organization. However, with the growth in the focus of knowledge management in an increasingly globalized economy, an organization might begin to increase focus and attention on the development and growth of its employees, who primarily create the intellectual capital of the organization.

The list of contributors to the development and advancement of the study of strategy is extensive. The preceding group is by no means intended to be all inclusive. Rather it attempts to touch upon those whose contributions, some argue, had the most impact, if by no other measure than their respective popularity and notoriety.

The preceding thinkers and authors shaped the discussion on strategy during the last half of the 20th century. Their respective contributions are indisputable and provide the foundation for any further discussion regarding strategy. However, with the transition from the 20th to the 21st century came a transformation.

The age of the Internet, the networked world, has brought about a major, some suggest a tectonic, shift in the way commerce is viewed and conducted. What became known as the "dot-com" world defied long-established economic principles. The rush was to "Web enable" the enterprise in some manner regardless of its economic value. The mantra of the time, to quote the movie *Field of Dreams*, was "if you build it they will come." However, the era of the "dot-com" quickly became the age of the "dot-gone." Although visibility on the Web was, and is, increasingly important, profits still matter. Carl Shapiro and Hal R. Varian in their work *Information Rules: A Strategic Guide to the Network Economy*,[36] stress that you ignore basic economic principles at your own risk. Technology changes, but economic laws do not. The book addresses a number of issues, including pricing and versioning information, rights management, recognizing and managing lock-in, switching costs, and how to account for government policy and regulation in strategy development.[37]

Although Shapiro and Varian examined the impact of the Internet, another phenomena had been entrenching itself in the landscape of commerce. Historically, capital was viewed as a physical or financial item—it manifests itself as building and equipment, or what could be found in corporate balance sheets. Beginning in the 1990s, the emergence of a more elusive form of asset, the intangible asset often identified as intellectual capital, began to command attention. Senge addressed the issue in *The Fifth Discipline: The Art and Practice of the Learning Organization*,[38] and in 1994 Drucker wrote that "the true investment in the knowledge society is not in machines and tools but in the knowledge of the knowledge worker."[39]

Intellectual Capital by Thomas Stewart[40] serves as a guide to understanding and managing intangible assets. Steward posits that merely understanding what intellectual capital comprises is only part of the issue. The real value of intellectual capital, and other intangible assets, comes from the organization's ability to capture and deploy these assets. The effective strategic utilization of intellectual capital can serve as a competitive differentiator in the market. "Knowledge assets, like money or equipment, exist and are worth cultivating only in the context of strategy. You cannot define and manage intellectual assets unless you know what you to do with them."[41,42]

It becomes increasingly evident that the field of strategy is a discipline that is still evolving and will continue to evolve to keep pace with the dynamic nature of modern commerce. There are no clear indications as to where strategy may be heading over the coming years. As Yogi Berra once famously said, "The future ain't what it used to be." There does appear to be a growing consensus in the strategy field that the world is unpredictable and by extension, the future is inherently unknowable because of the chaotic nature of events.

An area of potential applicability is the field of chaos theory. Chaos theory examines the underlying behaviors of systems, which are ruled by simple physical laws, but where the actual events appear so unpredictable they might as well be random. The field studies the complex relationships that underlie the "everyday" systems we encounter and observe in the real world. The greatest contribution of chaos theory is the revelation that even simple systems seem to create extraordinarily difficult problems of predictability. The universe is chaotic, ruled by entropy, and a never-ending tendency toward disorder. Long-term planning has been notoriously ineffective in predicting the future. In fact, detailed planning systems, and their underlying economic support systems, cannot be effective because of lack of certainty about what will happen next. Strategy needs to borrow from the physical sciences, most notably physics and biology. These lenses stress adaptability, flexibility, and speed of change. The old order of static positioning and long-term competitive advantage are no longer adequate. It is not just "running faster" but "thinking faster" that makes a difference.[43]

STRATEGIC THINKING VERSUS STRATEGIC PLANNING

The concept of strategy is often used interchangeably for the concept of strategy formation. Although it is easy to blend, even confuse the two, in reality, they are distinct, but related activities. In fact, the standard dictionary definition of the word strategy only contributes to the lack of clarity. On the www.merriam-webster.com/dictionary Website, the definition of strategy is as follows:

1a (1): the science and art of employing the political, economic, psychological, and military forces of a nation or group of nations to afford the maximum support to adopted policies in peace or war
(2): the science and art of military command exercised to meet the enemy in combat under advantageous conditions
b: a variety of or instance of the use of strategy
2a: a careful plan or method: a clever stratagem
b: the art of devising or employing plans or stratagems toward a goal

It is not until you get to 2a of the definition that the meaning of strategy as applied in the context of business becomes evident.

In order to clarify the definition, it becomes appropriate to consider the concept of strategy separately from the process of strategy formation. To start, strategy embraces almost all of the critical activities of a firm. That is, strategy provides a sense of unity, direction, and purpose, as well as accommodating the changes necessitated by the firm's environment. Hax[44] suggests that the following six dimensions need be included in any unifying definition of strategy:

1. Strategy as a coherent, unifying, and integrative pattern of decisions. Strategy gives rise to the plans that assure that the basic objectives of the enterprise are met, and that it is conscious, explicit, and proactive.
2. Strategy needs to be considered as a means of establishing an organization's purpose in terms of its long-term objectives, action programs, and resource-allocation priorities. This clearly indicates that resource allocation is a firm's most critical aspect of strategic implementation and effectiveness.
3. Strategy needs to be considered as a definition of a firm's competitive domain. One of the principal concerns of strategy is defining the businesses a firm is in or intends to be in, and relates back to dimension (1) mentioned earlier.
4. Strategy needs to be considered as a response to external opportunities and threats and in internal strengths and weakness as a means of achieving competitive advantage. A central objective of strategy is the achievement of a long-term sustainable advantage over a firm's key competitors.
5. Strategy needs to be considered as a logical system for differentiating managerial tasks at corporate, business and functional levels. This point recognizes the various hierarchical levels in most organizations, and that each level has differing managerial responsibilities in terms of their contribution in both defining and operationalizing the strategy of the firm.
6. Strategy is a definition of the economic and noneconomic contribution the firm intends to make to its stakeholders. It is easy for managers to fall into the trap of "bottom line/short-term" profitability as the ultimate driving force. Sustained profitability is the legitimate and desired outcome of a well-executed strategy.

It becomes apparent from the previously mentioned text that strategy encompasses the overall purpose of the organization. As such, defining it properly entails examining all of the multiple aspects that comprise the whole. Strategy becomes a framework by which an organization

asserts it continuity, while managing to adapt to the changing environment in order to achieve competitive advantage.[45]

Further examination of the literature on the difference between strategic thinking and strategic planning provides little clarity. Strategic planning is often associated with a programmatic, analytical thought process,
whereas strategic thinking refers to a creative, divergent thought process.
The source of the confusion lies in the fact that although the terms are
frequently used, they are often used in fundamentally different ways
by different authors. For some, strategic thinking and planning are distinct modes that are both useful at different stages in the strategic management process (e.g., Mintzberg); others posit that strategic thinking
is not so much creative as analytical (Porter). Still for some, strategic
planning remains an analytical activity, but the organizational practices
surrounding it have been transformed, whereas others believe the real
purpose of the analytical tools of strategic planning is to facilitate creativity, which is a part of strategic thinking. Last, for a select group, strategic planning is a useless activity that should be scrapped in favor of
strategic thinking.[46]

Heracleous[47] proposes that strategic planning and strategic thinking are two distinct thinking modes, and that strategic thinking needs
to precede strategic planning. This view is based upon the premise that
planning cannot produce strategies because its focus is programmatic,
formalized, and analytical. Planning is what happens after the strategy
has been decided upon, discovered or purely emerges. Mintzberg[48] en-
dorses this view by suggesting that the concept of strategic planning
is based upon three principal fallacies. First is the fallacy of prediction,
the belief that planners can accurately predict what will happen in the
marketplace. Second is the fallacy of detachment, the basis of which is
that effective strategies can be produced through formalized processes
by planners who are detached from business operations and the market.
Last is the fallacy of formalization, a disputable concept suggesting that
formalized procedures can produce strategies, whereas their appropriate
function is to operationalize existing strategies.

The preceding view stresses that strategic thinking and strategic planning involve distinctly different thought processes. Strategic planning
is analytical, systematic, and convergent, whereas strategic thinking is
synthetic and divergent. This view challenges conventional wisdom regarding strategic planning by seeking to limit planning to the operation-
alization of existing strategies as opposed to being able to generate new
or creative strategies. In contrast, Porter and others believe that strategic thinking is analytical. Porter supports this view with his analytical frameworks of five forces analysis, the value chain, the diamond
model of national competitive advantage, and strategy as an activity
system. In this view, strategic thinking is not a synthetic and divergent

thought process; rather, it is convergent and analytical, and therefore used interchangeably with the term strategic planning.[49]

In reality, although an organization may begin with a rational plan, what evolves may be something very different than what was actually intended. These "emergent" strategies evolve as part of a pattern in a stream of actions, as opposed to any preconceived plan.[50]

Liedtka[51] suggests that in the face of unpredictable, highly volatile, and competitive marketplaces, a capacity for innovative, divergent strategic thinking at multiple levels of the organization is central to creating and sustaining competitive advantage.

Liedtka's[52] examination of strategic thinking led her to present five major attributes of strategic thinking, as follows:

1. Strategic thinking reflects a system or holistic view that appreciates how the different parts of an organization influence each other, as well as their different environments.
2. Strategic thinking embodies a focus on intent. This contrasts with the traditional approach that focuses on creating a "fit" between existing resources and emerging opportunities. Strategic intent intentionally creates a substantial "misfit" between them.
3. Strategic thinking involves the ability to think in the time continuum. Strategic thinkers understand the interconnectivity of past, present, and future.
4. Strategic thinking is hypothesis driven. By asking the question "what if" followed by the critical question "if then," strategic thinking spans the analytical-intuitive chasm Mintzberg refers to in his definition of thinking as synthesis and planning as analysis.
5. Strategic thinking raises the capacity to be intelligently opportunistic. It means to recognize and take advantage of newly emerging opportunities.

The ability to think strategically facilitates another dimension of the process of strategy making. It recognizes that strategic thinking and planning are distinct, but interrelated and complementary thought processes.[53,54] Heracleous[55] asserts that thinking and planning must sustain and support each other for effective strategic management. He observes that creative groundbreaking strategies emerging from strategic thinking still must be operationalized through convergent and analytical thought (strategic planning).

The previously mentioned view suggests that the real purpose of strategic planning is to facilitate strategic thinking, where the structured planning tools of strategic planning are used to aid creative thinking. One of the principal tools associated with this view is "scenario planning," a process for examining appropriate responses to a spectrum of possible futures. The tool facilitates managers in questioning their underlying assumptions, and sensitizes their thinking to potential competitive arenas substantially different from their current ones. Schoemaker[56] describes scenario planning as a "thinking tool and communication devise that aids the managerial mind rather than replace it." It is particularly valuable in times of high uncertainty and complexity in that it challenges the status quo. Scenario planning is a tool that aids an organization's ability to identify trends and uncertainties in the macro-environment. It provides a means for sketching possible futures by capturing a range of options, stimulating thinking about alternatives, and challenging the prevailing mindset.[57] De Geus[58] suggests that value of planning does not reside in the plan itself, but in changing the mental models of managers involved in the process.[59]

The ability to think strategically gives meaning and insight to the process of strategic planning. It recognizes that strategic thinking and planning are "distinct, but interrelated and complementary thought processes," that must sustain and support each other for strategic management. Creative, groundbreaking strategies that emerge from strategic thinking still have to be operationalized through convergent and analytical thought (strategic planning). Planning is vital, but cannot produce unique strategies that challenge existing boundaries, unless it stimulates the creative mindset in the process.[60]

STRATEGIC PLANNING VERSUS STRATEGIC MANAGEMENT

The previous section discusses the differences between strategic thinking and strategic planning. Although the differences between the concepts seem subtle, it is important to understand and recognize them. The same is true when it comes to the differences between strategic planning and strategic management. Although very closely related, and to some interchangeable, there are important distinctions between them. One can actually look at the variations as a continuum, where strategic thinking begets strategic planning, which in turn begets strategic management. However, in reality the process is a continuous loop, not a continuum with a beginning and an end.

As discussed earlier, Mintzberg[61] calls the phrase "strategic planning" an oxymoron. He argues that real strategies are rarely the result of paneled conference room meetings, but are more likely to result informally from real-time hallway conversations, casual work groups, or casual moments of reflection.[62] Mintzberg sees strategic management as encompassing both strategic thinking and strategic planning, where strategic thinking is synthetic and divergent and strategic planning is analytical, systematic, and convergent. Taking this view, one can see that strategic management is the result of both the thinking and planning processes. However, it should not be viewed as the end; rather it is the action and subsequent checkpoint of the previous steps that then serves as the new beginning to the recursive cycle.

Having examined some of the differences between thinking and planning, with an emphasis on thinking, let's examine the more intricate aspects of planning. Hax and Majluf[63] suggest three levels of planning: corporate, business, and functional. The corporate strategic plan is the result of a disciplined and well-defined organization-wide effort aimed at completely specifying corporate strategy. Andrews[64] expressed corporate strategy as "the pattern of decisions in a company that determines and reveals its objectives, purposes, or goals, produces the principle policies and plans for achieving those goals, and defines the range of business the company is to pursue, the kind of economic and human organization it is or intends to be, and the nature of the economic and non-economic contribution it intends to make to its shareholders, employee, customers, and communities. . . . [it] defines the businesses in which a company will compete, preferably in a way that focuses resources to convey distinct competences into competitive advantages."

The planning process entails three major tasks that need to be updated and revised at every planning cycle. These three tasks are strategy formulation, strategic programming, and strategic and operational budgeting. Planning at the corporate level should not be considered a top-down or a bottom-up process. Rather, it is a complex, integrative activity requiring participation by all the key members of the organization who propose objectives from the top; and equally, participation from business and functional levels of the organization for specific pragmatic alternatives. It provides a rich communication mechanism giving voice to managers about their personal beliefs regarding the conduct of the firm. It offers key participants a valuable shared experience.[65]

A cornerstone of the strategic planning process involves segmenting the organization's various activities in terms of business units. This requires asking and answering the question: What business are we in? On the surface, this question is deceptively simple, yet in practice, it represents one of the most challenging and vexing questions faced by most organizations and requires creative and extensive analysis to fully answer. This criterion of segmentation may be valid for a vertically integrated, multidivisional corporation. However, most companies have difficulty breaking their businesses into totally unrelated units. In general, businesses within the same organization share resources in order to exploit economies of scale and maximize resource utilization. As such, most business activities need to be properly and adequately coordinated.[66]

It should be noted that "general planning" and strategic planning are not the same. Although the role of planning in general is indisputable, the value of formal strategic planning is subject to something less than unanimity. However, there seems to be little doubt that most managers find it extremely useful, if not outright essential. What then is the real value of formal strategic planning? The extant literature seems to conclude that its principal role is to help an organization make better strategies using systematic, logical, and more rational approaches to strategic choices.[67] Henry[68] describes the functions of a fully developed strategic planning system to:

1. Determine organizational purpose and management philosophy,
2. Identify internal strengths and weaknesses,
3. Monitor changes in the external environment,
4. Forecast future conditions and establish planning premises,
5. Determine threats and opportunities,
6. Formulate specific goals,
7. Identify and evaluate alternative policies and strategies,
8. Select the best strategic plan,
9. Prepare functional action plans, and
10. Prepare action plans.

The ultimate success of strategic planning is very much dependent upon the willingness and abilities of senior managers to make strategic decisions in the first place. It may well be that strategic planning is felt necessary by managers, analysts, and lower-level professionals in the organization because of a leadership vacuum. The call for strategic planning is really a call for leadership and direction. Because strategic planning is viewed primarily as a means for making strategic decisions, it is often mistakenly imagined that a mere formal process can generate a strategy.[69]

The path of strategic planning has been less than smooth. At the end of the 1970s, it had suffered a downturn in popularity and influence. This was attributable, in large part, to the apparent inability of strategic planning tools to deliver what was expected of them. The 1970s were a period of turmoil and firms had begun to learn that what was then called "long-range planning" and less ambitiously, "strategic planning," did not lead to the requisite adaptability or even survival. During the 1990s, strategy and strategic planning had regained some of the reputation and influence they previously lost. A contributing reason may well have been the increasing belief that practical strategic advice can be based on sound deduction and systematic observation.[70] This resurgence of practical strategy making may be attributable to the development of Barney's[71] resource-based view of strategy. The core implication to management of this view is that a firm may secure a strong performance with the acquisition of unique or scarce resources.[72]

Quinn[73] suggests that the real contribution of the corporate strategic planning systems is actually the process itself, rather than the decision. The main role of the planning session is to create a network of information, to force managers to focus on the future, to encourage rigorous communications about strategic issues, to raise the comfort level of managers, and to confirm earlier strategic decisions. Formal strategic planning and strategic planners do not make strategic decisions; rather, people and organizations make strategic decisions. Sometimes they use strategic planning as a discipline to facilitate the outcome. It appears that formal strategic planning is as much a social as a rational analytical process that varies according to organizational type. This view is supported by Boyd[74] who notes that strategic planning is one tool to manage environmental turbulence. Others, notably Sinha[75] and Ramanujam and Venkatraman,[76] argue that it is the act of planning that is the real value.

TOOLS OF THE TRADE

The paradigm of strategic management derived from the world of strategic planning is founded on a rational approach to provide strategic direction to the actions of an organization in an increasingly dynamic business environment.[77] Andersen[78] suggests that strategic management is often considered synonymous with strategic planning. This approach has become a dominant framework in the wide array of strategic literature as represented by: *Setting Strategic Goals and Objectives;*[79] *Setting Strategic Goals and Objectives;*[80] *Setting Strategic Goals and Objectives;*[81] *Competitive Strategy: Techniques for Analyzing Industries and Competitors;*[82] and *Setting Strategic Goals and Objectives.*[83]

Many of the contemporary textbooks on strategy support the duel theme of planning and emergence. These books usually present some formal strategic planning model while simultaneously recognizing that important strategic initiatives often emerge from within the organization; two among these are *Strategic Management: An Integrated Approach*[84] or *Crafting and Executing Strategy.*[85] Although the various aspects of strategic planning are generally recognized, it is also important to recognize, and attempt to understand, the complexities of the integrative strategy process and the dynamics of the interaction between emergence and planning.[86]

The spectrum of tools and techniques utilized by firms in strategic planning is extensive. An examination of these tools and techniques reveals four commonly utilized types. They include scenario or "what if" analysis, analysis of "key" or "critical" success factors, financial analysis of competitors, and SWOT analysis. The first, scenario or "what if" analysis is formed by describing a future situation and the corresponding course of events enabling the firm to progress from the original situation to the future situation. There are two major types of scenarios:

exploratory, starting from past and present trends and leading to likely futures, and anticipatory or normative, built on the basis of alternative visions of the future. The major activities of the scenario approach include: identifying the key variables, which is the purpose of a structural analysis, identifying and analyzing the potential actions of those external to the organization, thus identifying key questions about the future, and attempting to reduce uncertainty about those key questions and then to pick the most probable course of action or scenario.[87]

As demonstrated previously, the scenario approach requires the analysis of "key" or "critical" success factors internal to the organization. This coupled with financial analysis of competitors imply consideration for the external influences on the organization. These activities, when taken together, are also reflected in the assessment of the opportunities and threats driving the SWOT analysis often employed by firms. The internal analysis is that portion of the SWOT associated with the strengths and weaknesses, whereas the external analysis examines the opportunities and threats presented to the firm.

Another frequently used tool that expands the external analysis to the broader view of the industry is Porter's five forces/industry attractiveness analysis. At its simplest, Porter's five forces model examines existing rivals and the threat of new entrants, potential for substitutes, and the power or force exerted by the suppliers and customers on the organization. This approach provides integral components of the external appraisal of the organization, leading to a more considered view of the opportunities and threats facing the firm.[88]

Another tool that has contributed to the strategic planning process is the balanced scorecard, as conceptualized by Kaplan[89] and further expanded upon by Norton.[90] What the balanced scorecard does is to extend traditional financial measures of the firm's performance by injecting the perspective of the firm's customers, the performance of internal business processes, and the ability of the firm to continue to learn and grow. It enables companies to track their financial results while simultaneously monitoring their progress in building the capabilities and acquiring the intangible assets they need for future growth. The balanced scorecard is not a replacement for the financial measures of a firm. It rather complements them by integrating accounting and financial information into a management system that focuses the entire organization on implementing its long-term strategic plan and strategy.

The preceding text touches upon a few of the more prevalent tools used in the realm of strategic planning. It is by no means an all-inclusive study of the field of strategic planning, and the tools and approaches accompanying it continue to evolve and develop. Just as the environment in which business and commerce operates takes on new dimensions and complexities, so too must the tools that allow firms to successfully compete

adapt. Keeping in mind Gause's principle, as discussed at the very beginning of this chapter, competitors making their living in the same
way cannot coexist. Similar entities often required the same resources in
order to exist. As competition among entities for these common resources
became more intense, ways to achieve an advantage became increasingly
important. Each entity needs to develop "something," a feature, survival
mechanism, approach, or other means of differentiation, which provided
it a unique advantage. In other words, each organization needs a strategy, a strategic plan, and a strategic management approach that enables it
to survive among its competitors in its given environment.

NOTES

1. B. D. Henderson, "The Origin of Strategy," *Harvard Business Review* 67,
no. 6 (1989), 139–43.
2. M. McNeilly, *Sun Tzu and the Art of Modern Warfare* (New York: Oxford
University Press, 2003).
3. M. Matloff, *American Military History* (Cambridge, MA: Da Capo Press,
1996).
4. A. Wilden, *Man and Woman, War and Peace: The Strategist's Companion*
(London: Routledge, 1987).
5. Rich Horwath, *The Origin of Strategy* (Barrington Hills, IL: Strategic Thinking Institute, 2006).
6. C. Von Clausewitz and C.J.J. Graham, *On War* (Digireads.Com, 2008).
7. Horwath, *The Origin of Strategy.*
8. Jeffrey Bracker, "The Historical Development of the Strategic Management Concept," *The Academy of Management Review* 5, no. 2 (1980), 219–24.
9. A. D. Chandler, *Strategy and Structure: Chapters in the History of the American
Industrial Enterprise* (Frederick, MD: Beard Books, 1962).
10. A. P. Sloan Jr., *My Years with General Motors* (New York: Doubleday/Anchor,
1963).
11. C. I. Barnard, *The Functions of the Executive* (Cambridge, MA: Harvard
University Press, 1968).
12. Pankaj Ghemawat, "Competition and Business Strategy in Historical
Perspective," *Business History Review* 76, no. 1 (2002), 37–74.
13. H. I. Ansoff, *Business Strategy: Selected Readings* (New York: Penguin Books,
1969).
14. Bracker, "The Historical Development of the Strategic Management Concept," 219–24.
15. O. Morgenstern and J. von Neumann, *Theory of Games and Economic Behavior,* Vol. 3 (Princeton, NJ: Princeton University Press, 1947).
16. P. Drucker, *The Practice of Management* (New York: Harper & Brothers, 1954),
364.
17. Bracker, "The Historical Development of the Strategic Management Concept," 219–24.
18. P. Selznick, *Leadership in Administration: A Sociological View* (New York:
Harper & Row, 1957).

19. E. P. Learned, et al., *Business Policy: Text and Cases* (Homewood, IL: R. D. Irwin, 1969).

20. Chandler, *Strategy and Structure.*

21. H. I. Ansoff, *Corporate Strategy: An Analytic Approach to Business Policy for Growth and Expansion* (New York: McGraw-Hill, 1965).

22. Bracker, "The Historical Development of the Strategic Management Concept," 219–24.

23. E. Porter Michael, "How Competitive Forces Shape Strategy," *Harvard Business Review, Boston* 57, no. 2 (1979).

24. J. Middleton, *The Ultimate Strategy Library: The 50 Most Influential Strategic Ideas of All Time* (Oxford: Capstone Publishing, 2003).

25. K. Ohmae, *The Mind of the Strategist* (New York: McGraw-Hill Professional, 1982).

26. J. B. Barney, "Firm Resources and Sustained Competitive Advantage," *Journal of Management* 17, no. 1 (1991), 99–120.

27. H. Mintzberg, "Crafting Strategy," *Harvard Business Review* 65, no. 4 (July/August 1987), 66–75.

28. G. Santayana, *The Life of Reason; Or, the Phases of Human Progress: Introduction, and Reason in Common Sense* (New York: C. Scribner's Sons, 1917).

29. Middleton, *The Ultimate Strategy Library.*

30. H. Igor Ansoff, "Critique of Henry Mintzberg's 'The Design School: Reconsidering The Basic Premises of Strategic Management'," *Strategic Management Journal* 12, no. 6 (1991), 449–61.

31. Gary Hamel and C. K. Prahalad, "Competing for the Future," *Harvard Business Review* 72, no. 4 (July 1994), 122.

32. Middleton, *The Ultimate Strategy Library.*

33. M. Hammer and J. Champy, *Reengineering the Corporation* (New York: HarperCollins, 1993).

34. P. M. Senge, "The Fifth Discipline," *Measuring Business Excellence* 1, no. 3 (1993), 46–51.

35. Ibid.

36. C. Shapiro and H. R. Varian, *Information Rules: A Strategic Guide to the Network Economy* (Cambridge, MA: Harvard Business Press, 1999).

37. Middleton, *The Ultimate Strategy Library.*

38. P. M. Senge, *The Fifth Discipline: The Art and Practice of the Learning Organization* (New York: Doubleday, 1990).

39. Middleton, *The Ultimate Strategy Library.*

40. T. A. Stewart, *Intellectual Capital* (London: Brealey, 1997).

41. Ibid.

42. Middleton, *The Ultimate Strategy Library.*

43. Ibid.

44. Arnoldo C. Hax, "Redefining the Concept of Strategy and the Strategy Formation Process," *Strategy & Leadership* 18, no. 3 (1990), 34.

45. Arnoldo C. Hax and Nicolas S. Majluf, "The Corporate Strategic Planning Process," *Interfaces* 14, no. 1 (1984), 47–60.

46. Loizos Heracleous, "Strategic Thinking or Strategic Planning?" *Long Range Planning* 31, no. 3 (1998), 481–87.

47. Ibid.

48. Mintzberg, *Crafting Strategy*.

49. F. Graetz, "Strategic Thinking versus Strategic Planning: Towards Understanding the Complementarities," *Management Decision* 40, no. 5 (2002), 456–62.

50. Ibid.

51. J.M. Liedtka, "Linking Strategic Thinking with Strategic Planning," *Strategy and Leadership* 26, no. 4 (1998), 30–35.

52. Ibid.

53. Heracleous, "Strategic Thinking or Strategic Planning?" 481–87.

54. Graetz, "Strategic Thinking versus Strategic Planning," 456–62.

55. Heracleous, "Strategic Thinking or Strategic Planning?" 481–87.

56. P.J.H. Schoemaker, "When and How to Use Scenario Planning: A Heuristic Approach with Illustration," *Journal of Forecasting* 10, no. 6 (1991), 549–64.

57. Graetz, "Strategic Thinking versus Strategic Planning," 456–62.

58. A.P. De Geus, "Planning as Learning," *Harvard Business Review* (March–April 1988).

59. D.A. Nadler, "Collaborative Strategic Thinking," *Strategy & Leadership* 22, no. 5 (1993), 30–44.

60. Heracleous, "Strategic Thinking or Strategic Planning?" 481–87.

61. Mintzberg, *Crafting Strategy*.

62. Eric D. Beinhocker and Sarah Kaplan, "Tired of Strategic Planning?" *McKinsey Quarterly*, no. 2 (2002), 48–57.

63. Hax and Majluf, "The Corporate Strategic Planning Process," 47–60.

64. K.R. Andrews and D.K. David, *The Concept of Corporate Strategy* (Homewood, IL: R.D. Irwin, 1987).

65. Hax and Majluf, "The Corporate Strategic Planning Process," 47–60.

66. Ibid.

67. Ann Langley, "The Roles of Formal Strategic Planning," *Long Range Planning* 21, no. 3 (1988), 40–50.

68. H.W. Henry, "Strategic Management: A New View of Business Policy and Planning," in *Commentary on Lorange*, eds. D. Schendel and C.W. Hofer (Boston: Little, Brown, 1979), 245.

69. Langley, "The Roles of Formal Strategic Planning," 40–50.

70. N.J. Foss, *Resources, Firms, and Strategies: A Reader in the Resource-Based Perspective* (New York: Oxford University Press, 1997).

71. Barney, "Firm Resources and Sustained Competitive Advantage," 99–120.

72. K.W. Glaister and J.R. Falshaw, "Strategic Planning: Still Going Strong?" *Long Range Planning* 32, no. 1 (1999), 107–16.

73. J.B. Quinn, "Formulating Strategy One Step at a Time," *Journal of Business Strategy* 1, no. 3 (1981), 42–63.

74. B.K. Boyd, "Strategic Planning and Financial Performance: A Meta-Analytic Review*," *Journal of Management Studies* 28, no. 4 (1991), 353–74.

75. D.K. Sinha, "The Contribution of Formal Planning to Decisions," *Strategic Management Journal* 11, no. 6 (1990), 479–92.

76. Glaister and Falshaw, "Strategic Planning," 107–16.

77. D. Schendel and C.W. Hofer, *Strategic Management: A New View of Business Policy and Planning* (Boston: Little, Brown, 1979).

78. Torben Juul Andersen, "Integrating Decentralized Strategy Making and Strategic Planning Processes in Dynamic Environments," *Journal of Management Studies* 41, no. 8 (2004), 1271–99.

79. J.C. Camillus, *Strategic Planning and Management Control: Systems for Survival and Success* (New York: Simon & Schuster Trade Division, 1986).

80. M. Goold and J.J. Quinn, *Strategic Control: Establishing Milestones for Long-Term Performance* (Boston: Addison-Wesley, 1993).

81. P. Lorange, M.S.S. Morton, and S. Ghoshal, *Strategic Control Systems* (St. Paul, MN: West Group, 1986).

82. M.E. Porter, *Competitive Strategy: Techniques for Analyzing Industries and Competitors: With a New Introduction* (New York: Free Press, 1980).

83. M.D.V. Richards, *Setting Strategic Goals and Objectives, Vol. 2* (St. Paul, MN: West Group, 1986).

84. C.W.L. Hill and G.R. Jones, *Strategic Management: An Integrated Approach* (Independence, KY: South-Western, 2007).

85. A.A. Thompson, A.J. Strickland, and J.E. Gamble, *Crafting and Executing Strategy* (New York: McGraw-Hill, 2007).

86. Andersen, "Integrating Decentralized Strategy Making and Strategic Planning Processes in Dynamic Environments," *Journal of Management Studies* 41, no. 8 (December 2004), 1271–99.

87. Michel Godet, "The Art of Scenarios and Strategic Planning: Tools and Pitfalls," *Technological Forecasting and Social Change* 65, no. 1 (2000), 3–22.

88. Glaister and Falshaw, "Strategic Planning," 107–16.

89. Robert S. Kaplan, "Devising a Balanced Scorecard Matched to Business Strategy," *Strategy & Leadership* 22, no. 5 (1994), 15.

90. Robert S. Kaplan and David P. Norton, "Strategic Learning and the Balanced Scorecard," *Strategy & Leadership* 24, no. 5 (1996), 18.

BIBLIOGRAPHY

Andersen, Torben Juul. "Integrating Decentralized Strategy Making and Strategic Planning Processes in Dynamic Environments." *Journal of Management Studies* 41, no. 8 (2004): 1271–99.

Andrews, K.R. and D.K. David. *The Concept of Corporate Strategy*. Homewood, IL: R.D. Irwin, 1987.

Ansoff, H.I. *Business Strategy: Selected Readings*. New York: Penguin Books, 1969.

Ansoff, H.I. *Corporate Strategy: An Analytic Approach to Business Policy for Growth and Expansion*. New York: McGraw-Hill, 1965.

Ansoff, H. Igor. "Critique of Henry Mintzberg's 'The Design School: Reconsidering the Basic Premises of Strategic Management'." *Strategic Management Journal* 12, no. 6 (1991): 449–61.

Barnard, C.I. *The Functions of the Executive*. Cambridge, MA: Harvard University Press, 1968.

Barney, J.B. "Firm Resources and Sustained Competitive Advantage." *Journal of Management* 17, no. 1 (1991): 99–120.

Beinhocker, Eric D. and Sarah Kaplan. "Tired of Strategic Planning?" *McKinsey Quarterly* Special edition no. 2 (2002): 48–57.

Boyd, B.K. "Strategic Planning and Financial Performance: A Meta-Analytic Review*." *Journal of Management Studies* 28, no. 4 (1991): 353–74.

Bracker, Jeffrey. "The Historical Development of the Strategic Management Concept." *The Academy of Management Review* 5, no. 2 (1980): 219–24.

Camillus, J.C. *Strategic Planning and Management Control: Systems for Survival and Success.* New York: Simon & Schuster Trade Division, 1986.

Chandler, A.D. *Strategy and Structure: Chapters in the History of the American Industrial Enterprise.* Cambridge, MA: MIT Press, 1962.

De Geus, A.P. "Planning as Learning." *Harvard Business Review* (March–April 1988).

Drucker, P. *The Practice of Management.* New York: Harper & Brothers, 1954.

Eisenhardt, K.M. and S.L. Brown. "Competing on the Edge: Strategy as Structured Chaos." *Long Range Planning* 31, no. 5 (1998): 786–89.

Foss, N.J. *Resources, Firms, and Strategies: A Reader in the Resource-Based Perspective.* Oxford University Press, USA, 1997.

Ghemawat, Pankaj. "Competition and Business Strategy in Historical Perspective." *The Business History Review* 76, no. 1 (2002): 37–74.

Glaister, K.W. and J.R. Falshaw. "Strategic Planning: Still Going Strong?" *Long Range Planning* 32, no. 1 (1999): 107–16.

Godet, Michel. "The Art of Scenarios and Strategic Planning: Tools and Pitfalls." *Technological Forecasting and Social Change* 65, no. 1 (2000): 3–22.

Goold, M. and J.J. Quinn. *Strategic Control: Establishing Milestones for Long-Term Performance.* Boston: Addison-Wesley, 1993.

Graetz, F. "Strategic Thinking versus Strategic Planning: Towards Understanding the Complementarities." *Management Decision* 40, no. 5 (2002): 456–62.

Hamel, Gary and C.K. Prahalad. "Competing for the Future." *Harvard Business Review* 72, no. 4 (July, 1994): 122.

Hammer, M. and J. Champy. *Reengineering the Corporation.* New York: Harper Collins Publishers, 1993.

Hax, Arnoldo C. "Redefining the Concept of Strategy and the Strategy Formation Process." *Strategy & Leadership* 18, no. 3 (1990): 34.

Hax, Arnoldo C. and Nicolas S. Majluf. "The Corporate Strategic Planning Process." *Interfaces* 14, no. 1 (1984): 47–60.

Henderson, B.D. "The Origin of Strategy." *Harvard Business Review* 67, no. 6 (1989): 139–43.

Henry, H.W. "Strategic Management: A New View of Business Policy and Planning." In *Commentary on Lorange,* edited by D. Schendel and C.W. Hofer, 245. Boston: Little, Brown and Co., 1979.

Heracleous, Loizos. "Strategic Thinking or Strategic Planning?" *Long Range Planning* 31, no. 3 (1998): 481–87.

Hill, C.W.L. and G.R. Jones. *Strategic Management: An Integrated Approach.* Independence, KY: South-Western, 2007.

Horwath, Rich. *The Origin of Strategy.* Barrington Hills, IL: Strategic Thinking Institute. 2006.

Kaplan, Robert S. "Devising a Balanced Scorecard Matched to Business Strategy." *Strategy & Leadership* 22, no. 5 (1994): 15.

Kaplan, Robert S. and David P. Norton. "Strategic Learning & the Balanced Scorecard." *Strategy & Leadership* 24, no. 5 (1996): 18.

Langley, Ann. "The Roles of Formal Strategic Planning." *Long Range Planning* 21, no. 3 (1988): 40–50.

Learned, E.P., C.R. Christensen, K.R. Andrews, and W.D. Guth. *Business Policy: Text and Cases.* Homewood, IL: RD Irwin, 1969.

Liedtka, J. M. "Linking Strategic Thinking with Strategic Planning." *Strategy and Leadership* 26, no. 4 (1998): 30–35.

Lorange, P., M.S.S. Morton, and S. Ghoshal. *Strategic Control Systems*. Eagan, MN: West Group, 1986.

Matloff, M. *American Military History*. Cambridge, MA: Da Capo Press, 1996.

McNeilly, M. *Sun Tzu and the Art of Modern Warfare*. Oxford University Press, USA, 2003.

Middleton, J. *The Ultimate Strategy Library: The 50 Most Influential Strategic Ideas of all Time*. Oxford, England: Capstone Publishing Limited (a Wiley Company), 2003.

Mintzberg, Henry. "Crafting Strategy." *Harvard Business Review* 65, no. 4 (July/August 1987): 66–75.

Mintzberg, Henry. "Rethinking Strategic Planning Part II: New Roles for Planners." *Long Range Planning* 27, no. 3 (1994): 22–30.

Morgenstern, O. and J. von Neumann. *Theory of Games and Economic Behavior*. Vol. 3. Princeton, NJ: Princeton University Press, 1947.

Nadler, D. A. "Collaborative Strategic Thinking." *Strategy & Leadership* 22, no. 5 (1993): 30–44.

Ohmae, K. *The Mind of the Strategist*. New York: McGraw-Hill Professional, 1982.

Pearce, J. A., E. B. Freeman, and R. B. Robinson. "The Tenuous Link between Formal Strategic Planning and Financial Performance." *The Academy of Management Review* 12, no. 4 (1987): 658–75.

Porter, Michael, E. "How Competitive Forces Shape Strategy." *Harvard Business Review, Boston* 57, no. 2 (1979).

Porter, M. E. *Competitive Strategy: Techniques for Analyzing Industries and Competitors: With a New Introduction*. New York: Free Press, 1980.

Quinn, J. B. "Formulating Strategy One Step at a Time." *Journal of Business Strategy* 1, no. 3 (1981): 42–63.

Ramanujam, V. and N. Venkatraman. "Planning Systems Characteristics and Planning Effectiveness." *Strategic Management Journal* 8 (5): 453–468, 1987.

Richards, M.D.V. *Setting Strategic Goals and Objectives*. Vol. 2. Eagan, MN: West, 1986.

Santayana, G. *The Life of Reason; Or, the Phases of Human Progress: Introduction, and Reason in Common Sense*. New York: C. Scribner's Sons, 1917.

Schendel, D. and C. W. Hofer. *Strategic Management: A New View of Business Policy and Planning*. Boston: Little, Brown, 1979.

Schoemaker, P.J.H. "When and how to use Scenario Planning: A Heuristic Approach with Illustration." *Journal of Forecasting* 10, no. 6 (1991): 549–64.

Selznick, P. *Leadership in Administration: A Sociological View*. New York: Harper and Row, 1957.

Senge, P. M. *The Fifth Discipline: The Art and Practice of the Learning Organization*. New York: Doubleday, 1990.

Senge, P. M. "The Fifth Discipline." *Measuring Business Excellence* 1, no. 3 (1993): 46–51.

Shapiro, C. and H. R. Varian. *Information Rules: A Strategic Guide to the Network Economy* Boston: Harvard Business Press, 1999.

Sinha, D. K. "The Contribution of Formal Planning to Decisions." *Strategic Management Journal* 11, no. 6 (1990): 479–92.

Sloan Jr., A. P. *My Years with General Motors.* New York: Doubleday/Anchor, 1963.
Stewart, T. A. *Intellectual Capital.* London: Brealey, 1997.
Thompson, A. A., A. J. Strickland, and J. E. Gamble. *Crafting and Executing Strategy.* New York: Irwin/McGraw-Hill, 2007.
Von Clausewitz, C. and C.J.J. Graham. *On War.* Digireads.Com, 2008.
Wilden, A. *Man and Woman, War and Peace: The Strategist's Companion.* New York: McGraw-Hill, 1987.

Chapter 2

Marshaling Firm Resources in Order to Be a Successful Competitor

Franco Gandolfi

INTRODUCTION TO STRATEGIC MANAGEMENT

It is widely understood that strategic management, including strategic planning, is more than a set of managerial tools and techniques. In fact, strategic management is a way of thinking, a mental framework or approach, which continuously monitors, analyzes, and evaluates changes in the firm's internal and external environments. In order for strategic management to be used effectively, organizational leaders must develop a strategic mentality and outlook.[1] At its very core, strategic management represents the organization's efforts to *create and sustain competitive advantages.*

Essentially, this characterization of strategic management captures two fundamental elements. First, the strategic management aspects of any firm entail three ongoing processes: analyses, decision-making aspects, and organizational actions. Strategic management is concerned with the analysis of the firm's strategic intent, including its vision, mission, and strategic objectives, as well as with the ongoing monitoring and analysis of the internal and external environments of the firm. Second, executives must constantly engage in strategic decision-making activities. Broadly speaking, these decision-driven processes address two foundational questions: *what* industries and markets should we compete in, and *how* should we compete in those designated industries and markets? Evidently, these questions often involve a firm's domestic and global operations. Third, a firm's organizational actions need to be reviewed and evaluated constantly, as decisions alone are of *no or little use unless they are acted upon.* Thus, firms must take the necessary actions in order to implement and evaluate their strategies. Leaders need to allocate the necessary resources and design the organization to bring the intended strategies into reality. It is clear that this has to be an ongoing, evolving process requiring a great deal of interaction among those three defined processes.

Part of the DNA of strategic management is the inherent study of why some firms outperform others. Thus, organizational leaders need to determine how a firm is to compete so that it can create competitive advantages that are *sustainable* over a period of time. This, in itself, constitutes a significant challenge and poses a fundamental question: how should a firm compete in order to create competitive advantages in the marketplace? For example, a manager may find herself in a position where she needs to determine if the firm should position itself as a low-cost producer, or instead develop unique products and services that enable the firm to command premium prices. Managers may then ask themselves how such temporary advantages can be made sustainable in the marketplace. In other words, how can a firm create competitive advantages in the marketplace that are not only valuable *and* unique but also difficult for competitors to emulate or substitute?

Anecdotal evidence suggests that successful, workable business ideas are almost always imitable and emulated by competitive forces. Back in the 1980s, U.S. carrier American Airlines tried to establish a competitive advantage by introducing a frequent flyer program. Within weeks of its launch, all the major U.S.-based airlines had developed and launched their own programs. Literally, in a matter of weeks, instead of creating and boasting a competitive advantage, frequent flyer programs became an invaluable tool for competitive parity as opposed to creating a legitimate competitive advantage. Therefore, the key challenge for organizational leaders is to create a competitive advantage that is *sustainable.* Harvard Business School (HBS) strategist Michael Porter argues that sustainable competitive advantages cannot be achieved through the pursuit of operational efficiencies alone. Interestingly, most of the popular management innovations of the last three decades, including total quality management (TQM), just-in-time, benchmarking, business process reengineering (BPR), outsourcing, delayering, and employee downsizing, are concerned primarily with operational efficiencies. Operational efficiencies denote performing similar activities faster, cheaper, and better than those of a firm's rivals.[2] Admittedly, although each of these elements is important, none have shown to produce sustainable competitive advantages for firms over time. This is primarily because everybody is embracing similar management practices. The nature of strategy forces firms to articulate strategies that are distinct from those of competitors. Therefore, sustainable competitive advantage is possible only through performing activities that are different from those of rivals or performing similar activities in distinctly different ways.

Companies such as Southwest Airlines, Wal-Mart, Marks & Spencer, and IKEA have developed unique, internally consistent, and difficult-to-imitate systems and processes that have provided them with sustained competitive advantages. A firm must be very clear about what it wishes to accomplish. As a consequence, imitating rival products, services, and behaviors will not lead to long-term competitive advantages, but to an environment that is marked by mutually destructive price competition practices.

A BRIEF HISTORY OF STRATEGIC MANAGEMENT

Back in the 1960s and 1970s, strategic planning was seen as one of the finest tools to ensure high levels of employee effectiveness and corporate profitability. The underlying assumption was that decision-making aspects pertaining to strategic planning processes could be quantified, subjecting those measurements to quantitative models, which would then produce the best-possible strategies. It was during this time period that HBS professors Andrews and Christensen asserted that strategy could be made a powerful tool by linking it to business functions and by using it to assess a firm's strengths and weaknesses in relation with those of its rivals. General Electric (GE) emerged as a pioneer in the area of corporate strategic planning. With the assistance of consulting firm McKinsey, GE was organized into strategic business units (SBUs). During the same time, the Boston Consulting Group popularized a number of its own strategic approaches, including the "experience curve" and the "growth and market-share matrix."[3] Strategic planning gained further regard and popularity among executives during the 1970s, peaking in the early 1980s with HBS scholar Michael Porter's seminal book publication entitled *Competitive Strategy*.

In the early 1980s, a number of executives began voicing concerns regarding their investments in strategic planning processes. Their concerns were related to dramatic changes in the now-globalized landscape, as well as to the incredibly rapid technological developments leading to increased levels of complexities in the marketplace. It was once again GE that led the way; its charismatic chairman Jack Welch championed the cutting of his own firm's planning departments. Other corporate executives followed his lead throughout the 1980s and 1990s. In many ways, strategic planning was replaced by notions of improving quality and productivity through operational innovation. Some of those techniques included the *quality* philosophies of Deming, Juran, and Crosby. In the 1990s, firms shifted their focus and attention to improving efficiency,[4] resulting in the emergence of "strategic" tools, including delayering, BPR, downsizing, and rightsizing efforts.[5] In the 1990s, strategic planning experienced a renaissance. Specifically, new strategies emerged, focusing upon growth through joint ventures and mergers and acquisitions, the generation of innovative ideas through decentralized strategic endeavors within the firm, emergent strategies, and the leveraging of core competencies to create strategic intent.[6]

The dominant theme for firms in the early days of this new millennium has been strategic and organizational innovation. Current issues include reconciling a firm's size with its flexibility and responsiveness.[7] Strategic alliances infer cooperative strategies, complexity, and changes in commitments of corporate social responsibility (CSR). Today's strategic planning requires new forms and new models of leadership, more flexible organizational structures, and an increased commitment to self-direction.[8]

THE FAILURE OF TRADITIONAL STRATEGIC MANAGEMENT

Some management scholars contend that the traditional strategic management models have failed for a variety of reasons.[9] First, traditional models do not distinguish between strategic thinking and strategic planning. Indeed, traditional models rely heavily upon scientific and quantitative analyses, whereas strategic thinking methods focus upon the synthesis of a decision-maker's creativity, intuition, and experience in the selection of strategies. Second, traditional models overemphasize the role of strategy definition and formulation at the expense of aspects pertaining to strategy implementation, execution, and evaluation. This is particularly evident in business school curricula that focus heavily on strategy articulation and definition rather than the actual execution and evaluation of selected strategies. Moreover, those individuals who were traditionally tasked to translate strategy into workable tactics and operational action plans have been largely removed from organizational hierarchies in the 1990s and beyond. The "delayering" phenomenon promised many organizational benefits, yet, as we have come to understand, has left a deep vacuum in the translation and implementation of strategy.[10] Additionally, since traditional strategic planning occurs at the very top of organizations and often with the guidance of consultants, strategic plans frequently are handed down to managers with little or no material input and buy-in from lower-ranked employees. Therefore, deep commitment to the successful execution of a chosen strategy, especially among lower-level managers and nonmanagerial employees, remains questionable.

Management writer Mintzberg posits further reasons why traditional strategic planning efforts have failed, namely, the fallacy of prediction, the fallacy of detachment, and the fallacy of formalization:[11]

The fallacy of prediction: Traditional strategic planning is based on the premise that all variables relevant to the future of a business are measurable, analyzable, and predictable. Once the results are available, strategies could be based upon those predictions, thus ensuring future success. However, even the most sophisticated predictive models are unable to foresee economic, industry, market, and social shifts. Economic cycles do not behave in a linear fashion. The fallacy of prediction, according to Mintzberg, has contributed extensively to the downfall of traditional strategic planning since it was unable to deliver predictable success.

The fallacy of detachment: Traditional strategic planning is based on the notion that strategists ought to be detached from middle managers and employees when analyzing the data in order to remain objective and to prevent bias. However, this approach decontextualizes relevant data and detaches the strategy champions from the strategy implementers. Also, qualitative information is often ignored by the scientific community, creating blind spots in the overall strategy planning.

The fallacy of formalization: Traditional strategic planning is based on the belief that formal systems for information processing and decision making are superior to human systems. Although computerized systems are able to process large quantities of data, it is individuals who integrate, synthesize, and create new directions, patterns, and trends from such analyses.

Naturally, there are other management writers who have theorized about the failure of traditional strategic planning. For instance, the *Icarus Paradox*, which refers to Icarus of Greek mythology, who flew too close to the sun and melted his own wings, is a neologism coined and popularized by Danny Miller. The *Icarus Paradox* epitomizes an observed business phenomenon whereby the strengths and apparent victories of successful firms can be the very cause of their own strategic failures. Indeed, the paradox of Icarus was that his skill and technology, which in the story led him to freedom, ultimately also led him to his own death.[12]

Clayton M. Christensen, in his book *The Innovator's Dilemma,* reported that even if firms follow established management principles and practices, they are nonetheless exposed to events, problems, and complexities that can cause strategic failures. Christensen posits that the innovator's dilemma is that the logical and competent decisions of management that are critical to the success of their firms are also the reasons why they lose their positions of leadership. He asserts that "good" management practice involves sustaining the successes of services, products, and processes, and that firms generally succeed in this. These same companies, however, become vulnerable by the emergence of *disruptive* technologies, which appear harmless in the marketplace to the successful firm. Since they do not pose an immediate threat, they are ignored. As such, disruptive technologies may grow to become powerful forces and successful firms may be ill prepared to respond to the changed competitive landscape. Christensen affirms that successful firms are caught in the routine of maintaining the status quo (i.e., the current success) and often fail to perceive or understand the threat of disruptive technologies. The objective then is to build and sustain successful services, products, and processes, while possessing the ability to recognize, evaluate, and develop disruptive technologies.[13]

PORTER'S WORK

A review of the strategic management literature reveals that there is a great deal of interest in the study of environmental forces that impact upon the firm. In fact, there is even a greater interest in the *factors that can potentially be harnessed to provide competitive advantage.* Interestingly, the models, frameworks, and ideas that emerged during the 1970s and 1980s were primarily based upon the notion that a firm's competitive advantage was derived from its ability to earn a return on investment (ROI) that exceeded the average return for the industry sector.[14]

Porter's five forces model, one of the most recognized strategic frameworks for industry analysis and business strategy development, draws upon industrial organization (IO) economics to derive five forces that determine the competitive intensity and attractiveness of a market. At its core, Porter's five forces model deals with factors *outside* an industry that influence the nature of competition *within* the industry (i.e., macroenvironment), as well as the forces *inside* the industry (i.e., microenvironment) that affect the way in which organizations compete. Undoubtedly, a firm must understand the dynamics of its industry and markets in order to compete successfully and effectively in the marketplace.[15] Porter's competitive forces model identified five distinct forces that impact upon a firm's behavior in the market. They are the following:

- The threat of new entrants;
- The threat of substitute products or services;
- The intensity of competitive rivalry;
- The bargaining power of buyers; and
- The bargaining power of suppliers.

Porter's five forces include three forces from *horizontal* competition: the threat of substitute products (or services), the threat of established rivals, and the threat of new entrants; and two forces from *vertical* competition: the bargaining power of suppliers and the bargaining power of customers. It has been claimed that a deeper understanding of each of these forces provides firms with the necessary insights to enable them to formulate appropriate strategies to succeed in their respective markets.[16]

Force #1—The threat of new entrants: Average industry profitability is impacted by both existing and potential competitors. New entrants to an industry can raise the level of competition, thereby reducing its attractiveness. The threat of new rivals is based on the market's entry barriers, which can take various forms and may be used to prevent firms into the market. Strictly speaking, an entry barrier exists when it is difficult or economically unfeasible for an outsider to replicate the position of the incumbent. Common obstacles include cost of entry (e.g., investment into technology), economies of scale, access to industry distribution channels, and brand differentiation. Other aspects include legal barriers to entry, such as licensing laws, environmental regulations, and intellectual property rights. High entry barriers exist in certain industries (e.g., shipbuilding), whereas other industries tend to be easier to enter into (e.g., restaurants, real estate agencies).

Force #2—The threat of substitute products or services: The presence of substitute products or services can lower industry attractiveness and profitability by limiting price levels. The threat of substitute products or services depends upon the buyers' willingness to substitute, the relative price and performance of substitutes, and the costs of switching to substitutes.

Force #3—The intensity of competitive rivalry: The intensity or degree of rivalry will depend on the structure of competition (e.g., rivalry is more intense in the presence of small or equally sized rivals), the structure of industry costs (e.g., industries with high fixed costs encourage rivals to fill unused capacity by price cutting), degree of differentiation (e.g., industries where competitors can differentiate their products display reduced rivalry), switching costs (e.g., rivalry is reduced where buyers have high switching costs), strategic objectives (e.g., when firms pursue growth strategies, rivalry tends to be more intense), and exit barriers (e.g., when barriers to leaving an industry are high, rivals tend to exhibit greater rivalry).

Force #4—The bargaining power of buyers: Buyer power is determined by the size and the concentration of customers. The bargaining power of buyers tends to be greater when there are few dominant buyers and many sellers in the industry, products are standardized, buyers threaten to integrate backward into industry, and suppliers do not threaten to integrate forward into the buyer's industry.

Force #5—The bargaining power of suppliers: In many ways, supplier power mirrors buyer power in that the analysis of supplier power typically focuses first on the relative size and concentration of suppliers relative to industry participants and on the degree of differentiation in the inputs supplied. The bargaining power of suppliers is high when there are few dominant suppliers and many buyers, there are undifferentiated, highly valued products, suppliers threaten to forward integrate into the industry, and buyers do not threaten to integrate backward into supply.

Reflecting on Porter's Work

As one of the world's best known management strategists, Porter has significantly contributed to our understanding of organizational strategy and the competitiveness of nations and regions. Porter's five forces model, in particular, has established itself as a leading strategic tool that enables managers to determine whether new businesses, products, or services have the potential to be profitable.

It comes as no surprise that Porter's work has been subject to much criticism over the years. The main criticism stems from the historical context in which his models were created. Back in the 1980s, the global business landscape was characterized by strong competition, relatively stable market structures, cyclical developments, and predictable growth. Thus, the key focus was on the optimization of strategy in relation to the *external* environment, with the primary business tenets constituting profitability and corporate survival. Second, Porter's background is business economics and his theoretical work assumes a perfect market. Thus, it seems that his models are most applicable for analyses of simple market structures. Third, some authors have criticized Porter's work for its simplicity and unrealistically basic assumptions, which seem unable to deal with dynamic environments characterized by complex industries with a multitude of interrelations, products, and by-product groups. Fourth, the model is based on the notion of competition presupposing that firms try to obtain competitive advantages over *all* players in the market, including suppliers and customers. Thus, Porter's model does not take into consideration corporate strategic endeavors, such as strategic coalitions and alliances, as well as the pursuit of virtual enterprise-type networks. Fifth, Porter's work focuses upon the analysis of the actual situation (e.g., customers, suppliers, and competitors) and on predictable developments (e.g., new entrants and substitute products). Thus, Porter claims that competitive advantages develop from strengthening a firm's position within the framework. These criticisms suggest strongly that the models lack the capacity to explain today's unrelenting and ever-changing environment where seemingly subtle changes have the power to transform entire industries.

Beyond Porter

Porter's work was extended by Brandenburger and Nalebuff in the 1990s who added the concept of "complementary," enabling the authors to explain the reasoning behind the emergence of strategic coalitions and alliances. This sixth force is the relative power of other stakeholders, including "complementors" (i.e., businesses providing complementary products and services), the government, the public, and a firm's employees and shareholders.[17]

Downes claims that the basic assumptions underlying Porter's work are no longer viable. He identified three forces that necessitate a new framework and a new set of tools: digitalization, globalization, and deregulation. First, digitalization recognizes that the power of information technology will continue to expand and that all players in the market will have increased access to information. As a result, new business models will emerge, enabling external players—even rivals from outside the industry—to transform completely the basis of competition. Second, businesses and consumers are in a position to operate on a global scale. Therefore, everybody with access to modern-day technology can participate in the global marketplace even if they do not export or import themselves. Third, deregulation has taken place in many industries and countries, forcing businesses to restructure their businesses and to reemerge with new business plans and models. Downes concludes that the difference between the current technologically driven world and the old "Porter" world is technology. Furthermore, whereas in the past technology was used as a tool for implementing change endeavors, it is now the most important driver for change.[18]

Others have been more pragmatic about the limitations of Porter's work stating that it is not prudent to develop a strategy solely on the basis of Porter's model. What needs to be done is to adopt the model with the full knowledge of its limitations and utilize it as part of a larger framework of management tools, techniques, and theories, which is advisable for the application of any business model.[19]

THE RESOURCE-BASED VIEW (RBV) OF THE FIRM

An alternative perspective and a more recent entrant into the theoretical discussion of strategic management is the RBV of the firm. In essence, the RBV of the firm significantly differs from Porter's environmentally focused strategic management paradigm in that it emphasizes the firm's *internal* resources as the fundamental determinants of competitive advantage and performance. Thus, the RBV of competitive advantage is firm specific, whereas Porter's work had a decided industry-environment focus. With its historical roots in the organizational economics literature and the works of Ricardo, Schumpeter, and Penrose, one of the fundamental aspects of RBV is that the ultimate purpose of the firm is to maximize economic rent.[20] This encourages corporations to continually extract resources from less-valuable legacy operations and steer them toward profitable innovation.[21]

The traditional business literature, which includes Porter's work, assumes that firms competing in the same industry are homogenous and that the firm's adaptation to the characteristics of its product market is the key determinant of a firm's performance and success.[22] In stark contrast, the RBV of the firm is based on the notion that firms are unique and composed of distinct bundles of resources. Barney posits that a firm is regarded as a bundle of tangible and intangible resources and capabilities.[23] Within a pure RBV framework, internal resources are considered the *ultimate source of sustained competitive advantage.* Thus, strategy is primarily concerned with obtaining an alignment, or fit, between the organization's internal resources and external opportunities.[24]

At its core, the RBV of the firm operates on two assumptions. First, it assumes that firms within an industry are heterogeneous with respect to the resources they control. Second, it assumes that resource heterogeneity persists over time since the resources required to implement a firm's strategies are not perfectly mobile over time. Therefore, resources uniqueness, or heterogeneity, is considered a necessary condition for the resources to contribute to a competitive advantage. This is reflected in Dierickx and Cool's argument in that if all firms in a market have the same resources, no strategy is available to one firm that would not also be available to all other firms in the market.[25] As with the Chicago school tradition, the RBV of the firm presupposes an efficiency-based explanation for differences in a firm's performance.[26]

Critical to our understanding of the RBV of the firm is the definition of resources, competitive advantage, and sustained competitive advantage. First, Barney asserts that resources fall into three categories: physical-capital resources (e.g., a firm's plant, equipment, and geographical location), human-capital resources (e.g., experience, judgment, and intelligence of individuals), and organizational-capital resources (e.g., a firm's structure, planning, controlling, and coordinating systems).[27] Second, in the RBV of the firm, these resources can potentially be sources of competitive advantages. However, Barney warns that competitive advantages can only occur in situations of firm resource *heterogeneity* (i.e., resources vary across firms) and firm resource *immobility* (i.e., the inability of competing firms to obtain resources from other firms or resource markets). This is in stark contrast with the environmentally focused strategy models, as espoused by Porter, where resources are deemed mobile and where resources can be purchased or created by competing rivals. Third, a sustained competitive advantage is different from a competitive advantage in that a *sustained competitive advantage* only exists when rival firms are incapable of duplicating the benefits of a competitive advantage.[28]

A competitive advantage cannot be viewed as a sustained competitive advantage until all efforts by competing rivals to duplicate the advantage have failed. In the RBV of the firm, a source of sustained competitive advantage must meet four criteria: they must add *value* to the firm, they must be *rare* (or unique), they must be *imperfectly imitable,* and the resource *cannot be substitutable* with another resource.[29] In other words, when resources meet these criteria, they become potential sources of *sustained* competitive advantages. Barney and Wright add that whether or not such sustained competitive advantages are realized or not depends entirely on the extent to which a firm is organized to exploit them.[30]

Reflecting on the RBV of the Firm

The RBV of the firm is one of the most widely cited theories in the management literature. Its central proposition connotes that if a firm is to achieve sustainable competitive advantage, it is required to acquire and control resources that are valuable, rare (unique), inimitable, and nonsubstitutable.[31] Although the core theory of the RBV of the firm is appealing, it has been criticized for its weaknesses and shortcomings over the years. These criticisms fall into four categories:

Criticism #1: The RBV has no managerial implications: The RBV of the firm has been criticized for its lack of managerial implications and operational validity. Managerial leaders have been counseled to acquire and develop resources without a clear prescription of how this should be done. Thus, there is a tension between descriptive and prescriptive theorizing. However, the RBV of the firm aspires to explain why some firms have sustainable competitive advantages over others. As such, the theorizing was never intended to provide managerial prescriptions.[32] Selected writers assert that we should continue to focus on a discussion on the impact on managerial practice as opposed to a focus on a lack of managerial implications.[33]

Criticism #2: The RBV's applicability is too limited: A second criticism concerns the applicability of the RBV. Some authors argue that the notion of resource uniqueness denies the RBV of the firm any potential for generalization,[34] whereas others contend that it is feasible to create useful insights about degrees of resource uniqueness.[35] Another criticism pertains to the claim that the RBV insights are limited only to large firms with significant market power. However, a more realistic perspective is that insights from the RBV analysis are only applicable to firms that are not satisfied with their competitive position and actively pursue sustainable competitive advantages.

Criticism #3: Sustainable competitive advantage is not achievable: One of the key foci of the RBV of the firm is the notion of achieving a *sustainable* competitive advantage that exceeds other firms' capacity to duplicate or eliminate it. This has become a hotly debated issue. Can a sustainable competitive advantage really be achieved? A number of studies suggest that competitive advantages can only be sustained at the firm level through organizational learning or dynamic capabilities, which enable the firm to adapt faster than its competitors.[36] Other studies have demonstrated that static unique resources can lead to sustainable competitive advantages in static environments, whereas dynamic environments demand dynamic resources and capabilities.[37]

Criticism #4: The definition of "resource" is unworkable: A fourth criticism posits that the RBV of the firm may not adequately address the fundamental differences in how various types of resources contribute in a different manner to a firm's sustainable competitive advantage. Although the RBV of the firm recognizes three categories of resources, it treats them equally. In a recent publication, Barney and Clark suggest that the offered typologies are mere labels for which the basic logic of the RBV of the firm still holds.[38] They propose that different labels would only be appropriate if these referred to an alternative logic of linking a firm's assets with its sustainable competitive advantage favoring a single logic and terminology. These, for instance, could be labeled "resource based," "capability based," or "competence based." Other writers have concluded that the image and applicability of the RBV of the firm would improve if its basic logic would be refined by explicitly recognizing differences between types of resources, that is, static-dynamic; tangible-intangible; financial-human-technological; deployed-in reserve; and perishable-nonperishable, and between the types of resource ownership.[39]

An RBV of Human Resources and Competitive Advantage

Thus far, this chapter has established that, within an RBV of the firm, for a resource to qualify as a potential source of sustainable competitive advantage, the resource must add value to the firm, the resource must be rare or unique, the resource must be imperfectly imitable, and the resource cannot be substituted with another resource. Do human resources qualify as potential sources of sustainable competitive advantages?

Human resources add value to the firm: Most people would intuitively agree that human resources add value to the firm. Does this necessarily hold true? What does theory suggest? Firm-specific human-capital theory presents an explanation about the conditions under which human value creation is possible. Specifically, when the demand for labor is *homogenous* (i.e., individual employees are perfectly substitutable) and the supply for labor is also *homogenous* (i.e., all individual employees are seen as equal in their productive capacities), then there is no variance in the individual contributions to the firm and it is thus impossible to create value through human resources. Steffy and Maurer are of the opinion that the demand for labor is *heterogeneous* (i.e., different jobs require different skills) and the supply for labor is also *heterogeneous* (i.e., individuals possess different types and levels of skills), thereby arguing that human resources can add value to the firm.[40]

Human resources are rare: The RBV of the firm holds that human resources must be rare (or unique) in order to be viewed as a potential source of sustainable competitive advantage. With unemployment and underemployment at high levels, people would instinctively argue that there must be an excess of labor and that human resources are therefore not rare. Historically speaking, the scientific management paradigm has traditionally embraced the idea that firms need to focus on producing jobs that do not require employees with specialized skills. Therefore, within this mindset, the notion of special skills becomes largely irrelevant and employees are considered a commodity rather than a resource.

Assuming, however, that jobs do require specified skills and a variance in individual contributions, such rare, or unique, skills are distributed within the population. Therefore, human resources are believed to be a rare resource. Indeed, there are various measures on how to appraise the quality of human resources. Cognitive ability, for instance, is probably one of the most pervasive and consistent predictors of employee performance in firms.[41] Thus, it has been concluded that firms with employees holding high levels of cognitive ability possess more quality human resources than those of rivals. Furthermore, since the total human resource (HR) pool is believed to be finite, firms that have a high level of cognitive ability among their employees have gained this resource at the expense of rivaling firms.[42]

Human resources are inimitable: For a resource to be considered a source of potential sustainable competitive advantage, it must be inimitable. Indeed, if the competitive advantage derived from having high-skilled employees could be copied, then human resources would not be a source of sustained competitive advantage. How can rivals imitate human resources? First, competitors must be able to identify the exact source of competitive advantage. In other words, the actual components would need to be known in order to be imitated. Second, the rivaling firm would need to be able to copy the actual components *and* the contexts under which these human resources operated. Interestingly, it has been pointed out that having the necessary skills among individual employees per se does not ensure that the firm has gained a sustainable competitive advantage. What is pivotal then is that employees must possess the skills *and* have the ability to exhibit the required behaviors to exercise those skills.[43] A managerial implication in this discussion of resource inimitability is the notion of resource mobility. In certain countries, especially in the United States, human resources have historically been very mobile. However, employees are not perfectly mobile since there are sizeable transaction costs involved in moving individual employees.[44] As such, if employees are indeed highly mobile (or perfectly mobile), rivaling firms would not need to imitate them since they could simply lure and hire them away. However, firms may not know exactly which employees provide a source of competitive advantage. Thus, firms would need to hire away entire teams or groups of individuals. This, however, would still not guarantee that the competitive advantage could be imitated as the human resources might be coupled to other resources (i.e., physical and organization resources) within the firm.[45]

Human resources are nonsubstitutable: Human resources must not have substitutes if they are to be a source of sustained competitive advantage. Human resources are believed to have the potential to avoid obsolescence and to be transferable across technologies, products, and markets.[46] Ongoing training and development (T&D) among employees ensure that HR skills do not become obsolete. A brief study of human resources' practices reveals that cognitive ability is transferable across technologies, products, and services. A central element to this discussion is the question of whether or not technology has the potential for offsetting any competitive advantages that can be attributed to the utilization of human resources. It is probably safe to say that although technological changes have rendered certain technical skills obsolete, there is infinitely more to the inherent character of human resources than the technical elements that can be substituted. For any resource to replace human resources, it must be valuable, rare, inimitable, and nonsubstitutable. It appears that *only human resources* have the capacity to fulfill that requirement.

The Human Resource Equation: Cost versus Value

Firms feel increasingly compelled to invest significant resources into human capital in order to become successful and remain competitive. As the pressures of today's labor markets continue to intensify, the HR function is often perceived as a cost center within firms, although corporate rhetoric espousing that *our people are our most important asset* has remained conspicuously fashionable.

Wayne Cascio, a business professor at the University of Colorado, has examined the financial costs associated with employees. He argues that although firms recognize the financial value and benefit that people can bring into a firm, the unfortunate view that employees are *costs to be cut,* as opposed to *assets to be developed,* is still a widely held perspective. This view has seen the importance of accounting for the financial costs of employees become a vital part of the HR function and a newly found responsibility that firms owe to their respective investors.[47]

Labor costs can be extensive, especially in labor-intensive industries such as consulting firms, law firms, and universities. From a purely cost perspective, the people function often accounts for two-thirds or more of total operational expenses. Other factors, including cost per hire, wage-and-benefits' costs, cost per incident of absenteeism, and cost per incident of voluntary turnover are widely used metrics. On a more sobering note, there are immediate costs associated with the mismanagement of employees, including costs associated with lawsuits and costs associated with resolving industrial disputes. Thus, the role of HR has become linked to the accounting for such human-capital-related costs.[48]

An ongoing challenge for HR is to concentrate efforts on its people-investment approaches and steer away from models focusing primarily on the cost side of the equation.[49] The focus ought to be on *HR output as opposed to HR input*. Cascio contends that one of the greatest challenges for modern-day HR is to advance from a compliance-driven HR model to a service model. More specifically, in the former, HR focuses primarily on complying with laws and regulations and the policing of management processes. In the latter, HR provides HR-related service to support line managers in their operations. Finally, a movement toward a decision-oriented model focusing on the utilization and deployment of talent has been observed, thereby surpassing the traditional compliance and service frameworks.[50]

Research shows that firms struggle with the concept of ROI in the context of the HR functions. This thinking applies to a variety of HR activities, including career management, T&D, and work-life balance practices. What is pivotal is the ability to capitalize on those practices that create the highest value for the firm and employees and to identify HR practices that contribute positively to business performance and overall business strategy.[51]

Although it might seem good business practice to keep operational costs low and to reduce costs at all levels, this approach may not prove to be successful. Cascio stresses the importance of identifying and developing pivotal talent within the firm thereby fostering human-capital investment and creating strategic value for the firm. For example, a purposeful focus on staffing, training, and compensation in a call center where employees take orders for merchandise can provide positive financial returns for the firm and all stakeholders.[52]

Cascio posits that research has consistently shown that core quality employees are critical to the survival, growth, and overall success of a firm, and generate benefits that outweigh their operational costs. Treating employees well and reducing employee turnover may have a positive side effect. In his *Harvard Business Review* article, Cascio argues that firms can learn from the U.S. retail industry where "shrinkage" (i.e., losses due to employee theft, fraud, and administrative errors) account for up to two percent of annual sales, which, in some cases, can constitute millions of lost dollars. Research shows that retailers with low employee turnover also have a tendency to have low shrinkage rates. U.S. retailer Costco, for instance, maintains labor pay rates that average 40 percent higher than those of its rivals, yet its shrinkage rate is a mere 0.2 percent, which is significantly lower than that of its closest competitors. Therefore, there appears to be value in ensuring competitive pay rates. Cascio concludes that in Costco's case the costs that it does not incur, in the form of reduced employee turnover and reduced shrinkage, clearly offsets its higher labor rates. Thus, it has been shown at Costco that labor costs as a percentage of sales per employee are lower than those of Sam's Club, its closest rival.[53]

Human Resources Management (HRM) and Pfeffer's Work

HRM as an academic discipline has developed dramatically over the past two decades. There is ample evidence supporting the observation that the development of HRM theory and practice have transformed and elevated the HRM function from a purely reactive function—mainly on administration and bureaucracy—to a proactive function actively pursuing strategy and integration. Thus, HRM is increasingly seen as a legitimate business activity linked to organizational strategy and to the achievement of competitive advantages.[54] It has been noted that one of the reasons for such a shift in emphasis is that some of the traditional sources of competitive advantage, including technology, economies of scale, and patents, have greatly diminished in value over time.[55] At the same time, it is the employees per se, or the workforce in general, who have emerged as an important source of competitive advantage. This has had a direct impact on the practice of HRM in that effective HRM is widely considered to be the key to realizing this potential from the employees for the firm.[56]

In line with the perspective that human resources are a critical source of competitive advantage for a firm, HRM, as a discipline, has developed a strategic focus. Strategic HRM, or simply SHRM, is primarily concerned with the alignment of HRM policies, practices, and plans with the overall business strategy. More practically, the HR function looks at how the firm selects policies, practices, and structures that best fit the particular business strategies being pursued, enabling the effective management of people within the firm so that firm-specific goals can be pursued and attained.[57]

A number of "best practices" regarding the practice of implementation of SHRM have emerged. In fact, the overriding objective of best SHRM practice is to promote employee commitment and employee motivation that is expected to produce employee development and positive economic performance, thus yielding a competitive advantage for the firm.[58]

For some scholars the underlying guiding principle of best practice is the adequate valuing and rewarding of employee performance.[59] Huselid developed a list of 13 high-performance work characteristics that he believed constituted best practice.[60] Inspired by Huselid's work, Pfeffer outlined seven best HR practices of successful firms, including employment security, selective hiring, extensive training, communication, self-managed teams, high compensation relative to performance, and the removal of barriers.[61] These are further elaborated:

1. *Employment security:* Pfeffer argues that employment security is underpinned by the other six HRM elements asserting that it would be unreasonable to require employees to commit to the firm if the company in turn could not offer some form of ongoing employment security to the employee. A reciprocal arrangement fosters mutuality between the firm and the employee and has the propensity to contribute to the development of a positive psychological contract between the parties,[62] encouraging an employment relationship characterized by openness and trust.[63]

2. *Selective hiring:* Utilizing selective hiring practices is the second HR area addressed and viewed as a potent way to achieve competitive advantages.[64] Although Pfeffer asserts that firms must hire individuals who have the required knowledge, skills, and abilities, firms also need to ensure that prospective employees possess the necessary characteristics of trainability and commitment.[65] The latter has been a practice of high-performing firms in that they hire for attitude and train for skills.[66] Of particular relevance is the notion that firms need to employ candidates who fit the culture of the firm.[67]

3. *Extensive training:* It comes as no surprise that organizations expend considerable efforts and resources in ensuring that they are sourced with the best-possible talent. Once a pool of talent is hired, firms need to ensure that the employees are fully harnessed and utilized. In order to execute this well, firms must be in a position to provide T&D opportunities that enable the employees to remain at the cutting edge in their respective fields. Thus, a long-term orientation and commitment to T&D, although costly from a purely financial perspective, is an absolute *must do* for leading-edge firms.[68] Various scholars have pointed out different T&D emphases, including training in interpersonal skills and teamwork giving rise to "multiskilling," which enables them to perform across functions,[69] technical training,[70] and training in knowledge and skills suited to the nature and strategy of the business.[71] In any case, the provision of T&D generates a sense of mutuality, showcasing the firm's commitment to ongoing, purposeful, and involved employment longevity.[72]

4. *Communication:* Communication and information sharing is the fourth dimension outlined by Pfeffer. Open, honest two-way communication must be encouraged at all levels. This provides a number of benefits: First, it ensures that employees are informed about financial, strategic, and operational aspects. Second, it conveys both symbolic and substantive messages about equitable and fair treat-

ment of employees, thereby creating trust. Third, it encourages active employee contribution. Fourth, it has been noted that effective communication has the capacity to raise workforce awareness of organizational objectives and imperatives and to encourage greater commitment toward the attainment of strategic goals.[73]

5. *Team working:* The active utilization of self-managed teams and team-working aspects as the dominant modes of structuring work are deemed vital to organizational success. Specifically, the adoption of such structural elements encourages more efficient and faster decision making, promotes creativity and innovation, and fosters a culture of collaboration and inclusiveness.[74]

6. *Compensation:* Pfeffer presented the compensation element as the sixth dimension of best HR practices. At its most basic, compensation as a strategy rewards individuals with high compensation related to individual and/or team performance. Research shows that there are many forms of rewarding employees, including but not limited to stock ownership, profit sharing, merit pay, as well as a variety of individual- and team-performance-based compensation schemes. Such a strategy purports to convey a message to employees that their contributions to organizational goals are deeply valued and that a high compensation culture is consistent with a hiring approach that attempts to attract and retain the highest-quality workers.

7. *Removal of barriers:* The last dimension concerns the removal of barriers within firms, also called harmonization. Harmonization can be attained by implementing standardized terms and conditions of employment across the entire workforce. These uniform practices apply to benefits, including holiday entitlements, sick-pay schemes, pensions, and hours of work, which lead to the removal of artificial barriers between different groups, thereby encouraging a team-environment-type philosophy. Pfeffer asserts that organizational symbols such as language, labels, physical space, and dress convey messages to employees about their intrinsic value within the firm. For instance, symbols that purport to promote egalitarianism suggest that all employees are equally valued, thus promoting a culture of collaboration and ideas sharing.[75]

IMPLEMENTATION OF HR ACTIVITIES AND PRACTICES

Distinct perspectives on HR strategy and implementation aspects have emerged, namely, the universal, contingency, and configurational perspectives. First, the universal perspective holds the view that the adoption of "best HR practice" will inevitably result in improved organizational performance. Therefore, this perspective does *not* require the purposeful integration between organizational strategy and HR plans, policies, and practices.[76] Second, the contingency perspective suggests that the potency and effectiveness of HR aspects hinge upon corporate strategy in that a firm adopting HR elements that are fitting for its competitive strategies will be more effective. Organizational performance should thus be positively impacted when HR activities mutually reinforce the firm's choice of strategy.[77] Third, the configurational perspective embraces the view that a fit between HR activities and organizational strategy is vital. Thus, HR practices become a key factor in the attainment of organizational goals and performance.[78] The configurational view assumes that HR practices must be characterized by their consistency with external, organizational, and strategic conditions (i.e., vertical fit) and internally consistent (i.e., horizontal fit). This dual form of integration has a synergistic effect for the firm.[79] Hitherto, there is limited evidence regarding the role, relevance, and effectiveness of these three perspectives. Nonetheless, some evidence has been reported on the synergistic benefits from an alignment of HR policies and practices with one another and with the overall organizational strategy.[80] It has been reported that growth and profitability are ultimately the result of alignment between people, customers, strategy, and processes. More specifically, firms that consistently land on their feet during turbulent times are managed by people who keep everyone focused and centered on a few key business objectives. They do so in a way that creates a self-aligning and self-sustaining culture that distributes leadership and energy throughout their firms and unleashes a kind of organizational power and focus on "alignment."[81]

HR scholars have examined and questioned the basis of some of the universal claims made about a possible correlation between the implementation of HR strategies and improved organizational performance. There is concern about the prescriptive nature of HR interventions applicable to firms, irrespective of context and priorities, with the expectation of similar level responses and results.[82] There is still an ongoing debate among and between HR scholars and professionals as to what exactly constitutes "best practice."[83] In other words, what established HR methods and techniques will most likely produce superior organizational results? It has been suggested that organizational activities and practices that are designed to empower and develop the employee in addition to positively affect the bottom line of the firm are considered "best practice."[84]

THE ROLE OF ORGANIZATIONAL CULTURE

Organizational culture has traditionally been considered a form of organizational capital.[85] Researchers agree that the concept of corporate culture is difficult to imitate or duplicate[86] due to its inherent tacitness, complexity, and specificity.[87] Barney characterizes organizational culture as valuable, rare, and imperfectly imitable, thereby possessing high potential for creating sustainable competitive advantage for a firm.[88] It may be deduced that organizational culture can have a direct impact on achieving higher levels of firm performance.[89] Organizational culture is seen as an intangible component of a firm,[90] encompassing social phenomena, including beliefs, values, behaviors, and assumptions, which become entrenched within organizational members.[91] These social phenomena constituting organizational culture shape the way a firm conducts its business, how the firm interacts with the external environment, and how a firm deals with its internal processes.[92]

There is some debate within the management literature arguing that HR practices do not directly impact organizational performance.[93] There are assertions that there is a missing link between the two variables leading to the emergence of a "black box," which explains an interest in the study of organizational culture. It has been noted that organizational culture is entrenched in the everyday working lives of cultural members[94] and manifested in the behavior of a firm's employees.[95] The organizational culture of a firm is believed to have a significant impact on employees' job attitudes as well as their efficiency and productivity levels.[96] A firm's culture also has the capacity to help it execute its plans and meet its strategic goals.[97]

Barney, who championed the development of the RBV of the firm, argues that certain firm-specific resources and capabilities can lead to sustainable competitive advantages and, thus, increase organizational performance. He affirms that a firm's culture can in fact be one of these resources. If a firm's culture meets the four criteria of being valuable, rare, imperfectly imitable, and nonsubstitutable, then it has an enhanced opportunity to be a source of sustained competitive advantage.[98] An appropriate HR system has the capacity to create and foster capabilities that themselves become sources of competitive advantages.[99] For example, Nordstrom, an upscale department store in the United States, attributes its successes to its culture with a focus on customer service, thereby generating a source of sustainable competitive advantage for the firm and its stakeholders. Another prominent example is Southwest Airlines, which is one of the few U.S. airlines that have maintained profitability in an industry notorious for financial losses. Southwest Airlines stresses the importance of a strong work environment focusing on all its stakeholders, including employees. In the words of its current CEO Gary Kelly, "People aren't an expense—our People are our heart and soul."

Finally, it has been stated that a firm's culture and its HR systems can be a valuable resource for the firm.[100] Thus, they play a significant role in the overall performance and business success of the entire organization.[101] Although it has been stated that HR practices affect organizational culture, which in turn, impact a firm's performance, we need to be careful as to the exact nature of possible claims of correlations and relationships between organizational variables. Most likely, there are a number of other internal and external variables that explain possible links between HR systems and firm performance. What is certain, though, is that organizational culture shapes the work environment in which performance occurs, and it is this performance that drives the firm's bottom line.

NOTES

1. Dess, G. G., Lumpkin, G. T., & Taylor, M. L. *Strategic Management,* 2nd edition, (New York: McGraw-Hill Irwin, 2005).

2. Gandolfi, F., & Hansson, M. "Reduction-In-Force (RIF)—New Developments and a Brief Historical Analysis of a Business Strategy," *Journal of Management & Organization (Journal of the Australian and New Zealand Academy of Management),* 16:5 (2010): 727–43.

3. Mintzberg, H. "The Fall and Rise of Strategic Planning," *Harvard Business Review,* January–February (1994): 107–14.

4. Littler, C. R., & Bramble, T. "Conceptualizing Organizational Restructuring in the 1990s," *Journal of the Australian and New Zealand Academy of Management,* 1:1 (1995): 45–56.

5. Gandolfi, F. "New Developments in Reduction-In-Force: A Brief Historical Analysis of a Business Strategy," *The Journal of Management Research,* 10:1 (2010): 3–14.

6. Hitt, M. A., Ireland, D., & Hoskisson, R. E. *Strategic Management: Competitiveness and Globalization* (Toronto: Thomson South-Western, 2005).

7. Laiken, M. E. Models of Organizational Learning: Paradoxes and Best Practices in the Post Industrial Workplace, *NALL,* NALL Working Paper # 25 (2001). http://www.nall.ca/res/25modelsoforglearn.htm.

8. Gunasekaran, A., & Yusuf, Y. Y. "Agile Manufacturing: A Taxonomy of Strategic and Technological Imperatives," *International Journal of Production Research,* 40:6 (2005): 1357–85.

9. Mintzberg, H., Ahlstrand, B., & Lampel, J. *Strategy Bites Back* (Glasgow, Scotland: Prentice Hall, 2005).

10. Gandolfi, F. "Reflecting on Downsizing—What Have Managers Learned?" *SAM Advanced Management Journal,* 73:2 (2008): 46–56.

11. Mintzberg, H. "The Fall and Rise of Strategic Planning," *Harvard Business Review,* January–February (1994): 107–14.

12. Miller, D. "The Icarus Paradox: How Exceptional Companies Bring about Their Own Downfall," *Business Horizons,* January–February (1992).

13. Christensen, C. M. *The Innovator's Dilemma: The Revolutionary Book that Will Change the Way You Do Business* (New York: Harper Paperbacks, 2003).

14. Thurlby B. *Competitive Forces Are Also Subject to Change* (London: Management Decision, 1998).

15. Porter, M. E. *Competitive Strategy* (New York: Free Press, 1980).

16. Porter, M. E. *On Competition* (Boston: Harvard Business School Press, 1998).

17. Brandenburger, A. M., & Nalebuff, B. J. *Co-Opetition* (New York: Currency Doubleday, 1997).

18. Downes, L. "Beyond Porter," *Context Magazine* (Fall 1997). http://www.garyclarke.com/documents/CLARKE873-1.html.

19. Haberberg, A., & Rieple, A. *The Strategic Management of Organizations* (Essex: Pearson Education Limited, 2001).

20. Conner, K.R. "A Historical Comparison of Resource-Based Theory and Five Schools of Thought within Industrial Organization Economics: Do We Have a New Theory of the Firm?" *Journal of Management,* 17:1 (1991): 121–54.

21. Moore, G. *Dealing with Darwin: How Great Companies Innovate at Every Phase of Their Evolution* (New York: Portfolio, 2005).

22. Barney, J.B. "Looking Inside for Competitive Advantage," *Academy of Management Executive,* 9:4 (1995): 49–61.

23. Barney, J.B. "Firm Resources and Sustained Competitive Advantage," *Journal of Management,* 17 (1991): 99–120.

24. Conner, K.R. "A Historical Comparison of Resource-Based Theory and Five Schools of Thought within Industrial Organization Economics: Do We Have a New Theory of the Firm?" *Journal of Management,* 17:1 (1991): 121–54.

25. Dierickx, I., & Cool, K. "Asset Stock Accumulation and Sustainability of Competitive Advantage," *Management Science,* 35:12 (1989): 1504–13.

26. Peteraf, M., & Barney, J. "Unraveling the Resource-Based Tangle," *Managerial and Decision Economics,* 24 (2003): 309–23.

27. Barney, J.B. "Firm Resources and Sustained Competitive Advantage," *Journal of Management,* 17 (1991): 99–120.

28. Lippman, S., & Rumelt, R. "Uncertain Imitability: An Analysis of Interfirm Differences in Efficiency under Competition," *Bell Journal of Economics,* 13 (1982), 418–38.

29. Priem, R.L., & Butler, J.E. "Is the Resource Based View a Useful Perspective for Strategic Management Research?" *Academy of Management Review,* 26:1 (2001): 22–24.

30. Barney, J.B., & Wright, P.M. "On Becoming a Strategic Partner: The Role of Human Resources in Gaining Competitive Advantage," *Human Resource Management,* 37:1 (1998): 31–46.

31. Barney, J.B. *Gaining and Sustaining Competitive Advantage* (Upper Saddle River, NJ: Prentice Hall, 2002).

32. Barney, J.B. "Where Does Inequality Come From? The Personal and Intellectual Roots of Resource-Based Theory," in K.G. Smith & M.A. Hitt (Eds.), *Great Minds in Management: The Process of Theory Development,* 280–303 (Oxford: Oxford University Press, 2005).

33. Ghoshal, S. "Bad Management Theories Are Destroying Good Management Practices," *Academy of Management Learning & Education,* 4:1 (2005): 75–91.

34. Gibbert, M. "Generalizing about Uniqueness: An Essay on an Apparent Paradox in the Resource-Based View," *Journal of Management Inquiry,* 15 (2006): 124–34.

35. Levitas, E., & Ndofor, H.A. "What to Do with the Resource-Based View: A Few Suggestions for What Ails the RBV That Supporters and Opponents Might Accept," *Journal of Management Inquiry,* 15 (2006): 135–44.

36. Eisenhardt, K.M., & Martin, J.A. "Dynamic Capabilities: What Are They?" *Strategic Management Journal,* 21 (2000): 1105–21.

37. Helfat, C.E., & Peteraf, M.A. "The Dynamic Resource-Based View: Capability Lifecycles," *Strategic Management Journal,* 24 (2003): 997–1010.

38. Barney, J. B., & Clark, D. N. *Resource-Based Theory: Creating and Sustaining Competitive Advantage* (Oxford: Oxford University Press, 2007).

39. Kraaijenbrink, J., Spender, J. C., & Groen, A. "The Resource-Based View: A Review and Assessment of Its Critiques," *Journal of Management*, 36:1 (2010): 349–72.

40. Steffy, B., & Maurer, S. "Conceptualizing and Measuring the Economic Effectiveness of Human Resource Activities," *Academy of Management Review*, 13 (1988): 271–86.

41. Hunter, J., & Hunter, R. "Validity and Utility of Alternative Predictors of Job Performance," *Psychological Bulletin*, 86 (1984): 72–98.

42. Wright, P. M., McMahan, G. C., & McWilliams, A. "Human Resources and Sustained Competitive Advantage: A Resource-Based Perspective," *International Journal of Human Resource Management*, 5:2 (1994): 301–26.

43. Ibid.

44. Abelson, M. & Baysinger, B. "Optimal and Dysfunctional Turnover: Toward an Organizational Level Model," *Academy of Management Review*, 9 (1984): 331–41.

45. Jones, G. "Task Visibility, Free Riding, and Shirking: Explaining the Effect of Structure and Technology on Employee Behaviors," *Academy of Management Review*, 2 (1984): 684–95.

46. Wright, P. M., McMahan, G. C., & McWilliams, A. "Human Resources and Sustained Competitive Advantage: A Resource-Based Perspective," *International Journal of Human Resource Management*, 5:2 (1994): 301–26.

47. Cascio, W. *Managing Human Resources: Productivity, Quality of Work Life, Profits*, 8th edition (Burr Ridge, IL: Irwin/McGraw-Hill, 2010).

48. Cascio, W. *Costing Human Resources: The Financial Impact of Behavior in Organizations*, 4th edition (Cincinnati, OH: Southwestern, 2000).

49. Gandolfi, F. *Human Resource Management: Fundamentals, Concepts, and Perspectives* (Köln, Germany: LAP Lambert Academic Publishing, 2010).

50. Cascio, W. *Managing Human Resources: Productivity, Quality of Work Life, Profits*, 8th edition (Burr Ridge, IL: Irwin/McGraw-Hill, 2010).

51. Noe, R., Hollenbeck, J., Gerhart, B., & Wright, P. *Fundamentals of Human Resource Management*, 2nd edition (New York: McGraw-Hill, 2007).

52. Cascio, W. *Responsible Restructuring: Creative and Profitable Alternatives to Layoffs* (San Francisco: Berrett-Koehler Publishers and the Society for Human Resource Management, 2002).

53. Cascio, W. "The High Cost of Low Wages," *Harvard Business Review*, March 3, 2006: 23–26.

54. Alcazar, F. M., Fernandez, P. M. R., & Gardey, G. S. "Researching on SHRM: An Analysis of the Debate over the Role Played by Human Resources in Firm Success," *Management Revue*, 16:2 (2005): 213–41.

55. Browning, V., Edgar, F., Gray, B., & Garrett, T. "Realising Competitive Advantage through HRM in New Zealand Service Industries," *The Service Industries Journal*, 29:6 (2009): 741–60.

56. Haynes, P., & Fryer, G. "Human Resources, Service Quality and Performance: A Case Study," *International Journal of Contemporary Hospitality Management*, 12:4 (2000): 240–48.

57. Boselie, J., Dietz, G., & Boon, C. "Commonalities and Contradictions in HRM and Performance Research," *Human Resource Management Journal*, 15:3 (2005): 67–94.

58. Hutchinson, S., Kinnie, N., Purcell, J., Rayton, B., & Swart, J. *People Management and Performance* (London: Routledge, 2000).

59. Johnson, E. "The Practice of Human Resource Management in New Zealand: Strategic and Best Practice," *Asia Pacific Journal of Human Resources*, 38:2 (2000): 69–83.

60. Huselid, M. "The Impact of Human Resource Management Practices on Turnover and Productivity and Corporate Financial Performance," *Academy of Management Journal*, 38 (1995): 635–72.

61. Pfeffer, J. "Seven Practices of Successful Organizations," *California Management Review*, 40:2 (1998): 96–124.

62. Browning, V., Edgar, F., Gray, B., & Garrett, T. "Realising Competitive Advantage through HRM in New Zealand Service Industries," *The Service Industries Journal*, 29:6 (2009): 741–60.

63. Marchington, M., & Wilkinson, A. "High Commitment HRM and Performance," in M. Marchington & A. Wilkinson, *Human Resource Management at Work*, 71–98 (London: CIPD, 2005).

64. Oster, G. "Extreme Diversity," *Review of International Comparative Management*, 12:1 (2011): 18–29.

65. Browning, V., Edgar, F., Gray, B., & Garrett, T. "Realising Competitive Advantage through HRM in New Zealand Service Industries," *The Service Industries Journal*, 29:6 (2009): 741–60.

66. Heskett, J.L. "Beyond Customer Loyalty," *Managing Service Quality*, 12:6 (2002): 355–57.

67. Schneider, B., & Bowen, D.E. *Winning the Service Game* (Boston: Harvard Business School Press, 1995).

68. Gandolfi, F. *Human Resource Management: Fundamentals, Concepts, and Perspectives* (Köln, Germany: LAP Lambert Academic Publishing, 2010).

69. Redman, T., & Mathews, B.P. "Service Quality and Human Resource Management: A Review and Research Agenda," *Personnel Review*, 27:1 (1998): 57–77.

70. Browning, V., Edgar, F., Gray, B., & Garrett, T. "Realising Competitive Advantage through HRM in New Zealand Service Industries," *The Service Industries Journal*, 29:6 (2009): 741–60.

71. Schneider, B., & Bowen, D.E. *Winning the Service Game* (Boston: Harvard Business School Press, 1995).

72. Marchington, M., & Wilkinson, A. "High Commitment HRM and Performance," in M. Marchington & A. Wilkinson, *Human Resource Management at Work*, 71–98 (London: CIPD, 2005).

73. Browning, V., Edgar, F., Gray, B., & Garrett, T. "Realising Competitive Advantage through HRM in New Zealand Service Industries," *The Service Industries Journal*, 29:6 (2009): 741–60.

74. Gandolfi, F. *Human Resource Management: Fundamentals, Concepts, and Perspectives* (Köln, Germany: LAP Lambert Academic Publishing, 2010).

75. Marchington, M., & Grugulis, I. "Best Practice HRM: Perfect Opportunity or Dangerous Illusion?" *International Journal of Human Resource Management*, 11:6 (2000): 1104–24.

76. Alcazar, F.M., Fernandez, P.M.R., & Gardey, G.S. "Researching on SHRM: An Analysis of the Debate over the Role Played by Human Resources in Firm Success," *Management Revue*, 16:2 (2005): 213–41.

77. Boxall, P., & Purcell, J. "Strategic Human Resource Management: Where Have We Come from and Where Should We Be Going?" *International Journal of Management Reviews,* 2:2 (2000): 183–203.

78. Browning, V., Edgar, F., Gray, B., & Garrett, T. "Realising Competitive Advantage through HRM in New Zealand Service Industries," *The Service Industries Journal,* 29:6 (2009): 741–60.

79. Delery, J.E., & Doty, D.H. "Modes of Theorizing in Strategic Human Resource Management: Tests of Universalistic, Contingency, and Configurational Performance Predictions," *Academy of Management Journal,* 39:4 (1996): 802–35.

80. Haynes, P., & Fryer, G. "Human Resources, Service Quality and Performance: A Case Study," *International Journal of Contemporary Hospitality Management,* 12:4 (2000): 240–48.

81. Labovitz, G., & Rosansky, V. *The Power of Alignment* (New York: Wiley and Sons, 1997).

82. Guest, D. "Human Resource Management—The Worker's Verdict," *Human Resource Management Journal,* 9:3 (1999): 5–25.

83. Price, A. *Human Resource Management in a Business Context,* 2nd edition, (London: Thomson Learning, 2004).

84. Edgar, F. "Employee-Centred Human Resource Management Practices," *New Zealand Journal of Industrial Relations,* 28:3 (2003): 230–40.

85. Barney, J.B. "Organizational Culture: Can It Be a Source of Sustained Competitive Advantage?" *Academy of Management Review,* 11:3 (1985): 656–65.

86. Mueller, F. "Human Resources as Strategic Assets: An Evolutionary Resource-Based Theory," *Journal of Management Studies,* 33:6 (1996): 757–85.

87. Reed, R., & DeFillippi, R.J. "Causal Ambiguity, Barriers to Imitation, and Sustained Competitive Advantage," *Academy of Management Review,* 15:1 (1990): 88–102.

88. Barney, J.B. "Organizational Culture: Can It Be a Source of Sustained Competitive Advantage?" *Academy of Management Review,* 11:3 (1985): 656–65.

89. McKenzie, K. "Organizational Culture: An Investigation into the Link between Organizational Culture, Human Resource Management, High Commitment Management and Firm Performance," *Otago Management Graduate Review,* 8 (2010): 39–50.

90. Carmeli, A., & Tishler, A. "The Relationship between Intangible Organizational Elements and Organizational Performance," *Strategic Management Journal,* 25 (2004): 1257–78.

91. Chow, I., & Liu, S. "The Effect of Aligning Organizational Culture and Business Strategy with HR Systems on Firm Performance in Chinese Enterprises," *International Journal of Human Resource Management,* 20:11 (2009): 2292–310.

92. Mahal, P. "Organizational Culture and Organizational Climate as a Determinant of Motivation," *Journal of Management Research,* 8:10 (2009): 38–51.

93. Boxall, P., & Purcell, J. "Strategic Human Resource Management: Where Have We Come from and Where Should We Be Going?" *International Journal of Management Reviews,* 2:2 (2000): 183–203.

94. McKenzie, K. "Organizational Culture: An Investigation into the Link between Organizational Culture, Human Resource Management, High Commitment Management and Firm Performance," *Otago Management Graduate Review,* Vol. 8 (2010): 39–50.

95. Ngo, H., & Loi, R. "Human Resource Flexibility, Organizational Culture and Firm Performance: An Investigation of Multinational Firms in Hong Kong," *International Journal of Human Resource Management*, 19:9 (2008): 1654–66.

96. Mahal, P. "Organizational Culture and Organizational Climate as a Determinant of Motivation," *Journal of Management Research*, 8:10 (2009): 38–51.

97. Chan, L., Shaffer, M., & Snape, E. "In Search of Sustained Competitive Advantage: The Impact of Organizational Culture, Competitive Strategy and Human Resource Management Practices on Firm Performance," *Journal of Human Resource Management*, 15:1 (2004): 17–35.

98. Barney, J. B. "Organizational Culture: Can It Be a Source of Sustained Competitive Advantage?" *Academy of Management Review*, 11:3 (1985): 656–65.

99. Lau, C. M., & Ngo, H. Y. "The HR System, Organizational Culture, and Product Innovation," *International Business Review*, 13 (2004): 685–703.

100. Carmeli, A., & Tishler, A. "The Relationship between Intangible Organizational Elements and Organizational Performance," *Strategic Management Journal*, 25 (2004): 1257–78.

101. Platonova, E. "The Relationship among Human Resource Management, Organizational Culture, and Organizational Performance," Unpublished doctoral dissertation (Birmingham, AL: University of Alabama, 2005).

Chapter 3

SWOT Analysis and the Three Strategic Questions

Tom Hinthorne

Analysts use the SWOT analysis to identify the firm's strengths (S), weaknesses (W), opportunities (O), and threats (T). Strengths and weaknesses are associated with the firm's internal environment and are to some degree manageable by the firm (e.g., human resources). Opportunities and threats are associated with the firm's external environment and are beyond the control of the firm, although adaptation may be possible. Today, the SWOT analysis is one of several tools available to business analysts; it is widely taught in business schools; it continues to offer value-added opportunities to analysts; and it is equally applicable to for-profit and non-profit firms. However, its analyses tend to be qualitative and difficult to quantify, which makes rigorous application imprecise.

The purpose of the SWOT analysis is to use the strengths of the firm to capitalize on opportunities, diminish threats, and reduce weaknesses (e.g., fill resource gaps). Jay Barney traces the analysis of the firm's strengths (i.e., resources and capabilities) and weaknesses to the work of Edith Penrose (1959), whose analyses underlie the resource-based view (RBV) of the firm.[1,2] Other writers have traced the linking of strengths and weaknesses (i.e., SW) and opportunities and threats (i.e., OT) to the work of Kenneth Andrews (1971).[3] The SWOT analysis is typically an analytical platform for creating strategic plans. Ultimately, the firm seeks to answer three strategic questions: Where is the firm now? Where does it want it to be in 5 to 10 years? How does it plan to get it there?[4]

In the 1950s, 1960s, and 1970s, many large firms developed central planning operations, and the planning process was relatively formal and systematic. Analysts called this approach the *rational design* school, and the SWOT analysis was associated with this school. In ensuing years, as planning environments became more turbulent and unpredictable, senior management delegated more of the planning to its strategic business units and reduced or eliminated its central planning operations. Increasingly, analysts saw strategy as being *crafted* through some instinctive experiential-based process emerging out of *the weakly coordinated decisions of multiple organizational members.*[5,6] Analysts called this approach the *emergent process* school. Today, depending on the circumstances, both approaches have merit.

This chapter develops in four parts. First, to make it instructive and interesting it focuses on the Northrop Grumman Corporation (NGC) and its primary target market, the U.S. Department of Defense (DoD). Second, the chapter focuses on the external environment of the firm and the assessment of opportunities and threats facing NGC and the industry. This is the *top down—big picture* context for subsequent analyses. Third, the chapter focuses on the internal environment of NGC and the assessment of its strengths and weaknesses. Last, to show how the SWOT analysis structures the planning process, the chapter considers how NGC might answer the three strategic questions. The time of the SWOT analysis is late 2010/early 2011.

NORTHROP GRUMMAN CORPORATION

NGC and its global competitors and suppliers are in the aerospace and defense industry. They are in the early months of a retrenchment process, given pending cuts in DoD expenditures. Product extensions into the commercial and civil markets (i.e., nonmilitary government markets, such as law enforcement) offer new revenue opportunities. Thus, NGC and its competitors are perfecting unmanned aerial systems (e.g., NGC's Global Hawk and Fire Scout drones) and cybersecurity systems (e.g., protecting computer networks from attacks).

In February 2009, Wes Bush, NGC's president and chief operating officer (CEO), described NGC as a *diversified security company* serving the long-term needs of the DoD and related markets. The DoD's needs include: (1) "assure U.S. military dominance, (2) confront irregular challenges such as terrorism, and (3) safeguard populations and critical infrastructures."[7] Bush said, "The United States faces a complex and rapidly changing national security environment . . . requires the ability to respond to constantly evolving threats, terrorist acts, regional conflicts and cyber attacks."[8]

In January 2010, NGC's board appointed Wes Bush as the president and CEO of NGC. As of November 2010, NGC had revenues of $35 billion (trailing 12 months) of which about 78 percent were attributable to defense.[9,10] NGC had the fourth-largest market share in the aerospace and defense industry behind Lockheed-Martin (United States), BAE Systems (United Kingdom), and Boeing. The largest firms in the industry were conglomerates that tended to follow each other's actions (e.g., in unmanned aerial systems and cybersecurity systems). NGC had 120,000 employees in 50 states and 25 countries. Its supply chain was global. In December 2010, a prominent advisory service gave NGC an A+ financial rating. Its primary U.S. competitors had A+ or A++ ratings.

In October 2010, Bush gave further definition to the scope of the DoD's mandate. The U.S. military had to be able to fight "conventionally trained and equipped military adversaries," contend with "violent insurgencies" and conduct "humanitarian operations" (e.g., in Haiti). In addition, the U.S. military had to be prepared to fight adversaries that had nuclear and biological weapons, ballistic missiles, and space capabilities. Moreover, there was the threat of cyber-attack and multiple regional instabilities. Bush concluded saying, "the global commons now includes cyber-space, and energy, food and water-rich areas among a world population that grows every year in numbers, desperation, and technological savvy."[11]

In October 2010, Bush reviewed the third-quarter calendar results, which were good. He said, "Third quarter results demonstrate that our focus on sustainable performance improvement (*i.e., NGC's top policy directive*) continues to gain traction across the corporation" (emphasis added). Sales were up four percent to $8.7 billion and free cash flow was $817 million (i.e., the cash left after the business has paid all of its cash expenses). NGC had also repurchased $180 million of its shares, continuing its share purchase program of nearly $6.8 billion in the last six years. NGC was investing in NGC. Its business units included:

1. *Aerospace systems:* (e.g., manned and unmanned aircraft, spacecraft, high-energy laser systems, microelectronics, etc.). Its 2009 revenues were $10.4 billion.
2. *Electronic systems:* (e.g., airborne surveillance, aircraft fire control, precision targeting, electronic warfare, air and missile defense, etc.). Its 2009 revenues were $7.7 billion.
3. *Information systems:* (e.g., intelligence processing, decision support systems, cybersecurity, systems engineering and integration, etc.). Its 2009 revenues were $8.6 billion.

4. *Shipbuilding:* (e.g., designs, builds, and refuels nuclear-powered air-craft carriers and submarines for the U.S. navy, etc.). Its 2009 revenues were $6.2 billion.
5. *Technical services:* (e.g., logistics, infrastructure, sustainment support, training and simulation services, etc.). Its 2009 revenues were $2.8 billion.[12]

With the exception of shipbuilding, NGC's four other business units are involved with other firms and countries in developing the $382 billion F-35 Joint Strike Fighter program. Lockheed Martin is the contractor; NGC is a principal subcontractor. The DoD launched the program in the mid-1990s. The objective is to develop an *affordably stealthy* multirole fighter plane for three target markets: (1) the F-35A for the U.S. air force and its allies; (2) the F-35B short takeoff, vertical landing, for the U.S. marines and British Royal Navy; and (3) the F-35C carrier-launched version for the U.S. navy.[13] By January 2010, the consortium had produced 19 F-35s; it was still testing the planes; and the estimated cost per plane ranged from $95 million to $135 million.[14] The program is controversial, but NGC is well positioned to capitalize on its 20 percent to 25 percent share of the project revenues in the near future.

NGC is a 40 percent partner in the production of the F/A-18E/F Super Hornet, the U.S. navy's frontline carrier-based strike fighter and the world's most advanced multirole strike fighter. Boeing is the contractor, while NGC is the principal subcontractor. NGC manufactures fuselage sections and associated subsystems. Delays in the production of the F-35s would likely be offset by increased production of the Super Hornet. The F/A-18s have been sold to the air forces of Australia, Canada, Finland, Kuwait, Malaysia, Spain, and Switzerland.

In June 2010, Loren Thompson, defense analyst and CEO for the Lexington Institute, said NGC seemed "well-positioned in terms of its business lines and competencies." For example, in 1999, NGC purchased Ryan Aeronautical, inventor of the Global Hawk, it continued to develop the unmanned stealth plane, and in 2009, it had almost 45 percent of the $3 billion market.[15] The Hawk can fly at 60,000 feet for more than 30 hours, at speeds of almost 340 nautical miles per hour. Equipped with proven new technology, it can see through most types of weather, day or night, and identify simulated improvised explosive devices (IEDs).[16] In sum, the international market for unmanned aerial systems is small and growing; there are potential civil and commercial applications (e.g., agriculture and energy); and existing firms are already positioned to aggressively exploit these market opportunities.[17]

Thompson approved of the recent "replacement of CEO Ron Sugar with the younger, more numbers-driven Wes Bush" and NGC's renewed emphasis on "capital efficiency over revenue growth." He favored "divesting under-performing businesses like shipbuilding."[18] NGC was weighing the divestment of its shipbuilding unit (i.e., a sale or spinoff). The unit's operating income (i.e., income before interest and taxes) as a percentage of the unit's revenues was a 4.8 percent profit in 2009, a 37.5 percent loss in 2008, and a 9.3 percent profit in 2007.[19] In November 2010, NGC e-mailed its 30,000 shipbuilding employees to say that if it were to spinoff the newly named Huntington Ingalls Industries shipbuilding division, NGC's stockholders would own 100 percent of the outstanding shares of the independent, public traded, wholly owned NGC subsidiary. Moreover, NGC's board had approved the spinoff and appointed retired Admiral Thomas Fargo, a member of NGC's board, as chairman of the board of the spinoff—should the spinoff happen.[20]

This background description of NGC provides the context for a SWOT analysis of NGC and the aerospace and defense industry. Next, the chapter focuses on the external environment of the firm and the techniques used to analyze the opportunities and threats facing NGC and its industry and, by extrapolation, other firms and industries. This process begins with an analysis of societal forces, followed by an analysis of competitive (industry) forces, an analysis of scenarios, and an analysis of stakeholder forces.

ANALYSIS OF THE EXTERNAL ENVIRONMENT— OPPORTUNITIES AND THREATS

Opportunities and threats develop from forces in the external environment. These forces have the power to change the direction and economic viability of the firm and are beyond the control of the firm. However, successful firms align their strategies with these forces. Scanning the external environment for forces and their effects begins with the opinions of experts and develops from there. The objective is to identify and assess the forces that are "dealmakers" or "deal breakers." The "possible maybes" may be worth watching for the future, but it is important to keep the analysis simple, focused, and relevant.

The Analysis of Societal Forces

For strategic planning purposes, it is important to understand the societal forces that are creating the opportunities and threats facing the firm. To guide the analyst's thinking, most strategy books offer lists of societal forces (e.g., economic, legal, natural, political, sociocultural, and technological forces). Typically, only a few forces are truly decisive in shaping the direction of the firm. Here, the discussion focuses on the societal forces affecting NGC. These forces and their future manifestations (i.e., what they morph into) are likely to play a significant role in shaping the future of

NGC over the next three to five years. Thus, the forces discussed here (i.e., societal, competitive, and stakeholder forces) are generally not static.

It is important to remember that an opportunity for one group of stakeholders may be a threat to another. For example, NGC's management may see terrorist and cyber-attacks on the United States as a business opportunity with a moral imperative to protect the nation's interests and the people of the United States. Alternatively, the general population is likely to see terrorist and cyber-attacks on the United States as a threat. Thus, in the following analyses, the reader should interpret the labeling of forces as opportunities or threats as meaning "more threats than opportunities" or "more opportunities than threats."

Economic Forces—Threats

At the onset of 2011, economic forces dominated NGC's strategic planning environment. The recession that began in 2007 had unleashed powerful forces that significantly affected many firms and governments in the United States and Europe, and to lesser degrees, firms and governments in Asia, Africa, and South America. For most firms, the recession posed significant threats; for some it was fatal; and for a few, it created opportunities (e.g., merger and acquisition opportunities). Similarly, it brought some governments (e.g., Greece, Ireland, Portugal, and Spain) to the brink of potentially disastrous sovereign debt defaults.

In November 2010, the Federal Reserve Bank's Open Market Committee reviewed the U.S. economic situation and its plans to manage inflationary and deflationary pressures and keep the federal funds rate between 0 and 1/4 percent. It noted that the rate of recovery in output and employment was slow. Household spending was increasing slowly, but it was limited by high unemployment (9.4%), modest personal income growth, depressed home values and housing starts, and tight credit. Business spending on equipment was rising, but more slowly than earlier in the year, although investment in commercial and industrial real estate remained weak. Businesses were hesitant to add employees. Meanwhile, inflationary expectations remained stable. To encourage economic recovery the committee decided to purchase a further $600 billion of longer-term treasury securities by the end of June 2011.[21]

Global leaders gave the Fed's decision mixed reviews. Detractors said the injection of $600 billion would devalue the U.S. dollar, creating a revenue advantage for U.S.-based exporters (i.e., an opportunity) or a revenue disadvantage for U.S.-based importers (i.e., a threat). Others feared the injection of $600 billion would trigger inflation and speculation-driven asset bubbles. The minutes of the committee's December 2010 meeting confirmed that it planned to continue its controversial $600 billion bond purchases.

In November 2010, President Obama's commission on reducing the federal budget deficit recommended sweeping spending cuts and various increases and decreases in taxes.[22] At fiscal year-end, September 30, 2010, the U.S. budget deficit was $1.3 trillion, and the national debt was $13.7 trillion or about 97 percent of gross domestic product. The commission recommended a $100 billion reduction in the DoD's annual expenditures over the next five years. However, its recommendations were controversial and nonbinding.

The DoD's estimated budget for fiscal 2010 included $508 billion for defense programs plus $128 billion for the Global War on Terror (GWOT) for a total of $636 billion.[23] (In 2002, the comparable budget was $342 billion.) Additional appropriations for the GWOT in fiscal 2010 were expected to increase the actual expenditure to perhaps $700 billion.[24]

In January 2011, Secretary of Defense Robert Gates was told to reduce the DoD's expenditures by $78 billion over the next five years.[25] In sum, given the federal budget deficit and debt, DoD expenditures were likely to plateau or even decrease in the future. However, significant attacks on the United States (e.g., the 9/11 attacks) might result in renewed growth in the DoD expenditures despite the deficit and debt. In addition, the United Kingdom was planning to reduce its defense budget by 20 percent, and several European countries were analyzing similar reductions.

Military/Terrorist Forces—Threats

In the early days of 2011, U.S. security forces were engaged in two wars and ongoing terrorist activities. The 9/11 attacks in 2001 were history, and the president and some congressional representatives were questioning the need to spend $700 billion a year on national defense. This reticence posed a significant threat to firms in the aerospace and defense industry. However, a series of 9/11-magnitude terrorist attacks or the outbreak of another war in the Middle East or on the Korean peninsula could turn the threat into an opportunity for NGC and other firms in the industry.

In January 2011, pictures of China's J-20 stealth fighter's first test flight appeared on the Internet. Apparently, the development of the J-20 was more advanced than most analysts had estimated. Within days, Secretary of Defense Robert Gates met with China's president, Hu Jintao and asked him how the test flight went. From Hu's reaction it appeared he had not been briefed on the test flight, raising questions about the military's motives and the wisdom of putting President Hu in an embarrassing position. For more than 70 years, China's military had been under the control of the Chinese Communist Party.

Once in service, the J-20s could be based in the interior of China from which they could patrol Taiwan, the East and South China Seas, and the Western Pacific, threatening Japan, South Korea, and other Asian countries.[26,27] The J-20 looked similar to the U.S. F-22 Raptor, which is the only operational stealth fighter in the world. Manufacturing of the F-22 was halted in 2009, but production could be restarted.

Cyber Forces—Threats

In April 2009, Defense Secretary Robert Gates said the United States is "under cyber attack virtually all the time, every day." The Wikileaks saga tested the cybersecurity of companies such as PayPal, MasterCard, and Visa. Experts considered the attacks relatively primitive. In contrast, J. B. "Gib" Godwin, NGC's vice president, Cyber-Security and Systems Integration, said, "Everyday there are an estimated 360 million probes directed at Pentagon computers, looking for vulnerabilities."[28]

In July 2009, Linda Mills, corporate vice president and president of NGC's information systems segment provided another example of a cyberattack. "That attack involved nearly 170,000 zombie computers in 74 countries linked together . . . it managed to hit virtually every major federal agency, including the White House."[29] She explained how NGC's engineers connected a personal computer loaded with the best commercial security software to the Internet. Within four hours, they detected the first ping by a potential hacker. Within a week, a hacker had installed a *"root kit"* to control the computer. Within two weeks, NGC's computer was enslaved and run by a server in Canada that was run by a server in Singapore that was run by a server that could not be traced. Then, NGC's computer was used to attack a computer in Poland.

On September 6, 2007, in a remote area of eastern Syria, North Korean workers were constructing a large building that analysts surmised would house a nuclear facility. Shortly after midnight, when most of the workers had left the site, Israeli F-15 Eagles and F-16 Falcons swept in and obliterated the building. Initially, Syria said nothing about the attack. Its Russian-built air-defense system gave no warning of the attack. Israel had taken control of Syria's computers, so the Syrians saw what the Israelis wanted them to see, which was status quo. Later Syria and North Korea expressed outrage at the attack. Syria said Israel destroyed an empty building. Syria cleaned up the debris and plowed the area. Israeli news services said nothing about the attack.[30]

NGC has been engaged in cybersecurity research for 20 years.[31] The need for cybersecurity on NGC's networks led it to develop a high-tech network defense capability for the "management of vulnerabilities, intrusion detection and prevention, incident response, and forensics."[32] In July 2010, NGC opened its new Cyber Security Operations Center in Maryland, a cyber-threat detection and response center to protect NGC and extend the lessons learned to customers' networks. In October 2010, NGC opened its Fareham cyber range in the United Kingdom. NGC linked its U.K. range to its Maryland facility and other cyber ranges. The ranges simulate large complex computer networks and their responses to threats.

Political Forces—Opportunities

The president's and the Congress' agendas can have a significant effect on the prosperity of the aerospace and defense industry. The 9/11 attacks in 2001 led to a big increase in DoD expenditures. Today, President Obama's agenda is more oriented to domestic needs (e.g., improving education and healthcare). In addition, U.S. arms sales to other countries continue to have a significant political dimension and impact on the industry. Last, as Standard & Poor's explains, "weapons purchases are not based on price and performance alone, but also on political considerations."[33] For example, the F-35 Joint Strike Fighter program elected to use a Pratt & Whitney (P&W) engine. General Electric (GE) and its supporters were promoting a GE engine. The DoD estimated the cost savings of halting the continuing development of the GE engine at $2.9 billion.[34]

The industry relies on many lobbyists and political action groups for access to the DoD. The contract acquisition market is not perfectly competitive. Thus, the DoD may continue to support military contracts for political reasons, even though the military need has passed. In addition, the DoD may award new contracts to support a contractor who needs the business or to preserve competition among the contractors.

Protecting jobs is important to congressional members, and the defense contractors leverage this fact. For example, in November 2010, NGC had 4,800 employees in San Diego County, California. About 2,300 worked on the development of its Global Hawk. In response to anticipated funding cuts, NGC put advertisements in five area newspapers explaining the importance of the Hawk and enabling people to use a Website to communicate directly with their congressional representatives. In addition, in November 2010, NGC was moving its corporate headquarters from Los Angeles to northern Virginia to be closer to the DoD (i.e., the Pentagon).

Innovation Forces—Opportunities

To identify societal forces, it makes sense to turn to the experts and start with their projections. For example, in mid-2009, McKinsey & Company analyzed "The 10 Trends You Have to Watch."[35] Although such forecasts are useful, the trends are likely to affect firms and industries differently. For example, the McKinsey authors projected a trend they called "innovation marching on" and noted "innovation in fields such as information technology, biotechnology, nanotechnology, materials science, and clean energy." In these industries and the aerospace and defense industry, the saying is "innovate or die."

The aerospace and defense industry thrives on innovation, and the DoD contractors create innovative solutions that sometimes have civil and commercial applications (e.g., unmanned air systems). Thus, the McKinsey authors' claim that innovation will continue seems reasonable; innovation is a source of competitive advantage. However, following the end of the Cold War, large cutbacks in the DoD expenditures led to a major exodus of talent from the industry. According to Wes Bush, "As a result, across the industry, we have a population gap in our ranks between the ages of about 38 to 52 . . . simple rule . . . technology attracts talent."[36] In sum, reductions in DoD technology funding are likely to shift talent to other industries (i.e., a threat).

Conclusions

In late 2010/early 2011, NGC faced several powerful societal forces. First, *economic forces* were a significant threat, and firms in the aerospace and defense industry were crafting retrenchment strategies (i.e., reducing costs and assets) and developing recovery strategies.[37,38] Second, *military/terrorist forces* had not been able to mount a successful attack in several years, and this fact threatened the industry's funding and preparedness. Third, *cyber forces* were an increasing threat, and the possibility of a cyber-war was no longer a Hollywood fantasy. Fourth, *political forces,* which usually created opportunities, were focused on reducing the DoD's funding, clearly a threat to many firms in the industry. Fifth, *innovation forces,* which typically created opportunities, were on the verge of declining. The aerospace and defense industry was retrenching. Firms were putting their low-potential projects on hold, and some of the talent that fueled innovation was looking for opportunities in other industries. An exodus of talent could be crippling.

Unfortunately, there is no way to quantify the societal forces and calculate, for example, a scaled assessment of an opportunity or threat (e.g., 90 = excellent opportunity, low threat; 50 = balanced opportunity and threat; and 10 = low opportunity, high threat). Although threats may conceal opportunities, the foregoing analysis suggests the aerospace and defense industry faces a period of declining opportunities and rising threats.

The next step in developing a SWOT analysis is to evaluate the competitive forces that are shaping the firm's industry. Here again, the purpose of the environmental scanning is to identify and assess the forces that are truly "dealmakers" or "deal breakers" and avoid being mired down in the analysis of minutia.

The Analysis of Competitive (Industry) Forces

Competitive forces have the power to change the direction and economic viability of the firm. Michael Porter published his classic model of industry structure analysis in 1980.[39,40] The model focuses on five competitive forces arranged in an airport hub-and-spoke layout, that is: (1) the threat of new entrants (north terminal), (2) the intensity of competitive rivalry (hub), (3) the bargaining power of buyers (east terminal), (4) the bargaining power of suppliers (west terminal), and (5) the threat of substitutes (south terminal).

Entry barriers reduce the threat of new entrants (i.e., economies of scale, expected retaliation, high brand loyalty, etc.). If there are strategic groups within the industry, mobility barriers within the industry will inhibit or prevent movement from one strategic group to another. In an industry, firms within strategic groups follow similar strategies, whereas different strategic groups within the industry follow different strategies.

In Porter's analytical framework, the subject of the analysis (e.g., NGC) is positioned in the central box, and it is the center of the analysis. Rivalry determinants and the determinants of buyer power, supplier power, and substitution structure the nature of the industry and give the analysis depth and breadth. The five forces operate in the external environment of the firm and have the potential to create opportunities and threats for firms in the industry. The basic logic of the model argues that the more intense the competitive forces are, the lower will be the long-run return on investment and vice versa.

Analysts use the model to analyze the structure of industries and to position firms in their industries with the intention of creating sustainable competitive advantages (i.e., sustainable levels of excellence in free cash-flow generation). Free cash flow is the preferred measure because cash pays the bills; cash creates and sustains credit; and cash and credit secure assets that generate more free cash flow. Therefore, it is important to never run out of cash or credit.[41] Analysts typically use free cash flow in the valuation of assets (e.g., payback, net present value, and internal rate of return criteria). Otherwise, they use some form of asset valuation (e.g., replacement cost). Sometimes analysts focus on profit as opposed to free cash flow. However, as the statement of cash flows clearly shows, profit is only a partial measure of cash flow. It is the first line on the statement of cash flows, and it excludes significant sources (uses) of cash.

Analysts want to know how the industry creates value (i.e., free cash flow) and who captures the value created. They envision the firm competing with its competitors (i.e., the intensity of competitive rivalry). In addition, Porter argues that the firm is also competing with its buyers and suppliers. Buyers typically want lower prices, higher quality, longer warranties, etc. If the switching costs are favorable, they might buy a competitor's products or play one firm against another. The greater the bargaining power of buyers is, the greater is the buyers' share of the value created by the industry, everything else being equal.

By contrast, suppliers want higher prices, lower quality requirements, less onerous warranties, etc. The greater the bargaining power of suppliers is, the greater is the suppliers' share of the value created by the industry, everything else being equal.

Porter saw substitute products as coming from outside of the firm's industry (e.g., beef, pork, and chicken are substitutes). The substitute serves the same function (e.g., nutrition), yet it is different (e.g., in appearance and/or chemical composition). Thus, it can place a ceiling on the price the firm can charge for its product, thus limiting the producers' value-creation possibilities. Last, if the threat of new entrants is high and low prices are a barrier to entry, it could further limit the producers' value-creation possibilities. An industry with strong buyers and suppliers, economically viable substitutes, and entry-barrier pricing, could be very unattractive. Unattractive industries often find it difficult to raise capital—debt or equity.

Analysts use Porter's model to understand the structure of an industry and the forces shaping the development of the industry, past and future. Typically, they want to learn how to position the firm in the industry to create a sustainable competitive advantage. Thus, using Porter's model to analyze the aerospace and defense industry might reveal the following:

Bargaining Power of Buyers—High to Moderate

The contracting activities of the DoD drive the economic activities of the aerospace and defense industry contractors. The primary buyer is the DoD (i.e., the Pentagon), which represents the various military services. Thus, contracts are usually associated with a military service (e.g., a navy contract). NGC's other buyers include civil buyers (i.e., nongovernment buyers, such as police forces and border patrols), commercial buyers, foreign governments, and scientific institutions (e.g., NASA). The DoD's purchases are significantly influenced by economic forces, military/terrorist forces, and the president's and the Congress' agendas (i.e., political forces). In June 2010, Loren Thompson, defense analyst, pointed to "trends unfolding within the Pentagon . . . migration of funding out of high-end technology and into people skills . . . move to 'in-source' tens of thousands of jobs previously contracted out to industry."[42] This migration threatens NGC's ability to retain high-technology talent.

Intensity of Competitive Rivalry—High and Rising

In the aerospace and defense industry the annual revenues of the largest 25 firms range from $3 billion to $65.7 billion.[43] The world's largest aerospace and defense contractors are Lockheed Martin, BAE Systems (United Kingdom), Boeing, Northrop Grumman, General Dynamics, and Raytheon. The larger firms have invested heavily in proprietary product technology and building economies of scale and brand identity (e.g., in 2009, NGC spent $610 million on research and had 6,293 patents). There are also hundreds if not thousands of smaller firms in the global supply chain. Competition at all levels of the industry is increasing, putting downward pressure on profit margins and free cash flows. The DoD clearly favors competition. Firms will likely reduce their margin requirements to protect revenue generation. Well-positioned firms will purchase firms with distinctive competencies. Firms without distinctive competencies will exit the industry.

Bargaining Power of Suppliers—Moderate

The large firms in the aerospace and defense industry (e.g., NGC) depend on a global supply chain. Given that the large firms are developing, producing, and marketing relatively similar products and services, it appears there may often be alternative buyers for suppliers' products and services, giving suppliers more bargaining power than they would have as a sole (captive) supplier. In addition, the industry depends on a continuous infusion of research—its own and the research of universities and independent research facilities. The bargaining power of these facilities depends on the quality of their research (i.e., their reputation).

Threat of New Entrants—Low

New entrants add capacity to the industry. New entrants may bring new, even "leap-frog," technology and/or productive capacity. Given the expected decline in DoD contracting and intensifying competition, significant additions to industry capacity are unlikely. However, industry leaders and analysts are discussing the likelihood of mergers and acquisitions (e.g., Boeing and NGC) and the possibility that one of the large firms might exit the industry. They seem to agree that mergers and acquisitions among the largest firms are unlikely because of the associated antitrust issues, but they are already underway among the second- and third-tier firms. The administration and the DoD are not in favor of large-scale mergers and acquisitions.[44]

Threat of Substitutes—Unknown

Substitutes serve the same function as the products/services they displace. Research displaces technology, and some of the research may come from industries presently or historically not engaged in producing products/services for the DoD. The likelihood of displacement largely depends on the switching costs and value-added potential.

In the aerospace and defense industry, the pending cuts in DoD spending set the context for the high and rising intensity of competitive rivalry. The high-to-moderate bargaining power of buyers, primarily the DoD and congressional representatives fighting for a share of the DoD contracts and jobs for their home districts, increase the intensity of competitive rivalry. The moderate bargaining power of suppliers is explained by the industry's global supply chain and its dependency on a continuous infusion of research. By contrast, the threat of new entrants is low. The next section explains the use of scenarios for managing a host of complex, high stakes, and relatively unpredictable forces that shape NGC's and the industry's strategic plans.

The Analysis of Scenarios

Analysts typically assess the future of a firm by projecting a future state of the industry (i.e., a single scenario).[45] Then, they examine various cases within the scenario (e.g., most likely, worst-case, and best-case pro forma financial statements). Sometimes, however, the planning environment is more complex and less predictable, and analysts must examine multiple independent scenarios with different policy prescriptions (e.g., DoD expenditures under a Democratic- versus a Republican-controlled presidency and/or Senate). Historically, when Republicans controlled the presidency and/or the Senate, DoD expenditures usually increased. When the Democrats controlled the presidency and/or the Senate, DoD expenditures usually decreased.[46] In each scenario, analysts examine the opportunities and threats NGC uses in both planning processes. As Wes Bush explained:

> We face a shifting security environment shaped to a significant extent by unpredictable external events and the political responses that they motivate. . . . We look for . . . changes in global macroeconomics; the military actions and investments of America's peer competitors; patterns of terrorist events; events associated with key resources such as food and energy; and weather-related disasters or pandemics. Any of these could be indicators of a new, relevant reality. Understanding these early indicators and being able and willing to react to them is what turns risk into opportunity and competitive advantage.[47]

This powerful quote captures the reality of strategic planning at NGC. Strategic planning at NGC is driven by a multitude of complex, high stakes, relatively unpredictable events. NGC scans the external environment for "indicators of a new, relevant reality" and plans accordingly. The next step in developing a SWOT analysis is the analysis of stakeholder forces that are shaping the firm's opportunities and threats in its external environment.

The Analysis of Stakeholder Forces

Stakeholders create opportunities and threats in the external environment of the firm. A stakeholder is a person(s) or organization(s) that affects or is affected by the actions or inactions of another person(s) or organization(s). NGC has many stakeholder relationships whose enhancement and maintenance are critical to its success (e.g., stakeholder relations with the DoD and members of the F-35 Joint Strike Fighter program). More specifically, to accelerate its research and feed its never-ending search for talent, NGC announced plans in December 2009 to invest millions to fund graduate fellowships and other research for at least five years at Carnegie Mellon's CyLab, MIT's Computer Science and Artificial Intelligence Lab, and Purdue's Center for Education and Research in Information Assurance and Security.[48]

Edward Freeman initiated the seminal research in stakeholder analysis. In his 1984 book, his approach to strategic management focused on "creating mutually beneficial stakeholder relations" (i.e., win/win situations). He asked:[49]

1. *Who are our stakeholders?*
2. *How do stakeholders affect each division, business and function, and its plans?*
3. *What are our assumptions about critical stakeholders?*
4. *Have we allocated resources to deal with our stakeholders?*

In 1994, Freeman developed *the principle of who or what really counts. To whom (or what) do the managers of the organization have to pay attention?*[50] This principle moved away from Freeman's 1984 proposition and created the possibility of win/lose situations. Thus, it was not only a question of who the stakeholders were, but also which stakeholders controlled management's attention, to what degree, and why? In 1997, Mitchell, Agle, and Wood used Freeman's principle of *who or what really counts* to argue, "Stakeholders with powerful, legitimate, urgent claims gained preferential access to management."[51]

In 1996, Hinthorne proposed a "predatory view" of stakeholder relations in an analysis of deregulation in the U.S. airline industry.[52] The use of the predatory/prey analogy suggests a strategic management style oriented to acquiring assets and removing obstacles with little or no regard for the human element in stakeholder relations. Hinthorne argued that in complex, high-stakes situations, the leaders of some organizations developed predatory management styles to achieve their organizations' goals. These leaders used power and force relations (e.g. stakeholder coalitions), and legitimacy to secure their goals. For example, they used institutional structures of power (i.e., executive, judicial, legislative, and regulatory) at the federal, state, and local levels to secure organizational goals. They preferred win-win strategies, but they also had some power to select, exploit, and destroy stakeholders—also exclude or silence stakeholders—to secure organizational goals, albeit while giving the appearance of pursuing legitimate goals.

Obviously, stakeholder relations are not always amicable. In stakeholder disputes, there are essentially two options for resolving the disputes—collaboration or litigation. There may be appeal processes (e.g., in working with government agencies), and arbitration and mediation are used. Litigation tends to be the preferred process of dispute resolution in the United States, and it is costly and time consuming.

If the disputants are sincerely interested in avoiding litigation and resolving their dispute on amicable terms, they may find that collaboration is the preferred process. However, there is a caveat: the disputants must share some critically important superordinate goals. Muzafer Sherif (1958) defined "superordinate" (i.e., common) goals as goals that are "compelling and highly appealing to members of two or more groups in conflict but which cannot be attained by the resources and energies of the groups separately. In effect they are goals attained only when groups pull together."[53] Sherif's research validated two hypotheses: (1) in conflict situations, groups will tend to cooperate to achieve superordinate goals, and (2) the more frequently the groups cooperate successfully to secure superordinate goals, the lower the conflict will be.

Collaboration is widely used in stakeholder disputes over natural resources (e.g., forest restoration and the protection of endangered species). It is typically less costly and more flexible than litigation. It is time consuming but no less so than litigation. Wondolleck and Yaffee studied over 200 collaborative situations, and their book is a good reference.[54] Collaboration usually faces significant threats. First, there is competition (e.g., egos, turf wars, self-interests, and win/lose and us/them mentalities). Second, there are conflicting interests (e.g., different core values, objectives, and strategies). Third, there is mistrust. Fourth, there is the compliance with U.S. laws and regulations that create unnecessary project delays and paperwork. Fifth, there is ineffective management of the collaborative process (e.g., lack of process skills and resources). Sixth, there are comfort zones (e.g., fears of change, collaboration, public interaction, lawsuits, and taking risks). Seventh, there is the need to secure the input of all likely stakeholders.[55]

The SWOT analysis is not just about the analysis of societal forces, competitive forces, and scenarios. It is also about the analysis of stakeholder forces. Stakeholder forces have the power to change the direction and economic viability of the firm. Therefore, good stakeholder relations are important. Collaboration is usually preferable to litigation when the disputants have superordinate goals and can collaborate successfully. However, litigation may be the only option when the disputants do not have superordinate goals. It may also be necessary to protect the firm's assets (e.g., intellectual property or reputation). Next, the SWOT analysis turns to an assessment of the firm's external environment and its strengths and weaknesses.

ANALYSIS OF THE INTERNAL ENVIRONMENT— STRENGTHS AND WEAKNESSES

Analysts use the RBV of the firm to assess its strengths and weaknesses. The RBV enables a firm to identify and develop its internal strengths, so it can capitalize on external opportunities. It also enables the firm to identify and reduce its internal weaknesses (e.g., fill resource gaps) and thereby reduce external threats. Much of the information presented here reflects the work of Jay Barney.[56]

The Underlying Assumptions

The analysis reflects two assumptions: resource heterogeneity and resource immobility.

1. *Resource heterogeneity:* A firm's resources reflect its evolutionary path of development, so its collection of resources is "path dependent" and unique. As a result, its resources are "heterogeneous" despite surface similarities. Heterogeneity could be a strength and a source of competitive advantage or a weakness and a source of competitive disadvantage. For example, NGC shares similarities with its competitors. However, it and each of its competitors have traveled different development paths, and their resources are unique.
2. *Resource immobility:* Some resources are costly or impossible to imitate or acquire. Their supply curves are inelastic (vertical), and a potential buyer's willingness to pay higher prices does not increase supply. At the extreme, there are no sellers.

In addition, Michael Porter and the RBV see the business as a chain of cost-incurring and value-creating activities, beginning with some form of "raw materials" and ending with some form of "finished product/service."[57] At one extreme, the fully integrated firm's activities include the complete value chain (e.g., land + oat seeds ⇒ Quaker Oats on the grocery shelf). At the other extreme, the firm may have only one activity (e.g., farmers who provide only land). Analysts examine each cost-incurring and value-creating activity to see how and where the firm creates value to ensure the configuration of activities is functioning optimally. In addition, they look for ways of reconfiguring activities to create greater synergies.

The Analysis of Resources and Capabilities

The definition of resources excludes assets readily available in markets. Resources include financial, human, knowledge, physical, organizational, reputational, and technological assets. Knowledge ranges from "information" that is relatively easy to codify and transmit to "know-how" that is tacit. Knowledge creation and management are potential sources of competitive advantage, especially if they enhance valuable tacit "know-how" or provide information enabling a "first-mover" advantage.

The firm's resources are not static and may be emerging along a predetermined path as the firm follows a specific strategy (e.g., growth, stability, or retrenchment)[58] or simply drifts because the firm does not have an effective strategy. Moreover, the value of the firm's resources and competitors' resources change over time. Resources are firm-specific assets that to some degree must meet several criteria. Jay Barney called this the "VRIO Framework" with the acronym standing for valuable, rare, inimitable, and organization.[59]

1. Resources must be *valuable,* that is, capable of exploiting opportunities, reducing threats, and creating a sustainable competitive advantage (e.g., a sustainable level of excellence in cash-flow generation). For a resource to be truly valuable, the firm must be able to associate the resource with specific value creating opportunities. If a resource is not unequivocally valuable, then its ability to create value is suspect.
2. Resources must be *rare,* that is, not readily available in markets. Moreover, most if not all competitors do not possess them or have the means to create them, except perhaps at great cost. Resources that are valuable but not rare cannot produce a sustainable competitive advantage because they are readily available to competitors. At best, they can produce "competitive parity."
3. Resources must be *difficult to imitate,* otherwise, competitors could copy them. At the extreme, the more useful, albeit confusing, word is "inimitability." That is, the resource *cannot be imitated.* Perhaps the

technology is proprietary (e.g., intellectual property) or the technology is physically not available for reverse engineering. Resources must also have *few or no substitutes,* that is, other resources cannot replace them. "Causal ambiguity" (i.e., ambiguous cause-effect relationships) may preclude imitation. That is, the observable is not necessarily the source of competitive advantage. For example, firms may have socially complex networked resources (e.g., organizational culture, senior management synergies, tacit knowledge, transformational leadership, etc.).

4. The firm must be *able to exploit its resources.* Firms combine resources to create distinctive capabilities that they use to complete specific activities efficiently and effectively. As firms refine their distinctive capabilities, they develop processes and routines—repetitively used codified and tacit practices—to enhance their distinctive capabilities and ensure optimal execution. These are "complementary resources." They enhance the value, rarity, and difficulty of imitating the firm's primary resources.

Resources are typically evaluated in the preceding order of importance (i.e., how valuable (most important), how rare, how inimitable, and how exploitable). Thus, as a resource's value rises (↑), rareness (↑), inimitability (↑), and exploitability rises (↑), the more likely it is that the resource is a major strength, able to form capabilities, exploit opportunities, and diminish threats.

Example: NGC sees its "leading capabilities" in "climate and environment technologies, battle management, cyber-security, defense electronics, homeland security, information technology and networks, naval shipbuilding, public health, systems integration, and space and missile defense."[60]

Example: In October 2010, NGC opened the first commercial cyber test range in the UK. The cyber range will simulate "large infrastructures and global threats and evaluate how these networks, whether military, civilian or commercial, respond to an attack in order to develop capabilities that will make these networks more secure." The range is linked to NGC's Cyberspace Solutions Center in Maryland (United States).[61] Conclusion: Keeping in mind that NGC spends over $600 million a year on research, it appears many of NGC's resources would variously meet the four resource criteria. Moreover, NGC has combined resources to create capabilities that may produce sustainable competitive advantages.

Example: In February 2009, Wes Bush explained how NGC developed a portfolio approach to managing roughly 100 different business elements. He said, *"We fully characterize each of these in terms of*

its products, technologies, customers, competitors, competitiveness, finan-
cial performance, and balance sheet. We also consider impacts resulting
from the interdependencies of these business elements."[62] Conclusion: This
appears to be a "*best practices*" approach to managing the business.
NGC's competitors and suppliers would likely have similar analytical tools, so NGC's portfolio analysis, while valuable, is probably not
rare, inimitable, and exploitable.

The Qualification and Quantification of Resources and Capabilities

The identification and assessment of resources and capabilities are subjective. That is, how valuable, how rare, how inimitable, and how well is
the firm organized to exploit its resources. In the RBV, resources and capabilities must be unequivocally valuable, rare, and costly to imitate. In
addition, the firm must be able to exploit its resources. Many firms do not
have unequivocal resources. Thus, they do not have the strengths to capitalize on opportunities, diminish threats, and reduce weaknesses (i.e., fill
resource gaps).

Every participant in a SWOT analysis has a personal concept of what
the words valuable, rare, inimitable, and exploitable mean in any given
situation. In each person's mind there is an inherent subjective scaling of
the criteria (e.g., "valuable, absolutely," or "valuable, well maybe"). These
personal concepts become more useful when analysts quantified them for
comparative analysis. Here, an analyst might use a 100-point scale (e.g.,
"valuable, absolutely—100" or "valuable, well maybe—30"). Once the
participants quantify their personal concepts, they can debate the issues
and perhaps reach a useful consensus (e.g., valuable, within a consensus
range of 60 to 80 for the following reasons . . .). Quantification elevates the
analysis of resources and capabilities from a "yes"/"no"/"maybe" level
(e.g., "yes" it is valuable, "no" it is not valuable) to a more productive level
that facilitates serious debate and objectivity.

The trap in using the RBV is to identify undifferentiated assets as resources. The human tendency in a competitive managerial environment
is to protect one's turf, objectively if possible and subjectively if necessary.
To correct for this tendency, analysts can debate and quantify the assessment of resources and capabilities and match these strengths to opportunities in the external environment to see if there is a strategic fit. Table 3.1
uses a 100-point scale, with 100 being the best, to assess three of NGC's
capabilities relative to its primary competitors.

The numbers in the table reflect competitive barriers. The higher the
number is, the greater is the barrier. For example, NGC has an A+ financial rating. The assessment indicates this is a very valuable resource (90); it
is very rare (80); it is somewhat costly to imitate (40); and the firm is very

Table 3.1
A Hypothetical Assessment of Three of NGC's Capabilities

	NGC's A+ Financial Rating	NGC's UK Cyber Range Investment	NGC's Portfolio Analysis Tool
How valuable?	90	100	80
How rare?	80	80	10
How costly to imitate (inimitability)?	40	100	20
How exploitable by NGC?	90	90	90
Relative importance	250	370	200
Possible	400	400	400

well positioned to exploit it (90). In sum, the A+ rating is worth 250 points out of 400 possible points, perhaps indicating NGC's A+ rating gives it at least competitive parity. The columns compare three hypothetical NGC capabilities.

A comparison of the four columns indicates the U.K. cyber range has the greatest potential for creating a sustainable competitive advantage. Relative to its competitors' resources and capabilities, the cyber range is extremely valuable (100); it is very rare (80); it is extremely costly to imitate (100); and NGC is extremely well positioned to exploit it (90).

Last, NGC's portfolio-analysis tool is very valuable (80); it is not rare (10); it is not costly to imitate (20), but the firm is very well positioned to exploit it (90). Notice too, it is a complementary resource that sustains NGC's business units.

After the firm's analysts have assessed its resources and capabilities qualitatively and quantifiably as relative strengths or weaknesses, the remaining question is this: how and when will the firm fill its resource gaps? The purpose of the SWOT analysis is to use the strengths of the firm to capitalize on opportunities, diminish threats, and reduce weaknesses (e.g., fill resource gaps), so there should be plan to reduce the firm's weaknesses as well as a plan to capitalize on its strengths.

THE SWOT ANALYSIS—A PLATFORM FOR STRATEGIC PLANNING

The SWOT analysis is typically an analytical platform for creating strategic plans. To get an overview of the issues, analysts often pose and try to answer three strategic questions: Where is the firm now? Where does it want to be in 5 to 10 years? How does it plan to get there? These are challenging questions, particularly for an outside observer. Nevertheless, the foregoing analysis suggests some answers, bearing in mind that it is late 2010/early 2011, and everything might look very different in 3 years, 5 years, and 10 years.

Where Is the Firm Now?

NGC is well positioned in the aerospace and defense industry (S). Its annual sales are $35 billion of which 78 percent are attributable to defense, giving it the third-largest market share in the industry (S/W). NGC has a 20 percent to 25 percent share of the F-35 Joint Strike Fighter program revenues (S), and it is a 40 percent partner in the production of the F/A-18E/F Super Hornet (S). NGC has almost 45 percent of the unmanned aerial systems market, which has growth potential (O), but the market is still relatively small (T).

NGC had an A+ financial rating (S) and a global supply chain (S). Its third-quarter sales were up four percent to $8.7 billion; its free cash flow was $817 million (S); and over the last six years it had repurchased nearly $6.8 billion of its shares (S). NGC may have a sustainable competitive advantage (i.e., a sustainable level of excellence in free cash-flow generation). However, the largest firms in the industry are conglomerates that tend to follow each other's actions in good times and bad (W). Thus, it is likely that the largest firms have a high degree of competitive parity. NGC's management is numbers driven (S) and focused on capital efficiency over revenue growth (S), divesting underperforming businesses (S), and sustainable performance improvement (S). It uses a portfolio approach to manage 100 different business elements. NGC spent over $600 million on research in 2009 (S), and it has 6,293 patents (S).

Where Does It Want to Be in 5 to 10 Years?

NGC is planning to spin off its shipbuilding business (S); so presumably, it does not want to invest in low-margin manufacturing operations. The remaining business units, aerospace systems, electronic systems, information systems, and technical services, are involved in the F-35 Joint Strike Fighter program and presumably are businesses that the management wants to expand. Aerospace systems include unmanned aircraft, and information systems include cybersecurity. NGC is repurchasing significant quantities of its stock, which raises a question of intentions. In late 2010, NGC had 291,990,000 shares outstanding; at $60/share, its market capitalization was $17,519,400,000. Is there a move to take the company private and avoid the scrutiny of the Securities & Exchange Commission?

How Does It Plan to Get There?

NGC might have been in a retrenchment mode for several years. It appears to have a strong financial position, and it is well positioned in its industry. It seems to be more focused on the efficient use of capital as opposed to revenue growth (S), which the investors seem to favor. It will use its numbers-oriented portfolio analysis to decide what operations to keep and build and what operations to divest. It looks like NGC has made a decision to spin off its shipbuilding segment, which is consistent with retrenchment. As it retrenches, it will develop a recovery strategy, building on the expertise of its four remaining business units. However, NGC faces several challenges over the 5- to 10-year period, including:

Societal forces: Economic forces (e.g., federal debt and deficit levels), military/terrorist forces (e.g., the probability of a 9/11-scale attack), and their interdependencies will drive NGC's scenarios. Cyber forces are likely to become more threatening; political forces will continue to shape scenarios; and unforeseen forces are likely to emerge. Innovation will continue to move forward; however, the level of innovation in the aerospace and defense industry is problematic.

Competitive forces: It appears that the aerospace and defense industry is facing declining market opportunities. As a result, firms in the industry are implementing retrenchment strategies and mulling over recovery strategies. The structure of the industry appears rigid and unlikely to change significantly in the near future. The bargaining power of the buyers is likely to remain high to moderate. Political forces may keep some firms and product/service offerings operating beyond their economic life to maintain competition in an industry sector or for political reasons (e.g., protecting jobs in a congressional district). The intensity of rivalry is likely to remain high and rising, precipitating firm closures, mergers, and acquisitions. The bargaining power of suppliers is likely to be moderate and global, and the threat of new entrants is likely to remain low.

Stakeholder forces: The aerospace and defense industry appears to face stakeholder forces that could affect its strategy choices. Creating win/win relations is important, and Freeman's four questions are worth considering.[63] The industry could probably improve its stakeholder relations through collaboration. However, there are significant barriers to collaboration. Unless the stakeholders can find common ground (i.e., superordinate goals), collaboration simply will not happen. Mutual trust is also critical. Beyond collaboration, there is litigation, which is costly and lessens the likelihood of successful collaboration in the future but may be necessary to protect the firm's assets.

In closing, the SWOT analysis provides a useful tool. However, none of the components, with the possible exception of the analysis of resources and capabilities, is measureable on a commonly understood scale. As a result, communication remains subjective and imprecise. However, an opportunity to make a valuable contribution to the research literature beckons.

NOTES

1. Edith Penrose, 1959. *The Theory of the Growth of the Firm.* Oxford: Oxford University Press.

2. Jay B. Barney, 2011. *Gaining and Sustaining Competitive Advantage.* Upper Saddle River, NJ: Prentice Hall.

3. Kenneth Andrews, 1971. *The Concept of Corporate Strategy.* Homewood, IL: Richard D. Irwin.

4. Thomas Wheelen & David Hunger, 2010. *Concepts in Strategic Management & Business Policy, Achieving Sustainability.* (paraphrased from p. 6), Upper Saddle River, NJ: Prentice Hall.

5. Henry Mintzberg, 1987. Crafting Strategy. *Harvard Business Review,* July–August, 66–75.

6. Robert M. Grant, 2003. Strategic Planning in a Turbulent Environment: Evidence from the Oil Majors, *Strategic Management Journal,* 24: 491–517.

7. Wes Bush, President and Chief Operating Officer, Northrop Grumman Corporation, 2009. Wes Bush Addresses the Wharton Aerospace Forum, February 6.

8. Northrop Grumman Corporation, 2010. Securities & Exchange Commission, Form 10-K: 27, February 9.

9. Yahoo, Inc. 2010. Northrop Grumman Corporation, November.

10. Standard & Poor's, 2010. *Industry Surveys, Aerospace & Defense,* February 11.

11. Wes Bush, 2010. Wes Bush Addresses the Center for Strategic and International Studies, October 19.

12. Northrop Grumman Corporation, 2010. 10-K, February 9.

13. *Defense Industry Daily,* 2010. F-35 Joint Strike Fighter: 2009–2010, December 15.

14. David Pugliese, 2010. F-35 Purchase Plan Based on a Wing and a Prayer, Opposition Says, *Postmedia News,* December 11.

15. Helen Kaiao Chang, 2009. Northrop Grumman's Success Formula, San Diego News Network, May 27.

16. Northrop Grumman Corporation, 2010. Northrop Grumman's ASTAMIDS Proves It Can Detect IEDs from the Air in Near-Real Time, NGC Press Release, December 6.

17. Bruce Gerding, 2010. Bruce Gerding Addresses Aerospace & Defense Industry Suppliers Conference, May 4.

18. Loren B. Thompson, 2010. Remarks to the BB&T Capital Markets Defense Teleconference, June 22.

19. Northrop Grumman Corporation, 2009. Form 10-K, March 11, p. 45.

20. Karen Nelson, 2010. Northrop Picks Name, Leader for Company It May Spin Off, www.sunherald.com, November 24.

21. Federal Reserve Bank, 2010. Open Market Committee, November 3.

22. John D. McKinnon, Corey Boles, & Martin Vaughan, 2010. Deficit Panel Pushes Cuts, *Wall Street Journal,* November 11: A1.

23. Standard & Poor's, 2010. Industry Surveys—Aerospace & Defense, February 11.

24. Loren B. Thompson, 2010. Remarks to the BB&T Capital Markets Defense Teleconference, June 22.

25. Nathan Hodge & Julian E. Barnes, 2011. Pentagon Faces the Knife. *Wall Street Journal.* January 7: A1.

26. Jeremy Page, 2011. Test Flight Signals Jet Has Reached New Stage, *Wall Street Journal,* January 12: A10.

27. Jeremy Page & Julian E. Barnes, 2011. Test Flight Upstages Gates, Hu, *Wall Street Journal,* January 12: A1.

28. J.B. "Gib" Godwin, 2009. J.B. "Gib" Godwin Addresses AFCEA TechNet Asia-Pacific on Cyber-Security, November.

29. Linda Mills, 2009. Linda Mills Addresses the National Press Club on Cyber Security, July.

30. Richard A. Clarke & Robert K. Knake, 2010. *Cyber War: The Next Threat to National Security and What to Do About It.* New York: HarperCollins Publishers.

31. Reuters, 2009. Northrop Grumman Launches Cyber Defense Team, December 2.

32. Linda Mills, 2009. Linda Mills Addresses the National Press Club on Cyber Security, July.

33. Standard & Poor's, 2010. Industry Surveys—Aerospace & Defense, February 11.

34. Editorial, 2011. Flying the GE Skies, *Wall Street Journal,* January 7: A1.

35. Eric Beinhocker, Ian Davis, & Lenn Mendonca, 2009. The 10 Trends You Have to Watch, *Harvard Business Review,* July-August, 55–60.

36. Wes Bush, 2006. Wes Bush at the Strategic Space and Defense 2006 Conference, October 11.

37. Keith D. Robbins & John A. Pearce II, 1992. Turnaround: Retrenchment and Recovery. *Strategic Management Journal,* 13: 287–309.

38. John A. Pearce II & Keith D. Robbins, 1994. Retrenchment Remains the Foundation of Business Turnaround. *Strategic Management Journal,* 15: 407–17.

39. Michael E. Porter, 1980. *Competitive Strategy: Techniques for Analyzing Industries and Competitors.* Cambridge, MA: Harvard University Press.

40. Michael E. Porter, 2008. The Five Competitive Forces that Shape Strategy, *Harvard Business Review,* January, 79–93.

41. Tom Hinthorne, 1994. Evaluating Business Practices: Linking Purpose, Practice and People, *Industrial Management,* 36(4): 5–7.

42. Loren B. Thompson, 2010. Remarks to the BB&T Capital Markets Defense Teleconference, June 22.

43. Standard & Poor's, 2010. Industry Surveys—Aerospace & Defense, February 11.

44. Strategic Discourse, 2010. Comments by Boeing's Dennis Muilenburg Indicate Massive Defense Merger, September 12.

45. Michael E. Porter, 1985. *Competitive Advantage: Creating and Sustaining Superior Performance,* Cambridge, MA: Harvard University Press.

46. Loren B. Thompson, 2010. Remarks to the BB&T Capital Markets Defense Teleconference, June 22. Thompson was citing the research of Ron Epstein at Merrill Lynch.

47. Wes Bush, President and Chief Operating Officer, Northrop Grumman Corporation, 2009. Wes Bush Addresses the Wharton Aerospace Forum, February 6.

48. Grant Gross, 2009. Northrop Grumman Launches Cybersecurity Research Group, IDG News, December 1.

49. Edward R. Freeman, 1984. *Strategic Management: A Stakeholder Approach.* Boston: Ballinger.

50. Edward R. Freeman, 1994. The Politics of Stakeholder Theory: Some Future Directions. *Business Ethics Quarterly,* 4: 409–21.

51. R.K. Mitchell, B.R. Agle, & D.J. Wood, 1997. Toward a Theory of Stakeholder Identification and Salience: Defining the Principle of Who and What Really Counts, *Academy of Management Review,* 22(4): 853–86: 95.

52. Tom Hinthorne, 1996. Predatory Capitalism, Pragmatism, and Legal Positivism in the Airlines Industry, *Strategic Management Journal,* 17: 251–70.

53. Muzafer Sherif, 1958. Superordinate Goals in the Reduction of Intergroup Conflict, *American Journal of Sociology,* 63(4): 349–56.

54. J.M. Wondolleck & S.L. Yaffee, 2000. *Making Collaboration Work: Lessons from Innovation in Natural Resource Management.* Washington, DC: Island Press.

55. Tom Hinthorne & Patricia Holman, 2009. Wildfire Protection: Conflict in the Bitterroot National Forest, *Case Research Journal,* 29(1): 47–61, Winter.

56. Jay B. Barney, 2011. *Gaining and Sustaining Competitive Advantage.* Upper Saddle River, NJ: Prentice Hall.

57. Michael E. Porter, 1985. *Competitive Advantage: Creating and Sustaining Superior Performance,* Cambridge, MA: Harvard University Press.

58. Thomas L. Wheelen & David Hunger, 2010. *Concepts in Strategic Management and Business Policy: Achieving Sustainability,* 12th Edition. Upper Saddle River, NJ: Prentice Hall.

59. Jay B. Barney, 2011. *Gaining and Sustaining Competitive Advantage.* Upper Saddle River, NJ: Prentice Hall.

60. Robert F. Brammer, Vice President and CTO, Northrop Grumman Information Systems, 2010. 2010 MIT Europe Conference, Brussels, Belgium, October 13.

61. Ken Beedle, Northrop Grumman Corporation, 2010. PRNewswire, London, October 22.

62. Wes Bush, President and Chief Operating Officer, Northrop Grumman Corporation, 2009. Wes Bush Addresses the Wharton Aerospace Forum, February 6.

63. Edward R. Freeman, 1984. *Strategic Management: A Stakeholder Approach.* Boston: Ballinger.

Part II

The Strategic Environment

Chapter 4

The Economy, the Government, and Managerial Decision Making

R. Scott Harris

INTRODUCTION

This chapter originally was titled "The Economy and Managerial Decisions." The emphasis and bulk of the discussion would have been on how managerial decisions are impacted by various "free market" phenomena. Many such discussions tend to offer general advice and warnings centered around various macroeconomic indicators—such as interest rates, inflation, unemployment, etc. They sound erudite but usually prove to be pretty useless where the rubber hits the road. For example, the national and even local unemployment rates are of little help to the personnel managers who are having a difficult time filling positions with qualified workers. Likewise decisions to resize are in response to many factors that are idiosyncratic to a firm's particular products and relevant micromarkets and often are totally independent of national trends. Sure, there is a correlation: in bad times, more firms will be downsizing. But the point is that there will be *some* firms—perhaps even a sizable minority—that will have expansion opportunities and generalized advice based on economy-wide macrotrends will be wrong for them. Even if the macrovariables seem relevant, the specifics of one's circumstances usually are critical in determining how and the extent to which a business unit should react.

Giving advice that must be applied in specific ways from the distance and comfort of the professorial chair is both presumptuous and rather arrogant, if not insulting to the knowledge of those who are in the trenches of business and industry making the hard, bottom-line, day-to-day choices that will affect the lives and choices of workers, suppliers, and customers in untold numbers of ways. At first blush, it may seem that I am merely reiterating the old stereotypical differences between the ivy tower and practicality that have given rise to such unhelpful "truths" as "that may work in theory, but it doesn't work in the 'real world'."[1] The stereotype is rooted in a misunderstanding of the fundamental differences in types of knowledge that must be employed in making any decision. Each place, the academy and the workplace, has different but crucial contributions to make that managers need to recognize.

TYPES OF KNOWLEDGE: A USEFUL TAXONOMY

Nobel Laureate Friedrich von Hayek astutely categorized types of knowledge as being "scientific" or "of specific time and place."[2] The category labels require brief explanation. "Scientific" knowledge is general knowledge that has universal application. An easy example would be the "law of gravity" and its consequences—definitely "scientific." Other examples are less stereotypically "scientific," such as the knowledge of knowing how to type using a QWERTY keyboard, or the knowledge of double-entry bookkeeping, or knowledge of the relationships between elasticity of demand and marginal revenue, or knowledge of inventory models, or knowledge of the psychology of colors, etc. Though emanating from many branches of the traditional classifications of knowledge by subject matter, and ranging from the very general to the highly refined, all these fall into the category of Hayek's "scientific knowledge." They have several important commonalties: they are in and of themselves nonspecific, but useful in many diverse specific applications. They are the types of knowledge that are commonly taught in schools. We discuss gravity in physics courses, double-entry accounting in accounting courses, learn to type in typing (or keyboarding) classes, etc.

There are many useful things that we cannot teach in schools. Those often fall into Hayek's other type of knowledge category, "the knowledge of specific time and place." This is the knowledge that one gains through intimacy with one's "immediate" surroundings. Though it often is the case, "immediate" need not always be thought of in a physical or spatial sense. Immediacy is more an idea of knowing the specific things that are "important" factors to take into account as one applies the more general "scientific" knowledge. One may have graduated from the most prestigious of universities, but the degree will be of little value if it cannot be used—and its use invariably will require good specific knowledge of time and place. I still remember as a youth coming home to tell my dad that I had learned in my foreign language class that Castilian Spanish is spoken with a lisp compared to Mexican Spanish. Dad was unimpressed. He was concerned that, were I ever to visit a Spanish speaking country, I would be able to ask someone where the bathroom is. Much later, I made the acquaintance of a gentleman who was the president of a multistate supermarket chain. After earning an MBA from a top-tier school, his first job was stocking shelves in an urban grocery store. Though the MBA program provided a great depth of scientific knowledge, it could only be applied after he learned the grocery business literally by starting at the bottom throwing cans on the night shift. What should be apparent is that both forms of knowledge that were described by Hayek are crucial to good decision making; neither can be said to be more or less important than the other.

My purpose in bringing this up is to recognize that each manager must possess both types of knowledge and that across the economy, the specific knowledge that will be employed is so diverse, specific, and sometimes multifaceted and complex that what works for one will almost certainly not work (or at least work as well) for another. So, a chapter of cookie-cutter advice would be of little help if indeed we were truly looking at the impact of macroeconomic variables on specific managerial decisions.

FREE MARKET MACROECONOMICS—ALL YOU REALLY NEED TO KNOW IN 30 SECONDS

An often overlooked fact of pure free market behavior only adds fodder to my contention that there would be little of particular use for me to say in a discussion of "markets and management." Markets have an uncanny and nasty habit of doing things that were not expected or anticipated; it would be the likely case that almost anything I say would be shallow or simply moot. The whole idea of market risk is a direct acknowledgement of this. People are innovative, and innovation, by definition, is "outside of the box" and hence does not yield predictable results. Entrepreneurship, the acceleration of technological achievements, and the resulting advances in communication and the spread of all forms of knowledge create a soup of unknown digestibility. Things are changing, and what those changes portend make our future both exciting and risky. So, if I were to focus on our economy as a "free market," it would be proper to end this chapter here with a salute and a heartfelt earnest set of best wishes on your ongoing voyage.

A CHANGE OF PARADIGM

Fortunately for me, the critical assumption in the foregoing discussion is false: the economy within which managerial decisions are and will be made is becoming less and less legitimately characterized as a "free market." Recognizing the fact that government is playing an ever-increasing role in the economy changes the paradigm in significant ways. Unfortunately it is predictable that the expansion of government's activity in the economy will yield a whole new slew of unintended consequences that will both increase risk and decrease overall productivity and the well-being of our citizens. But it also presents new opportunities for those savvy enough to identify how the game is fundamentally changing and act accordingly. Therefore, the bulk of this chapter will be devoted to the topic of "The Economy, the Government, and Managerial Decision Making." Discussion of the ramifications of the addition of the two words, "the government" into the title could fill up several books the size of this one. So, it will fall on me to highlight just some of the implications. That hopefully will allow me to be general in a meaningful way so that the reader hopefully will be able to readily apply their own knowledge of time and place to determine their own best courses of action.

The Myth of Free Market U.S. Capitalism

The first "lesson" is that we recognize that the U.S. economy is not and never has been a true "free market" economy. In his 1963 book, *The Triumph of Conservatism*, about the so-called called "Progressive Era" at the beginning of the 20th century, historian Gabriel Kolko wrote, "[T]he answer is that the federal government was *always* involved in the economy is various crucial ways, and that laissez faire never existed. . . . This has been known to historians for decades, and need not be belabored."[3] This fact may be well known, yet it most decidedly needs to be belabored as it is conveniently ignored all too often in public discourse. Whenever any Tom, Dick, or Mary runs for public office, increasingly there are identified economic issues where something is claimed to be amiss with our "free market" economy. Having erected such a straw man, the inevitable "fix" proposed by the political wannabes will be more government oversight, regulation, or outright management of the offending businesses. So pervasive is the faith that ours is an imperfect but "free market" system that it is almost never suggested that the offensive behavior could be the result (intended or not) of government intervention itself in the marketplace. And, in those rare instances when blame is laid on the government's doorstep, the solution offered is to change or increase government involvement rather than to examine it for being the fundamental source of the problem. The continued duplicity, complicity and "imperfection" of the "free market" is implicitly assumed as an article of faith; the only mistake those who subscribe to that faith made was that they didn't get the proper amount of government intervention right the first time. Politicians do not get elected on the "mea culpa" platform.

Some may point out that even in the best of all worlds, there is a legitimate role for government to play in the economy. In its simplest form, the government role would be to set the ground rules and be an impartial referee of last resort in the economy, but otherwise let the chips fall where they may. There would seemingly be a role for the government in granting and enforcing copyrights and patents. Then there would be a role in dealing with "natural monopolies" and the provision of "public goods." All of these are generally accepted as "proper" roles of government in the economy. My argument is not whether these are proper or improper, but rather that the government unmistakably is involved in the economy. That is a fact. Further, it is a fact that the involvement of the government in the economy has consequences that are often far from the intent of the involvement. Even the most traditional roles we have assigned to government are not untainted. For example, many claim that copyright and patent protection is needed to encourage innovation and growth by protecting intellectual property. Actually the example of copyright and patents provides several interesting lessons to which we will turn later. However, now it is sufficient that we understand that government is not a neutral benign, staid, and static arbiter in the economic affairs of the nation. Rather, it is an alternative stage where managers must have a presence—whether they like it or not.

Lessons from Microsoft and History

Microsoft Corporation is a place of legends. Harvard dropout Bill Gates and his cohorts parlayed their passion for computer programming, a lot of hard work, a fortuitous misstep by IBM, and a little luck into the world's largest software producer. They made wealth the old-fashioned way: they produced something of value, took it to market, and the market responded. As Microsoft grew, so did the scrutiny of their business practices not just from competitors and the press, but also from government regulators. In 1990, the Federal Trade Commission started an investigation into the relationship between Microsoft and IBM Corporation.[4] Things simmered along for a few years with no huge push from regulators. The earlier issue ended in a consent decree and there was a Justice Department denial of a proposed acquisition (Intuit Corp.), but other than those and similar bumps in the road, the company focused on its core competencies and strove to stay ahead of its competition in the marketplace. Then, in 1997, the Department of Justice initiated full-blown antitrust proceedings against Microsoft. In 2000, it was found guilty and the order was issued to break Microsoft into two companies. Though the breakup order was reversed on appeal and eventually things got settled by late 2002, the cost of defending themselves was huge. Further, it never was clear that Microsoft had done anything wrong other than try to compete in the marketplace by "building a better mousetrap" (or, in this case, software). Professor Ben Klein of UCLA carefully analyzed all of the charges and arguments against Microsoft and was able to demonstrate that virtually all of Microsoft's alleged missteps were perfectly consistent with competitive behavior.[5]

What is interesting about this Microsoft example is not what went on in the trial, but rather something else. The Center for Responsive Politics was founded in 1983 by two U.S. senators with the goal of "tracking money in politics and [showing] its effect on elections and public policy."[6] The center publishes its information on its OpenSecrets.org Website. Its information on the political contributions of Microsoft Corporation includes the following:

> Prior to 1998, the company and its employees gave virtually nothing in terms of political contributions. But when the Justice Department launched an antitrust investigation into the company's marketing of its popular Windows software, things changed. The company opened a Washington lobbying office, founded a political action committee and soon became one of the most generous political givers in the country.[7]

Microsoft's political contributions in 1990 were a grand total of $3,800, divided among five candidates, all but one of whom were part of the Washington state congressional delegation. That grew to a total of $251,474 for the 1996 election cycle. Then in 1998, the amount jumped to $1,366,821 and hit $4,628,893 in 2000! Amounts have ranged from $2 million to over $4 million in each two-year election cycle since 2000.[8] In addition, lobbying efforts, which had been limited prior to 1998, jumped to almost $4 million in 1998 and hovered between $8.5 and $9.5 million each year from 2003 through 2008. In 2009 and 2010, the lobbying expenditure hovered between $6.7 and $6.9 million (presumably due to the recession).[9]

The coincidental occurrence of the Justice Department's antitrust lawsuit and Microsoft's decision to enter the political fray is telling. Some (who choose not to speak for attribution) opine that the Justice Department suit was a wake-up call to the company for not paying proper attention to "rendering unto Caesar." Whatever the reason, one thing is clear: Microsoft discovered that its success depended on both how it competed in the marketplace as well as how it competed in the political arena. In contrast to how Microsoft cofounder Bill Gates is managing his personal fortune, the corporate entity Microsoft is not (and never was) in business to spend millions on charity or goodwill. Those lobbying efforts are at a very minimum designed to fend off challenges that emanate from politically inspired changes in the ground rules. More likely would be the situation where Microsoft has discovered that it sometimes can be easier to beat the competition through political means than it is to meet them head on in the marketplace.

The art of using government to mold the playing field in one's favor is nothing new and is quite ubiquitous. A visit to a hearing of a local government board that is deciding whether or not to grant a liquor license often reveals that those speaking most fervently against approval are those who have been lined up and orchestrated by someone who already holds a liquor license and would face additional competition if the new license were approved. In Billings, Montana, each of the two hospitals separately and independently saw fit to petition the city to abandon a block of city street so the hospitals could expand. Each hospital wished to acquire a separate block (three blocks apart) of the same street that would primarily adversely impact access to their *own* emergency rooms. But at the hearings, each hospital rose in opposition to allowing the other to acquire the rights to the street because of claimed blockage of access to *their* emergency room three blocks away.

Federal regulatory agencies were set up to regulate business activity, often at the behest of and with the cooperation of the very businesses they were destined to regulate. For example, the Interstate Commerce Commission originated because competition had an uncanny way of destroying the railroad's attempts to cartelize the industry, resulting in pricing and pooling agreements that were highly instable and unpredictable. Although customers found this volatility to be disconcerting, the railroads were apoplectic. "Fortunately," they found sympathizers in the halls of Congress who not only crafted stability in the form of the Interstate Commerce Commission, but then also have effectively shielded the industry from the provisions of the Sherman Antitrust Act.[10] To be effective in their charge of regulating the railroads, the commission needed to have intimate knowledge of the operation of railroads—not at the abstract level, but at the nitty-gritty level; the "specific time and place" type of knowledge mentioned earlier. Accordingly, they put the proverbial fox in charge of the henhouse in what turned out to be a magnificent opportunity for the railroads to use the government as a vehicle to further their own ends. This phenomenon is so well known and often repeated that it is commonly referred to as the "capture theory of regulation," wherein the companies that are subject to regulation "capture" the regulatory body to work on their behalf.

In a rare instance of deregulation, the foxes didn't guard the henhouse adequately. The Civil Aeronautics Board (CAB) was dissolved in the later 1970s and interstate passenger air carriers were cut adrift from the agency and its predecessors that had effectively cartelized them since the 1930s. So effective was the CAB at protecting those whose job it was to regulate that during the entire time the CAB existed, no new interstate airlines entered the business in the United States. So, when Cornell University Professor Alfred Kahn was appointed by President Carter to head the CAB, a great deal of complacency about how to compete in the marketplace was pervasive in the industry. Those few airlines that had come into existence while the CAB reigned avoided CAB oversight by restricting their routes to intrastate flights entirely within California or Texas, the only states large enough and populous enough to sustain an airline. Kahn was well aware that the unregulated intrastate airlines offered fares at a fraction of the prices that were regulated by the CAB. The author recalls ads for Pacific Southwest Airlines (PSA) that offered one-way fares between San Francisco and Los Angeles for $12.50, whereas fares for the same interstate distance between New York and Boston were several times the price. Further, the intrastate carriers were generally reporting profits, whereas the cartelized interstate carriers struggled. Kahn's push to abolish the CAB fare structure and ultimately the agency itself thrust the interstate carriers into a completely new competitive paradigm—the marketplace.

The transition for most airlines was painful. Many, Eastern, Western, and Pan American, to name a few, did not survive. All found the challenges of upstart newcomers or old intrastate carriers such as Southwest who now could expand into the interstate market to be formidable. At least one of the "old guard" airlines returned to familiar territory where they maintained a competitive advantage, the halls of the Capitol in Washington, D.C., where they could engage in aggressive lobbying. This was important to Dallas-based American Airlines, because it was particularly vulnerable to Southwest who was using nearby Love Field as its base of operations. Likewise, supporters of the new Dallas/Fort Worth (DFW) international airport were chagrined that Southwest had successfully sued to stay and compete with them from Love Field, an airport that DFW had supposedly replaced for commercial flights. The type and extent of lobbying and by whom will never be truly known, but we do know that the then majority leader of the U.S. House of Representatives (and future Speaker of the House) Jim Wright, a congressman from Fort Worth, Texas, inserted an amendment to the International Air Transportation Act of 1979. The act was passed by both houses of Congress as amended and was signed into law. The amendment, infamously known as "the Wright Amendment," had virtually nothing to do with international air transportation; its sole purpose was to alter the ground rules by which Southwest (and Love Field) could compete with the airlines operating out of DFW. It did so by restricting Southwest's normal interstate flights from Love Field to states contiguous to Texas: Oklahoma,

Arkansas, Louisiana, and New Mexico. It did allow for interstate flights to other states but only if done on commuter aircraft with a maximum capacity of 56 passengers. Later amendments to various bills expanded the allowable states to which nonstop flights could be made. In 2006, the Congress passed "the Wright Amendment Reform Act of 2006" that would phase out the restrictions by 2014.[11]

These examples are diverse yet consistent in showing the degree to which government affects competitive outcomes. I reiterate: It is simply not enough to do your best at outperforming your competition in the marketplace (as Microsoft almost found out the hard way); you must always be cognizant of both opportunities and threats that come from the regulatory and legislative processes. To do so, you must be well versed in the way governmental regulatory and legislative processes work and try to stay as far ahead of the competition in that game as possible. It takes considerable resources. The small businessperson must be willing to log in nights at local government hearings to get to know the ropes. Managers of larger companies need to have eyes and ears in local, county, and state halls of government, and often at the federal level.

If nothing else opens your eyes to the importance of having skin in the game at the governmental level, try this: since 1998 the annual spending on lobbying at the federal level alone has increased from $1.44 billion (with a b!) to $3.47 billion in 2010. Those who spend that kind of money consider it an investment; they wouldn't spend it if they didn't think it was worth it. And, if you still are not convinced, consider the process of how many of the recent important laws came to be enacted. Senate and House staffers are generally young; they do not have the expertise or the "knowledge of time and place" necessary to craft the mountains of legislation that come out of Washington, so they have to rely on others whose presence is strategically orchestrated by lobbyists to be in the right place and just the right time. I recall a viral YouTube video that was released at the height of the debate over the health-care bill.[12] It showed a town hall meeting with Senator Arlen Specter and Health and Human Services Secretary Kathleen Sebelius. In it Senator Specter basically admitted that he might not have time to learn the written details of even the most important bills that he was going to vote on. That admission is telling in several ways: If the health-care bill was over 1,000 pages in length and was so quickly cobbled together that those who voted on it did not have time to read it—let alone understand its far-reaching implications—who did we entrust to write and approve of the bill? We are told that the insurance companies were frozen out of the final bill, but I wouldn't take either that bet or one that denies that the pharmaceutical companies and the AMA or the American Hospital Association had significant influence in crafting the final bill. Perhaps that explains why a record amount of money was spent on lobbying that year—the year following the election of a President who promised to bring transparency to government.

At this point you may be forgiven if you think I am belaboring this point, but the facts are that the importance of keeping close watch on and being prepared to influence government decision makers is *not* something business schools prepare managers for. Sure, we teach courses that acknowledge that we all must comply with various regulatory and legal constraints, but usually that environment is presented as static, when we know that nothing could be further from the truth. Government involvement in the economy is becoming increasingly fluid and those who understand the dynamics of the processes by which regulations and laws are formed will have a dramatic advantage over those who sit on the sidelines and react. If business schools really mean what they say about training tomorrow's managers for the challenges they will face, we need to develop meaningful courses in how governmental actions are formulated, rendered, and administered. A former colleague (who will remain nameless) took a stab at creating such a course in an MBA program a few years ago. He took the students to Washington, D.C., and divided them into teams, each one of which would pass the course only if they were successful in getting a specific piece of (usually trivial) legislation of their making introduced and enacted into law with the President's signature. Time was short—only one semester—but during that time the students had to get their bills introduced and manage their passage through committees and both houses of Congress. There was only one rule: students were absolutely forbidden to let anyone know that they were doing it for a class project.

With the major exception of the dismantlement of the CAB in the 1970s and incidental adjustments such as the Wright Amendment Reform Act of 2006, the general trend over the years has been for the influence of government to become increasingly larger factors in managerial decisions. Until quite recently, most of the action was still practiced at the microlevel with earmarks and specific lines in legislation inserted to benefit specific interests either through grants, subsidies, or tilting the playing field in favor of someone (and against someone else). A few years ago, that changed.

THE GAME IS CHANGING—NOW

In 2004, economists Harold Cole and Lee Ohanian published an article in the prestigious *Journal of Political Economy*[13] that was lauded by Nobel Laureate Robert E. Lucas Jr. as "exciting and valuable research" that recast our understanding of the Great Depression of the 1930s.[14] The exercise was not just academic because understanding the past hopefully will enable us to avoid making the same mistakes again. A significant finding of the research was summarized by Professor Cole:

The fact that the Depression dragged on for years convinced generations of economists and policy-makers that capitalism could not be trusted to recover from depressions and that significant government intervention was required to achieve good outcomes. Ironically, our work shows that the recovery would have been very rapid had the government not intervened.[15]

Fast forward to 2008: As a result of years of arm twisting from Capitol Hill and various occupants of the White House to make housing affordable, banks and mortgage brokers who caved to the political pressure found themselves in a bit of a pinch. The house of cards that had underpinned their success to date—namely, a shortsighted faith in continued appreciation of housing values—was starting to collapse. It started with the subprime mortgage market. But rather than recognizing this for what it truly was, namely, a pool of mortgages that constituted about 15 percent of total mortgages where only 20 percent were in serious payment arrears (more than three or four months behind in payments), the "Chicken Littles" put this together with a few other bad decisions by some large companies and sounded the alarm. Three to four percent of the mortgage market that was concentrated in the highest-risk group would normally not seem to constitute a crisis worth summoning the financial equivalent of the horse cavalry, but the call went out for the entire army, navy, air force, and marines. From a macroeconomic standpoint, this was a mere blip in the economy, but none of that matters if your company has a lot of wealth tied up in that particular blip. And, if your company has a lot of political clout and friends in high places, well, you know what happened.

A few years prior, the seventh-largest company in the United States, Enron, had imploded and had been allowed to fail. Now, the worry was that there might be some more failures. Indeed, some did pay the price—Indymac Bank, Bear Stearns, and Lehman Brothers—but others, still standing, albeit with their pants down around their ankles, made the desperate call to be saved from their past missteps. Let's face it: too many of these strategically placed folks had abandoned good management practices and basic common sense and succumbed to the allure of questionable accounting practices and flimflam leveraging in their appeasement of pressure from Capitol Hill to make housing affordable and in their ubiquitous quest to make a quick buck. They had been caught. And they knew the market would render summary judgment and mete out uncompromising punishment. They knew that there were long-established and robust institutions in place to deal with them. Takeovers of depreciated assets by others occur all the time subsequent to bad decisions or bad luck. Failing that, bankruptcy laws have evolved over decades to handle these situations in an orderly but predicable way that minimizes the impact on the rest of the economy. There simply was no good reason from a macroeconomic point of view at that time for anyone to panic;[16] those who were panicking were trying to save their own skins and had a vastly inflated view of their importance in the overall scheme of the economy, and they found friends in the highest places.

Once Treasury Secretary Paulson got on board, President Bush was not far behind. Both chorused the "sky is falling" refrain and promised swift remedies. Now, most of us were on the outside looking in. Those at the highest levels of government were clearly panicking. Some possibly believed that the crisis was indeed severe and that we were on the brink. Others, in a cynical power grab went to great lengths to recast their past complicity in overtly pressuring lenders to issue risky mortgages and tried to pin all of the blame on "free markets." The cacophony from the banks of the Potomac was heard across the country, and folks rightfully grew uneasy. People reacted rationally by battening down the hatches and preparing for the rainy day. Large purchase decisions were delayed, spending was curtailed. Banks and lenders normally would adjust and tighten lending procedures, but the noises from Washington, D.C., on how the government would react to all of this were ones nobody had heard before. That added even more uncertainty to the mix and the credit markets rationally decided to put decisions on hold until they could figure out what was going to happen. That signal was generally misinterpreted as further evidence that the economy was on the brink, resulting in still more panic—and a recession was born. Basically the recession was caused by policy makers who possess the lethal combination of ignorance regarding the overall and strategically complex ways that markets work, combined with unflagging egos that they alone know how to make things right. It helps that in the process they are saving their own hides.

All of the political processes that fell out from the subprime mortgage blip couldn't have been better orchestrated to produce a new phenomenon: bailouts taken to heretofore unimaginable heights. As if it were some new special technological breakthrough, "too big to fail" has now become the standard. Bank and auto company executives invoked it while ignoring their own miscalculations or even misdeeds. In a supreme gesture of disdain for the pain others were suffering as a consequence of their errors in judgment, they flew in corporate jets to Washington, D.C., to claim their indulgences.

As this is being written, the administration is, naturally, playing up the good news that they can claim for their interventionist actions while downplaying or ignoring those that didn't work out so well. The emphasis seems to be on when General Motors will pay us back and whether the government (aka, the taxpayers for publicity purposes) will actually make a "profit." The same goes for the banks. So far, there hasn't been much said about how the taxpayer has fared with Freddie Mac and

Fannie Mae. From an economic point of view, this is all nice, but it truly ignores the long-lasting legacy from the bailout precedent. Nobody has enunciated this legacy better than Neil Barofsky, the man the Obama administration named to be the special inspector general of the famous Troubled Asset Relief Program (TARP). On January 27, 2011, Mr. Barofsky was interviewed by Steve Inskeep on National Public Radio's (NPR) Morning Edition. The following is excerpted from that interview:

> **Inskeep:** Let's talk about whether the problem has been fixed, here. Why have you been saying that more bank bailouts are more or less inevitable?
>
> **Mr. Barofsky:** Well, it's not just me saying it. It was really information that was provided to us by Secretary Geithner in an interview that we did with him in December with respect to a recent audit. And the problem is that the notion of too big to fail—these large financial institutions that were just too big to allow them to go under—since the 2008 bailouts, they've only gotten bigger and bigger, more concentrated, larger in size. And what's really discouraging is that if you look at how the market treats them, it treats them as if they're going to get a government bailout, *which destroys market discipline and really puts us in a very dangerous place.*
>
> **Inskeep:** Let me make sure I understand what you're saying. You're saying that credit rating agencies and investors, when they look at the risk of investing in a bank, they say, well, they can do whatever they want because the government will bail them out. That's what you think?
>
> **Mr. Barofsky:** Exactly. And it's not just what I think. Recently, just this past month, S&P, one of the largest of the rating agencies, did something remarkable. They said that they're intending to change their rating methodology *to make it a permanent assumption that the government will bailout the largest institutions,* give those banks higher ratings. Which means they're going to be able to borrow money more cheaply. They're going to be able to access credit and capital and debt more easily.[17]

In a later interview on February 18, 2011, with NPR's Chris Arnold, Mr. Barofsky indicated that the TARP program, which was originally designed in part to help between 3 and 4 million people stay in their homes by avoiding foreclosure, has only reached about 500,000 people and that "many people are being rejected for the wrong reasons . . . [because] the government didn't put the right incentives in place to really bring the banks on board."[18]

Not only is this bailout not meeting its intended purpose, it is also setting a huge precedent that the market is already adjusting for. On one hand, it raises the expectations that "too big to fail" businesses will be exempt from the discipline of market forces, allowing them to take bigger risks and act with greater impunity toward their stakeholders. On the other hand, it portends an increasing substitution of government regulation for the discipline that would otherwise be meted out by the market. There are two aspects to regulation that need to be understood: (1) Regulation by government oversight is a much more expensive proposition than regulation in the marketplace. Taxpayers foot the bill to (supposedly) keep businesses in line while preventing them from failing; no such burden is borne when the discipline of the markets force a business into insolvency and failure. (2) Regulators, if they are not "captured" by industry as discussed earlier, are necessarily outsiders. They will never be privy to the degree of "knowledge of time and place" concerning the everyday operations of those they are charged to regulate. In the vast majority of instances, meaningful decisions are made "where the rubber hits the road" and those often are very specialized decisions made in response to very specialized "knowledge of time and place." In that environment, regulators are pushing the proverbial strings uphill. Things will "slip through the cracks" (like several million people whose mortgages are being foreclosed!). Inefficiencies will occur as businesses expend resources to get around regulations or avoid their consequences. And, on the bottom line, taxpayers will pay for it.

The lesson for managers is one of peril, especially those who are not "Washington insiders" or who are "small potatoes"; in other words, most of us. You will not only experience increased demands for complying with new regulations, and in dealing with regulatory oversight from people who often will have no clue about the special circumstances you face in your business environment, you will also have to adjust how you interface with other businesses, especially those deemed "too big to fail." Doubtless a new "equilibrium" will be found, but it will be a frustrating one. Products that before would have been valuable to customers but marginally profitable for you will become unprofitable as you absorb increased overhead when your costs of regulatory compliance increase. To become nimbler at responding to the increase in unpredictability associated with heretofore uncharted expansion of government in the economy, long-term decision processes will be abandoned in favor of a less efficient series of short-term decisions, as the business and regulatory environment becomes riskier. In sum, look for managers' plates to have more heaped on them while given fewer resources with which to respond. Doing the groundwork now that will allow for rapid adjustment, and understanding of the new operating environment and what it portends will allow most astute managers to prepare. In this changing environment, it is imperative that you reassess and understand where the threats (and any opportunities) are likely to come from and alter your strength/weakness profile to best prepare. Be realistic and you will improve your chances of staying ahead of the tsunami.

There is one postscript to this section that I truly hope will not come to pass, yet fear it may. Over the past several years we have seen an increase in the number of high-profile cases of "white collar" crime. There always have been snake oil vendors and opportunists in our midst. On the frontier and in common law, miscreants of this sort were "run out on the rails" or otherwise dealt with on a case-by-case basis. As technology and communication improved, it became practical and cost effective to codify increasing numbers of acts that would be considered criminal. As with most things, there is a point of decreasing returns in writing laws and establishing regulations. We are told that ignorance of the law is no defense, but with increasing numbers of laws and regulations, it will be nigh impossible for managers not to sooner or later find themselves committing some sort of violation—often that they didn't know about. This creates a new dimension of liability and risk for managers. Since laws and regulations are always subject to interpretation, overzealous regulators could advance their careers by casting very wide nets that entangle managers whose activities are fundamentally blameless, but may be in technical violation. Although such charged managers are entitled to their day in court, defending oneself is costly in terms of resources, time, and ultimately reputation. The chilling effect that this will have on innovation and thinking outside of the safest boxes will only increase as regulation multiplies.

FOLLOW THE LEADER? NEW RISKS IN FOLLOWING OLD RULES

Predictable increases in the number and scope of government mandates and regulations will not only increase the uncertainty that managers will face vis-à-vis their dealing with government, they will also make it harder to decipher information that is gleaned from the marketplace. As all managers are well aware, they must constantly make decisions based on information they possess. Much of that information will fall into the "knowledge of time and place" category and will be very specific to the particular circumstances the manager faces. In making decisions, experience can be of great value. Recall that the experience of throwing cans on a night shift served well the president of a grocery chain. So, too, will the experiences of others serve in predicting your success or failure in a similar venture. But, since no two decisions can ever be made under absolutely identical circumstances, the trick is to know what circumstances encountered in the past or by others are relevant to the decision at hand. Although there are some commonalities everywhere, the experiences of the manager of a rock quarry are likely to be less helpful in managing a Mexican restaurant than the experiences of a manager of a delicatessen.

If more regulations are imposed, the chances increase that some of those regulations will become critical in making certain decisions. So, managers will not only have to differentiate between potential variation in specific market conditions in seeking experiences to guide decisions, they will also have to additionally decide if the regulatory environment is similar enough to make a past experience useful. The more regulations there are, the harder it will be to rely on simple and direct experiences to guide future decisions. Instead, one will have to identify and control for all relevant differences in circumstances and make suitable adjustments. Good decision making will become both costlier and riskier.

Two examples show how the regulatory environment can affect managerial decisions in what otherwise would be considered similar businesses. The first takes us back to the days when the CAB regulated interstate airline fares. The regulated fare prices were set so high that airline seat capacity far outstripped the demand to fly. As a consequence the industry average occupancy rate was right around 50 percent of capacity. In an unregulated market, the affected airlines would have cut fare prices to compete for customers and thereby enticed a greater number of people to fly. But, they couldn't do that. Instead, they tried to lure customers through other forms of competition that were not regulated. They increased the amenities associated with flying—meals, champagne, leg room, the sex appeal of the cabin attendants, etc., with each airline not only trying to outdo the others in these established ways, but they also kept trying to find new and innovative ways to compete that would get around the controlled fare prices. One of the airlines discovered that purchasing high-end hotels at popular destinations to which they flew could be helpful. Since the CAB did not control hotel rates, the airlines found they could effectively lower prices on travel packages by discounting hotel prices to customers who flew on their airlines. The first airlines that did this experienced a boom in sales, so everyone else in the industry was forced to do the same or lose out to competitors. Even though airlines were not especially adept at running hotels— the differences in business models were not inconsequential—even with less-than-perfect management, the hotel programs became a critical part of the airlines' competitive strategies. Along these same lines, some airlines found it profitable to acquire rent-a-car companies.

As mentioned earlier, there were a few airlines that operated within the states of California (PSA and Air California) and Texas (Southwest Airline) that were not subject to the CAB controls (since the U.S. Constitution only allows the federal government the right to regulate interstate commerce). These intrastate airlines charged fare prices considerably below those charged by their interstate brethren and were generally profitable. Although some paid attention to the amenities that the interstate airlines offered, most discovered that they were unnecessary. Air California, for example, discovered that it could cut recruiting and training costs of its cabin attendants if it picked up stewardesses (yes, they were all women at that time!) who had been let go by other airlines because they had grown too old, had gotten married, or otherwise lost their sex appeal. Folks flying Air California from Orange County (before it was named John Wayne) airport to San Francisco showed much more interest in the low fares and good service from experienced cabin attendants than with fantasizing. Since none of the intrastate airlines could fly long hauls (the flights between Los Angeles and San Francisco took less than an hour), it did not make sense to offer meals in any case.

It is important to understand that both the intra- and interstate airlines were subject to government regulations. Both groups were subject to the safety requirements of the FAA, and although interstate airlines were regulated by the CAB, in California the intrastate airlines were "regulated" by the state Public Utilities Commission. So sorting out what was good for one group and not another was not evidently apparent to the upper management of PSA as they noticed the bottom-line impact of hotels and car-rental businesses on their competitors. Given those experiences, PSA dove into the hotel and car-rental business—and promptly lost a ton of money. The psa-history.org Website describes the situation:

> Back in 1967, PSA started the "Fly! Drive! Sleep!" campaign. The goal was to fly people, have them get a PSA rent-a-car, and stay in a PSA hotel—similar to United's 1987 "Allegis" plan. So PSA bought ValCar rent-a-car from Thrifty. However, PSA was still a commuter airline, and the traffic base wasn't there to support the idea—ValCar was never profitable, and shuttered in September 1971.
>
> The plan was expanded with hotel purchases. The Islandia in San Diego, San Franciscan in SFO, Queen Mary Hotel at LGB (Long Beach service started in 1971), and PSA Hollywood Park hotel were all acquired or built. Again, the hotels lost money and were leased to Hyatt in 1974 (later divested). PSA's checkbook was used toward other acquisitions, like 4 radio stations, 2 background music creation companies, and even a 70-foot long catamaran (catering to J. Floyd Andrews' love of fishing). Two jet leasing firms were created to dispose of PSA's excess aircraft. All of the acquisitions took

their toll, causing a $16.7 million loss in 1975 (even after most were disposed of).[19]

Even in hindsight, the authors of the history attribute at least part of the losses to the fact that PSA was a "commuter" airline, and not to the fact that the rent-a-car and hotel business gave them no competitive advantage because, unlike the interstate airlines, their fares were not kept artificially high. Low hotel and car-rental prices for their customers could only be losers.

This example shows how important it is when looking to others' experiences to understand what differences between you and them are critical when making specific managerial decisions. With increasingly selective regulation, it will become progressively difficult to know when to emulate others' successes and when not to.

A second example may be more familiar to you. Federal Express and United Parcel Service (UPS) are both in the package delivery business. From many customers' standpoints, they are direct competitors. Yet, their business models are built around very different regulatory environments. UPS is subject to operating under the National Labor Relations Act (NLRA), whereas FedEx works under the aegis of the Railway Labor Act (RLA). This has an impact on the two companies' labor relations strategies in quite different ways. It is much easier for labor to unionize under the NLRA than it is under the RLA and consequently, UPS has a more costly labor agreement than does FedEx. Both companies are duking it out in Washington, D.C., with FedEx spending about $9 million a year in lobbying expenses to protect its interests, whereas UPS is paying about $5 million a year to lobby the government to "level the playing field."[20] It is interesting to note that UPS's efforts appear more designed to bring down FedEx to their level rather than to lift themselves to the same level as FedEx.

Though both FedEx and UPS deliver packages on your and my streets, because one started primarily as a truck deliverer and the other as an air deliverer, they fall under different regulations. So, regardless of how similar two companies appear to be in product and structure, one cannot assume that they are treated similarly by the government regulatory agencies. This is yet another instance where appearances can be deceiving and confusing, especially if they don't seem to make sense.

ALL IS NOT AS IT SEEMS

Patents and copyrights are explicitly addressed in the U.S. Constitution: "To promote the Progress of Science and useful Arts, by securing for limited Times to Authors and Inventors the exclusive Right to their respective Writings and Discoveries."[21] The flip side of that is that patents and copyrights, by their definition, bestow government enforced monopoly rights upon their holders. As we learn in economics 101, monopoly stifles social-wealth production and transfers wealth to the monopolist from the rest of society. The stated intent of copyrights and patents is to promote wealth production, but in applying them, we create institutions that work contrary to that intent. The history of congressional debate and enactments of copyright and patent law clearly shows there was recognition of the double-sided nature of the laws.[22] Despite the recognition that copyrights and patents grant extended monopoly rights to their holders, it may seem curious that there was an unchecked trend during the 20th century and culminating with the Copyright Term Extension Act of 1998 for the term of copyrights to be extended *retroactively.* Thus a work copyrighted in 1924 that would have entered the public domain 56 years later in 1980 under the terms of the original copyright will continue to enjoy protected monopoly status until January 1, 2020. Clearly the balance envisioned by the framers of the constitution when they explicitly called for limiting the monopolistic effects of copyrights and patents is tilting in favor of extending monopoly rights. Although it is conceivable that an argument can be made that such an extension is warranted in modern times "to promote the progress of science and useful arts," no such argument exists for *retroactively* extending the monopoly power since the affected items subject to patent and copyright were already produced under the aegis of the old laws. The only effect the retroactive coverage of these laws could have is to further extend monopoly power and perpetuate windfall wealth transfers to those now fortunate enough to have inherited a copyright. Novelist Cory Doctorow cites a specific descendant of an author (who will go unnamed here because of his litigious bent) when he blogged, "The professional descendants making millions off a long-dead writer have become a serious impediment to living, working writers—and readers. If this isn't the greatest proof that extending copyright in scope and duration screws living creators and impedes the creation of new works, I don't know what is."[23]

The discussion of patents and copyrights brings us to an admonition for managers. Successful business strategies must take into account all aspects of government involvement in the economy. Government itself is "old technology" characterized through the claim of monopoly rights to use force and violence.[24] The rules by which these monopoly rights are administered are what separate democracies, republics, dictatorships, and other manifestations of government. So, in our example, copyrights and patents are enforced by the government through the threat of fines and/or incarceration for those who violate the rights of the patent or copyright holders. It is important to note that those whose wealth is protected by government-issued and enforced patents and copyrights do not pay for that protection; that burden befalls the general taxpayer who also is likely to be the person paying monopoly tribute to the copyright or patent holder.

Though we will shortly turn to issues involving the benefits of lobbying government for special consideration—in this case the retroactive extension of copyrights—there is another point that pops out of this example. As I write this, new technologies are being credited with mobilizing citizens in the Middle East to demand changes in the old technology of government. Just as electronic and information technology render it more difficult for despots to enforce their will on the people, so too will it become more difficult for any government to enforce laws that can both easily be circumvented and are judged to be meritless even by those who impute ethical considerations into their decision making. Cheap and widely available technology and safe-haven Website locations allow people to circumvent royalty or copyright payments almost at will. Although the government's response of imposing astronomical fines on those it catches and charges may have some deterrent effect, every governor and police official knows that laws simply cannot be enforced in the face of general civil disobedience—at least not in a society that generally sees itself as civil and free. Therefore, it would be wise for managers and businesses that seek special favors and protection from the government to focus their attention on the pulse of the public mood and be aware of how far people can be pushed to comply with edicts.

Examples are all around us of how technology is allowing innovative people to (often legally) circumvent monopolistic practices resulting from copyrights and patents. College students who feel the pinch of escalating costs of education have learned that textbooks are often published in both U.S. and international editions. The two editions are usually identical in content, but the U.S. edition typically is a hardback text, whereas the international has a soft cover. The quality of paper in the books may or may not differ. Pictures and diagrams in the international edition may be in black and white as opposed to color in the U.S. edition, but not always. The salient difference is the price of the textbook—and with it, the price of the knowledge it contains. Students have discovered that it is worth their while to learn what book is being used in a course far enough in advance so they can order it from foreign mail-order sources. This market has become significant enough that students can occasionally find U.S. mail-order suppliers who make international editions available.

On another domestic front, in an effort to make ethical drugs more cheaply available to medical patients, folks have learned that drugs that are pretty pricey in the United States are considerably cheaper in other countries. Bowing to constituent pressure, some politicians are looking into the possibility of allowing U.S. residents to purchase drugs from foreign retailers.

The issues of copyright protection afford a case study in "thinking outside of the box." The old-school mentality would be to "pass a law and enforce it," come hell or high water. In contrast, over the past several years, there has evolved another approach to production. The notion that copyright protection is necessary to foster inventiveness, growth, and progress is being challenged by events we are all familiar with. The "open source" movement in computer programming and technology has refuted the argument that copyright protection is necessary to spur innovation. A few years ago a young author named Cory Doctorow (whom I cited earlier) decided to publish a book he had written. He put the entire book online and made it generally available through free downloads. He only asked readers to honor a "Creative Commons" license for his book. To use modern lingo, the book "went viral" and was subsequently published on "real" paper. It spent seven weeks on the *New York Times* bestseller list even while it remained as a free download. It is interesting to note that the book, *Little Brother,* was written for a young adult audience, precisely the type of person who could hack a Website or "pirate" the book at will. But this is also the type of person who would have been on the frontlines in Egypt.

Predating and independent of Doctorow's act of rebellion, David Levine, a highly respected economist and now John H. Biggs Distinguished Professor of Economics at Washington University in St. Louis started examining the assumptions behind intellectual property rights, especially those having to do with patents and copyrights. Along with colleague Michele Boldrin, Levine critically examined the theoretical underpinnings of intellectual property using the lens of history and as much data as they could gather. Their findings stunned them because the evidence they found ran counter to the received wisdom regarding the social-incentive effects of protecting intellectual property. Going back to the dawn of the Industrial Revolution, they discovered that patents and copyrights have generally been used to inhibit progress rather than incentivize it. Having started the investigation with the same predisposition toward patents and copyrights as the framers of the constitution, Boldrin and Levine had to completely rewrite significant portions of their book on the subject as the evidence became increasingly clear. Like Cory Doctorow, they published their book, *Against Intellectual Monopoly,* online,[25] followed by a hardcover version published by Cambridge University Press. Ironically the hardback version is copyrighted (presumably at the insistence of the publisher rather than the authors).

The lesson to be learned is that managers must be nimble and become aware of the practical limits that technology is placing on the extent to which traditional government power can be exercised on their behalf. As we shall now see, this does not mean that government involvement in the economy will likely be waning in the near future. Far from it. What it does mean is that managers must be careful not to get on the wrong side of uncontrollable civil disobedience. An unenforced law is no law at all. It also means that there will be new opportunities for managers to exploit new social trends that open daily as a result of technological innovations. Many of those opportunities will involve disenthralling oneself of the old paradigm of relying on government to protect one from competition.

CONCLUSION

If there is a theme in this chapter, it is that government involvement in the economy only serves to lessen confidence and the degree of certainty that one can have about the success of business outcomes. The admonition is that managers have to be on top of things increasingly in order to avoid pitfalls and missteps. In a competitive market economy, success is achieved by keeping ahead of your competition. Sure, one can be blindsided by an unforeseen entrepreneur building the proverbial "better mousetrap." But the main focus is on providing customers with better products and service than one's competitors. Adding government to the mix changes the focus of the manager as well as the modus operandi. The goals associated with maximizing wealth are largely unchanged, but the methods of doing so may be profoundly changed. Managers face options: do they concentrate on outperforming their competition in the marketplace or do they try to outmaneuver them in the halls of government? And, as we have seen, they have to be aware of the risk that the government will be a fickle master/servant or that the old benefits from alliances with government will be rendered moot by advances in technology and/or consumer consciousness.

Postscript

In his farewell address to the nation on January 17, 1961, President Eisenhower foresaw the dangers we are facing. The speech is most famous for its warning about allowing the "military-industrial complex" to acquire too much influence in the halls of government. I leave you with another excerpt from the address, but invite you to read the speech in its entirety.

> . . . Today, the solitary inventor, tinkering in his shop, has been overshadowed by task forces of scientists in laboratories and testing fields. In the same fashion, the free university, historically the fountainhead of free ideas and scientific discovery, has experienced a revolution in the conduct of research. Partly because of the huge costs involved, a government contract becomes virtually a substitute for intellectual curiosity. For every old blackboard

there are now hundreds of new electronic computers. The prospect of domination of the nation's scholars by Federal employment, project allocations, and the power of money is ever present—and is gravely to be regarded.

Yet, in holding scientific research and discovery in respect, as we should, we must also be alert to the equal and opposite danger that public policy could itself become the captive of a scientific-technological elite.[26]

NOTES

1. The test of any theory *is* whether it works in the "real world." If a theory doesn't add to our understanding of how things work, it is simply a bad theory that either needs fixing or discarding. Ultimately *any* prediction must be based on *something*—and that *something* is, by definition, a theory. So, while the old saw about theories and the "real world" sounds nice, in reality it is just a red herring.

2. Friedrich von Hayek, "The Use of Knowledge in Society," *American Economic Review,* 35, No. 4. (1945): pp. 519–30. American Economic Association. Available at http://www.econlib.org/library/Essays/hykKnw1.html.

Hayek used his knowledge categories to buttress his thesis that central economic planning and socialism cannot work because it would be impossible for a central planner to possess the requisite specific knowledge of time and place to make good decisions. More recently, professors William Meckling (late; of the University of Rochester) and Michael Jensen (emeritus at Harvard) extended Hayek's knowledge taxonomy to apply to business leadership and the various managerial roles within an organization. So, while Hayek's original purpose was to discuss macroeconomic policy, Jensen and Meckling have taken the same ideas and applied them to the microeconomic levels of organizational management.

3. Gabriel Kolko, *The Triumph of Conservatism: A Reinterpretation of American History, 1900–1916* (London: The Free Press of Glencoe, 1963), 4.

4. This and subsequent timeline information were taken from the U.S. *v.* Microsoft: Timeline at http://www.wired.com/techbiz/it/news/2002/11/35212 (accessed February 19, 2011).

5. Benjamin Klein, "An Economic Analysis of Microsoft's Conduct," *Antitrust* (Fall 1999): 38–47.

6. http://www.opensecrets.org/about/tour.php (accessed February 19, 2011).

7. http://www.opensecrets.org/orgs/summary.php?id=d000000115 (accessed February 19, 2011).

8. http://www.opensecrets.org/orgs/totals.php?id=d000000115&cycle= 2000 (accessed February 19, 2011).

9. http://www.opensecrets.org/lobby/clientsum.php?year=2010&lname=M icrosoft+Corp&id= (accessed February 19, 2011).

10. For a complete history and evaluation of the Interstate Commerce Commission, see George W. Hilton, "The Consistency of the Interstate Commerce Act," *Journal of Law and Economics,* 9 (October 1966): 87–113.

11. The actual text of the Wright Amendment used to be posted on the Southwest Airlines Website but has apparently been taken off following Southwest's

current détente with DFW and American Airlines and the passage of the Wright Amendment Reform Act of 2006. The full text of the 2006 act is available at http:// www.gpo.gov/fdsys/pkg/BILLS-109s3661enr/pdf/BILLS-109s3661enr.pdf and a discussion of the original and reform bills is available at http://rsc.jordan.house. gov/UploadedFiles/LB_092906_suspensions.pdf starting on page 3 (both Websites accessed on February 19, 2011).

12. http://www.youtube.com/watch?v=J-Bpshk5nX0&NR=1&feature=fvwp (accessed February 19, 2011).

13. Harold L. Cole and Lee E. Ohanion, "New Deal Policies and the Persistence of the Great Depression: A General Equilibrium Analysis," *Journal of Political Economy,* 112, No. 4 (August 2004): 779–816.

14. http://newsroom.ucla.edu/portal/ucla/FDR-s-Policies-Prolonged-Depression-5409.aspx?RelNum=5409 (accessed February 20, 2011).

15. Ibid.

16. Economist Lee Ohanian explains how the fundamentals of the economy were still robust in a video interview: http://reason.tv/video/show/585.html (accessed February 20, 2011).

17. http://www.npr.org/2011/01/27/133264711/Troubled-Asset-Relief-Program-Update (accessed February 20, 2011). Italics added.

18. http://www.npr.org/templates/transcript/transcript.php?storyId= 133839730 (accessed February 20, 2011). Quote is reporter Arnold paraphrasing Mr. Barofsky's response. Barofsky later made this direct response: "This is a product of poor program design, of poor oversight by the Treasury Department, or poor execution of compliance. Treasury designed this program and its failings are its failings."

19. http://www.psa-history.org/articles/hist.php (accessed February 20, 2011).

20. http://washingtonexaminer.com/op-eds/2009/06/ups-vs-fedex-labor-law-corporate-weapon (accessed February 20, 2011).

21. U.S. CONST. art. I, § 8, cl. 8.

22. For a discussion of the history of copyright and patent legislation, debate, and case law, see Tyler T. Ochoa "Patent and copyright term extension and the Constitution : a historical perspective," *Journal of the Copyright Society of the U.S.A.,* 49 (2001): 19–125. Also available at http://homepages.law. asu.edu/~dkarjala/opposingcopyrightextension/constitutionality/OchoaJCS-TermExtArt.pdf (accessed February 18, 2011).

23. http://www.boingboing.net/author/cory-doctorow-1/ Blog entry 8:21 AM Fri (February 25, 2010) (accessed February 27, 2011).

24. The founding fathers of the United States recognized this when they attempted to craft a constitution for the government that restrained the scope and application of force and violence. The Bill of Rights would otherwise be unnecessary.

25. http://levine.sscnet.ucla.edu/general/intellectual/againstfinal.htm (accessed February 19, 2011).

26 Dwight D. Eisenhower, "Farewell Address," January 17, 1961. Audio and text available at http://www.americanrhetoric.com/speeches/dwightdeisen howerfarewell.html (accessed February 27, 2011).

Chapter 5

Navigating the Political Environment

Ronald J. Hrebenar

After all, the chief business of the American people is business.
—President Calvin Coolidge, January 17, 1925,
in an address to the United States Press Club,
Washington, D.C.

. . . for years I thought what was good for the country was good for General Motors and vice versa.
—Charles E. Wilson at his 1953 congressional
confirmation hearings to become secretary of
defense in the Eisenhower administration

Money is the mother's milk of politics.
—Jessie Unruh, speaker of California's state assembly
quoted in *Time* magazine, December 14, 1962

On being a politician dealing with lobbyists. . . . "If you can't eat their food, drink their booze, screw their women and still vote against them, you have no business being up here."
—Jessie Unruh, quoted in Lou Cannon's
Ronnie and Jesse: A Political Odyssey. Garden
City, NY: Doubleday, 1969, p. 101.

U.S. business and government have always existed in a symbiotic relationship. Business needs government to provide the services, policies, contracts, preferments and, yes, the protection it needs to make the profits necessary to survive and prosper. Government (and more clearly, the politicians and bureaucrats that run the government) need business for election support in their political campaigns or for post-politics jobs. They needed each other in the 1800s, the 1900s and now, especially, in the 21st century. However, it would be true to note that the need for business to be much involved with governments on all levels of U.S. politics greatly increased beginning around 1900, when government began to be much more involved with business. Today, every business, no matter how small, has to deal with governmental regulations and concerns on an almost day-to-day basis. Clearly, the business of the federal government is business and that the business of Washington, D.C., is lobbying. Washington is filled with lawyers, and many of these lawyers are also lobbyists—lobbyists who mostly work for the world of business.

In addition, one can see this in a brief walk around the famous K Street in Washington, D.C., where thousands of corporations, trade associations, interest groups, and lobbyists have their offices.[1] smaller versions of K Street exist around many state capitals and some city and county halls. Lobbying is a growth business in the United States even in these times of economic doldrums because whether the economy is good or bad, government and business remain intertwined.

This chapter addresses that essential relationship between business and government. Unfortunately, many, if not most, businessmen and corporate executives know little or nothing about how to deal with government and the people who make the decisions for the government. An MBA, although a wonderful degree to have on one's resume for leading a major corporation in the United States, does not prepare a business leader for making his or her claims on the city council, state legislature, or the Congress. Dealing with government from a businessman's perspective might seem to be very easy, but it isn't. Lobbying, the process of communication between the interest and government, can be very complicated. It's an art, not a science.[2] Well, it seems to be more of an art than a science. It does have a large number of "dos and don'ts" which are so widely agreed on that they seem to approach the level of "laws or theories." Even if lobbying is studied by scholars from political science from colleges of social and behavioral science, the practice of lobbying is still considered an "art."

The nation is filled with an enormously wide range of interests who have concerns and demands to make at the various levels of the U.S. government. We do know that the great majority of these interests come from the world of business. At the state level, business dominates the debates in the legislatures and in the various offices of the bureaucracy. Compared to the other interests that may seek to influence public policy, business is the "300-pound gorilla" in state politics. No other interest comes even close to rival the power of the business lobbies

A PLAN, THAT'S WHAT WE NEED, A PLAN!

Any organization that feels it needs to play the game of politics in its state's capital or in Washington, D.C., needs to have in mind a set of goals or objectives. You need to clearly state what you want and why you want it. Politics is often called the politics of compromise, so you need to also have in mind your fallback position or compromise position. You should be aware of the resources you may already have in-house (within the organization) or access to these resources from previous ventures in the world of politics (if any) and special relationship your organization may have with politicians or governmental agencies that may be useful. One should be aware of the potential time frame in which the political goals need to be achieved. Is this a long-term goal? Or does it have to be done right now? Often, like purchasing airline tickets, right now can be very expensive. Some sense of possible costs is also essential to consider. Start with the costs of failure to your company or association. Some outcomes from governmental decision making can be extremely costly—maybe even fatal—to an interest. Other costs may involve only a minor inconvenience. If it is the latter case, then a low-cost lobbying campaign may be just fine. But if it is the former, substantial costs may be completely justified. Finally, consider what information and data need to be collected and evaluated that might be useful in the upcoming campaign. OK, now we have the elements of a plan. The next step is implementation.

OUR BUSINESS NEEDS PROFESSIONALS—WHERE ARE THE LOBBYISTS?

Just like a military general in a war, today's business leaders need intelligence and experience in order to deploy the army's resources in such a way as to maximize the prospects of victory. For a CEO to try to make his or her case to the government unassisted is like trying to do your own brain surgery. You can try, but it is not recommended. Think of the lobbying team as your intelligence branch, or G-2 in military slang. Large corporations have their own in-house lobbying team in their public relations (PR) or government affairs division. The larger the corporation, the more specialized that team may be: some specialize in state and local lobbying and others may specialize in federal lobbying, and the company, if it has concerns with the federal government, may have its own office in Washington, D.C., or lobbying firms it has on retainer.

What do these lobbyists do? There are specialized roles that lobbyists have developed over the decades. One of the most important roles is that of *watchdog*—lobbyists who are assigned to specific sites in government watch for potential problems that may emerge that may impact, negatively or positively, their employer. Not the most exciting job, day in and day out, but just like a nation's spy in a neutral country, the information they find can make the difference between being ready to deal with a threat or opportunity and being surprised and perhaps, suffering defeat. Around Congress or a state legislature, these watchdogs attend committee meetings and political party discussions and listen and follow up on bits of information. It is important that these watchdogs know the vital interests of the company so they can understand when something that may sound quite disassociated really might be important down the road.

A second and very frequent type of lobbyist role is that of *contact man*—someone who knows key people in government and other interest groups and is able to identify who to talk to about a certain type of issue at this particular moment of the public-policy process. From the viewpoint of major law and lobbying firms, these lobbyists are often called "rainmakers" because of the big-money clients they are expected to bring into the firm. Many contact lobbyists are high-level former officials in government—some are former senators and House members, whereas others have worked in the executive branch offices of the president or governors. The biggest names in this category can demand and get salaries that run well over a million dollars a year. Their real value lies in the unique access they retain to communicate a client's interests and concerns directly to the people in the government who have the power to accomplish policy objectives. The policy process is filled with veto points and roadblocks that can affect a policy or a piece of legislation. The policy process is also filled with many actors who can assist or hinder one's interests in many different ways—many of them hidden behind the scenes and nearly invisible to even the decision makers in the process. Government at all levels, but especially at the federal and state levels, has gotten just too complicated and the people who understand that the best are often the lobbyists who specialize in the very narrow and complex pieces of the process.

A third role for lobbyists is that of the *persuader.* Persuaders are the lobbyists we think of when we think of them in the popular mass media—the ones with the thousand-dollar suits and the Gucci shoes. These are the lobbyists out front in the policy battles. They go from office to office. They shepherd people from the home districts back to the state capitols and Congress. They are the ones sitting up in the balcony on the last night of the session hoping that the bills they support are on the calendar and will be heard and voted upon before the session is adjourned. They are the experts on the members of a legislature or Congress and their staff. They know who your friends and enemies are, who needs campaign funds in the next election, what arguments and facts will be effective, and who is persuadable and who isn't.

Other lobbyists are *specialists* in certain parts of modern lobbying campaigns. Some specialize in *grassroots* campaign organization, where the lobbyist attempts to create pressure on political decision makers by getting people in their districts or home states to make demands on these decision makers to support certain policies or issues. Others organize *coalitions* of several or many interest groups or corporations to join together on a specific issue campaign. This has become a much more common strategy in recent years and affords the advantage of both economies of scale and specializations of access. Five groups, for example, can contact many more decision makers in a legislature than just one, but each group will often have very specialized relationships with specific legislators, which facilitate access that one group could never achieve.

WHERE CAN OUR COMPANY FIND SOMEONE TO LOBBY FOR US?

Where does one find an effective lobbyist? Good news, your company or association may have a good one already working for you. In smaller trade associations, the executive director will often have the lobbying experience and skills to represent your interests. Larger associations and corporations will often have one or more "governmental liaisons" or governmental relations specialists. These should be your first choices unless there is something out of the ordinary involved in your particular situation. Maybe, for example, this particular fight is sited in a governmental agency or legislative committee that your in-house lobbyist has never worked before. If that is the case, then you will probably need to seek out a lobbyist or lobbying firm who has experience in dealing with this decision-making site. Many of America's giant corporations and powerful trade associations have lots of in-house lobbying expertise; many have major lobbying firms or law firms on retainer in Washington, D.C.; and they still will go out and hire a specialist lobbyist or firm when necessary. Washington and many of the larger state capitals have small boutique lobbying firms that specialize in one particular issue area, such as energy law, or even one specific unit of government such as the House Agriculture Committee. A great advantage offered by these small firms is that a client will be only one of a small number of clients the firm must take care of. The big firms have dozens of clients and many of them may be paying much more than what you may want to spend. The big firms are big for a reason. They have a track record of success, lots of special contacts, many talented lobbyists, and great expertise in many of the strategies and tactics of a multifaceted lobbying campaign. Some firms or associations like being the big fish in a small pond and others love playing in the ocean.[3]

As Bertram Levine, a former lobbyist for Johnson & Johnson and now a professor of political science at Rutgers University, has said:

There is no official set of criteria for determining what is and what is not quality lobbying. It follows that there is no authoritative ranking system for the profession—no top to bottom list ranging from the best to the worst.[4]

It is important that the corporate or association leader designate someone to be the contact person between you and the lobbyist or lobbying firm.[5] During any lobbying campaign, things may change very quickly and rapid decisions may often have to be made to take advantage of an unexpected opportunity or to avoid a potential setback. One decision that most do not like to think about is the decision "to pull the plug" on either a successful or unsuccessful lobbying campaign. Since such campaigns can cost as much as tens of thousands of dollars a month, it is a waste of money to keep a campaign running after you have won or lost. On the other hand, even if you won—this round—future dangers to your goals may lie in different venues. Some lobbying campaigns have had hundreds of battles in many different arenas over decades.

LOBBYING FOR YOUR OWN INTERESTS

Let's assume for financial reasons you have decided to lobby for yourself. My strong recommendation is to find an experienced lobbyist who has knowledge of your lobbying topic and the governmental unit that will be making the decision. But, maybe your organization is a little strapped for money in its budget and has a governmental affairs department or an executive director that can manage the lobbying. That's fine, many corporations and associations have decided to do just that. You have a wide range of options open to you to help you achieve your goals, but let's do some background thinking first. Which institution or institutions of government have the power to achieve or block the policy decision you are concerned over? *Know your target* is the first major piece of intelligence you need. Since most of us are concerned about new laws or ordinances that impact our businesses, we might assume that our focus should be on the city council, county commission, state legislature, or even the Congress. Find out where the decision that affects you will be made and then focus on that institution. You might want to spend a little money up front to discuss with a lobbyist who has worked with that institution and is knowledgeable about *the norms of behavior and expectations regarding lobbying* and the members of the decision-making body. Make no mistake; there is often a great range of what is considered to be "the rules of the game," even among similar level units in the same state. Urban and rural, religious and secular, Republican or Democratic, and professional and amateur—each comes with a different set of informal rules regarding what is normal and what is "outside the norms." So before you do anything, make sure what you think you should do is acceptable.

As was mentioned previously, it is very important to designate one person as the lobbying coordinator for your corporation or association. The reason for this is to avoid multiple messages or lobbying efforts that may be confusing or worse, counterproductive. The key to good and often successful lobbying is staying on the message as much as possible and making sure that all the personnel involved in the message are trained and coordinated. If legislators hear multiple or conflicting messages, they start to get worried and often decide to avoid the issue as much as possible since it could be politically dangerous to them. One of the tasks performed by the coordinator is the collection of materials and information that will be useful in the campaign. This can include information from your own organization as well as from other similar organizations, as well as information about the legislators or bureaucrats you wish to lobby. You will also want to gather information from other organizations that may be lobbying the body since they may be potential coalition allies that may work together with you to help achieve your goal. Finally, you will want to explore what other states or governmental units have done on the same issue to see if you can strengthen your argument for action or learn what to fight against or just what to avoid. There is no sense of reinventing the wheel, if you can avoid it. The next step after the information is gathered is the packaging of it in forms that can be easily understood and effectively packaged. The refined information can be distributed in one-page hand-outs during one-on-one visits, on Websites, in mass media appeals, and in media interviews.

One extremely important set of rules involves the creation of access to the decision makers. Usually, the lower the level of government is, the easier is the access to the decision makers. City council and county commission members are usually pretty easy to approach and to communicate your interests to them. Up a level and depending on the state, the members of the state houses of representatives and senates may be accessible in small, rural states or really tough to meet in those states with so-called professional style bodies, such as California. I recommend the direct approach, don't send e-mails or letters, but try to set up face-to-face meetings. As you already know, e-mails get trashed very easily and the people you want to talk to may get hundreds of e-mails every day. The key to access to legislators in many cities and states is going to their office, talking with their secretaries, and setting up a short (and I mean short) meeting. These people are always busy. Even those who are not very busy, act like they are and so when asked the question, "How much time do you need?" the answer should always be, "Five to ten minutes would be fine." Actually, that is all the time you need. I know that your office has collected lots of information to support your position, but this is not the time to dump it on the legislator. You need a *printed one-page summary.* Yes, boil your entire argument down to a single page. It should identify the problem, note its seriousness, link it to the legislator by explaining its impact on his/her district or the state in general, and clearly state the action that you want done. If you want a bill introduced, indicate you already have a copy of the proposed bill. If you want an already introduced bill passed or killed, clearly identify that bill and indicate where it is in the legislative process. If the legislator is really interested, the meeting may last longer than a few minutes and he/she may ask you for additional information, which you can provide at a later time. Play it by ear and always respond to questions with honesty and in a positive manner. Never threaten! Statements such as "if you don't support this, we will get you!" are the kiss of death for your company *unless you can carry out the threat.* In reality, the tactic of burning bridges in the political game is rarely an effective path to follow. Even opponents on the specific bill you are concerned about this time may be potential allies in future lobbying campaigns or future years. Don't burn bridges!

After you have finished the meeting, take a few minutes and make some notes about who you saw and what you discussed. Be sure to write down if you were asked for additional information or any supporting action. Always follow up on any such requests. Be known as a reliable and responsible participant in the political decision-making process. The notes will help you remember the meeting and facilitate future meetings and maybe help you and your organization to decide if you want to get involved in the campaign finance part of lobbying and maybe even put together a political action committee (PAC) to provide for even easier access in the future.

Let's discuss the possible situation where access is not as easy as it may be at the local government level. Lobbying political decision makers is always easier if the interest has developed a personal relationship that facilitates the making of lobbying appointments easier. Over the years, a number of "access-creating activities" have been tried and tested. Access creation in the 19th century and the first half of the 20th century usually was male dominated and involved smoke-filled rooms, alcohol, food, poker, and, sometimes, female companionship. By and large, those days are gone now. Today's access-creating techniques center on the offer of campaign support and campaign money and certain types of limited social activities. On the national level, major interest groups are constantly being asked to "buy a table" at some reception to "honor and support" a particular member of Congress. The implication is if you attend or "buy a table," you will have a much easier time meeting the congressman and making your case. Major interests also will make campaign contributions at key moments in a legislative or election cycle that may be even better at getting attention for your group. At the state level, some states, such as California, have very stringent laws on how much can be given to a candidate or even how much can be spent on a reception or other types of entertainment. The infamous Delay-Abramoff golf trips to Scotland in the 1990s resulted in many new rules on the federal level that limited the spending on such access-creating activities. Some states, such as Utah, have few such laws other than ones that may require the reporting of such expenditures, although Utah passed a new law in 2010 that prohibited campaign fund raising during the annual state legislative session from January to early March. Even the wild west of Utah political fund raising finally got some restrictions. This is an important point to remember: the rules change all the time and you want to be on the right side of these rules. You will want to be very clear about what the rules require or prohibit in your state. It is very embarrassing to be featured in the local newspaper as a violator of such laws. One basic informal rule is that specific lobbying does not happen at such events. If you invite a state legislator to a football game, performance of a symphony, or a dinner, enjoy the time together and discuss common general interests, but don't lobby. Formal lobbying occurs later. Don't worry, the good time you all spent together will not be forgotten.

DIRECT LOBBYING VERSUS INDIRECT LOBBYING

There are two basic lobbying strategies: direct and indirect lobbying. The resources of the organization should be contrasted. The following is a menu of tactics available for selection in a direct-indirect lobbying plan. The listing of tactics is from the more effective to the less effective tactics.

Direct Lobbying Tactics

1. Face-to-face personal lobbyist visits to elected officials.
2. Personal visits to the staff of public officials.
3. Bringing influential constituents to meet with public officials.
4. Writing letters to public officials. Personal, individual letters are best.
5. Phone calls to public officials or their staff.
6. Sending e-mails to public officials.

Indirect Lobbying Tactics

1. Grassroots lobbying campaigns.
2. Mass media advertising.
3. Public opinion polls.
4. Mass public opinion molding efforts.
5. Elite opinion molding efforts.

Direct face-to-face lobbying is "the gold standard" of lobbying. Every-thing else is done to support the basic form. Face-to-face lobbying is con-sidered to be the most effective because it allows the interest to directly communicate its concerns, needs, and demands directly to those who pos-sess the power to do something politically. The lobbyist and the public of-ficial exist in a mutually symbiotic relationship. Each has something the other desperately needs. The interest seeks governmental assistance and the public official seeks political support for future elections or political issue campaigns. The environment for such lobbying discussions is usu-ally the spaces outside the legislative chambers or perhaps the offices of the legislators. The legislative arena has characteristics that facilitate the lobbying process. It is complex and chaotic. Out of the thousands of bills that might be introduced in a legislative session, sometimes fewer than a hundred are actually passed. There is never enough time to complete the work on the agenda—not even a fraction of the work. The political pro-cess tends to be a winner-takes-all game—often a zero-sum game given the limited resources available and seemingly endless lists of demands that request some allocation of resources. Everyone in the process desper-ately needs information and the most frequent (and most useful) source of information is the lobbyist. The exchange is simple: the lobbyist helps out the governmental officials by providing them with information and the government official reciprocates by helping the interests gain their ob-jectives. There is a cycle to every governmental decision-making site. At crucial times in those cycles the needs of the officials or the lobbyists may dominate. For lobbyists in a legislative site the crucial moments are as the session goes down to its final hours. For legislators, the closer they are to the next election, the more responsive they are to lobbyists who possess resources that may help them win the next election. In the old days, bribery was very important to many legislators; those days are al-most completely gone now. The danger of exposure and personal disaster is too great to risk in today's mass media–dominated society. In today's political world, the public officials' greatest interest is in getting the re-sources they need to stay in office and lobbyists are crucial to getting those resources.

The important thing to remember is that lobbyists need public officials and the public officials need the lobbyists. As was mentioned earlier, the process is chaotic. Lawmaking could be described as making sausage in the dark. In one aspect, this is very true. Much of what happens in the pro-cess is hidden from public view. Deals are made in closed meetings and the public events are often largely symbolic. Many casual observers of the legislative process—think public events, such as committee meetings with interest-group testimony—are crucial to success or failure of a cause. Oc-casionally it may be, but much more often, the hearings and testimony are staged events to justify the decisions that have already been made by party, legislative, and interest-group leaders. These decisions are important in the public framing of the legislative decision-making process, but the real decisions are usually made by interest-group leaders and lobbyists in private meetings off the legislative floors.

The general rules of direct lobbying are pretty simple. Keep it short in terms of time and the one-page handout with the information you want to communicate to the official. Be clear and direct. Mention the problem, why it is important, what is desired, and what the political implication may be. Provide honest information of either a technical or political nature. Just like location, location, location is the key to a successful business, the key words for a lobbyist are absolute honesty, honesty, honesty. If an interest-group leader or lobbyist is seen as offering dishonest or wrong information, his or her days in that profession are at an end.

The transfer of information process is usually preceded by some preliminary meetings with the legislator's or bureaucrat's staff. This should not be bypassed because in many venues, the staff controls access to a wide variety of information and has a great influence on the official's decisions. Many times, the legislators are inundated with issues in a legislative session and they look to their staff or the party caucuses for guidance on many votes. Thus it is important to learn the ins and outs of the legislative process. There are many veto points in the complex process. There are many places to bury a proposal and many decision points that have to be overcome to make something happen. The legislative process is often a death march of legislation. In short, there are many places a bill can be altered or left to die.

There will be times when you may be invited to give testimony at a formal hearing of a legislative, executive, or regulatory body. Such invitations are seldom random; they are usually carefully planned and set up in consultation with the legislative leaders of the convening body. Often the hearings are done to justify decisions that are already made or to show the various organizations involved that they are really playing an important role in the decision-making process. There are a couple of simple rules for you if you are asked to make such a presentation: (1) write two presentations, one to insert into the written record and one for the oral presentation; (2) one page—keep it short; (3) thank everyone for the opportunity to present before their organization; and (4) make your presentation, give a summary, make a clear request for specific support, and then close.[6]

INDIRECT LOBBYING, GRASSROOTS, AND MEDIA

Organizations and businesses often may decide to try more indirect techniques in order to make their direct lobbying more effective. Indirect lobbying involves attempts to sway public opinion to be more supportive of the group's lobbying objectives. Businesses often have difficult PR problems. And, of course, there are a variety of ways for dealing with them. Some of them involve efforts to improve the corporate image. Support of various charities or sporting teams is often a good move that casts a good glow on the corporate identity that can be useful in later lobbying efforts.

Issue framing or spinning is often initiated prior to a lobbying campaign. Issue framing are efforts to alter public perceptions or attitudes regarding a specific issue. One can initiate issue framing by submitting opinion pieces to local newspapers—either the state's major newspapers or even better, the smaller and less-urban papers. Newspapers are often looking for "filler," and you should view it as a great opportunity to communicate your message to the general public.

A much more expensive step in issue framing involves the use of paid media and professional PR firms. Paid media can be the use of billboards to bring your issue to the attention of a larger percentage of the general public. If you want to get attention to your cause and a more favorable public response to your business or organization, you may have to invest in hiring a PR firm. On the other hand, if you have the access to the legislature or the relevant government agency that controls the fate of your issue, you probably do not need to spend any money on PR. Remember, this can be a very expensive tactic. At the expensive end of the category is placing your company's name on a sports arena or community building. At the bottom is sponsoring a little league or five-kilometer run. All such efforts get your name in front of the public in a positive manner. The goal is to create a positive response for your company when you come to make your case.

Real media lobbying is extremely expensive. As is common knowledge to everyone involved in election campaigns, the decision to use electronic media greatly multiplies the cost of a campaign. Of course, campaign media, or in this case, the cause- or issue-related media continuum has many stops along the way. Radio ads are relatively cheap to run during a legislative session; television is much more expensive and may be beyond the budgets of all but the largest corporations or associations. One consideration in the use of paid electronic media in an issue campaign involves the careful determination of your target audience. Using the radio to target very narrow segments of the population, such as Hispanics or those listening to conservative talk radio, can be a very inexpensive option. Frequently, your targeted audience will be the political elite who make the decision that has an impact on your issue. In Washington, D.C., this may involve ads in the D.C. newspapers or the Capitol Hill political media. The more expensive approach is to place ads on the D.C. radio or television stations. During the Clinton administration, the famous "Harry and Louise" ads that killed the Clinton health-care reforms in 1993–1994 were basically shown just in the Washington, D.C., media markets. Planned public rallies in support of your issue can be done on the steps of the capital or the city hall, and handouts to watchers or media representatives are often the cheapest possible form of issue-campaign media.

Recent Supreme Court decisions have freed corporations and groups to spend unlimited amounts of money during political campaigns in media advertising on issues.[7] The Citizens United *v.* the Federal Election Commission, decided in 2010, was the landmark court decision that eliminated legal restrictions on the use of unlimited corporate funds in federal elections. The Supreme Court held that corporations must be afforded the protection of the freedom of speech provision of the First Amendment of the U.S. Constitution. The 5–4 decision, with the five conservative justices in the majority, overturned provisions of the 2002 federal Bipartisan Campaign Reform Act. The door has been opened for a huge inflow of corporate (and labor union) money into federal election campaigns and the disclosure of donors and expenditures in these campaigns by these organizations has been largely eliminated in any meaningful way. Of course, it is the huge financial muscle of national-level corporations or associations that allows them to play this game. But that may be impossible for you. However, on the state and local levels, when public opinion is in flux, even small media efforts can have a big impact on election campaigns and attitudes toward public-policy issues.

Some companies have found it to be effective to work with think tanks and research groups as well as local colleges and universities. Sponsoring research projects that may support your lobbying effort is quite common as is the sponsoring of seminars to raise the visibility of your issue. Such think-tank or higher-education activities may also raise your respectability and legitimacy as a major player in the lobbying game. Most states have a number of such think tanks—some liberal and some conservative—that often are looking for "sponsors" to help pay the rent on their quarters.

Grassroots lobbying can be a cheap way to put pressure on governmental decision makers. This approach is a common form of lobbying for corporations and groups seeking to invoke indirect pressures. Instead of communicating directly with decision makers, indirect lobbying seeks to go to the grassroots to outside the "beltway" to activate different types of constituents to communicate the group's message to the decision makers. The process starts with a corporation or group deciding that additional political pressure on the decision makers may be useful in achieving the lobbying objective. There is no reason to do grassroots lobbying if the lobbying objective is easy to achieve as it may be in some cases. The next decision involves a determination of what part of the grassroots the corporation or group may want to activate. There are two general strategies: shotguns and rifles. The shotgun approach is to mobilize as many constituents as possible to communicate their concerns, demands, or requests. The shotgun approach can use either a "natural" or an "artificial" style of communication. Take, for example, a natural shotgun campaign that asks local level real estate agents to send a message (e-mail, letter, or telephone call) to their city council members who are considering a new ordinance restricting the placement of "house for sale" signs. The campaign would be "natural" because each of the messages would be written in a unique, individualistic way. An "artificial shotgun" campaign would seek to overwhelm a political office with relatively large numbers of messages. Perhaps most, if not all, of the messages are identical, but it is the numbers that may have the greatest impact.

The "rifle grassroots" is a much more focused indirect lobbying campaign. Its goal is to seek out influential or important constituents to communicate personal messages to the decision makers. The most expensive, and probably the most effective, way to do this is to bring a handful of important constituents to the decision maker's office. An example would be a company, such as a bank, that has a number of branches in a particular state. In this instance the company would organize trips to the state capital by bankers with offices in the districts of members of the state legislature holding seats on a committee deliberating a proposed law that would impact the banks. Less expensive would be a company or association having key members write, call, or e-mail their messages. Even a U.S. senator or powerful House member pays attention when a letter comes to his office from the president of the biggest bank in his or her district. We know that governmental officials gets thousands and even millions of messages, but their office staff always culls out the "important ones" to place in the folder on their boss's desk to read.

The very well-organized groups or corporations have a grassroots campaign already set up on their computers and they can activate the campaign in very short time. The less well-financially endowed corporations and associations can play the same game with a much cheaper and less well-organized effort. Associations such as the League of Women Voters and Common Cause, that do not have millions of dollars to run such campaigns, have in the past run effective grassroots campaigns using telephone trees, where 10 people call 10 people each, who then call 10 more and so forth.

THE LAST SITE OF LOBBYING—THE COURTS

Finally, we should discuss the site for the final stand of organizations that have played the lobbying game in the legislative and executive branches and lost at both battlegrounds. The U.S. judicial system and the courts can be the final site for protecting your interests. Most people do not think of the courts as a site for political battles, but they clearly can be and often are. We also know that legislators and bureaucrats often make decisions that violate existing law and even constitutional law. One good example would be the aforementioned proposed city ordinance regulating lawn signs for realtors. Such a law could easily be a violation of the First Amendment's protection of the freedom of speech, and in this case, commercial speech. Unless you are a huge corporation or powerful national association, you probably do not have the resources to pursue a case all the way to the U.S. Supreme Court, but there are ways to play the judicial lobbying game on the cheap. A corporation or association can file a suit challenging an ordinance, law, or regulation. That is the costly version of judicial lobbying because it may cost hundreds of thousands of dollars. A much less costly form is to file an *amicus* brief in an already existing case. This piggybacking on to another case is very common and some cases will end up with dozens of amicus briefs seeking to add their wisdom and reputations to a cause. Another recent form of judicial lobbying has been the financial activity of corporations and groups in elections involving judicial selection and retention. Especially at the state supreme court level, elections have attracted millions of dollars from interests seeking to influence the judges who may have to vote on issues and interests that impact the corporations and interests in the state. This lobbying tactic has always been possible, but has become more often used in recent years as the costs of even judicial elections has risen in the world of electronic campaigning.

CONCLUSIONS

The key to lobbying on the state or local level is really quite simple. Hire a good lobbyist who knows your issues and has good access to the decision makers your organization wants to influence. It is also possible to do your own lobbying. If you do, you may not be able to spend all your time in the capital city or the decision-making site. That's all right, but make sure you are diligent in monitoring the important developments that may impact your interests. This is especially important during legislative sessions or on the days the legislature at the local level may be meeting. You should be building up a collection of relevant information of both a political and a technical nature that may be of use in the future lobbying you will be doing. You will also want to build up a useful set of important contacts that you can go to if necessary. These can include legislators, legislative staffers, officials in the executive branch, relevant agency personnel, in-the-know media, and significant actors from other organizations that may share your interests and may join you in future coalitions. One must always remember that although the official legislative session is the place where many final decisions affecting success or failure are made, most of the important work in framing the issue and even drafting proposed legislation or regulations is done prior to the session or in the legislative interim. There is much more free time in the interim and thus more opportunity to gain access and present your case. Remember, government is a 365-days-a-year operation and important planning and decision making is occurring nearly every day on a formal or informal basis. You need to be aware of what is happening and try to influence it when you can.

There is no "secret" to successful lobbying and it is not so difficult that educated individuals cannot learn how to do it and be successful in a relatively short period of time. Successful lobbying involves contacts and trust; technical and political information; having resources and using the resources in a manner that is politically effective; and having reasonable political objectives and reasonable plans to achieve them. Lobbying is an "art," not a science and thus there is no ironclad set of laws that must be followed. "Correct lobbying" is based on the unique pattern of resources your group may have and the political environment you have to operate with and the goals you are seeking to accomplish. There are many choices to be made and many of them seem to be reasonable. Like many aspects of real politics, the key to success is political management or the careful application of power to achieve the desired results. Don't assume all the important decisions are being made by one governmental entity to the exclusion of other governmental entities. In other words, don't have such a singular focus on the decision making at one site, such as one chamber of a legislature, that you miss important events occurring at other sites.

Good lobbying requires flexible decision making. The political environment is very fluid—changing every day because of the impact of previous decisions, economic changes, or world events. As the political environment changes, your lobbying must also adapt or risk failing. There is nothing worse than having a cause or an objective that has been made obsolete by changing events. This is why your organization really needs someone who knows what is happening on any given day.

Finally, allow me to mention one other aspect of successful lobbying: group unity or at least the appearance of group unity. Your group, at least in public, must speak with one voice, and hopefully the voice of authority or expertise on the topic you are lobbying for. A group that appears to be divided on an issue loses influence very quickly. Even worse, the group's reputation as a lobbying force will be damaged for a very long time.

Remember, lobbying is a communications process. It is your constitutional right to communicate with government and make your needs and concerns known to government officials.[8] If you have not gotten into the game, you may want to reconsider your interests and your relationship with government and how you can take political action to protect your interests.

APPENDIX: SEVERAL THINGS TO REMEMBER WHEN LOBBYING

1. You are dealing with political decision makers who have a wide range of ambitions, motivations, and goals. The key to effective lobbying is aligning your interests and goals to the decision makers.

2. Most government officials want to succeed in their jobs, keep their jobs, or get even better jobs. Any way you can connect with these decision makers and help fulfill everyone's goals will help you to be a winner.

3. The reality of politics is *compromise*. Almost never does anyone get everything they want in a lobbying exchange. Remember that lobbying success means accomplishing your goals a little bit at a time. Be prepared to compromise and don't have a short-term time horizon. Be aware of the changes that can impact your interests, and be flexible.

4. Know the decision-making process. In any legislature, there are lots of dark spots where legislation can be killed, severely altered, and even advanced to law status. The same is true in the governmental bureaucracy. Many different actors can play a critical role that profoundly affects your interests. Think of the decision-making process like an assembly line with different actions along the line. If one of these stations breaks down, the chances of the final product reaching the end of the line are small.

5. A good lobbying process requires lots of time and effect and planning long before the line starts humming. Start as early as you can on your lobbying campaign in terms of the basic preparations.

6. Lobbying can be hard work. Be prepared. Sometimes it is tedious and even boring. Sometimes you have wait for long as the decision makers deal with one issue after another and meet others before they find time to meet with you and discuss your issue.

7. Be courteous and positive—no matter how you may feel at a given moment. Remember, you are asking for someone to do something for you and your organization. No one wants to interact with a grumpy or bad-tempered individual. It is OK to be committed and maybe even a bit intense in terms of your commitment to your cause, but rudeness or excessive aggressiveness is often a negative in the lobbying process. Remember, mutual respect often works very nicely.

NOTES

1. Allan J. Cigler and Burdette A. Loomis, *Interest Group Politics.* Washington, DC: Congressional Quarterly Press, 2007, 214–32.

2. Bertram J. Levine, *The Art of Lobbying: Building Trust and Selling Policy.* Washington, DC: Congressional Quarterly Press, 2009.

3. Ronald J. Hrebenar, *Interest Group Politics in America.* Armonk, NY: M. E. Sharpe, 1997, chapter 4.

4. Levine, op. cit. p. 34.

5. Clive. S. Thomas. *Dealing Effectively with Alaska State Government: Lobbying the Legislature, the Governor's Office and State Agencies.* University of Alaska: Corporate Programs.

6. AARP, "You Can't Fight City Hall," quoted in Hrebenar, *Interest Group Politics in America,* op. cit. pp. 112–13.

7. *Citizens United v. Federal Election Commission,* 558 U.S. 08-205 (2010). Other recent federal decisions that have significantly impacted the rights of corporations in federal campaigns; *McConnell v. Federal Election Commission,* 540 U.S. 93 (2003), which earlier upheld most of the BICRA, and *Federal Election Commission v. Wisconsin Right to Life, Inc., 551 U.S. 449* (2007), which began the process of freeing corporate money to buy ads in federal election campaigns.

8. The First Amendment to the U.S. Constitution's least-known clause is the one that protects the citizen's right to lobby—the "right to petition government for redress of grievances." Of all the clauses in the First Amendment, this one has been least addressed by the Supreme Court and has the most absolute levels of protection.

SELECTED BUSINESS LOBBYING BIBLIOGRAPHY

deKieffer, Donald E. 1997. *The Citizen's Guide to Lobbying Congress.* Chicago: Chicago River Press.

Gray, Virginia and Russell L. Hanson. 2008. *Politics in the American States: A Comparative Analysis.* Washington, DC: Congressional Quarterly Press.

Guyer, Robert L. 2003. *Guide to State Legislative Lobbying.* Gainesville, FL: Engineering THE LAW.

Hrebenar, Ronald J. 1997. *Interest Group Politics in America.* Armonk, NY: M. E. Sharpe.

Hrebenar, Ronald J. and Bryson B. Morgan. 2009. *Lobbying in America.* Santa Barbara, CA: ABC-CLIO.

Opensecrets.org. The Website of Center for Responsive Politics. This site has a lot of information on Washington, D.C., lobbying, data on major interest groups, and lobbyists.

Rosenthal, Alan. 1993. *The Third House: Lobbyists and Lobbying in the States.* Washington, DC: Congressional Quarterly Press.

Thomas, Clive S. 2011. *Dealing Effectively with Alaska State Government: Lobbying the Legislature, the Governor's Office and State Agencies.* University of Alaska: Corporate Programs.

Wittenberg, Ernest and Elisabeth Wittenberg. 1994. *How to Win in Washington: Very Practical Advice about Lobbying the Grassroots and the Media.* Cambridge, MA: Blackwell.

Chapter 6

The Influence of Social Forces on Firm Strategy

Tracy L. Gonzalez-Padron

> The "dual economic and social project" was born of a simple
> fact that remains just as true today: a company cannot succeed
> in the long run if it turns its back on the society it is a part of, if
> it only looks to its short-term economic gain. Danone's founder
> understood very quickly that creating economic value and so-
> cial value are both essential to a company's solidity.
> —Frank Riboud, CEO Danone[1]

Forces external to the organization's boundary challenge managers to
adopt business practices while continuing to meet the company's objectives. A firm's success depends on understanding the economic, political, technological, and social forces that influence an industry. One of
the most complex and intangible forces that affect business are those of
a social nature—embedded in the values and norms of a society. However, as the opening quote illustrates, responding to social forces is instrumental for long-term company success. Social forces are the effects from
changes in demographic patterns, tastes and habits, and concerns for the
environment and health. For example, there are increasing demands for
businesses to take responsibility for negative externalities—social costs

such as pollution, health care, and unemployment that firms do not bear. Governments are responding through regulations to minimize effects or through taxation to recover costs.

In a 2006 survey of executives, responses highlight how companies continue to struggle with tactics for addressing multiple social issues effectively.[2] Approaches to address social issues range from reactionary to strategic. Successful companies view growing social concerns of climate change, human rights, and corporate responsibility as opportunities for innovation and growth. Porter and Kramer propose a strategic approach to address social issues that have a direct impact on the business, either through a reliable supply chain or competitive product offerings.[3] The authors expand on this theme in a 2011 article that redefines business as creating shared value with its communities. They stress, "The competitiveness of a company and the health of the communities around it are closely intertwined"[4] and call for businesses to consider the social and economic impact on the community when making business decisions. The significance of this shift is evident with the proliferation of evaluative firm rankings based on corporate social performance (*Business Ethics* magazine's "100 Best Corporate Citizens"), environmental performance (*Newsweek*'s "America's Greenest Companies"), and corporate reputation (*Fortune*'s "World's Most Admired Companies").

How best to respond to societal expectations of business in firm strategy? First, managers need to understand the social forces that generate salient social issues influencing their organization's performance through environmental scanning. Second, social and environmental issues should be included in firm strategy through sustainable business practices measured by a triple bottom line. Third, an organizational structure for a strategic approach to sustainability requires top management commitment, an ethical culture, stakeholder engagement, and functional integration. The resulting organizational policies and procedures lead to product innovation, customer satisfaction, and a positive reputation that influence financial performance of the firm.

SOCIAL FORCES INFLUENCING BUSINESS

Traditions, values, and attitudes of a changing population are social forces that guide employee and consumer behavior. Social issues such as privacy, obesity, offshore supply, and pharmaceutical product safety challenge organizations to adapt to changing ground rules that can influence financial and reputation performance. Social and environmental issues generally fall into three categories: (1) general social issues important to society; (2) value chain social effects from the company operations; and (3) social dimensions of competitive context that affect competitive advantage of a company, such as labor, environmental, and regulatory influences.[5] A company should focus on those social issues that have a direct impact on the business. For example, Danone identifies the following social issues for their company requiring strategic responses:

- *Employment downturn:* Influences the income of the family, individual identity and social integration, sense of personal achievement, and employee commitment.
- *Product safety and health concerns:* Influences demands for food safety, scientifically proven health claims, the quality, and conformity of products marketed with respect to nutrition.
- *World food-related health situation (including undernutrition, malnutrition, excess-weight, obesity, and chronic food-related diseases:* Influences voluntary programs to improve products' nutritional value, provide nutrition labeling, and communicate valid health claims to avoid regulatory demands.
- *Increasing population effect on food requirements:* Influences pressures on natural resources (soil and water) needed for agricultural production.[6]

However, not all social problems escalate to an issue requiring managerial attention. Social issues obtain meaning through the interpretation of the public and other interested parties such as individuals, organizations, associations, governments, and governmental agencies. Managerial attention heightens when stakeholders capable of influencing governmental action or company policies define social issues as problematic to society, often because of a triggering event.[7] For example, popular business press reveals the power of activist groups in escalating a social issue for corporate and regulatory attention. Student activist demonstrations against Coca Cola's worker conditions in Colombia cost the beverage company millions of dollars in college contracts.[8] Health and wellness trends and concerns of obesity pressured snack and fast food companies such as Pepsi, McDonald's, and KFC to change their product offering and marketing strategies.[9] Timberland established supplier guidelines for leather supply in response to a Greenpeace guerrilla e-mail attack.[10]

The challenge for managers is to identify those social trends that warrant company attention and resources. One approach is to understand how your company affects the environment and quality of life of the community in which it operates. Authors Christopher Meyer and Julia Kirby developed the "ripples of responsibility" that outlines firms' accountability, remediation competence, and brands' credence for a particular social issue.[11] They argue that the trend toward greater corporate accountability for negative effects is inevitable. Companies have the option of acting proactively on their own terms or being coerced by outside forces to solve social issues related to their business. Therefore, the level and type of response to a particular social issue correlates to three characteristics: (1) the extent that the business is responsible for the social consequence; (2) whether the organization has expertise for addressing the issue; and (3) brand-reputation effects from consumer attitudes. Ripples of responsibility reference three concentric circles surrounding the core business of a firm:

Take Ownership

These are effects that can be directly traced to your operations.

Take Action

These are effects that you contribute to and in relation to which you have particular problem-solving competence.

Take Interest

These are distant ripple effects, and you have no special competence to ameliorate them. Channel efforts through other trusted parties.[12]

Adding complexity for managers is the dynamic nature of social issues that influence corporate attentiveness and responsiveness. Studies show that societal expectations follow a path from a period in which an issue was unthinkable, to a period of increasing awareness and expectations for action, and then to a period where dealing with the issue becomes ingrained in the normal functioning of the company.[13] Shareholder resolutions over time show that some issues, such as human rights and energy, endure at a consistent level, whereas environmental and diversity issues follow an interrupted pattern as interests rise and fall.[14] Understanding this "social issue cycle" can help organizations to identify emerging social issues, respond quickly, and influence legislative or regulatory action.

THE TRIPLE BOTTOM LINE

Competitive companies are managing social forces through a sustainability strategy, including in their "bottom line" an assessment of effects on the broader social, economic, and ecological resources of the community in which they operate, and seeking to lessen the negative effects while continuously improving upon the positive ones. Sustainability is often defined as "development that meets the needs of the present without compromising the ability of future generations to meet their own needs."[15] This definition appeared in the 1987 World Commission on Environment and Development report that also stresses the role of industry as "the main instrument of change that affects the environmental resource bases of development both positively and negatively" and calls for greater collaborations between the private sector and governments.[16]

Many companies view social and environmental issues through a triple bottom line, incorporating economic, environmental, and social dimensions in reporting performance. The triple bottom line furthers a company focus on value creation by reporting, "not just on the economic value that they add, but also on the environmental and social value that they add—or destroy."[17] The economic dimension represents the financial impact of the organization in contributing to economic viability of the surrounding community and includes the sales of products and services; profits paid to investors or reinvested into the firm; and taxes paid. The environmental dimension centers on the company stewardship of natural resources and includes reducing waste that fills landfills and pollute waterways, reducing energy use and carbon emissions, and complying with environmental regulations. Finally, the social dimension focuses on the influence the company has on people and includes encouraging an inclusive approach to employees, customers and suppliers, respecting the human dignity of the workforce, and supporting community projects for addressing social issues.

The real synergy of the triple bottom line occurs when the dimensions interact, providing firms a competitive advantage by improving quality of life for employees and suppliers and by offering different products that fill customer demand. For example, focusing on the economic and social dimensions generates employment, employee commitment, and sales from marketing campaigns for customers to contribute to solutions of social issues. Meyer and Kirby encourage companies to channel efforts through other organizations to address general social issues for which they have no special competence.[18] For example, Procter & Gamble partners with UNICEF to combat the fatal maternal and neonatal tetanus by donating the cost of one tetanus vaccine for every purchase of specially marked Pampers diapers and wipes.[19] The program also offers employees a three-month paid sabbatical to volunteer with UNICEF, increasing employee commitment and retention for the firm while providing valuable knowledge to a nonprofit organization. Danone addresses the social issue of unemployment and subsequent influence on family consumption through a program jointly managed with an NGO. The company describes the program:

The *Semilla project in Mexico* is a different type of approach: it is inspired by the Danone's experiences in South Africa with Danimal and the Daniladies, and with the Grameen Ladies in Bangladesh, and entails distributing products door to door to create jobs for local residents. This is a perfect illustration of the relationship between economic and social value creation. Adapting to the realities of different countries means taking into account their social concerns and, for the poorest among them, coming up with new distribution models to do as much as possible to create jobs and combat poverty.[20]

Likewise, a competitive advantage evolves from a focus on the economic and environmental dimensions that lower costs, protect supplies of critical raw materials, and generate revenue from innovative product solutions. Perhaps the most visible economic outcome from environmental management programs is lower operating costs, including savings from greater resource efficiency and lower litigation or regulatory costs.[21] For example, Ecolab, Inc. reports that resource-efficiency efforts in plant operations save 6,500 gallons water daily, reduce material- and waste-removal costs by $320,000 annually from product scrap reuse, and $260,000 annually from better controlling chemical use in production.[22] Companies realize that emerging environmental regulations can influence their production operations. An example of a company that anticipated government bans on lead solders used in electronics production is Hewlett-Packard, which invested in developing a soldering process that eliminated lead well before the July 2006 European Union's Restriction of Hazardous Substances Directive regulating the use of lead in electronics products.[23] Another outcome of responding to environmental issues is protecting natural resources critical to production of a product or service. For example, Danone identifies the environmental impact from increased agricultural food production as a major social force. In response, they implemented strategies to protect water resources by reintroducing clean water as waste, reducing water consumption, and collaborating with organizations that promote the conservation and restoring of wetlands.[24]

Revenue from innovative products and services considering the environmental impact on consumers and the community represents another intersection of economic and environmental dimensions. For example, when research showed that laundry care was a leading household expense due to water-heating energy costs, P&G developed cold-water specialty detergents, helping the company enter a new market.[25] Similarly, Ecolab Inc. develops new products by assessing how environmental variables affect customer costs associated with water use, energy, and waste treatment in food-production processes.[26] The result of their sustainability product review is a series of cleaning and food-processing products that appeal to customers for economic reasons (lowering long-term total costs) while meeting environmental-oriented goals. One such product developed by Ecolab is waterless lubricant for bottle processing that reduces water use at one large processing plant by 1.5 million gallons annually and results in cleaner and more efficient bottling lines.

Social forces related to the environment affect communities through employee safety and health, product safety, and supplier integrity. The toxicity of materials in product manufacturing and use is a major social environmental issue influencing companies in many industries. Major chemical exposures, such as at the Three Mile Island nuclear plant and the Bhopal India chemical spill, highlighted fears of health risks from toxins used in industry. As one article states, "It is a rare morning paper or evening broadcast that does not contain news of acid rain, polluted waters, tank-car derailments, toxic waste dumps, or malfunctions at nuclear power plants."[27] As a result, the United States formulated regulations relating to the use and disposal of toxic chemicals in the manufacturing process; these regulations were aimed at improving the health of people working in polluting industries and of communities neighboring these industries.[28] A series of subsequent state regulations improved the health of workers and citizens substantially. However, companies find that communities are holding them responsible for past environmental practices, as in the case of a New Jersey's community lawsuit against Ford Motor Company for property damage and personal injuries from hazardous paint sludge and toxins dumped almost 40 years earlier that continues to contaminate the soil, air, and groundwater.[29]

Today, global supply chains increase the urgency for companies to address environmental issues that influence employees and customers. Production in emerging countries to reduce costs can result in unsafe working conditions, environmental pollution, and incentives for using the cheapest and toxic materials. In a 2011 audit of suppliers, Apple found that 137 workers at a Chinese factory "had been seriously injured by a toxic chemical used in making the signature slick glass screens of the iPhone."[30] Likewise, Mattel discovered unapproved leaded paint in its supply chain, resulting in a recall of over 2 million toys in 2007.[31]

Chemical exposures from household, personal care, and food products may increase health risks such as cancers, developmental disorders, and obesity. Consumer product sources with potentially dangerous toxins include pesticides, fabrics, foam, plastics, electronics, toys, cleansers, lotions, and our food. Companies have to redesign products to remove banned toxins from their production, while consumers are becoming more educated on the dangers of continual exposure to the accepted level of chemicals in daily product use. Therefore, advocates for product safety call on industry to develop consumer products that replace harsh chemicals with gentler, natural ingredients. Examples include products such as Clorox Greenworks and Seventh Generation that clean effectively, while eliminating chemical fumes or residue. Companies may certify their products as meeting standards set by the Natural Products Association for foods, dietary supplements, home-care products, and health/beauty aids. Standards focus on four dimensions: natural ingredients, safety, responsibility, and sustainability:

- *Natural ingredients:* A product labeled "natural" should be made up of only, or at least almost only, natural ingredients and be manufactured with appropriate processes.
- *Safety:* A product labeled "natural" should avoid any ingredient that has peer-reviewed, scientific research showing human health or environmental risk.
- *Responsibility:* A product labeled "natural" should use no animal testing in its development except where required by law.
- *Sustainability:* A product labeled "natural" should use biodegradable ingredients and the most environmentally sensitive packaging.[32]

The triple bottom line provides companies a framework for responding to dynamic social forces influencing their business. Successful strategies require understanding the direct effects of company operations on the environment and communities and emerging trends in societal expectations of business. Companies that develop capabilities to include societal goals strategically report improvements in innovative products or services, access to new markets, reliable supply chains, and the shaping of the industry's competitive structure.[33]

SUSTAINABILITY STRATEGY IMPLEMENTATION

Although sustainability clearly is growing in importance, organizations struggle in how to integrate sustainability into decision making and new product development. To remain competitive, companies need to translate societal trends in environment or social issues into specific product offerings, while still meeting customer demands for performance. A powerful barrier against investing in sustainable products is the lack of demand for products that have a positive social and/or environmental impact.[34] Studies show that consumers are less likely to purchase sustainable products and services in product categories that value strength or aggressiveness, especially the cleaning product category.[35] Therefore, a strategic approach to sustainability requires that organizations solve two problems simultaneously. They must (1) formalize and execute a vision for customer value creation and (2) recast how they operate to execute new management structures, methods, executive roles, and processes tailored to sustainability demands.[36]

An example of strategic social and environmental sustainability efforts would be the steps undertaken by Procter & Gamble, a leader in consumer packaged goods with sales in about 80 countries in 2011. The magnitude of the effects that P&G has on its customers relates to the scale and scope of its 50 leading brands in beauty and grooming, health care, snacks and pet care, fabric care and home care, and baby care and family care. The P&G 2011 Sustainability Overview titled "Commitment to Everyday Life" begins with the following statement:

> At P&G, we're committed to delivering products and services that make everyday life better for people around the world. Our opportunity to touch and improve lives comes with a responsibility to do so in a way that preserves the planet and improves the communities in which we live and work. We're continuing to make progress in our focus areas of Products, Operations and Social Responsibility, enabled by our employees and our stakeholders.[37]

Another company receiving awards for sustainability is Ecolab, Inc., the global leader in industrial cleaning and food-safety products and services with $6 billion in global sales.

> At Ecolab, making the world a cleaner, safer place is our business. We are committed to providing our customers with the most effective and efficient cleaning, food safety and infection control programs available. Sustainability is inherent in our products and services. From concentrated, solid formulations to innovative packaging and dispensing methods, our products are designed to help increase safety, lower the use of water and energy, and reduce the chemicals and waste released to the environment. Strengthened by the expertise of our associates and combined with our dedication to social responsibility, these offerings provide value to our customers and the global economy—and help foster a more sustainable world.[38]

Both of these examples illustrate the importance of considering all aspects of the business in a sustainability strategy, including product offerings, employee engagement, and internal operations. What are the cornerstone business dimensions for a successful sustainable business strategy? A three-year assessment of 183 companies by MBA students from a leading university provides insights into dimensions that are evident in a sustainable business. Each assessment included management interviews and completion of a self-assessment survey of 113 items. Out of the 183 companies, only 45 (24.2%) feel that their organization's current efforts in environmentally and socially sustainable business make them leaders in their industry, although almost half (92 firms) are making substantial progress in their sustainability efforts. The sample includes companies that are relatively small (49% with less than 500 employees) and large (51% with over 500 employees, including 41 companies with more than 3,000 employees). The findings from the project showed little difference in the success factors for a sustainable business strategy due to size. From the initial survey, four dimensions of a sustainable business emerge that include top management commitment; an ethical culture; stakeholder engagement; and functional integration. These form the organizational structure to support policies and procedures for producing products and services that provide economic and social value. There are key questions for management relating to each of these dimensions for assessing organizational opportunities for a sustainable business.

Top Management Commitment

Top management commitment in stressing environmental and social programs positively influences employees in the organization. Putting emphasis on areas other than the financial bottom line signals to the organization that these social goals are equally valid, and offers opportunities for creative programs and integrative solutions that work to meet the triple bottom line. Lack of emphasis, on the other hand, communicates apathy toward social responsibilities and an unwillingness to devote time or effort into anything other than maintaining the profit margin of the organization. Industry leaders in creating social and economic value demonstrate their commitment in the following ways:

Top Management Commitment

- Does management emphasize environmental and social programs?
- Has the company developed a formal policy statement that addresses environmental practices?
- Has the company developed a formal policy statement that addresses social issues (i.e., human rights, diversity)?
- Does the top management provide the resources required to meet environmental/social goals or objectives?
- Does the top management seek periodic audits of environmental/ social activities?

The CEO, senior management, and the board of directors express the company's position on social and environmental issues through annual reports, letters to shareholders, and corporate mission statements. A formal policy statement demonstrates a public commitment by an organization to take responsibility for their social and environmental imprint. It communicates to members of the organization that environmental and social efforts are an organizational priority, positively influencing the corporate culture and encouraging individuals to present solutions. For example, the CEO of P&G states in a letter in their 2011 Sustainability Overview report:

> The opportunity to make a difference that lasts generations—whether through our brands and services, our operations, our environmental sustainability efforts, or our philanthropy—is what attracts people of remarkable character and caliber to P&G. We are committed, together, to improving life every single day. We're proud of the progress we make year after year, and we are inspired by the challenge to do more. (Robert A. McDonald, Chairman of the Board, President and Chief Executive Officer)[39]

Incorporating environmental and social goals into the corporate culture through the positive communication of top management is essential, but without monetary and human resources, such communication becomes irrelevant. Of the top management questions in the survey, this is the one topic where the majority of all businesses see room for improvement. In particular, smaller companies view any programs beyond regulations for social and environmental responsibilities as an expense that would inflate costs and lose customers. One company states, "If you're smart about balancing, then you can really drive most of the way there without incurring much cost, but if you're not careful you can spend lots of money and not get any real return out of it. You can be a good corporate citizen but you won't be around. That's not sustainable."

Articulating a sustainability strategy entails leadership to develop measures to identify and manage the social and environmental effects of corporate activities in order to gain reputational advantages. For example, the auditing of these activities by an outside agency can provide corporations with expert measuring techniques and perspectives that benefit from experience with similar corporations. Top management encouragement of, and cooperation with, such practices is crucial in order to properly examine how the company environmental and sustainability efforts are improving over time. Consequences of not delivering on promises of sustainable business practices can be long lasting. As Meyer and Kirby state, "When the public perceives that a company is producing an externality that it could take greater responsibility for but isn't, that's when mechanisms of compulsion are brought to bear, from regulation to riots."[40] Thus, top management emphasis on social and environmental issues through formal policies, resources, and auditing is a critical success factor for implementation of a sustainability strategy.

Ethical Culture

A strong ethical culture that encourages fair and honest practices is another characteristic of industry leaders in sustainability. The ethical climate of an organization refers to the degree of organizational commitment to ethical responsibilities of corporate citizenship and defines appropriate behaviors of its employees and suppliers. Ethics is not often considered in discussions of corporate social responsibility; yet a culture that promotes and monitors ethical standards is the founding principle for responsible companies.[41] Companies establish an ethical culture through business ethics programs that guide employees, suppliers, and distributors to understand expected conduct through training and communications, advice and reporting mechanisms, and monitoring through auditing systems. The following questions identify key characteristics of industry leaders in sustainability:

Ethical Culture

- Does the organization have a comprehensive code of ethics?
- Does a confidential procedure exist to report misconduct?
- Is fairness toward employees an integral part of processes?
- Do employees follow professional standards?

A comprehensive code of ethics sets the bar for the way in which a corporation handles its relationships with customers, employees, suppliers, government, and the community. The strength of an ethics code depends on how much it is encouraged and implemented by the upper management; when executed by all of a company's employees, it can enhance the reputation of the company, while reducing risks. Larger companies are more likely to have a formal code of ethics than small and medium-sized enterprises. A lack of a code of ethics puts the company at risk of employee or supplier actions, resulting in criminal prosecution, product recalls, toxic waste spills, or harassment claims. Therefore, a formal statement of a code of ethics includes the social and environmental issues that influence the business.

Businesses globally are creating an infrastructure for reporting wrongdoing through ethics hotlines or ethics' officers to comply with legislation such as the Federal Sentencing Guidelines and Sarbanes-Oxley Act in the United States and with similar legislation in Europe. Studies have found five employee responses when exposed to ethical misconduct in the workplace: inaction, confronting the wrongdoer(s), reporting to management, calling an internal hotline, and external whistleblowing.[42] However, many employees remain silent from fear that speaking up will damage relationships and cause others to view them negatively.[43] Employees must feel confident that they are free to voice their concerns or report when they witness misconduct taking place.

A strong indicator of an ethical culture is the employee perception of fairness in the workplace. An emphasis on fair treatment of workers is necessary to demonstrate responsiveness to social issues relating to human rights and diversity. Studies show that the ethical leadership of the immediate supervisor demonstrates the degree of concern for others, fairness, and trustworthiness for employees that contributes to an environment that values ethical conduct.[44] Ethical leadership reduces employee stress and affects job satisfaction. For example, a worker in a multinational company states: "I am thankful that I am at a company that I don't have to 'go there' (meaning compromise his/her ethics)—I'm fortunate enough that I don't have to make those decisions. It is something that the company is very proud of."[45]

Along with organizational codes of ethics, employees of ethical companies abide by professional standards for their discipline, whether it is accounting, finance, marketing, or engineering. Of all the questions relating to ethical culture, this is the only one that is not significantly higher in larger companies. Companies in highly regulated industries, such as financial services, governmental contracting, and health care, value compliance with professional standards in order to maintain legitimacy in the market.

Companies may comply with voluntary standards and codes of conducts to address the legal, ethical, social responsibility, and environmental issues they face. Particularly over the past two decades, a number of prominent business associations, NGOs, and international government institutions developed a body of global standards for a responsible business. For example, a global network of business leaders committed to principled business leadership provides principles for responsible business. The Caux Round Table believes that business has a crucial role in developing and promoting equitable solutions to key global issues. The International Organization for Standardization has an environmental management standard (ISO 1400) and social responsibility standard (ISO 26000), both assisting companies to operate in the environmentally and socially responsible manner that society increasingly demands. The Global Reporting Initiative provides globally applicable guidelines for reporting on economic, environmental, and social performance.

Stakeholder Engagement

Sustainable companies recognize salient stakeholder groups, their key issues, and their potential for helping or harming the business. A widely accepted and popular definition of a stakeholder is that "any group or individual who can affect or is affected by the achievement of the organization's objectives."[46] Stakeholders exhibit at least one of these characteristics: (1) the potential to be positively or negatively affected by organizational activities and/or is concerned about the organization's impact on his or her or others' well-being, (2) can withdraw or grant resources needed for organizational activities, or (3) is valued by the organizational culture.[47] Industry leaders develop expertise in stakeholder engagement and are able to address their concerns and interests. Key questions companies may ask include the following:

Stakeholder Engagement

- In my organization do units engage with external stakeholders (e.g., suppliers, customers, local communities) in order to carry out their projects?
- Does the company have an assessment tool to evaluate social and environmental performance of its key suppliers?
- Does the company educate and/or assist its suppliers in meeting environmental/sustainability goals?
- Does the company measure its customers' demands for environmentally and socially responsible products (and/or services)?

Stakeholder engagement includes processes for information gathering about the interests and expectations of stakeholders, information giving to share activities and performance, and dialogue and consultation. Nearly half of the respondents indicated that they engaged stakeholders by communicating with them. Tactics varied from engaging in formal dialogue or surveys to informal engagement (staying in touch with customers, discussing sustainable issues during other communiques, etc.). Although a company benefits from such communication processes, a collaborative effort with stakeholder groups provides greater opportunities "to become better aligned with their stakeholders and better positioned to become sustainable enterprises."[48]

Industries vary in the degree of engagement with specific stakeholder groups—especially customers, regulatory agencies, and suppliers. Manufacturers tend to have a greater focus on suppliers than nonmanufacturers. Although consumers and employees receive the largest attention overall, services and retail are most attentive to these two groups. Highly regulated industries, such as utilities (e.g., energy and air travel) and industrial manufacturing, have the greatest focus on regulatory groups. One interesting story from the interviews relates to a multinational corporation working with a regulatory agency. Prior to starting business in Costa Rica, the company discovered deficient chemical and environmental regulations. Rather than take advantage of a lack of regulatory oversight, the company immediately collaborated with the government to design and pass environmental legislation modeled by the most stringent U.S. guidelines.

Suppliers are important stakeholders for a firm, yet many companies do not consider the supply chain in social and environmental programs. Social issues relating to suppliers relate to diversity, the environment, and labor concerns. The complexity of the global supply chain suggests a greater likelihood of accepting responsibility for the actions of their suppliers. Firms with a larger percentage of their sales or supply from outside of the United States should pay particular attention to address employee concerns. A need to focus on employees is a reflection of the various legal and regulatory issues with labor in international markets, as well as the difficulty in managing and controlling supplier labor practices. Industry leaders in sustainability select and evaluate suppliers based on their social and environmental performance, helping competent vendors become socially responsive, and helping socially responsive vendors to become competent. Inclusion of social and environmental issues in vendor selection has far-reaching effects in an industry. Of the companies interviewed, more than a quarter of respondents require their suppliers to meet government regulations, industry standards, or voluntarily codes for sustainability. Other respondents implement social and environmental programs to continue to supply a major customer.

Understanding customer demand for products that have a positive social and/or environmental impact is critical for a strategic sustainability strategy. Consumer expectations regarding health and safety, marketing and advertising, and product performance influence buying habits. Industry leaders seek customer input for developing solutions that address social or environmental issues. For example, at Ecolab they survey field sales staff to understand their customers' operations, collect quantitative and qualitative research on customer satisfaction and perceptions, and encourage customers to meet with management to build mutually beneficial relationships.[49]

Functional Integration

When instituting a top-down initiative to institute environmental awareness and social programs, employee engagement at all levels is imperative for a successful sustainability strategy. Through sharing of information and resources, companies can generate an organizational culture that encourages innovative approaches to environmental and social issues. However, each function within an organization faces unique social and environmental challenges. Providing education and training enables employees to achieve positive results company wide, while sharing experiences encourages crosspollination of ideas throughout the organization.

A review of five cases of employee engagement finds the following best practices: (1) inviting all levels of an organization into dialogue and acting on resulting ideas; (2) having a clear and compelling vision that everyone creates and supports; (3) integrating sustainability concerns into fundamental human resource practices, product design, and corporate facilities; (4) proving consistent messages through peer partners, lunch-time discussions, newsletters, and community service events; and (5) training the managers to train others in safe and proper practices.[50] The questions where *leaders of sustainability* scored the highest reflect these best practices:

Functional Integration

- Does the company integrate social and environmentally conscious practices across product/service lines?
- Is staff at all levels educated concerning environmental awareness and sustainability?
- Is the spirit and vision of social responsibility communicated to all levels in all locations?
- Are department managers trained to understand environmental/sustainability programs and policies in order to achieve the environmental/sustainability goals and issues of their departments?
- Does the company provide a method for communication between departments within the company (e.g. sales/marketing, product design, purchasing, etc.) regarding sustainability/environmental issues and practices?

Although you may expect functional integration to be more difficult for larger companies, results of the sample surveyed show the opposite. Companies with more than 500 employees indicate more emphasis on training, communication, and crosspollination among functions. At least one organization includes social and environmental activities in job descriptions, with a closed-loop feedback system created by auditors and agencies. They state: "as the auditors make findings related to processes or sustainability, changes and improvements are incorporated and the process repeats itself."

Management research shows that awareness, understanding, and demand from managers and employees are key success factors to implementing a sustainability strategy.[51] However, some of the survey respondents admit that sustainability discussions are primarily in the upper levels of the company and communication to other levels is too strategic and not practical enough for the mid-level manager or front-line employee. In one organization, the management expressed that social and environmental activities were only the responsibility of a sustainability department and therefore only communicated within that group. Company training and communication initiatives need to consider all levels and locations of the organization. One company interview includes upper management stressing effective communication of their sustainability strategy, although a lower manager of the same company is not able to recall communicating sustainability concepts to their employees. Successful companies invest in integrating environmental, social, and economic goals across the organization expecting each functional area to understand the effects of their activities, accept the responsibilities for implementation, and develop policies and practices for achieving these goals.

Policy and Practice

With an organizational structure for social and environmental responsibility, functional areas can implement practices that drive sustainability performance. Formal policies encourage employees to consider social and environmental issues in the design, production, and marketing of products and services. However, sustainability performance only improves with continuous learning through monitoring the effects practices have on all stakeholders. Offering products and services that provide social and economic value to consumers requires coordination of policies and practices among research and development, procurement, production, and marketing departments. At Ecolab Inc., new product innovation involves collaboration with sales, marketing, R&D, and engineering employees through an assessment of customer needs, product data, sales and financial projections, and sustainability effects.[52] For a successful implementation of a sustainability strategy, companies can assess the extent to which employees incorporate and measure social and environmental issues through the questions relating to product design, purchasing, marketing/packaging, operations, and facilities. From results of the 113 items in the initial survey, industry leaders put a significantly greater emphasis on the following policies and practices than those with little or no sustainability efforts:

Product Design

- Is there a formal policy to reduce the dependence on nonrenewable natural resources through design of the products or services?
- Is life-cycle thinking made an integral aspect of product design?
- Is the product designed to reduce the amount of materials and packaging required?
- Does the product design achieve a high recycled content?
- Are materials evaluated for upstream and downstream energy and fuel intensity?

Purchasing

- Does the company have an environmentally preferred purchasing policy or guidelines?
- Does the company provide socially diverse suppliers the opportunity to participate in sourcing opportunities?
- Does your organization assess human rights conditions of your first-tier suppliers and suppliers beyond the first tier?
- Does purchasing identify and purchase sustainable products (recycled, recyclable, bio based, climate neutral, nontoxic)?
- Does the purchasing department promote minimization, reuse, or recyclability of packaging from suppliers?
- Are local products/suppliers given preference in purchasing decisions?

Marketing/Packaging

- Has the company developed and implemented environmentally oriented packaging guidelines for customer shipments?
- Does the company promote minimization of packaging?
- Are incoming and outgoing packaging material reused or recycled?
- Are marketing claims periodically evaluated and substantiated to avoid inaccurate or misleading claims (i.e., "green washing")?
- Do marketing and sales strategies accurately reflect company sustainability policies?
- Does the company educate its customers about sustainability issues?

Operations

- Has the company developed a pollution-prevention program for its operations?
- Does the company ensure business and administrative operations (papers, toners, marketing materials, etc.) comply with sustainable guidelines?
- Does the company dispose of its waste in an environmentally responsible manner?
- Has the company developed a system to identify and reduce air emissions?
- Has the company developed a system to identify, reduce, and/or eliminate hazardous materials?
- Does the company require and promote recycling throughout its operations?

- Are waste-minimization procedures implemented and tracked in all processes?
- Does the company have policies in place to minimize transportation emissions in employee transportation or product delivery?
- Does the company have policies in place to minimize energy use in the receiving or delivery of its products and/or services?

Facilities

- Does the company track the consumption and reduction of energy?
- Does the company track the consumption and reduction of water in its facilities?
- Are electrical, mechanical, plumbing, and lighting fixtures chosen for maximum efficiency?
- Are green spaces and native landscaping incorporated at the site as a means of reducing water usage?
- Do the parking facilities accommodate alternative fuel vehicles, carpoolers, and cyclists?
- Does the company's new/recent facilities meet a nationally recognized green building standard (LEED, Green Globe, etc.)?

Although not a comprehensive list of policies and practices for implementing a triple bottom line, the chosen activities focus on offering products and services that minimize the impact on the environment, while increasing the health and safety of consumers, employees, suppliers, and the community. They represent organizational competences for becoming a market leader by realizing sustainability as an opportunity for innovation to address social and environmental issues.[53] Questions relating to nonrenewable natural resources, energy and water use, recycling, and waste management address the environmental and economic dimensions of the triple bottom line by increasing efficiency throughout the value chain. Additionally, increased revenues result from the focus on developing innovative product solutions through a life-cycle analysis that addresses the overall impact of the product through raw material acquisition, manufacturing, distribution, use and reuse, and end-of-life management. Marketing questions relate to customer perceptions of innovative products or packaging that requires "the ability to generate real public support for sustainable offerings and not be considered as 'greenwashing'."[54]

Likewise, a number of the questions relate to social issues for business. For example, purchasing and operations departments focus on eliminating hazardous and toxic materials to address social and environmental issues of product safety and employee health. Policies for sourcing from socially responsible suppliers illustrate a commitment to incorporate diversity and human rights into the procurement function. As a whole, the survey questions provide a starting point for companies struggling to address social and environmental issues that affect its customers, employees, suppliers, and surrounding communities.

MANAGERIAL IMPLICATIONS

Understanding the social forces influencing firm strategy is both important and complex with increasing demands for companies to take responsibility for social costs. Social forces are dynamic, reflecting shifts in demographics, lifestyles, attitudes, and social norms. Issues that evolve from societal trends include social (i.e., human rights and diversity) and environmental (i.e., energy use and climate change). The triple bottom line approach views social issues in three dimensions: economic, environmental, and social. The interactions among these three dimensions highlight emerging social issues, such as job creation, employee welfare, product safety, supplier integrity, and waste management, which arise from the attention of the press, government, and activist groups. Management must prioritize attention and resources on the social issues that have the most impact on their industry.

Companies gain a competitive advantage if able to anticipate and respond to social trends that guide consumer and employee behavior. Therefore, management of leading firms emphasize their commitment to addressing social and environmental issues through a formal strategy that encourages ethical practices in engaging with key stakeholders, including customers, employees, suppliers, regulatory agencies, and the community. Collaborative efforts with customers or the government can result in innovative product and service solutions to pressing social issues. Integration of the vision for social responsibility to management and employees at all levels aligns business activities to achieve organizational social and environmental goals. Through implementation of sustainable business practices that consider influences of social forces, the company reduces risks of regulation and litigation, enhances efficiency, and increases revenues by creating economic and social value for customers.

Why is it so important to attend to social and environmental issues in business? Because the degree to which a company addresses social trends in its strategy influences its overall reputation, customer satisfaction, and innovation, which in turn affects financial performance.[55] Although "doing good" creates customer satisfaction and a positive reputation, irresponsible actions lower customer satisfaction and overall reputation that have lingering effects. An unethical practice that exploits or harms another party reduces the customer's satisfaction, whether or not the firm is directly responsible. For example, consider a retailer who prides themselves on animal rights, and a supplier was found to use animals for testing products. High customer ethical expectations of the retailer may result in higher dissatisfaction.[56] Unfortunately, a poor reputation for corporate social responsibility discredits social and environmental initiatives. Some firms recognize this in their annual reports; as the tobacco company, Altria Group, states:

> We know that this is an evolving process and continually strive to improve our efforts to earn public trust and strengthen our reputation through a commitment to responsible marketing, quality assurance, ethical business practices and by giving back to our communities.[57]

As shown, social trends relating to health, safety, energy, waste, and employment influence firm strategy by expecting responsible business practices throughout the value chain. Negative social and environmental effects from company activities become targets for activist groups, creating detrimental reputational effects, and impending regulation. Through constructive dialogue with stakeholders, companies can anticipate and respond to emerging issues to create both economic and social value. Sustainable businesses recognize that strategic responses to social forces are instrumental for long-term company success.

NOTES

1. Danone. "Danone Sustainability Report 2010," Available from: http://www. danone.com/images/pdf/danone_uk_24mai.pdf.

2. Bonini, Sheila M. J., Lenny T. Mendonca, and Jeremy M. Oppenheim, "When Social Issues Become Strategic," *The McKinsey Quarterly,* 2006. 2: pp. 19–31.

3. Porter, Michael E. and Mark R. Kramer, "Strategy and Society: The Link between Competitive Advantage and Corporate Social Responsibility—Response," *Harvard Business Review,* 2007. 85(6): pp. 136–37.

4. Porter, Michael E. and Mark R. Kramer, "Creating Shared Value," *Harvard Business Review,* 2011. 89(1/2): pp. 66.

5. Porter and Kramer, "Strategy and Society: The Link between Competitive Advantage and Corporate Social Responsibility—Response," *Harvard Business Review,* 2007. 85(6): pp. 136–37.

6. Danone. "Danone Sustainability Report 2010," Available from: http://www. danone.com/images/pdf/danone_uk_24mai.pdf.

7. Mahon, John F. and Sandra A. Waddock, "Strategic Issues Management: An Integration of Issue Life Cycle Perspectives," *Business and Society,* 1992. 31(1): p. 19.

8. Foust, Dean, Geri Smith, and Elizabeth Woyke, "'Killer Coke' or Innocent Abroad?" in *Business Week.* 2006. p. 46.

9. "Business: The Blog in the Corporate Machine; Corporate Reputations," in *The Economist.* 2006. p. 66.

10. Swartz, Jeff, "Timberland's CEO on Standing up to 65,000 Angry Activists," *Harvard Business Review,* 2010. 88(9): pp. 39–127.

11. Meyer, Christopher and Julia Kirby, "Leadership in the Age of Transparency," *Harvard Business Review,* 2010. 88(4): pp. 38–46.

12. Ibid., p. 44.

13. Zyglidopoulos, Stelios C., "The Issue Life-Cycle: Implications for Reputation for Social Performance and Organizational Legitimacy," *Corporate Reputation Review,* 2003. 6(1): p. 70.

14. Graves, Samuel B., Sandra Waddock, and Kathleen Rehbein, "Fad and Fashion in Shareholder Activism: The Landscape of Shareholder Resolutions, 1988–1998," *Business and Society Review,* 2001. 106(4): pp. 293–314.

15. World Commission on Environment and Development, *Our Common Future.* 1987, Oxford, New York: Oxford University Press.

16. Ibid., Chapter 12: Towards Common Action: Proposals for institutional and Legal Change.

17. Elkington, John, *Cannibals with Forks : The Triple Bottom Line of 21st Century Business.* Published 1997 by Capstone Publishing Limited, Oxford Centre for Innovation, Oxford, UK; Stony Creek, CT: New Society Publishers.

18. Meyer, Christopher and Julia Kirby, "Leadership in the Age of Transparency," *Harvard Business Review,* 2010. 88(4): pp. 38–46.

19. Procter & Gamble. "Social Responsibility: Pampers Vaccinations," Available from: http://www.pg.com/en_US/sustainability/social_responsibility/pampers_vaccinations.shtml.

20. Danone. "Danone Sustainability Report 2010," Available from: http://www.danone.com/images/pdf/danone_uk_24mai.pdf, p. 34.

21. Epstein, Marc J., *Making Sustainability Work: Best Practices in Managing and Measuring Corporate Social, Environmental and Economic Impacts,* 1st ed. 2008, Sheffield, UK: Greenleaf Pub.; San Francisco: Berrett-Koehler Publishers. 288 pp.

22. Ecolab, Inc. "Sustainability Report 2010," Available from: http://www.ecolab.com/Publications/SustainabilityReport/sustainreport2010_40pp.pdf.

23. Nidumolu, Ram, C. K. Prahalad, and M. R. Rangaswami, "Why Sustainability Is Now the Key Driver of Innovation," *Harvard Business Review,* 2009. 87(9): pp. 56–64.

24. Danone. "Danone Sustainability Report 2010," Available from: http://www.danone.com/images/pdf/danone_uk_24mai.pdf, p. 34.

25. Nidumolu, Ram, C. K. Prahalad, and M. R. Rangaswami, "Why Sustainability Is Now the Key Driver of Innovation," *Harvard Business Review,* 2009. 87(9): pp. 56–64.

26. Milliman, John, Tracy L. Gonzalez-Padron, and Jeffrey Ferguson, "Sustainability-Driven Innovation at Ecolab, Inc.: Finding Better Ways to Add Value and Meet Customer Needs," *Environmental Quality Management,* 2012. 21(3): pp. 21–33.

27. Erikson, Kai, "Toxic Reckoning: Business Faces a New Kind of Fear," *Harvard Business Review,* 1990. 68(1): p. 123.

28. Dunagan, Sarah C., et al., "Toxics Use Reduction in the Home: Lessons Learned from Household Exposure Studies," *Journal of Cleaner Production,* 2011. 19(5): pp. 438–44.

29. Stodghill, Ron, "Can Ford Clean up after Itself?" *New York Times*. 2007. p. 1.

30. Barboza, David, "Workers Poisoned at Chinese Factory Wait for Apple to Fulfill a Pledge," *New York Times*. 2011. p. B1.

31. Becker, Monica, Sally Edwards, and Rachel I. Massey, "Toxic Chemicals in Toys and Children's Products: Limitations of Current Responses and Recommendations for Government and Industry," *Environmental Science & Technology*, 2010. 44(21): pp. 7986–91.

32. Natural Products Association. "NPA Quality Assurance Programs," October 25, 2011; Available from: www.npainfo.org.

33. Gonzalez-Padron, Tracy L., and Robert W. Nason, "Market Responsiveness to Societal Interests," *Journal of Macromarketing*, 2009. 29(4): pp. 392–405.

34. Wirtenberg, Jeana, Wiliam G. Russell, and David Lipsky, "Introduction and Overview," in *The Sustainable Enterprise Fieldbook*, Jeana Wirtenberg, Editor. 2009, New York: Greenleaf Publishing, pp. 2–24.

35. Luchs, Michael G., et al., "The Sustainability Liability: Potential Negative Effects of Ethicality on Product Preference," *Journal of Marketing*, 2010. 74(5): pp. 18–31.; Sheth, Jagdish, Nirmal Sethia, and Shanthi Srinivas, "Mindful Consumption: A Customer-Centric Approach to Sustainability," *Journal of the Academy of Marketing Science*, 2011. 39(1): pp. 21–39.

36. Lubin, David A. and Daniel C. Esty, "The Sustainability Imperative," *Harvard Business Review*, 2010. 88(5): pp. 42–50.

37. Procter & Gamble. "2011 Sustainability Overview Report," Available from: http://www.pg.com/en_US/sustainability/overview.shtml.

38. Ecolab, Inc. "Sustainability Principles"; Available from: http://www.ecolab.com/CompanyProfile/GlobalSustainabilityPrinciples.

39. Procter & Gamble. "2011 Sustainability Overview Report," Available from: http://www.pg.com/en_US/sustainability/overview.shtml, p.2.

40. Meyer, Christopher and Julia Kirby, "Leadership in the Age of Transparency," *Harvard Business Review*, 2010. 88(4): p. 43.

41. Epstein, Marc J., *Making Sustainability Work: Best Practices in Managing and Measuring Corporate Social, Environmental and Economic Impacts*, 1st ed. 2008, Sheffield, UK: Greenleaf Pub.; San Francisco: Berrett-Koehler Publishers, pp. 36–37.

42. Kaptein, Muel, "From Inaction to External Whistleblowing: The Influence of the Ethical Culture of Organizations on Employee Responses to Observed Wrongdoing," *Journal of Business Ethics*, 2011. 98(3): pp. 513–30.

43. Milliken, Frances J., Elizabeth W. Morrison, and Patricia F. Hewlin, "An Exploratory Study of Employee Silence: Issues That Employees Don't Communicate Upward and Why," *Journal of Management Studies*, 2003. 40(6): pp. 1453–76.

44. Mayer, David, Maribeth Kuenzi, and Rebecca Greenbaum, "Examining the Link between Ethical Leadership and Employee Misconduct: The Mediating Role of Ethical Climate," *Journal of Business Ethics*, 2010. 95: pp. 7–16.

45. Gonzalez-Padron, Tracy, "Ecolab Inc.: How a Company Encourages Ethical Leadership," in *Learning from Real World Cases—Lessons in Leadership*, D.D. Warrick and Jens Mueller, Editors. 2011, Oxford, UK: Rossi Smith Academic Publishing, pp. 41–48.

46. Freeman, R. Edward, *Strategic Management: A Stakeholder Approach*. 1984, Englewood Cliffs, NJ: Prentice Hall.

47. Ferrell, O.C., et al., "From Market Orientation to Stakeholder Orientation," *Journal of Public Policy & Marketing*, 2010. 29(1): pp. 93–96.

48. Sloan, Pamela, "Redefining Stakeholder Engagement: From Control to Collaboration," *Journal of Corporate Citizenship*, 2009(36): p. 35.

49. Milliman, John, Tracy L. Gonzalez-Padron, and Jeffrey Ferguson, "Sustainability-Driven Innovation at Ecolab, Inc.: Finding Better Ways to Add Value and Meet Customer Needs," *Environmental Quality Management*, 2012. 21(3): pp. 21–33.

50. Fairfield, Kent D., et al., "Employee Engagement for a Sustainable Enterprise," in *The Sustainable Enterprise Fieldbook*, Jeana Wirtenberg, Wiliam G. Russell, and David Lipsky, Editors. 2009, New York: Greenleaf Publishing, pp. 141–61.

51. Wirtenberg, Jeana, Wiliam G. Russell, and David Lipsky, "Introduction and Overview," in *The Sustainable Enterprise Fieldbook*, Jeana Wirtenberg, Editor. 2009, New York: Greenleaf Publishing, p. 17.

52. Milliman, John, Tracy L. Gonzalez-Padron, and Jeffrey Ferguson, "Sustainability-Driven Innovation at Ecolab, Inc.: Finding Better Ways to Add Value and Meet Customer Needs," *Environmental Quality Management*, 2012. 21(3): pp. 21–33.

53. Nidumolu, Ram, C.K. Prahalad, and M.R. Rangaswami, "Why Sustainability Is Now the Key Driver of Innovation," *Harvard Business Review*, 2009. 87(9): pp. 56–64.

54. Ibid., p. 60.

55. Brammer, Stephen and Andrew Millington, "Corporate Reputation and Philanthropy: An Empirical Analysis.," *Journal of Business Ethics*, 2005. 61(1): pp. 29–44; Luo, Xueming and C.B. Bhattacharya, "Corporate Social Responsibility, Customer Satisfaction, and Market Value.," *Journal of Marketing*, 2006. 70(4): pp. 1–18; Mcwilliams, Abagail and Donald S. Siegel, "Corporate Social Responsibility: A Theory of the Firm Perspective," *Academy of Management Review*, 2001. 26(1): p. 117.

56. Rhea, Steven J. Skinner, and Valerie A. Taylor, "'Consumers' Evaluation of Unethical Marketing Behaviors: The Role of Customer Commitment," *Journal of Business Ethics*, 2005. 62(3): p. 237.

57. "Altria Group, Inc. 2004 Annual Report." 2004, Altria Group, Inc.: New York, p. 8.

Chapter 7

Business-Government Dynamics in the Global Economy

Drew Martin and Loren M. Stangl

INTRODUCTION

When analyzing foreign market opportunities, a major pitfall is making incorrect assumptions about a country's external environment. Managers tend to assess foreign market conditions using a self-reference criterion, thus unconsciously referencing their own values and experiences when appraising new environments. However, decisions based on self-reference criterion limit a manager's ability to accurately assess foreign market conditions. In the United States, business decision makers tend to follow neoclassical economic assumptions about how businesses and government affect competitive market conditions. Yet, the roles businesses and governments play in the marketplace vary by country, by industry, and over time. Capitalism comes in many shapes and sizes with no dominant form. This chapter develops a four-cell model of business-government relations to explain differences that marketers encounter in foreign environments. The model contributes to research on varieties of capitalism (VOC) by framing the discussion around foreign entry decision-making criteria. This chapter advocates that managers approach foreign market opportunities with awareness of personal bias and openness to various business-government configurations.

Strategy recommendations offer possible solutions for the various economic conditions.

Interdependencies between business organizations, industrial sectors, and economic institutions vary by country and evolve over time. For firms considering international expansion, competitive advantages and awareness of industry competitive structure may not be enough for success. Firms need to understand the underlying mechanisms that define the business-government dynamics within the home and host countries to effectively create successful international strategies.[1]

The strategy tripod approach considers firm, industry, and institutional perspectives to create a holistic evaluation of foreign market opportunities. As such, a strategy tripod approach considers the embedded nature of strategic decision making in international business environments.[2] Integrating the resource-based view,[3] industry-based view,[4] and institutional theory[5] into a single perspective, the strategy tripod approach recognizes that a firm's embedded environment affects both domestic and international strategies.[6] This chapter advocates an awareness of both home and host country institutional environments as preconditions for firms considering international expansion.

Institutional theory builds upon the recognition that firms operate within a social framework representing a country's idiosyncratic economic, social, and political history. A country's institutional matrix includes formal institutions (e.g., laws and regulations) and informal institutions (e.g., social norms and shared cultural beliefs). Institutional theory also recognizes that interacting regulatory, normative, and cultural-cognitive forces support and maintain stable behavior.[7] Regulatory forces establish the "rules of the game" by which firms operate.[8] In contrast, social norms and values define proper[9] and admired behavior.[10] Cultural-cognitive forces relate to preconscious cultural behavior affecting regulatory and normative conditions.[11] DiMaggio and Powell maintain that institutions exert pressure on both firms and individuals to conform through coercive, imitative, and normative expectations.[12] In addition, the government's cooperation or involvement directing economic growth and facilitating international trade also develops as part of the institutional matrix. As a result, expectations regarding appropriate business-government interaction and cooperation vary by country.

Globally, various capitalist configurations exist that display complementary firm-institutional environments.[13] Institutional theorists debate whether isomorphic forces shape homogeneous firm strategies based on a country's institutional comparative advantage, or heterogeneous firm strategies coincide and thrive within any given institutional architecture.[14] In either case, institutional theory recognizes that national environments operate differently and the firm's domestic environment influences firm strategy.

Business relationships with government-directed economic institutions develop through repeated interactions based on historical events and cultural expectations. Economic institutions both enable and restrict firm activities.[15] According to Boyer, "Firm's organizational choices are actually informed and constrained by the overall institutional architecture, not the other way around."[16] Hall and Soskice support this proposition by contending, "In sum, and in many respects, [firm] strategy derives from [institutional] structure."[17] This line of thinking advances the notion that institutional expectations become embedded in the firm's organizational activities. For example, China and the United States have different ideas about the role of business and government. The Chinese government takes a more obvious and active role in business planning whereas the U.S. government attempts to follow a laissez faire approach to business activity involvement, until forced to intercede (e.g., the recent financial crisis).

Does government involvement in trade impede or improve free trade? The answer to this question depends on how one views the role of government in the economy. From the U.S. perspective, government interventions in business activities create market-entry barriers and provide industry subsidies that negatively affect the competitive market. U.S. business leaders and government policy makers operate under the assumption that markets should be free and unfettered. Do free markets actually exist in the neoclassical sense? Neoclassical economists assume that government's role should be minimal. Businesses should be free to make revenue-maximization decisions without government intervention. Assuming market information is available to all participants, the neoclassical market is the most efficient because businesses operate in their own best interest. How can governments be involved in centralized planning? Too many variables affect the market conditions. Only individual businesses operating within the market have the ability to move quickly enough to capitalize on market changes.

Do businesses operate in a purely competitive, global market? The evidence suggests pure competition died long ago with Adam Smith. Not surprisingly, American businesses that base their strategies solely on neoclassical economic theories struggle both internationally and domestically. For example, U.S. leadership in solar-panel manufacturing has been lost to Chinese companies heavily subsidized by their national government. Even a $535 million government-backed loan to Solyndra did not make the solar-panel manufacturer immune from low-cost Chinese imports resulting in the company's bankruptcy.[18] China's government continues to tilt the playing field by turning a blind eye to working conditions and currency manipulation. Last year, seven Chinese workers took their own lives because working conditions in their Shenzan factory included illegally long hours and draconian rules for a daily

wage of $11.[19] These workers spent up to 80 hours of monthly overtime
to meet consumer demands for Apple's new iPad.

Concerns about China's undervalued currency led some government
policy makers to consider actions to correct the trade imbalance.[20] Historically, the U.S. Congress is not comfortable with government involvement in "free trade" as evidenced by vetoes of previous efforts to fast
track presidential authority to negotiate on international trade issues.[21]
In recent years, greater support has emerged for government involvement in trade negotiations.

Structural and cultural rationales offer explanations as to why some
nations develop competitive advantages in certain product areas.[22] Assuming these differences contribute to trade advantages, these competitive advantages are treated like national security interests. To level the
playing field, the World Trade Organization and regional trading areas
(e.g., North American Free Trade Association and the European Union)
reduce some barriers; however, the road to consensus among member
nations is slow.[23] Also, trade zones potentially present barriers for non-
member countries.

The preceding text suggests that the business and government dynamic vary by country. Even businesses not considering foreign markets
need to be concerned about how their domestic market is influenced
by government policies as well as domestic and foreign competitors. To
help in understanding these differences, the following framework offers
a model to explain different market conditions in both industrialized
and developing countries. A four-cell model outlines the different roles
played by businesses and governments in market formation. First, the
discussion reviews the mainstream theories of business and government
relations. Understanding these different forms of capitalism provides
a background about the variety of global perspectives. These perspectives influence the formation of market structures. By understanding
these differences, businesses can better understand the global business
environment and they will be better prepared to succeed in overseas
markets.

FORMS OF CAPITALISM—CURRENT AND PAST

A wide and diverse body of literature debates the causes, consequences, and typologies of global capitalism.[24] According to Baumol
and his colleagues, "no single and pure form of capitalism is likely to
dominate any economy to the exclusion of elements of the other, the mix
of different systems being what is the most important for the country's
growth."[25] A common theme to most research on capitalism varieties
is an exploration of the influences of governance, employment, and/

or investment institutions on business activities.[26] This chapter explores capitalism's variations based on business-government dynamics.

Depending on the philosophical foundation, one arrives at very different conclusions about the appropriate level of public sector involvement in business and economic development. National differences stem from government's role in business-development activities. These differences offer guidance to categorize the different forms of capitalism. Economic and political science literatures examine the growth of industrialized nations in terms of these relationships. Specifically, the literature focuses on a variety of institutional,[27] industrial,[28] and organized labor,[29] or, a combination of all three characteristics.[30]

Lazonick[31] and Pitelis[32] provide a framework relating to the strength of business and national governments in industrialized nations' market formation. This framework shows four basic capitalism forms. Placement of nations within this model depends on the relative control public (government) and private (organized groups) have on the market.

Proprietary Capitalism

The movement from a monarchy to a more democratic form of governance supports the transition from mercantilist to free market theory. A weak government's role assures that markets remain transferable so participants are not hindered from making transactions. Governments operating under the proprietary form of capitalism would not be considered a "principal" beneficiary of policies and laws. Adam Smith is one of the first to present a weak-state model.[33] Under proprietary capitalism, individuals are free to make economic production and consumption decisions. The government's role is limited to performing tasks for the public good (e.g., national security) and to maintaining an environment that allows for a free-flowing economic system.

Smith's invisible hand assumes that the nation is composed primarily of small, sole-proprietary businesses. Each small business serves a small percentage of the total market. Government action interferes with the market's spontaneous order. Since small businesses dominate the competitive environment, organized societal groups also are assumed to be weak. No dominant group controls enough resources to influence the market (monopoly power). Chandler coins the term "proprietary" to describe this "weak state-weak society" capitalism form.[34]

Theory expansion from classical economics to neoclassical economics is sometimes credited to the Alfred Marshall's work on marginal analysis.[35] The fundamental idea of Marshall's work is that the power of supply and demand generates market equilibrium. Market-price equilibrium occurs when the quantity demanded equals the quantity supplied at a given price and given time (the point where the market clears). This school of economics assumes that the market is free of imperfection.

An important variant stemming from the neoclassical theory is attributed to John Keynes.[36] Keynesian economic intervention responds to high unemployment in England that contradicted the classical assumption of full employment (Say's Law). According to Say's Law, a wage rate always exists that makes full employment possible in a capitalistic system.[37] Keynes argues that the employment level has no relationship to the cost labor; instead, an increase in aggregate demand serves as the primary incentive to hire more workers, which directly relates to the level of investment. Businesses will not hire more people to produce more products unless a demand for the surplus exists. The investment decision requires inducements such as: (1) the marginal efficiency of the capital (e.g., the best return for idle cash); or (2) the risk related to the loan payoff to finance the production that makes the rate of return acceptable. Through monetary (e.g., prime lending rate) or fiscal policy (e.g., state procurement policy) manipulation, the government affects total spending and total employment.

Support for proprietary capitalism comes from the Chicago and public choice schools. Milton Friedman and the Chicago School proponents express concern about any concentration of power. Essentially, they believe affecting trade for a public good is impossible.[38] Unlike the Keynesian use of demand as an employment-level determinant, Milton Friedman focuses on the equilibrium of the money market (known as quantity theory). Equilibrium in the money market is believed to be the necessary market condition for expenditures on goods, services, and securities. The public choice school also supports a limited state role. Public choice proponents are critical of any government intervention. In the minimal-state model, the state's role should be limited to protection against force, theft, fraud, and enforcement of contracts.[39] All other state actions violate individual rights.

Although the proprietary form is considered the theoretical foundation for United States' capitalism, this form has several shortcomings.[40] At least three shortcomings associate with neoclassical theory.[41] These shortcomings suggest that the existence of this form of capitalism is problematic.

First, neoclassical theory assumes preexisting markets where one individual or group has oligopoly or monopoly power. The automobile and commercial aircraft manufacturing as well as consumer retailing are examples of oligopolies. General Motors, Boeing, and Walmart complete against Toyota, Airbus, and Target, respectively. Small businesses trying to enter these competitive environments face insurmountable barriers. For example, Walmart's 9,700 retail stores had fiscal year 2011 sales of $419 billion.[42] Even Walmart's suppliers are kept in line by the retail's purchasing power. In the mid-1990s, Rubbermaid raised the price charged for the company's products because a key ingredient's price increased by 80 percent. Walmart's solution was to give more shelf space to lower-priced competitors, forcing Rubbermaid to merge with rival Newell.[43] Clearly, Walmart's size creates economies of scale enabling the company to sustain a cost leadership position.

Second, Pareto efficiency assumes rationality of buyers and sellers. Retail shopping behavior studies suggest buyer behavior does not support rationality. According to Point-Of-Purchase Advertising International, 70 percent of retail purchase decisions are made in the store; in-store displays encourage between 1.2 percent and 19.6 percent product lift.[44] John Bargh's research on unconscious behavior helps explain this behavior.[45] According to Bargh, most brain functions are done unconsciously and automatically and people are on autopilot for most functions. Rather than making decisions deliberately or rationally, consumers use their instincts.[46]

Third, neoclassical economics assumes state action neutrality toward all individuals or groups. What is government neutrality? Any governmental subsidy offers one stakeholder group an advantage. Do all members of society benefit equally from government intervention? The government-guaranteed loan to solar-panel maker Solyndra created 1,100 jobs and supported the clean-energy development. In this case, government policy makers felt the loan guarantee served national interests. Solyndra's recent bankruptcy filing leaves taxpayers and law makers with questions about whether or not all stakeholders benefited equally from the government-guaranteed loan.

Some evidence suggests that industrialized nations are moving even further away from proprietary capitalism. Examining Western European and U.S. economic growth from the 1930s to 1960s, Andrew Shonfield concludes government planning increased regardless of the country's historical relationship between business and government.[47] Shonfield suggests centralized planning helps to take some fluctuations out of the market and allows for wider benefit distribution. The rewards appear to be even greater in the future as state and business planning methods improve.

Despite the proprietary model's limitations, the governmental trade policies remain influenced by neoclassical economic assumptions. For example, negotiations for a free trade agreement between Australia and China include the recognition the latter is a market economy, a condition for free trade negotiations.[48] Arguably, free trade agreements are a two-edged sword. Ignoring these arrangements put domestic businesses at a disadvantage when competing against other foreign firms.[49] Entering the free trade agreement exposes domestic businesses to foreign competition on equal footing. Countries with lower production costs have price advantages, and domestic production moves overseas to remain competitive. In this case, not all stakeholders benefit equally from government action. For example, organized labor unions see jobs disappear overseas from outsourcing related to free trade agreements.

Managerial Capitalism

In *The Visible Hand*, Alfred Chandler discusses the transition from "proprietary" to "managerial" capitalism.[50] Between the 1840s and 1920s, the economy of the United States transformed from agrarian and rural to industrial and urban. Modern multiunit business enterprises replaced small, traditional, sole-proprietary businesses. Controlling more resources enabled the new industrialists to increase productivity and lower costs. These industry consolidations resulted in greater market control by large, vertically integrated corporations. Big business arrived in the United States, seizing control of resources including raw materials, production technology, labor, and ultimately the government. A managerial capitalism artifact is oligopolistic price fixing, which results in market inefficiencies.

Organized groups are the principal beneficiaries of managerial capitalism.[51] Governmental assistance varies proportionately by the resources each group controls. Under managerial capitalism, the government's primarily role is to support these groups as an act of self-preservation. Satisfying large corporations helps the government to retain the existing structure and size (e.g., funding from tax revenues). Atomized societal members find their roles reduced. Marginalized groups controlling fewer resources receive far fewer benefits than people belonging to powerful and well-organized groups. The U.S. Congress's approval of the 2003 tax bill created $350 billion savings for tax payers. This legislation passed despite less than one-third of the public feeling these tax cuts were the best way to increase economic growth and increase jobs.[52] One estimate found only 22 percent of tax payers with incomes less than $100,000 would benefit by President Bush's 15 percent maximum dividend tax rate.[53] Who benefits the most by low dividend tax rate? Clearly, big business owners gain the most from such policies.

A pluralist society enables organized groups to exert too much influence on government trade policies. Capital's growing interests eventually control the activities of government, even at the expense of the long-term interests of society.[54] Big capital's development into transnational corporation threatens the existence of the nation-state as well as labor unions and small capital. Following this line of thinking, growth trends in large corporations come at the expense of higher unemployment and a decline in small businesses.

Despite the apparent shortcomings of managerial capitalism, this form best represents the dominant state of U.S. capitalism.[55] Managerial capitalism also has proponents; for example, Austrian economist Joseph Schumpeter argued that a production system dominated by big businesses is superior to one with only small businesses.[56] Government regulation should not be based on the principle that big business must operate under a system of perfect competition. While Schumpeter's mention of government regulation seems to suggest the need for some big business limitations, he encourages market development beneficial to big capital. Another argument is big business represents the lesser of two evils.[57] Capitalism stands with federalism, the separation of powers, and the antitrust tradition in the deep suspicion of authority.

Cooperative Capitalism

The "strong state-strong societal" form of capitalism can be characterized by both collectivist and neocorporatist theories. Whereas the former has historical roots in U.S.-state theory, the latter can be traced back to Europe. The European version has little in common with the U.S. style of capitalism due to organized labor's inclusion in the model. Jeffrey Hart's analysis of capitalism highlights this difference by distinguishing between cooperative governance based on organized labor's relative strength.[58]

The collectivist theory can be traced back at least to Alexander Hamilton. Hamilton provides recommendations for strong government guidance and protection of domestic industry.[59] Hamilton states that the nation as a whole should support industry development. He warns that small manufacturers in the United States could never catch up with the larger and more-advanced manufacturers of Europe unless they are protected and subsidized. Government needs to provide a strong role to ensure the economic well-being of citizens. Arguably, England's fall in manufacturing competitiveness is attributed to government failure to protect domestic industries from foreign competitors.[60]

Some distinguishing collective-capitalism features include: (1) the organizational integration of a number of distinct firms, (2) the long-term integration into the enterprise of personnel below the managerial level, and (3) the state's cooperation in shaping the social environment to reduce the uncertainty of facing private sector investments.[61] During the 1980s and 1990s, Japan's phenomenal economic growth and success were credited by some authors to collectivist policies where business and government work closely together for national interests.[62] As was the case historically in the United States and the United Kingdom, the Japanese state played an important role in protecting the home market. Government protection allowed business organizations to develop to the point where they could attain a comparative advantage in international markets.

Another cooperative form of governance is the neocorporatist system, where societal interests are represented by formal, compulsory, noncompetitive groups.[63] Neocorporatism should be understood in terms of degrees instead of absolutes. Comparative studies on industrialized capitalist nations conclude that the United States is the weakest in terms of its level of neocorporatism.[64] Due to legal limitations on industry collusion and cartels as well as the lack of a unified group representing labor interests at the national level, the United States lacks the foundation to develop a neocorporatist style of capitalism.[65]

Collective-capitalism critics express concerns about the limitations of centralized planning and increasing the power of government. Austrian school proponent Friedrich Hayek argued that a centralized authority cannot possibly acquire all the dispersed knowledge required for decision making.[66] Other arguments against a more formalized relationship between government and business come from the proponents of propriety capitalism, such as the Chicago and public Choice schools.[67]

Also, most big business interests likely will resist a call for more government coordination. For example, interviews with the negotiations team involved in a joint venture to build commercial aircraft in Japan and China confirms that big businesses feel better qualified to conduct their own foreign affairs. Businesses only want government assistance if it is in their best interest.[68] An example of this governmental role can be seen when U.S. presidents visit Japan to lobby for more-open automobile markets.[69] On the other hand, these same businesses try to distance themselves from U.S. national policies when human rights violations surface.[70]

In recent years, some economists have called to formalize the relationship between business and government.[71] Increasing government-assisted foreign competition successfully is penetrating the U.S. market. At the same time, U.S. businesses have difficulties entering foreign markets. Perhaps U.S. businesses are beginning to realize they are mismatched when competing against nations with more formalized business and government's relationships. Lester Thurow sees the United States as using an individualistic strategy against countries that have a more cooperative form of capitalism.[72] Robert Reich echoes similar sentiments; he recommends that a more formalized business and government partnership be supported.[73] In the early 1990s, the Clinton administration advocated a more active role for government and international trade. President Bush tried to continue this trend, but he had more difficulty getting congressional approval.[74] The U.S. government started to assert itself in overseas markets on behalf of U.S. businesses.

This trend trickled down to the local level as well. Even U.S. state governments started sending representatives abroad for trade missions. Starting in the 1980s, many U.S. state governments opened overseas promotion offices in Asia and Europe.[75] In particular, Japanese economic growth led state government policy makers to believe that market opportunities existed and local government was best positioned to help businesses. Most overseas offices were understaffed and underfunded. Annual or biannual office budgets make long-term planning difficult. Some offices became part-time ventures for English-speaking local business people. Other offices closed when state budgets required balancing. No compelling evidence supports the assertion that these state offices did much to help U.S. businesses enter Japan's tightly controlled market.[76] Little evidence suggests alliances between business and government resulted in a stronger position for the U.S. economy. These "cooperative" efforts appear to serve other purposes, such as offering state governors a bit of international experience to enhance their political portfolios in the event of them having aspirations for a role in politics at the national level.

Authoritarian Capitalism

Although the "strong state-weak society" form is not found in many industrialized nations, this model of capitalism has a record of rapid growth in today's global economy. An authoritarian system provides a strong centralized government to discipline disorderly and aggressive societal impulses. Authoritarian capitalism gives the head of government extraordinary powers. Government organizes societal interests from above, and prohibits the formation of autonomous groupings that might resist state leadership. Late-developing nation-states with weak industrial infrastructure are historically excellent candidates for this interventionist form of capitalism.[77]

Authoritarian capitalism first emerged in the early 1900s and, to varying degrees, continues to shape newly industrialized nations during times of war. Some early corporatist models were found in Italy and Germany during the World Wars.[78] The primary difference between today's neocorporatist systems and the former corporatist systems is that the government of the latter used coercive behavior to control societal elements (labor and capital). To distinguish corporatism from neocorporatism (the latter also is referred as corporatism in the literature), the former will be called "authoritarian" capitalism.

Compared to other forms, authoritarian capitalism is relatively new. The other three forms of capitalism emerged in response to commerce; however, the authoritarian variation appears to have roots in conflict or unstable political systems. Under an authoritarian system, tight resource control is necessary to build a power base. Whatever reason for authoritarian capitalism's emergence, the market is structured so that the principal beneficiaries are government élites.

The economic growth in South Korea and Taiwan represent some variation found within the authoritarian form of capitalism.[79] In both cases, these nations have had high degrees of political autonomy in postwar economic development; however, differences exist in how businesses are organized in these countries. In South Korea, large business conglomerates (*chaebol*) remain operational, but Taiwan's private business groups (*guanxiqiye*) primarily are composed of smaller businesses. Arguably, South Korea's *chaebol* provide evidence of a different type of market structure. Some evidence suggests that government planning and directing is still prominent in South Korea. For example, the South Korean government still has the ability to slow the international expansion of domestic firms.[80]

Although authoritarian control by the state suggests an antidemocratic decision-making structure, some evidence does support this form's effectiveness. During the early 1990s, a number of Southeast Asian economies had tremendous economic growth. In particular Indonesia, Thailand, Malaysia, Singapore, and the Philippines seem to fit within an authoritarian style of capitalism.[81] The recent enterprise expansion in China also seems to parallel other recent Asian nation transitions to authoritarian capitalism.

Today, a growing segment of the world is adopting some variant of an authoritarian mode of capitalism. Newly emerging democracies and longstanding dictatorships are both trying to rapidly catch up with industrialized nations. Authoritarian capitalism offers a possible solution to their goal of a more-prosperous national economy. Although industrialized nations unlikely will evolve into this form of capitalism, business leaders need to understand the authoritarian mode's structure because today's economy is global.

WHEN CAPITALISM'S FORMS COLLIDE

The preceding model shows how differences in the competitive environment can be explained by the dynamics of business and government relations. The model emphasizes some important differences in business-government relations. The model complements previous VOC discussions. Hall and Soskice classify capitalism as a dichotomy between two modes of organization: liberal market economies (LME) or coordinated market economies (CME).[82] They argue that institutional complementarities cluster countries into identifiable groups based on either market or strategic coordination modes of governance. The United States and United Kingdom classify as LMEs, whereas

Germany and the Nordic countries fall under the CME classification. The current model extends Hall and Soskice's model by considering LMEs to contain both proprietary and managerial forms of capitalism and CMEs to contain both authoritarian and cooperative capitalism forms.[83]

Managers with an eye on overseas markets face problems from their marketing mix, and economic, political, and sociocultural conditions in the foreign markets. U.S. managers particularly are naive when assessing the relationship between the government and competitive environment. In the United States, business and government seem to be obsessed with the notion that free and unfettered markets exist and that the government should have a minimalist role in the economy. As a result, these assumptions may be relied upon when assessing the overseas competitive environment. While collecting information about foreign countries, marketing managers need to take care not to use a neoclassical economic assumption in their analyses. Reliance on neoclassical market assumptions may result in incorrect conclusions about opportunities and threats in the external environment. Business opportunities to enter foreign markets depend upon the interaction between internal and external environmental factors.[84]

In the United States, the managerial variant has been the dominant form of capitalism for the last 100 years. As markets have become more global, the United States seems to respond slowly to different forms of capitalism. Evidence of serious trouble began surfacing between the years 1997 and 2000 when trade imbalance more than doubled from $215 billion (1997) to $482 billion (2000) and imports increased to over $1.1 trillion.[85] The trade imbalance's effect has been increasing difficulties for U.S. businesses to compete domestically as well as internationally. To decrease costs, U.S. businesses outsource production. While this model lowers costs, domestic unemployment has soared to over nine percent.[86] Consumers fearful of losing their jobs have cut back on spending. Declining sales force retailers to downsize further. Arguably, the U.S. strategy has backfired.

Meanwhile, state-assisted businesses from other nations seem to be successful when trying to sell goods and services in the United States. In 2010, the United States had negative goods trading imbalances with China ($273 billion), South Korea ($10 billion), and Taiwan ($9.8 billion).[87] South Korea rose to become the world's eighth-biggest exporter of goods in 2010 and a tenth-ranked gross domestic product growth rate of close to four percent.[88] At the same time, China's gross domestic product rose by 10.5 percent and forecasts for 2015 predict a 10 to 12 percent annual growth.[89] The evidence suggests that the United States may be mismatched when competing against nations with more formalized business and government relations.

Understanding nuances of business-government relations are important for reforming a business strategy to compete in domestic and foreign markets. The next challenge for U.S. businesses and government is to find the right balance between assisting and interfering with commerce. Finding this balance is problematic because neoclassical economic thought influences state policies. Global markets dictate that something needs to be done to improve the effectiveness of U.S. businesses to enter foreign markets. Proprietary capitalism's influence makes this proposition more challenging. Each foreign market also offers a different competitive dynamic. Michael Porter's study of national competitive advantages shows evidence of industry clusters in various industrialized countries.[90] Large multinational corporations reach most markets affecting markets without major domestic competitors. For example, even though New Zealand's business base does not include any companies in the top global 500 firms, a number of these top foreign firms have a market presence. New Zealand's economy is considered to be one of the least corrupt and transparent, thereby creating an environment where foreign businesses can easily enter and compete with smaller, local firms.[91] Foreign and domestic firms lobby New Zealand's government, suggesting managerial capitalism is not contained by national borders.

The United States is the headquarters for 133 of the top 500 global businesses, compared to 61 in China.[92] On the other hand, another U.S. trading partner, Mexico, only has three companies in the global 500 list. These large global companies pay taxes, employ people, and finance political campaigns. These companies also employ professional lobbyists to try and influence government policies to protect their self-interests. Goldman Sachs spent $4.6 million lobbying the U.S. federal government last year to try and influence the overhaul of financial regulations because key reforms will directly affect their bottom line.[93] Corporate lobbyists in the Australia, Canada, Japan, European Union, United Kingdom, and United States sometimes are former elected officials or retired government employees with links to top policymaking officials. In the United Kingdom, some observers argue a revolving door exists between parliament and industry.[94]

While measures such as the government corruption scale developed by Transparency International and domestic influence serve as proxies for big business and government involvement, the evidence is startling.[95] Managerial capitalism exists in both the United States and United Kingdom. Between 2005 and 2011, these economies show declines in transparency and big businesses. Such changes suggest more government involvement, either directly or indirectly in economic planning. Dramatic increases in government spending serve as subsidies for businesses affected. For example, between 2005 and 2011, the U.S. federal percentage of spending increased from 19.9 percent to an estimated 25.1 percent of the nation's gross domestic product.[96] At the same time,

U.S. private sector unemployment increased from 5.2 to 9.2 percent.[97] The U.S. total of the global 500 businesses shrank five percent from 176 to 133.[98]

Japan's cooperative capitalism also shows some changes. Like the United Kingdom and United States, the number of global 500 big businesses dropped from 81 to 68.[99] Interestingly, the transparency score for Japan's government shows improvement, suggesting less government involvement and fewer barriers for foreign businesses. These changes likely reflect ongoing efforts by the Japanese national government to boost economic growth. Government spending as a percentage of gross domestic product continues to hover around 37 percent.[100]

Finally, China's business sector has increased considerably since 2005. China now has 61 of the global 500 businesses, an increase from 16 in 2005.[101] The Chinese government owns all large financial institutions and the four state-owned banks account for over 50 percent of the total assets.[102] A combination of high corruption, a weak judicial system, and a strong central government control that limits foreign investment makes foreign business investment challenging. Although China's recent economic growth outpaces the industrialized nations, wages for workers remains low. Businesses from other countries find price-based competition against Chinese businesses difficult.

Business and government leaders need to recognize free market economies do not exist. The competitive environment includes both domestic and foreign big businesses. These giants have economies of scale advantages and perhaps institutional arrangements with local governments to protect their interests. Any action or inaction by government affects the playing field as well. To be successful in global markets, businesses need to understand that differences exist and develop strategies taking these differences into account.

DEVELOPING STRATEGIES FOR FOREIGN MARKETS

Foster's Lager is a global beer brand. Despite being an industry leader, the firm misread how capitalism works in China. Foster's purchased majority shares of local breweries in Shanghai, Guangdong, and Tianjin in 1993. While consumer price sensitivity was an issue, Foster's could have avoided an expensive lesson had executives understood that the Chinese beer industry was highly fragmented and each town has at least one brewery.[103] Foster's could not develop a national distribution network because the numerous local breweries slowed the development of an intermediary distribution system in China. The company experienced additional problems working with the Chinese government because economic growth was more important than protecting foreign business interests. Four years and $70 million in losses later, Foster's sold the Guangdon and Tianjin breweries and took a $100 million write-off.

Borden learned Japan's growing preference for premium ice cream did not equate to market success.[104] Borden's market-entry options included foreign direct investment, joint venture, or licensing. High foreign investment costs and Japan's multilevel distribution system influenced the company's decision to enter into a limited term licensing agreement with Meiji Milk, Japan's leading ice cream maker. Furthermore, market success would be challenging because Häagen Daz owned 90 percent of Japan's premium ice cream market.[105] This licensing agreement served Meiji better than Borden. As the licensing agreement approached its end, Meiji's Aya premium ice cream line was launched domestically. Borden had trained a new competitor.

While Internet businesses are not new ideas, companies using technology to deliver products need to recognize that market entry occurs at the speed of light. Waiting for even a few months to make a market-entry decision is a costly decision. eBay executives learned that they missed an opportunity by delaying the company's expansion into Japan. Used consumer goods waiting for garbage pick-up suggests that Japanese people tend to shy away from used items. Yahoo Japan discovered Japanese consumers buy collectables just like everyone else. Yahoo's four-month head start allowed the company to capture 95 percent of the market.[106] Two years later, eBay abandoned the company's three percent market share and gave up on Japan.[107]

Firms operating in dynamic, knowledge-intensive industries need to develop strategic networks to help improve their success in foreign markets.[108] International business research finds that firms operating in emerging or transitional institutional environments tend to substitute strong network relationships for unstable institutions. Small businesses experience different challenges, particularly when they are isolated geographically from major international markets. In this case, the industry type affects the expansion rate. Both small and large businesses seem affected equally when innovation and change are rapid. Network relationships serve as potential market-entry strategies, particularly if the industry's innovation rate is rapid.[109] In one case, a New Zealand computer software firm discovered that time spent raising capital for international expansion resulted in losing their competitive advantage.[110]

The preceding examples highlight challenges businesses face competing globally. While Foster's holds a strong, global position in the beer industry, the firm's resources did not overcome competitive and governmental differences experienced in China. The Chinese beer industry is fragmented, thus making market growth challenging. China's strong government created additional challenges because centralized planning emphasizes economic growth and the country's legal system lags economic growth. The lack of legal transparency creates challenges for foreign companies attempting foreign direct investment options.

Borden found oligopoly-level competition in Japan's ice cream market. Japanese businesses have an institutional tradition of business linkages called *keiretsu*. These linkages include overlapping boards of directors involving related businesses, a practice considered collusive and illegal in the United States.[111] The larger *keiretsu* arrangements evolved from pre–World War II *zaibatsu* (Mitsubishi, Mitsui, Sumimoto, and Yasuda). These business organizations have existed since the 1920s and include close relationships with government officials. Retiring, high-ranking government officials are hired as executives by these *keiretsu* organizations, creating a partnership between business and government. In this case, Japan's tradition of close business and government relationships made Borden's foreign market success difficult.

eBay just dropped the ball. A lack of Japanese domestic competition and a global advantage over Yahoo may have made eBay executives complacent. Technology-related firms need to recognize that market opportunities open and close at the speed of light. While eBay is a market leader and the Japanese market was wide open for opportunity, eBay executives failed to see a growth opportunity. When the company did launch in Japan, little effort was made to change their operations to adapt to Japanese consumers.[112] Yahoo's executives recognized their market entry as an opportunity to brand the company as Japanese and product adaptations were made. Either eBay's executives felt the brand name would encourage Yahoo customers to change loyalty, or they just wanted to test the market without spending too much money. Regardless of their intent, the results were not good.

Finally, small firms suffer from a lack of resources to enter foreign markets, or to compete once they arrive. Creating strategic networks help these firms move quickly and compete effectively. The New Zealand software company provides an example of what happens in a fast-changing business climate if capital cannot be raised quickly. In this case, technological innovation moved faster than the firm's ability to raise capital and the product was no longer competitive. Finding the right company for these alliances is critical. As the market moves quickly, good partners become scarcer over time.[113] Without these partners, the chances of success for small firms are slim. Bigger businesses will develop similar products, and competing in foreign countries without insider help is expensive and difficult.

To develop an effective market-entry strategy, a firm needs to consider the embedded nature of both domestic and foreign markets. This chapter identified differences in government's cooperation or involvement directing economic growth and facilitating international trade. Recognizing that differences exist helps to prevent making incorrect assumptions about the target market. Firms need to assess their own capabilities, the industry's competitive nature, and the host country's institutional environment.

NOTES

1. Peng, Mike W., and Jessie Q. Zhou. "How Network Strategies and Institutional Transitions Evolve in Asia." *Asian Pacific Journal of Management* 22 (2005): 321–336.

2. Peng, Mike W., Dennis Y. L. Wang, and Yi Jiang. "An Institution-Based View of International Business Strategy: A Focus on Emerging Economies." *Journal of International Business Studies* 39 (2008): 920–936.

3. Barney, Jay. "Firm Resources and Sustained Competitive Advantage." *Journal of Management* 17, no. 1 (1991): 99–120.

4. Porter, Michael E. *Competitive Strategy* (New York: Free Press, 1980).

5. DiMaggio, Paul J., and Walter W. Powell. Introduction to *The New Institutionalism in Organizational Analysis,* vol. 17, eds. Walter W. Powell and Paul J. DiMaggio (Chicago: University of Chicago Press, 1991), 1–38; North, Douglass C. *Institutions, Institutional Change, and Economic Performance* (Cambridge: Cambridge University Press, 1990); Scott, W. Richard. *Institutions and Organizations* (Thousand Oaks, CA: Sage, 1995).

6. Gao, Gerald Y., Janet Y. Murray, Masaaki Kotabe, and Jiangyong Lu. "A 'Strategy Tripod' Perspective on Export Behaviors: Evidence from Domestic and Foreign Firms Based in an Emerging Economy." *Journal of International Business Studies* 41 (2010): 377–396.

7. Scott, W. Richard. "Approaching Adulthood: The Maturing of Institutional Theory." *Theory and Society* 37, no. 5 (2008): 427–442.

8. North, *Institutions, Institutional Change, and Economic Performance,* 1990.

9. Bruton, Garry D., David Ahlstrom, and Han-Lin Li. "Institutional Theory and Entrepreneurship: Where Are We Now and Where Do We Need to Move in the Future?" *Entrepreneurship Theory and Practice* 34, no. 3 (2010): 421–440.

10. Busenitz, Lowell W., Carolina Gómez, and Jennifer W. Spencer. "Country Institutional Profiles: Unlocking Entrepreneurial Phenomena." *The Academy of Management Journal* 43, no. 5 (2000): 994–1003.

11. Meyer, John W., and Brian Rowan. "Institutionalized Organizations: Formal Structure as Myth and Ceremony." In *The New Institutionalism in Organizational Analysis,* eds. Walter W. Powell and Paul J. DiMaggio (Chicago: University of Chicago Press, 1991), 41–62.

12. DiMaggio, Paul J., and Walter W. Powell. "The Iron Cage Revisited: Institutional Isomorphism and Collective Rationality in Organizational Fields." *American Sociological Review* 48, no. 2 (1983): 147–160.

13. Baumol, William J., Robert E. Litan, and Carl J. Schramm. *Good Capitalism, Bad Capitalism, and the Economics of Growth and Prosperity* (New Haven, CT: Yale University Press, 2007); Hall, Peter A., and David Soskice. *Varieties of Capitalism: The Institutional Foundations of Comparative Advantage* (New York: Oxford University Press, 2001); Whitley, Richard. *Divergent Capitalisms: The Social Structuring and Change of Business Systems* (Oxford: Oxford University Press, 1999).

14. Boyer, Robert. "How and Why Capitalisms Differ." *Economy and Society* 34, no. 4 (2005): 509–557; Carney, Michael, Eric Gedajlovic, and Xiaohua Yang. "Varieties of Asian Capitalism: Toward an Institutional Theory of Asian Enterprise." *Asian Pacific Journal of Management* 26 (2009): 361–380.

15. Lazonick, William. "Varieties of Capitalism and Innovative Enterprise." *Comparative Social Research* 24 (2007): 21–69.

16. Boyer. "How and Why Capitalisms Differ," 2005, 543.

17. Hall and Soskice. *Varieties of Capitalism*, 2001, 15.

18. Koch, Wendy. "End of Subsidies Sets Off 'Solar-coaster Ride; Once a World Leader, U.S. Industry at a Crossroads." *USA Today*, October 4, 2011, 1B.

19. "High Tech Demand Creates Living Hell." *New Zealand Herald*, May 7, 2011.

20. Krugman, Paul. "Holding China to Account." *New York Times*, October 3, 2011, Section A, p. 25; Helderman, Rosalind S. "Bill on Chinese Valuation Policy Advances on Hill." *Washington Post*, October 7, 2011: A12.

21. "Free Trade over a Barrel." *Wall Street Journal*, July 9, 2002: A18.

22. Porter, Michael E. *The Competitive Advantage of Nations* (New York: Free Press, 1990).

23. World Trade Organization. "Update of WTO Dispute Settlement Cases" (February 6, 2002). http://www.wto.org/english/tratop_e/dispu_e.htm.

24. Both Boyer and Whitley offer two good examples. See: Boyer, Robert. "How and Why Capitalisms Differ." *Economy and Society* 34, no. 4 (2005): 509–557; Whitley, Richard. *Competing Capitalism: Institutions and Economies*, vol. 1: (Cheltenham, UK: Edward Elgar Publishing, 2002).

25. Baumol, Litan, and Schramm. *Good Capitalism, Bad Capitalism, and the Economics of Growth and Prosperity*, 2007; Hall and Soskice. *Varieties of Capitalism*, 2001.

26. Lazonick. "Varieties of Capitalism and Innovative Enterprise," 2007.

27. Zysman, John. *Governments, Markets, and Growth: Financial Systems and the Politics of Industrial Change* (Ithaca, NY: Cornell University Press, 1983).

28. Chandler, Alfred D. *The Visible Hand: The Managerial Revolution in American Business*, 1977; Shonfield, Andrew. *Modern Capitalism: The Changing Balance of Public and Private Power* (New York: Oxford University Press, 1969).

29. Turner, Lowell. *Democracy at Work* (Ithaca, NY: Cornell University Press, 1991).

30. Wilson, Graham. *Business and Politics* (Catham, NJ: Catham Publishers, 1985); Hart, Jeffrey A. *Rival Capitalists: International Competitiveness in the United States, Japan, and Western Europe* (Ithaca, NY: Cornell University, 1992).

31. Lazonick, William. *Business Organization and the Myth of the Market Economy* (New York: Cambridge University Press, 1991).

32. Pitelis, Christos. *Market and Non-Market Hierarchies* (Oxford: Basil Blackwell, 1991).

33. Smith, Adam. *An Inquiry into the Nature and Causes of the Wealth of Nations*, vol. 1, eds. Roy H. Cambell and Andrew S. Skinner (Oxford: Clarendon Press, 1776/1976).

34. Chandler. *The Visible Hand*, 1977.

35. Marshall, Alfred. *Principles of Economics*, 8th ed. (London: Macmillan (1920/1890). Other classical economists who contributed to the transition from classical to neoclassical economics include David Ricardo and John Stuart Mill.

In addition to Marshall, other founders credited with the development of the neoclassical system were John Clark, Francis Edgeworth, Irving Fisher, Vilfredo Pareto, Léon Walras, and Knut Wicksell.

36. *The General Theory of Employment, Interest, and Money* is arguably Keynes's greatest work. The four main contributions of this work are: (1) a reformation of monetary theory by emphasizing the difference between a monetary and barter economy, (2) the creation of a general equilibrium theory that is relevant to problems of economic policy, (3) an explanation of why a competitive capitalist economy does not automatically maintain full employment, and (4) a revolution in orthodox thinking about the role of government in a competitive capitalist economy. See: Keynes, John M. *The General Theory of Employment, Interest, and Money* (New York: Classic Books, 2009/1936).

37. Say, Jean-Baptiste. *A Treatise on Political Economy* (New York: Cosimo, 2007/1803).

38. Friedman, Milton and Rose Friedman. *Free to Choose* (Orlando, FL: Harcourt Brace, 1979).

39. Nozick, Robert. *Anarchy, State, and Utopia* (New York: Basic Books, 1974).

40. Many economic theories contradict the neoclassical assumption of free and widespread "market" information. For example, Kenneth Arrow's discussion of consumer rationality and societal good concludes that society is too complex for people to understand the ramifications of their actions. This conclusion implies that people cannot possibly take all factors into consideration when making consumption decisions. Ronald Coase also looks at "market" information and concludes that efficiency cannot be achieved without planning within organizations. Organizations not employing some sort of centralized planning have higher transaction costs and no longer be competitive in the market. See: Arrow, Kenneth J. "Rationality of Self and Others in an Economic System." *Journal of Business* 59, no. 4 (1986): 385–399; Coase, Ronald H. *Essays on Economics and Economists* (Chicago: University of Chicago Press, 1994).

41. Pitelis, *Market and Non-Market Hierarchies*, 1991.

42. "Walmart announces FY2013 global capital expenditure program of $13 to $14 billion; Company sets five-year commitment for greater operating expense leverage" Walmart.com, October 12, 2011. http://walmartstores.com/pressroom/.

43. Hopkins, Jim. "Wal-Mart's Influence Grows." *USA Today,* January 29, 2003. http://www.usatoday.com/money/industries/retail/2003-01-28-walmartnation_x.htm.

44. Vence, Deborah L. "Point of Purchase Displays." *Marketing News* 41, no. 18 (2007): 8.

45. Bargh, John A. "Losing Consciousness: Automatic Influences on Consumer Judgment, Behavior, and Motivation." *Journal of Consumer Research* 29, no. 2 (2002): 280–285.

46. Malcolm Gladwell proposes people save time making decisions by trusting their gut feelings. In *Blink,* Gladwell describes a case where museum curators spent months deciding whether or not a piece of art was real or fake. One curator's initial gut feeling was that the art is a fake. At the end of their deliberations, the committee of experts concluded that are was a forgery. See: Gladwell, Malcolm. *Blink: the Power of Thinking without Thinking* (New York: Back Bay Books, 2005).

47. Shonfield. *Modern Capitalism,* 1969.

48. Grattan, Michelle and Hamish McDonald. "China Ties More Than Free Trade: Howard." *The Age,* April 19, 2005, 1.

49. Shapiro, Gary. "Pass Free-trade Agreements to Create U.S. Jobs; Every Day Congress Does Nothing, American Workers and Business Lose." *Washington Times,* July 13, 2011, 3.

50. Chandler, *The Visible Hand,* 1977.

51. Lowi, Theodore J. *The End of Liberalism,* 2nd ed. (New York: W.W. Norton, 1979).

52. A *Wall Street Journal/NBC News* poll showed only 29 percent of the public considered the tax cuts as "the best way to increase economic growth and create jobs," and 64 percent of respondents thought "better ways" exist. See: Rosenbaum, David E. "Large Tax Cut a Bush Victory; Against Odds, President Wins Using Popularity and Strategy." *New York Times,* May 24, 2003, 5.

53. Milbank, Dana. "Bush Signs $350 Billion Tax Cut Measure; Some Americans Will Get Refunds in July; Payroll Deductions to Drop in June." *Washington Post,* May 29, 2003, A6.

54. Pitelis, *Market and Non-Market Hierarchies,* 1991.

55. O'Connor, James. "The Fiscal Crises of the State, Part II." *Socialist Revolution* 1, no. 2 (1970): 34–94; Lazonick. *Business Organization and the Myth of the Market Economy,* 1991.

56. Schumpeter, Joseph A. *Capitalism, Socialism and Democracy* (New York: Harper & Brothers, 1942).

57. Rostow, Eugene. *Planning for Freedom* (New Haven, CT: Yale University Press, 1959).

58. Hart. *Rival Capitalists,* 1992.

59. Hamilton, Alexander. "Report on the Subject of Manufacturers." In *The Papers of Alexander Hamilton,* vol. 10, ed. Harold C. Syrett (New York: Columbia University Press, 1791/1966), 230–341.

60. List, Friedrich. *The National System of Political Economy,* trans. Sampson S. Lloyd (Kitchener, Ontario: Batoche, 1885/2001).

61. Lazonick. *Business Organization and the Myth of the Market Economy,* 1991.

62. Fallows, James. *Looking at the Sun* (New York: Pantheon, 1994); Johnson, Chalmers. *MITI and the Japanese Miracle* (Stanford, CA: Stanford University Press, 1982); Tsuru, Shigeto. *Japan's Capitalism: Creative Defeat and Beyond* (New York: Cambridge University Press, 1993).

63. Schmitter, Philippe J. "Still the Century of Corporatism?" in *Trends toward Corporatist Intermediation.* eds. Peter J. Schmitter and G. Lehmbruch (Beverly Hills, CA: Sage, 1979), 7–53.

64. Salisbury, Robert H. "Why No Corporatism in America?" in *Trends toward Corporatist Intermediation,* eds. Peter J. Schmitter and G. Lehmbruch (Beverly Hills, CA: Sage, 1979), 213–230; Wilson, Graham. "Why Is There No Corporatism in the United States?" in *Patterns of Corporatist Policy-Making,* eds. G. Lehmbruch and Peter C. Schmitter (Beverly Hills, CA: Sage, 1982), 219–236; Wilson. *Business and Politics,* 1985; Streeck, Wolfgang, and Philippe C. Schmitter. "Community, Market, State—and Associations?" In *Private Interest Government: Beyond Market and State,* eds. Wolfgang Streeck and Phillippe C. Schmitter (Beverly Hills, CA: Sage, 1985), 1–29.

65. Reich's (1992) *Work of Nations* discusses the rise of unionization in the early 1950s, and its relation with the "core" of big business in the United States. Together with the government, these three groups controlled prices, inflation, and wages. Although this arrangement was not formalized, the evidence supports some organization along the lines of the neocorporatist model. See: Reich, Robert B. *The Work of Nations* (New York: Vintage, 1992).

66. Hayek, Friedrich A. *The Road to Serfdom* (Chicago: University of Chicago Press, 1944).

67. Nozick. *Anarchy, State, and Utopia,* 1974; Friedman, Milton & Rose Friedman. *Free to Choose* (Orlando, FL: Harcourt Brace, 1979).

68. Reich, *The Work of Nations,* 1992.

69. Sullivan, Kevin. "For Clinton in Japan, Accord and Smiles: 'Feeling Good', and the Trade Talks are Easy." *Washington Post,* April 19, 1996, A27.

70. Interviews with Boeing's negotiation team for a sale in China were concerned about the impact of human rights discussions on the sale of airplanes in that country. Neil Standal, interview by Drew Martin, Kobe, Japan, April 4, 1992.

71. Thurow, Lester. *Head to Head: The Coming Economic Battle among Japan, Europe, and America* (New York: Warner Books, 1993).

72. Ibid.

73. Reich, Robert B. *The Next American Frontier* (New York: Crown Publishing, 1983).

74. "Free Trade over a Barrel," 2002, A18.

75. National Association of State Development Agencies (NASDA). *NASDA 1994 State Export Program Database Analysis* (Washington, DC: NASDA, 1994).

76. Martin, Drew. "What Do State Trade Offices Do Best?" *International Journal of Commerce and Management* 13, no. 2 (2003), 54–73; Martin, Drew, Tim Wilkinson, and Michael d'Amico. "Export Promotion and FDI Attraction in Japan: The Impact of U.S. State Based Industrial Policy," *International Journal of Management Practice* 1, no. 3 (2005): 251–262.

77. Gershenkron, Alexander. *Economic Backwardness in Historical Perspective* (Cambridge, MA: Belknap, 1962); Gershenkron, Alexander. *Continuity in History and Other Essays* (Cambridge, MA: Belknap, 1968).

78. Wilson. *Business and Politics,* 1985.

79. Wade, Robert. "East Asia's Economic Success. *World Politics* 44 (January 1992): 270–320; Ungson, Gerardo R., Richard M. Steers, and Seung Ho Park. *Korean Enterprise: The Quest for Globalization* (Boston: Harvard Business School Press, 1979); Fields, Karl. *Enterprise and the State in Korea and Taiwan* (Ithaca, NY: Cornell University Press, 1995).

80. Nakarmi, Laxmi. "Seoul Yanks the *Chaebol's* Leash." *Business Week,* October 1995, 20–21.

81. Woodside, Alexander. "The Idea as a Mobilization Myth." In *What's in a Rim?: Critical Perspectives on the Pacific Regional Idea,* ed. Arfic Dirlik (New York: Westview, 1993).

82. Hall and Soskice. *Varieties of Capitalism.*

83. Ibid.

84. Andersson, Savante. "Internationalization in Different Industrial Contexts." *Journal of Business Venturing* 19, no. 6 (2004): 851–875; Madsen, Tage Koed,

and Per Servais. "The Internationalization of Born Globals: An Evolutionary Process?" *International Business Review* 6, no. 6 (1997): 561–583.

85. U.S. Census Bureau (2011). "Real Exports, Imports, and Balance of Goods, Petroleum and Non-Petroleum End-Use Commodity Category Totals." http://www.census.gov/foreign-trade/statistics/historical/realpetr.pdf.

86. United States Department of Labor. "Labor Force Statistics from the Current Population Survey." http://www.bls.gov/cps/.

87. U.S. Census Bureau. "U.S. Trade in Goods by Country" (October 13, 2011). http://www.census.gov/foreign-trade/balance/#T.

88. Economy Watch Content. "South Korea Economy" (March 30, 2010). http://www.economywatch.com/world_economy/south-korea/.

89. Economy Watch Content. "The Chinese Economy" (June 30, 2010). http://www.economywatch.com/world_economy/china/?page=full.

90. Porter, *The Competitive Advantage of Nations,* 1990.

91. Transparency International (2009), *Global Corruption Report 2009.* http://www.transparency.org.

92. Global 500, 2011 Rankings. CNN Money. http://money.cnn.com/magazines/fortune/global500/2011/countries/US.html.

93. Puzzanghere, Jim. "Wall Street; Goldman Boosts D.C. Lobby Force; Departing From Its Under-the-Radar Style, the Investing Giant Is Putting More Money and Muscle into Its Capitol Presence." *Los Angeles Times* (July 5, 2011): B1.

94. Whitehall, Polly C. "New MPs' links to Lobbyists Worries Anti-Spin Group." *The Guardian,* July 3, 2010, 6.

95. Transparency International's scale ranges from 0 to 10. To make the scale's axis similar, the government transparency score is divided by 10 to represent a percentage of transparency. Sources: Transparency International (2011), *Global Corruption Report 2005* and *Global Corruption Report 2011.* http://www.transparency.org.

96. *Historical Tables: Budget of the U.S. Government* (2011), p. 27. http://www.gpoaccess.gov/usbudget/fy11/pdf/hist.pdf.

97. United States Department of Labor, Bureau of Labor Statistics (2011). Labor Force Statistics for Nonagriculture, Private Wage and Salary Workers. http://www.bls.gov/webapps/legacy/cpsatab14.htm.

98. CNN Money. http://money.cnn.com/magazines/fortune/global500/2011/countries/US.html.

99. Ibid.

100. Heritage Foundation. (2011), *2011 Index of Economic Freedom.* http://www.heritage.org/index/country/Japan#government-spending.

101. CNN Money. http://money.cnn.com/magazines/fortune/global500/2011/countries/US.html.

102. Heritage Foundation (2011). "2011 Index of Economic Freedom," http://www.heritage.org/Index/Country/China.

103. Tanzer, Andrew "Over a Barrel." *Forbes* 162, December 14, 1998, 156–159.

104. The Japan Ice Cream Association reports a growing preference for ice cream from 47 percent in 1997 to 88 percent in 2008. See: Japan Ice Cream Association, "Ice Cream Hakusho 2008," May 9, 2009. http://www.icecream.or.jp/data/pdf/hakusho2009.pdf; Japanese Ice Cream Association. "Ice Cream Hakusho 1999." http://www.icecream.or.jp/data/pdf/hakusho1999.pdf.

105. Taiga Uranaka. "Ice Cream Companies Turning to High-end Treats," *Japan Times,* June 19, 2003.

106. Belson, Ken, Rob Hof, and Ben Elgin. "How Yahoo! Japan Beat eBay at Its Own Game," *Business Week,* 3735 (June 4, 2001): 58.

107. Lane, Greg. "Failed Businesses in Japan," *Japaninc* 73 (September/October, 2007): 6–8. http://www.japaninc.com/mgz_sep-oct_2007_issue_failed-businesses.

108. Pittaway, Luke, Maxine Robertson, Kamal Munir, David Denyer, and Andy Neely (2004). "Networking and Innovation: A Systematic Review of the Evidence." *International Journal of Management Reviews* 5/6, no. 3–4 (2004): 137–168; Eisenhardt, Kathleen M., and Claudi Bird Schoonhoven (1996). "Resource-Based View of Strategic Alliance Formation: Strategic and Social Effects in Entrepreneurial Firms." *Organization Science* 7, no. 2 (1996): 136–150.

109. Laanti, Riku, Mika Gabrielsson, and Peter Gabrielsson. "The Globalization Strategies of Business-to-business Born Global Firms in the Wireless Technology Industry." *Industrial Marketing Management* 36 (2007): 1104–1117.

110. Chetty, Sylvie K. and Loren M. Stangl. "Internationalization and Innovation in a Networking Relationship Context." *European Journal of Marketing* 44, no. 11–12 (2010): 1725–1743.

111. Sheard, Paul. 1997. "Keiretsu, Competition, and Market Access." In *Global Competition Policy,* eds. Edward M. Graham and J. David Richardson (Washington, DC: Institute for International Economics): 501–546. http://www.piie.com/publications/chapters_preview/56/16ie1664.pdf.

112. Lane, Greg. "Failed Businesses in Japan," 2007, 6–8. http://www.japaninc.com/mgz_sep-oct_2007_issue_failed-businesses.

113. Chetty and Stangl. "Internationalization and Innovation in a Networking Relationship Context," 2010.

Part III

Approaches to Strategic Management

Chapter 8

Serendipity as a Strategic Advantage?

Nancy K. Napier and
Quan Hoang Vuong

Who, over the age of 20, hasn't experienced a serendipitous event: unexpected information that yields some unintended but potential value later on? Sitting next to a stranger on a plane who becomes a business partner? Stumbling onto an article in a journal or newspaper that helps tackle a nagging problem? Creating a new drug by accident?

Serendipity, defined as the ability to recognize and leverage or create value from unexpected information, appears in all parts of life,[1] and especially in professional fields, including science and technology,[2] politics and economics,[3] education administration,[4] library and information science,[5] career choice and development,[6] and entrepreneurship and management.[7] Interestingly, although scientists have moved from reluctant to open acknowledgement that serendipity is behind many an invention or discovery, few business scholars or managers have systematically studied or applied serendipity in any direct fashion. The topic, though, may be gaining more visibility and attention: a new book on luck, for example, looks at how individuals and organizations have turned good or bad luck into something of value ("return on luck").[8]

Thus, in this chapter, we seek to understand serendipity in a business context, examine what it could mean for management and strategy, and how it could be used in business. We divided the chapter into three sections. First, we examine the concept of serendipity and its importance and then review literature about it, in terms of definitions, conditions that encourage or hinder serendipity at different levels (the level of the individual, the level of an organization, and external conditions), and the process of serendipity. Next, we propose a tentative framework that seeks to incorporate the literature and existing models, and which draws upon discussions with executives who have begun to track and analyze how they might use serendipity in their ongoing management practices. Finally, we close with suggestions for how to develop the notion of serendipity as a competitive advantage, both in practice and in research.

SERENDIPITY—WHY WORRY ABOUT IT?

In the early 1950s, two eminent medical researchers—Drs. Lewis Thomas from New York University and Aaron Kellner from Cornell University—separately noticed an unusual anomaly in their research labs: the ears of rabbits "flopped" when the animals received injections of the enzyme papain.[9] Each researcher considered the phenomenon to be abnormal and dramatic, but for each of them at the time, not worth spending much energy on. They were both pursuing other research and this unexpected event did not peak their interests (or fit into their budgets) enough to follow up. The same phenomenon consistently occurred on subsequent occasions whenever they injected papain; again both researchers noticed it, but they did not pursue it.

But some years later, in 1955, when Lewis was showing the phenomenon to a group of medical students, he finally decided to follow up on why the rabbits' ears flopped. At that time, he was able (more interest, time, and money) to pursue what had caused the odd result. When he at last studied what was happening, the pursuit resulted in research that was revolutionary, more significant than the research he had been pursuing when he initially noticed the "floppy ears." The floppy-eared-rabbit research eventually led to a Nobel award. In contrast, the other researcher, Professor Kellner, never pursued the floppy-ears anomaly, as it did not fit into his research interest. Barber and Fox[10] described what happened as "serendipity gained" (Thomas's decision to look into the phenomenon) and "serendipity lost" (Kellner's decision not to pursue it). The example offered a striking illustration of the potential benefit of investigating some unexpected information or discovery, as Thomas (finally) did.[11]

More famous examples abound of unexpected scientific discoveries that have become lifesaving or revenue-generating products (e.g., penicillin, Velcro). Interestingly, and perhaps because the results are easier to measure, scientists have unabashedly accepted the value of looking for the unexpected or anomaly that may be more interesting than the expected findings.[12] In contrast, whereas most management scholars generally ignore, at best, or scoff, at worst, the notion of serendipity as an ability to cultivate and use to organizational advantage, some management literature has begun to examine the concept. For instance, Brown[13] argues that it could play a role in entrepreneurs' actions. Dew[14] draws upon Sarasvathy[15] to argue that "surprises are usually relegated to error terms in formal models. Instead . . . they *may be the source of opportunity for value creation,* but only if someone seizes upon them in an instrumental fashion and imaginatively combines them with . . . inputs to create new possibilities" (italics added). Interestingly, when questioned, many managers will say "it happens all the time," but are reluctant to admit basing major decisions or directions upon serendipity.

Yet, some business strategic moves may depend more on serendipity than managers or scholars have acknowledged in the past. Meyer and Skak[16] studied the decisions of small- and medium-sized enterprises that were considering and/or moving into Eastern Europe. The networks that managers had developed sometimes offered "unanticipated opportunities by providing complementary resources, knowledge, or contacts." Given that the networks were outside of the firm's control, an important aspect was that the managers were open and ready to consider and then take advantage of the unexpected opportunities that arose. In particular, Meyer and Skak[17] found that for small firms, such "elements of chance" could affect a firm's growth path and direction because of the networks, contacts, and opportunities that the managers could pursue as a result of those serendipitous events. When the small firms responded quickly, they could in some ways leverage such unexpected information better and faster than competitors.

Finally, Collins and Hansen,[18] in describing the idea of "return on luck," note that events—good and bad—happen in any organization. The ability to take advantage of them, to execute an action that generates good value, has benefited some firms in major ways.[19,20]

As the management literature increasingly begins to open to the possibility that serendipity may have value in business, perhaps the way Taleb[21] and others have discussed it in relation to scientists could be applied to management: "successful scientists search for something they know but generally find something unexpected."[22]

WHAT DO WE KNOW ABOUT SERENDIPITY?

Serendipity as a concept has been around for hundreds of years. Serendipity as a "studied" concept is rather recent. In this section, we review some of what has been examined and studied about several aspects of or affecting serendipity. First, we review definitions, characteristics and "types" of serendipity. Next, we look at the contextual factors influencing it, particularly at the organizational, individual, and external/environmental levels. Third, we examine literature that offers insight into how serendipity happens, or the process that seems to occur once unexpected information appears. Finally, we review literature on the types of actions resulting from leverage serendipity.

Most discussions on definitions of "serendipity" start with some version of the story reported by Walpole (1754). Hundreds of years ago, a king named Giaffer educated his three sons to a level that nearly satisfied him, but felt they needed a bit more "seasoning" before assuming the duties of the throne. He sent them into the countryside of what was then called Serendip, later Ceylon, now Sri Lanka. In the course of their walks, they noticed and made observations about information they had not sought or expected, ranging from grass eaten and not, spit wads on one side of the road, bees and flies, and footprints. When they arrived at one town, a farmer asked if they had seen his lost camel.

"Is the camel blind in its right eye? Is it missing a tooth on the left side of its mouth? Is it lame in one leg? And is it carrying honey and sugar?"

The astounded farmer at once accused the three princes of stealing his camel and demanded that the emperor punish them. But the wise emperor asked first to hear the princes' story.

"We noticed along the way that the grass on the left side of the road had been eaten, while the right side was still covered with fresh grass (so we assume the camel is blind in one eye). We saw wads of grass that had dropped onto the ground, through a hole where a tooth should be in the camel's mouth. Bees like honey and flies like sugar, which the camel was carrying in packs on either side of its back and, as it swayed, must have left drops in the road. And finally, we noticed three footprints and a drag where a fourth would be, suggesting the camel was lame in one back leg."

The princes' notoriety came from their ability to notice unexpected information that they were not searching for and, later, turn it into something of value. At the time, their curiosity caused them to notice, but lacking context, they did not connect the various pieces of information. Once they had a context for understanding the unexpected information and a problem (the lost camel), they were able to connect the pieces of a puzzle and offer and explain how they knew about the camel.

Definitions

The Walpole story is useful, but often not useful enough for people who have tried to define serendipity over the years. In the management literature that has tackled the concept, typical characteristics that emerge include:

- Unsought, unexpected, unintentional, unanticipated event or information,[23]
- Out of the ordinary, surprising, anomalous, inconsistent with existing thought, findings or theory,[24] and

- An alertness or capability to notice what others do not, to recognize, to consider, and to connect previously disparate or discreet pieces of information[25] to solve a problem or find an opportunity.

Unsought, Unexpected . . . Anomalous and Inconsistent with Existing Thought

The definitions range from being quite broad—unsought discoveries, unexpected events, or information—to being more specific and narrower in the nature of the event or information. In particular, the literature makes it clear that the unexpected information should be an "anomalous," incongruous, or inconsistent discovery or finding, at odds with existing theory or ways of thinking.[26] Scientists, especially, appear to conscientiously seek the inconsistent or anomalous information or event because that forces review of existing theory and can, perhaps, lead to new directions with possible major payoffs.[27]

In some cases, an individual may be searching for a new idea, problem, solution, or opportunity. In combinatorial chemistry, for instance, which often yields new drugs, the notion of "a blind search" is part of the process,[28] with "serendipity mistakes" just a likely stage in the experiment. Going down a blind alley in search of some answer but finding another one, then, is almost built into the research process itself.

Dew[29] describes serendipity as the intersection of three "domains" or elements: search, knowledge/preparation, and chance. He claims that an individual needs to be looking for something, such as a solution to a problem or an opportunity. She needs to approach the search with existing knowledge and preparation so that she will be able to recognize an event or information. In addition, the unexpected event or information has to emerge by chance. Thus, according to Dew,[30] serendipity occurs only when all three elements are present and overlap (a search, prior knowledge, and chance event).

Yet, if we return to the three princes of Serendip story (or to the floppy-eared-rabbit story, for that matter), perhaps the search can come "after" the information appears. In their case, it seems that two of Dew's[31] three conditions existed on the part of the princes—prior knowledge and preparation and the chance occurrence of unexpected information (e.g., the grass eaten on one side of the road, the footprints, and rut in the sand). The princes—and often scientists—were not "looking for something," but rather were able to solve a problem once they were presented with it, not because they were seeking information to solve it.

An Alertness or Capability

Finally, a group of researchers note that the ability to notice or be aware of unexpected information is critical. De Rond[32] talks of scientific discovery as beginning with the "awareness of anomaly and unsought factors." Van Andel[33] defines serendipity as the experience of observing an unanticipated, anomalous, and strategic piece of data, which then allows for developing new theories or expanding existing ones.

Other definitions focus on the capacity or ability to see and leverage unsought information or discovery. In other words, serendipity is not just the unexpected information or event but rather the ability to recognize and do something with it. Specifically, it is an individual's or organization's ability to recognize and capitalize upon an unexpected event or information and turn it into something that adds value for the organization—or, in the case of scientists, the research community.[34]

Characteristics and "Types"

For scholars, scientists, and practicing managers, serendipity can appear in several "types," depending partly upon whether there is a search "intent" and whether the unexpected information solves some problem or opens the door to new problems/opportunities. In particular, several researchers use a 2 by 2 matrix to clarify these options. Essentially, they break serendipity into two categories: (1) whether there is explicit intent to find something or a search exists to solve a problem or find an opportunity,[35] and (2) whether unexpected information solves an existing problem or reveals solutions to unknown problems or opportunities.[36] (*Note:* A situation where there is an intent and a solution to the problem at hand is a traditional problem-solving (A to B) situation, not serendipity.) Thus, this generates three types of serendipity, illustrated in Figure 8.1.

Type I

First, the most common type of serendipity is when an individual seeks a solution to problem A and it does not come from "expected" sources, but rather from an unexpected event or piece of information, (B). For instance, when researchers sought an explanation for obesity, initial assumptions were that physiological or economic reasons were base causes; individuals had genetic tendencies toward obesity or they purchased cheaper food, which tended to be higher in fat content. In fact, two researchers studying data from a small town in Massachusetts found another unexpected explanation, from a completely different direction. Put simply, they found that "your friends can affect your health." People who are overweight tend to associate with others who are overweight, as do smokers with other smokers. Christakis and Fowler[37] argue that social networks and friendships may influence health, which was a completely unexpected explanation or solution to the initial problem of obesity.

Figure 8.1
Types of Serendipity

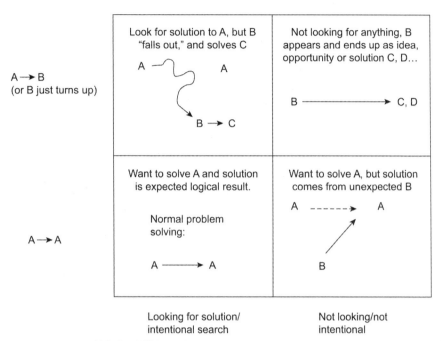

Note. Modified from M. De Rond, 2005, "The Structure of Serendipity," Cambridge Judge Business School Working Paper.

Type II

Type II serendipity happens when an individual searches for a solution to problem A, but rather than finding a solution to A, uncovers something unexpected and unsought (B). Well-known examples of Type II serendipity include the floppy-eared rabbits we mentioned previously, as well as penicillin and Post-It notes. Fleming was not looking for penicillin, but accidently discovered a "mold" in his lab that of course had many implications and uses. For Post-It notes, a 3M researcher was trying to create a glue that would stick well and instead, accidentally discovered one that did not stick so well, but then uncovered many uses for the newly discovered product.

Type III

The story of the three princes of Serendip reflects a final and, as some might say, the truest form of serendipity. This occurs when a chance or unexpected event or piece of information appears, and an individual then begins to think about what it might mean, and along the way, solves a problem or discovers a new opportunity he or she had not intended or thought of previously. In this case, no intent or overt searching happens, but to gain the benefits of the unexpected event, the individual must still have knowledge and a prepared mind to notice and then realize its potential value. The legend of the apple falling on Newton's head—combined with his knowledge of science—led to his serendipitous discovery of gravity's properties. Likewise, the also now famous story of the invention of Velcro: a man who found insistently sticky burrs on his dog was led to wonder whether there might be anything of value that could be made from such an unexpected bit of information.

In Type III serendipity, some scholars insist that there must also be a "metaphorical leap" to uncover a possible value or use in the information or event. In Newton's case, a falling apple came to represent gravity's pull on any object; the "burrs on the dog" could be extrapolated to "some sort of material that holds tight."

CONTEXT FOR SERENDIPITY

It is not just the merit of the discovery that counts per se but also the context in which it emerges.[38]

If a tree falls in the forest and no one hears it, does it make a sound? If an unexpected and unsought event happens and no one notices, did it really happen? Context is critical for serendipity. In the floppy-eared-rabbit example, one scientist did not and one (finally) did pursue an unexpected observation, yielding major research implications for the one who did. The key is that both researchers *noticed* the unusual event. Thus, for unexpected information to be of any potential value, it has to be noticed.

The scholarly literature suggests that two factors influence the possibility of unexpected information being noticed and leveraged. Those factors exist at two levels: the organization and the individual. Most literature relating to organizational context refers to how culture can enhance (or hinder) the chances of serendipity occurring. At the individual level, the literature discusses characteristics and traits that individuals need to have or acquire to take advantage of serendipity. We briefly review each of the context factors further on.

Enhancing Organizational Serendipity

By far, the most important aspect at the organizational level for enhancing the chance that serendipity will be leveraged is organizational culture.[39] At least four elements of culture emerge often as being important for increasing and facilitating serendipity.[40]

First, the notion of finding ways to help dissimilar individuals inter-act with one another is critical, especially when they come from differ-ent disciplines.[41] As the book *The Power of Pull* suggests, if knowledge is dispersed,[42] it is harder to find desired information with a formal search; rather, it is more likely that individuals will "discover something useful through a chance encounter." That requires infrastructure—both physical but also cultural—to encourage those encounters. Cunha et al.[43] talk of the need for "free flow of information" through different types of social net-works, such as when smokers meet outside a building. (One must wonder, as smoking disappears, what interesting ideas and social networks have also disappeared). When people come from diverse units and hierarchi-cal levels, the opportunities for exploring the "periphery" of some field or discipline can grow, and that unexpected information and chance for exchange is high.

Following closely along with the importance of diverse groups that interact is the need for trust, willingness to share knowledge, and so-cial capital within an organization.[44] In a culture that allows risk taking, withholding of blame, and openness to a range of ideas, the likelihood is greater that serendipitous events will be noticed and considered. Only then can they be leveraged or used to an advantage. If a culture thwarts open discussion or some amount of "directionless activity,"[45] the chance for gaining value from serendipity disappears.

Third, in addition to encouraging opportunities for cross-discipline ex-changes and trust to happen, the literature suggests that an organizational culture needs to tolerate a degree of autonomy for experiments,[46] "con-trolled sloppiness,"[47] and minimal structure.[48] When some amount of in-efficiency, dissent, and failure are allowed to occur, unintentional events may happen, which may in turn generate ideas, opportunities, or solu-tions to problems.

Fourth, for members of an organization to actively look for serendipity in their fields, it has to be perceived as relevant and important for that orga-nization.[49] The value of noticing unexpected information needs to be built into the institutional routine, and then, when some information has been recognized, it needs to be leveraged and implemented. As that cycle occurs and individuals see the results, the notion of serendipity gains credibility and legitimacy. That allows the organization to focus on hiring or devel-oping people with a "serendipity disposition," with diverse search styles (looking for unexpected events), peripheral vision, and "weirdness."[50]

Obstructing Organizational Serendipity

The factors within organizations that encourage serendipity can, of course, hinder its likelihood if they are lacking.[51] Without openness and trust, the chance of self-censorship increases and individuals will be less alert to unexpected information. If power comes into play in deciding who "owns" a great idea, or if vested interests dominate within an organization, ideas or observations could be "interrupted" or quashed somewhere in the organizational hierarchy, making it improbable that ideas and the opportunity to leverage unexpected information will emerge in the future. If the organization does not value or allow a certain amount of experimenting or sloppiness, a discovery may be recast as one that was rational, leading to potential loss of other discoveries in the future. Finally, if the right people do not support the process and notion of serendipitous events having possible value, they certainly will go unnoticed.

ABILITIES NEEDED TO BE ABLE TO RECOGNIZE AND TAKE ADVANTAGE OF SERENDIPITY

Chance is an event, serendipity is a capability.[52]

In "the science of serendipity, luck can be 'caught,' corralled, coached, and created."[53] For organizational leaders to leverage unexpected information, the capability of doing so must exist. This is the arena where education, training, and building of skills are most likely and most promising. Scientists training students routinely discuss the importance of looking for unexpected findings, following paths that peak curiosity and may (or may not) have potential payoff.[54] In this section, we discuss the broad categories of skills that individuals need so they may develop the ability to notice and take advantage of unsought information or events. The skills fall roughly into three broad groupings: general characteristics, those relating to openness and curiosity, and those relating to preparedness and alertness, including stage of development. Finally, we close the section with a review of the types of obstacles that can thwart the capability of serendipity.

General Characteristics

The literature suggests that individuals who possess several fundamental characteristics are more likely to be able to see and pursue serendipitous events. Four broad groups of characteristics or skills come through: (1) motivation to work hard and perform well; (2) a social network used effectively; (3) willingness to take risks; and (4) a good "grip on reality" in terms of what is possible or not in the marketplace.

First, regardless of the literature discipline—whether education, career development, or business—the research focuses on characteristics that start with the most basic, including intelligence and competence, a strong work ethic, persistence, diligence, and motivation to succeed.[55] Next, the literature suggests that individuals who more often benefit from serendipity have strong and diverse social networks,[56] which matches with the need for a culture that encourages cross-discipline interactions. Third, a willingness to take risks and pursue untested ideas is critical for creative ventures of any sort, and particularly with regard to unexpected events or information.[57]

Finally, and again critical for any endeavor where evaluation of unexpected events is necessary, it is an ability to assess "realities." In examining differences between alert and nonalert people who noticed events in the marketplace, Gaglio and Katz[58] supported Kirzner's[59] alertness principle in their findings that "shrewd and wise assessment of the realities" helped to encourage flashes of insights, which in turn led to identification of market opportunities. Such a grip on reality[60] enhances the likelihood that an individual will notice (by being alert) and be able to assess the information or event for its possible value.

Openness and Curiosity

As we reported in the commonly told story about the three princes of Serendip, one of their foremost qualities was simple curiosity and the ability to notice.[61] They were open to what they found out later were clues to a lost camel, which they had no knowledge of at the time they made their observations along the way. They simply noticed because they were curious.[62]

Such openness to unsought events and information has been noted in career development, even to the point where Williams et al.[63] suggest that women are more open to serendipity in their careers than men. In addition, Van Andel[64] includes openness and curiosity as critical factors in people who "find" serendipity. Often the curiosity is coupled with a willingness to look for the surprise or the anomaly in a situation.[65] Such counterfactual thinking becomes useful later in assessment of the information or event as well.

Preparedness and Alertness

Was there ever a more trite saying than the often repeated comment attributed to Louis Pasteur: "chance favors the prepared mind"[66]? Yet, if this holds, then training, reading, and experience could help foster serendipity. And indeed, one of the most frequently mentioned characteristics needed for taking advantage of serendipity is the notion of being ready and prepared.[67] Kirzner[68] defined alertness as being able to notice an event without searching for it and in the process identifying opportunities that had been overlooked. Cunha et al.[69] note that serendipity thrives on alertness and as a result depends upon mindfulness.[70] The opposite, an unprepared mind, discards the unusual observation and hence loses the chance for leverage.[71]

But simply being alert or prepared may not be enough. In a study of corporate executives and new venture managers, Busenitz[72] found that inexperienced founders of firms were intense and alert in their search for information—unexpected and otherwise—but that they were less focused in how they searched, and sometimes let curiosity take them further afield (and wasted time) more than the experienced managers did. In other words, they were open, but perhaps not prepared or alert in the right manner.

Closely tied to being prepared and alert is, for some individuals, the stage of their own development, whether that is in careers, knowledge base, or personal lives.[73] For instance, Betsworth and Hansen[74] found that factors both personal and professional influenced the degree to which, and direction that, serendipitous events played in the lives of college graduates. Gaglio and Katz,[75] as we mentioned previously, found that experience (i.e., later stage of career or profession) factors into the ability of new venture founders to notice and take advantage of serendipity.

Finally, the two medical researchers who noticed the floppy ears in rabbits (Lewis and Kellner) were well-established scientists, with solid reputations, and thus at stages of their careers where they could, if they desired, be more able or willing to take risks by following a path that could have led to nothing. Of course, Lewis did not pursue the anomaly until several factors contributed to his being ready to look at the question. He pursued the floppy-ears question only later, when he had more resources (rabbits to test), when he was frustrated with his other research (which had hit a snag, so he was looking for new areas to pursue), and when he was, as he put it bluntly, "showing off" a bit to his students. At that point, Thomas realized he should be doing a more systematic comparison of injected and noninjected rabbits.[76] Thus, his stage of career and stage of research projects influenced his readiness to look into the rabbit ears.

Obstacles

As we noted at the start of this section, sometimes "serendipity lost" wins the day. Several obstacles can impede serendipity. In fact, one could wonder how it ever occurs! The obstacles range from a culture (discussed earlier) that neither encourages nor celebrates the ability to notice and take advantage of unexpected information, to individual inability or unwillingness to be open, courageous, and timely about what events or information might be of value. Barber and Fox's[77] comparison of the medical researchers identified distraction (with other projects) and lack of resources (not enough rabbits to test) as obstacles to Lewis and Kellner pursuing the unusual observation when they both first noticed it.

But perhaps even more important and more devious are the preconceptions, expectations, and convictions that those researchers held, as do others, when they encountered an unexpected or unsought finding.[78] Essentially, once expectations and assumptions are set, it becomes hard to see something differently. In the rabbit ears' cases, each scientist had a research focus in an area unrelated to cartilage (which is finally where Lewis realized the impact of the enzyme). One focused on proteins, the other on muscles, and as a result, when the out-of-the-norm observation occurred, and did *not* fit within their frameworks of how to evaluate it, they could not explain it (and refrained from pursuing it any further). Thus, a very large obstacle, which ties back to the willingness to be open, is preconceived notions of the meaning of some observation.

HOW DOES SERENDIPITY HAPPEN?

How does the act of serendipity occur? What happens when individuals—or organizations—leverage serendipitous information or events? Is there a process or framework to help us understand it, follow it, shape it, or learn it?

In this section, we review three frameworks from the business management literature (although one comes from information technology) that suggest stages or steps in a process of understanding and using serendipitous events or information. Although 50–60 years ago it was not common, the science disciplines today, as we have suggested earlier, more readily acknowledge that serendipity is a normal part of operations. In contrast, Cunha et al.[79] note that even now, few management scholars explicitly research serendipity in organizations.

The frameworks have in common the notions of some sort of precipitating conditions or situation, whether at the level of the individual,[80] the organization,[81] or the external environmental level.[82] They also comprise the need for an individual to *notice* an unusual event or anomaly, to *recognize* there might be some possible value, and to *connect seemingly disparate ideas or data* (also known as "connecting the dots"), which some scholars refer to as "bisociation."[83] This stage refers to the ability to identify "matching pairs" of events that are meaningful, and which may be, but are not necessarily, causally related.[84] Finally, the frameworks generally include some type of evaluation and resulting action that emerges from the process.[85] We describe the three frameworks in more depth further on.

Looking for A but Finding B

Mendoca et al.[86] and Cunha et al.[87] focus on what we might call Type II serendipity, where an individual searches for a solution to problem A, but in the process, discovers something quite unexpected, a solution for a completely different problem B. The framework has four major variables: (1) precipitating conditions, or those that will encourage or hinder likelihood of serendipity occurring; (2) the process of searching for a solution to problem A, including how organizational members go about the search, and how open and focused they are; (3) bisociation, or the ability to connect information, improvise, or make do with what is available to solve problems; and (4) reaching an unexpected solution for a different problem, including how open the organization and individuals are to ambiguity and imperfection.

Stages

Two other frameworks[88] are stage models that focus more on the acts of noticing or recognizing an unsought or unexpected event or information. Consultants Lawley and Tompkins[89] propose a very straightforward framework that argues for the importance of preparation (E minus 1), before some unexpected event (E), and the steps that follow (called E + 1, E + 2, and so on): recognition, choosing an action, and understanding its consequences. These steps may be iterative and happen repeatedly over time before the final evaluation and assessment of the outcome is clear.

A second stage model comes from Gaglio and Katz.[90] They focus especially on the impact of unexpected events in terms of their likelihood to lead to moderate or innovative opportunities. They offer a series of steps that an individual would experience, where several types of evaluation occur. First, an individual determines whether an event is normal and expected, or unusual and unexpected. For the "normal event," typically the individual and organization will continue with its status quo plans and operations, and the event then will very likely yield small or imitative new opportunities, if any. If the event is unexpected, then a first assessment determines whether to ignore, discount, or pursue it. If the organization chooses to ignore or discount the event, then the outcome is similar to what occurs with a normal, expected event: following the status quo. If an unusual event that is noticed and then assessed, subsequent stages include trying to understand what it means for the industry, society, or market, and then trying to explain it and put into the organization's context. This happens through what Gaglio and Katz[91] call "counterfactural thinking" and "mental simulation," or trying to sense whether the event is analogous to something already experienced. From that analysis may come a big breakthrough that would lead to innovative or quite different opportunities.

For all three frameworks, the final outcome or action likewise tends to be something that is unexpected or unsought.[92] Those could be, for example, finding a solution to a different problem, discovering a new solution to an existing problem, or identifying a new opportunity (that ultimately will save or make money).

DEVELOPING A TENTATIVE FRAMEWORK FOR SERENDIPITY

Our tentative framework for the serendipity process incorporates many ideas from existing models and adds a few twists. Some of the "twists" emerged from attempts to apply "serendipity as a competitive advantage" within a sample business firm. Recently the former CEO of a manufacturing firm, Randy Hales, raised the question in his senior management group of whether the organization could develop serendipity as a capability and leverage it to their competitive advantage. The firm, Mity-Lite, based in Salt Lake City, Utah, produces high-quality office furniture—chairs and tables—for use worldwide. The initial reaction by the top executives was, not surprisingly, skepticism. Yet the executive suggested that the managers experiment (curiosity and openness!), spend 30 minutes every two weeks to identify unexpected information, how they noticed and evaluated it, and then decide what, if any, actions they might take to leverage it. That very small experiment, in addition to existing research and literature, helped us shape a tentative framework, presented further on. We begin with a definition and its elements and follow with the framework itself.

Definition

The definition of serendipity that we use is the *ability* to *recognize* and *evaluate unexpected information* and generate *unintended value* from it. Four aspects in the definition are critical to dissect: (1) the ability; (2) to recognize and evaluate; (3) unexpected information; and (4) generate unintended value.

Ability

First, serendipity as a *capability* more closely mirrors others' definitions that it is an alertness or capability to notice what others do not.[93] It is not a "happy accident" or an unanticipated discovery. Those are data points, events, or pieces of information that exist, whether or not they are noticed. But data points, facts, or information on their own are worthless without the action or ability to leverage them. Thus, our definition of serendipity supports others in its focus more on the *action taken as a result of observing* or uncovering information, rather than simply on the discovery or event or piece of information itself.

Recognize and Evaluate

The ability *to recognize and evaluate* comprises several pieces. First, recognizing includes two critical acts: noticing and connecting information.

The three princes of Serendip observed or noticed bees circling droplets of honey, grass that had been eaten on one side of the road, and three hoof prints and one groove in the sand. Those bits of information, noticed and filed away then, became important only later, within a context of the problem of a lost camel. In a sense, the bits of information were "clues" that they did not realize were "clues." Only within that context of a problem did the princes *connect* the disparate pieces of unexpected information, and put those clues together.

After noticing or observing comes evaluation of information. The ability to *evaluate* encompasses both "flash evaluation" and more systematic evaluation in pursuit of creating value. Flash evaluation starts with a "gut feel" that moves toward fuller alertness, which in turn can go to a more systematic evaluation that confirms the initial gut feel. The reliance on information—whether from internal (personal or organizational) or external (environmental) sources—may vary, however, and we discuss that in more depth further on.

Unexpected Information

Serendipity assumes the appearance of some type of information that is unanticipated, unexpected, unplanned, or unsought.[94] In a sense, it is the reverse of what happens during the insight experience. Insight occurs typically after a conscious search for (and then sometimes and unconscious mulling of) information to learn or a problem to solve. During the time we wrestle with the problem, or try to learn a new concept, we must assertively put forth effort and work, absorb information and sort it, before the insight occurs. Thus, in the case of encouraging insight or aha moments, we assertively pursue information.

Serendipity, on the other hand, begins more passively. It does not necessarily presume any "work" or attempt to solve a problem, other than noticing and having a prepared mind. It *can* include a search (Type I serendipity that we discussed earlier in this chapter), but it does not require it (Types II and III). Rather, it contains the notion of unexpected information appearing, even when there is no immediate problem to solve. Information could be data, an event, or an observation or clue. Again, to refer to the three princes, they came across unsought, unexpected, and unplanned information or clues. They made note, but did nothing with the information until they encountered a context—problem—which allowed them to connect disparate clues or pieces of information into something of (unintended) value.

Unintended Value

Finally, the serendipitous experience includes the element of *creating unintended value*, which refers to the potential outcome of a problem solution, new opportunity, idea, or other direction that was unintended. In other words, serendipity implies the lack of intension to solve a particular problem or find a particular opportunity. Rather it suggests the ability to take unexpected information and create value that, before the information appeared, would not have happened.

Tentative Framework

The tentative framework (Figure 8.2) offers a process that individuals appear to follow as they apply the ability to recognize, evaluate, and create value from unexpected information. The model has many steps, but we have clustered them into four broad stages, with subparts in some. The four stages include: (1) setting the stage or conditions that will increase the likelihood that unexpected information will be noticed (A, B, C, and G); (2) noticing unexpected information and beginning to connect it to other information (D); (3) evaluating the information—flash evaluation and, sometimes, more systematic evaluation—in terms of whether it could create unintended value (E); and (4) taking action upon the information to generate that value (F).

Figure 8.2
Tentative Framework of Serendipity Process

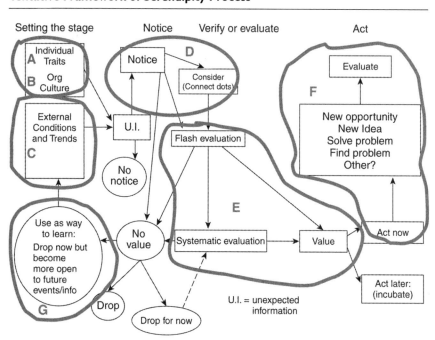

Setting the Stage (A, B, C, and ... G)

The model suggests that conditions at three levels may enhance the likelihood of unexpected information being noticed. First, the characteristics or conditions of an individual (A) that will make her more or less likely to notice anomalous information (e.g., openness, confidence, curiosity, alertness) are ones that many scholars have covered.[95] Organizational culture (B), including an openness to new ideas, a cross-discipline mix of people, and an allowance for "sloppiness," are similarly ones that research has addressed.[96]

Finally, external conditions (C) have been less widely considered and yet could well be more important for different types of settings or industries.[97] In the case of the Mity-Lite executives, once they agreed to try and "track" unexpected information and analyze how they could deal with it, the openness in their culture and willingness to notice unexpected information was critical for them to generate potential future value. As they became assertively alert to unexpected information, they began to see or find information that they may have dismissed or not noticed before they began their tracking exercise.

For example, in one case, the executives were launching a new product and had market analysis in preparation. In the process, they uncovered unexpected information that suggested their pricing methodology was inaccurate. Because they had been alerted to the notion of unexpected information and were looking for ways to recognize and leverage whatever they might find, they did notice unexpected information about their pricing methodology, and evaluated and acted upon it. In the discussion about their experience, they claimed that because they had been alerted to the notion of unexpected information, they were more receptive to noticing and otherwise might have missed it without those "conditions" being favorable to noticing.

Interestingly, even when information is seen to be of "no value," the simple act of noticing and recognizing possibilities may in turn enhance the openness for setting the stage for future noticing (G). Thus, the act of noticing and considering and then doing a flash evaluation may heighten awareness and increase alertness for more unexpected information later.

Noticing and "Connecting" Unexpected Information (D)

The process of noticing or being alert to unexpected information[98] and then beginning to connect or "bisociate"[99] unexpected bits of information is one of the most critical steps in the serendipity process and framework. Gaglio and Katz[100] call this the "What's going on?" step, which involves noticing an unusual piece of information and then beginning to wonder (and follow through) what it might mean. Critical in this phase, of course, is the willingness to pursue the anomaly.[101]

The Mity-Lite executive team offered several examples of unexpected information that they connected that led to new directions, some more strategic than others. One example involved a former employee who had left the firm to gain expertise in a very different area than his previous job. He joined another organization and realized he missed working at the manufacturing firm; so he contacted the head of operations saying that he would like to return to the firm, and was willing to go back to his former job. Simultaneously, the operations executive had been considering the question of how to help the firm develop and move into the very expertise arena that the former employee had developed while he was away from the firm. The executive had decided that he had no option but to develop an internal candidate since finding an external candidate was deemed likely to be too difficult and costly. Then, boom! Unexpected information (the former employee with the desired expertise) calls. His re-emergence thus solved a problem from an unexpected direction (Type I serendipity).

Evaluating—Flash and Systematic (E)

The evaluation stages comprise both flash evaluation and more systematic evaluation.

Flash Evaluation. Initially, and coupled with the early connecting of information bits is a flash evaluation, in which an individual does a quick, almost gut feel assessment of the unusual information. The manufacturing executives refer to this as using their "experienced eyes" to assess quickly some unexpected information. That initial gut feel then may lead the individual to become more alert to whether there are ways to connect the observed information to other already known information, both internal and external.

More Systematic Evaluation. A more systematic evaluation would include analytical assessment that leads toward a clearer confirmation of the information's possible value. That process of assessing unexpected information for potential value is affected by factors such as risk tolerance, level of uncertainty surrounding the information and evaluation, timing, and finding additional information that will help confirm or dispute the initial unexpected information. Depending upon how evaluators/decision makers take those factors into account when assessing unexpected information may lead to better or worse outcomes.

The systematic evaluation part of the model has three critical elements: (1) the distance between perceived or anticipated *opportunity* from the unexpected information and the *reliability of the evaluation* of the unexpected information (in the middle), (2) the general *evaluation process* from "gut feel" to a firmer belief about the evaluation, and (3) the *factors* that may influence the process of evaluation. Those elements also determine the extent to which the information used in making decisions is weighted internally or externally.

The result of evaluation could take on at least three outcomes or decisions of whether to pursue an opportunity. First, when the unexpected information is evaluated in the context of both internal and external factors, when the evaluator/decision makers are not "swayed" too strongly by any of those sources, the evaluation is "balanced" and the outcome may well be an opportunity that the decision maker leverages when competitors do not.

In the second situation, the decision maker notices unexpected information but mostly because others point it out and suggest that there is a way to leverage it. The decision maker then essentially follows the herd to try and take advantage of the unusual information, resulting in what might be called a "herd" outcome. In this case, there is no competitive advantage to the organization because a herd of organizations is trying to leverage the information.

Finally, internal decision makers may be pressured from sources, such as government policy makers (e.g., Vietnam's Ministry of Finance or the U.S. Treasury during the financial crisis) to act. In this case, the organization may act on unexpected information without thoroughly considering external factors or repercussions. During the 2008 financial crisis, for example, large U.S. banks were forced to take sell toxic assets to the U.S. government, which affected their leverage ratios; most ultimately and quickly repaid the money. Unexpected information, evaluated "for them," and the outcome was not necessarily in their favor. This "do it my way" approach is less common but does exist.

Creating Unintended Value (F)

The ability to recognize and evaluate unexpected information is not valuable in itself. To be a competitive advantage, the assessment must yield value and action: the unintended value is thus a critical part of the process. Whether it results in solving an existing or not-yet-tackled problem, finding an opportunity, or generating new ideas for future use, the use of serendipity (as an ability) must be that individuals and the organization as a whole can leverage it to create value. The manufacturing firm executives, for example, realized that by responding to a request for just one sample product, they ended up with an "unexpected customer" that could become major part of the firm's business. Since the orders (and revenue) were not anticipated in the current fiscal year plan, the firm has decided to incur premium labor (overtime) to fill the demand, with the expectation later of increasing the price point for the products. Unexpected information/request created an initial problem (finding a way to fill orders), but ultimately became an opportunity.

WHAT NEXT?

The reaction of managers to the idea of "watching for" serendipity has been mixed—most say they understand the concept immediately, once they move beyond initial skepticism or even outright laughter ("how can you use something so unpredictable?"). Others say, "of course, it happens all the time." Some have embraced the idea of actively being open to serendipity and looking for ways to use it. As we mentioned, one firm's senior executives who began to track unexpected information and notice how, if at all, it could take advantage of it, found at least six cases of "serendipity gained" during their first two months of looking for it. As they described the incidents, it became clear that they experienced what they referred to as different types (i.e., people and process based), but they also experienced all three forms of serendipity: Type I (looking for a solution to A but finding a solution from an unexpected source); Type II (looking for a solution to problem A but discovering something completely unexpected that, in turn, led to an opportunity and solution to an, as yet, unidentified problem); and Type III (finding something unexpected and unsought that later turned into an idea for an improved product). Although the executives did not categorize the events as being "different types of serendipity," they recognized the value of noticing and being aware of unexpected information, whereas they had not before their CEO presented the idea to them. As they have begun to calculate the economic impact, their skepticism about the rather fuzzy notion has dissipated.

This small example of the application and use of serendipity, or the ability to notice, evaluate, and create value from unexpected information, is a first step for both managers and scholars to learn more about it. As organizations seek new ways to improve performance, and as the existing techniques (e.g., lean manufacturing) become widespread, firms will look for avenues that are less tapped and more difficult to execute well, such as using creativity and innovation, insight, and serendipity. Being an early tester, if not an early adapter, may help some of them move into the lead.

NOTES

1. Van Andel, Pek. 1992. "Serendipity; Expect also the Unexpected," *Creativity and Innovation Management* 1(1): 20–32.

2. Barber, B. and Renee C. Fox. 1958. "The Case of the Floppy-Eared Rabbits: An Instance of Serendipity Gained and Serendipity Lost," *American Journal of Sociology* 64(2): 128–136; Custers, Ruud and Henk Aarts. 2010. "The Unconscious Will: How the Pursuit of Goals Operates Outside of Conscious Awareness," *Science* 329, July 2: 47–50; Peterson, Gail B. 2004. "A Day of Great Illumination: B. F. Skinner's Discovery of Shaping," *Journal of Experimental Analysis of Behavior* 82(3): 317–328; Roberts, Royston M. 1998. *Serendipity: Accidental Discoveries in Science.* New York: John Wiley & Sons.

3. Taleb, Nassim N. 2007. *The Black Swan. The Impact of the Highly Impossible.* New York: Random House; Kirzner, I. 1979. *Perception, Opportunity, and Profit.* Chicago: University of Chicago Press.

4. Delcourt, Marcia A. B. 2003. "Five Ingredients for Success: Two Case Studies of Advocacy at the State Level," *Gifted Child Quarterly* 47(1): 26–47.

5. Foster, Allen and Nigel Ford. 2003. "Serendipity and Information Seeking: An Empirical Study," *Journal of Documentation* 59(3): 321–340; LeClerc, Amanda. 2010. "Seeking Serendipity: The Inspiration Hunt of a Creative Professional," *Faculty of Information Quarterly* 2(3) May/June: 1–8; Nutefall, Jennifer E. and Phyllis Mentzell Ryder. 2010. "The Serendipitous Research Process," *Journal of Academic Librarianship* 36(3): 228–234.

6. Betsworth, Deborah G. and Jo-Ida C. Hansen. 1996. "The Categorization of Serendipitous Career Development Events," *Journal of Career Assessment* 4(1): 91–98; Diaz de Chumaceiro, Cora L. 2004. "Serendipity and Pseudoserendipity in Career Paths of Successful Women: Orchestra Conductors," *Creativity Research Journal* 16(2 and 3): 345–356.

7. Brown, Stephen. 2005. "Science, Serendipity, and Contemporary Marketing Condition," *European Journal of Marketing* 39(11/12): 1229–1234; Dew, Nicholas. 2009. "Serendipity in Entrepreneurship," *Organizational Studies* 30: 735; Pina e Cunha, Miguel, Stewart R. Clegg, and Sandro Mendoca. 2010. "On Serendipity and Organizing," *European Management Journal* 28: 319–330; Svensson, Goran and Greg Wood. 2005. "The Serendipity of Leadership Effectiveness in Management and Business Practices," *Management Decision* 43(7/8): 1001–1009; Van Andel, 1992.

8. Collins, Jim and Morten T. Hansen. 2011. *Great by Choice: Uncertainty, Chaos, and Luck—Why Some Thrive Despite Them All.* New York: HarperBusiness.

9. Barber and Fox, 1958.

10. Barber and Fox, 1958.

11. Van Andel, 1992.

12. Hauser, Stephen L. 2008. "Translational Research for a New Administration: What Sort of Change to Believe In?" *American Neurological Association* 64(4): A5–A6.

13. Brown, 2005.

14. Dew, 2009.

15. Sarasvathy, Saras D. 2007. *Effectuation: Elements of Entrepreneurial Expertise.* Cheltenham: Routledge.

16. Meyer, Klaus and Ane Skak. 2002. "Networks, Serendipity and SME Entry into Eastern Europe," *European Management Journal* 20(2): 179–188.

17. Ibid.

18. Collins and Hansen, 2011.

19. Graebner, Melissa, E. 2004. "Momentum and Serendipity: How Acquired Leaders Create Value in the Integration of Technology Firms," *Strategic Management Journal* 25: 752.

20. Nonaka, Ikujiro. 1991. "The Knowledge Creating Company," *Harvard Business Review* 69(6): 94.

21. Taleb, 2007.

22. Hauser, 2008.

23. Cunha et al., 2010.

24. Brown, 2005; Van Andel, Pek and Daniele Bourcier. 2002. "Serendipity and Abduction in Proofs, Presumptions, and Emerging Laws," *Studies in Fuzziness and Soft Computing* 94:273–286.

25. De Rond, M. 2005. "The Structure of Serendipity," Cambridge Judge Business School Working Paper; Gaglio, C. M. and J. A. Katz. 2001. "The Psychological Basis of Opportunity Identification: Entrepreneurial Alertness," *Small Business Economics* 16(2): 95–111; Hafner, Katie. 2010. "Think the Answer's Clear? Look Again." *New York Times,* August 31: D1, 4; Kirzner, 1979.

26. Brown, 2005; De Rond, 2005.

27. Barber and Fox, 1958.

28. Garcia, Pio. 2009. "Discovery by Serendipity: A New Context for an Old Riddle," *Foundations of Chemistry* 11: 33–42.

29. Dew, 2009.

30. Dew, 2009.

31. Dew, 2009.

32. De Rond, 2005.

33. Van Andel and Bourcier, 2002.

34. Cunha et al., 2010; De Rond, 2005; Gaglio and Katz, 2001; Hafner, 2010; Kaish, S. and B. Gilad. 1991. "Characteristics of Opportunities Search of Entrepreneurs versus Executives: Sources, Interests, General Alertness," *Journal of Business Venturing* 6(1): 46–61; Kirzner, 1979.

35. Foster and Ford, 2003.

36. Cunha et al., 2010; De Rond, 2005; Roberts, 1998.

37. Christakis, Nicholas and James Fowler. 2009. *Connected: The Surprising Power of Social Networks and How They Shape Our Lives.* New York: Little, Brown.

38. Cunha et al., 2010: 325.

39. Cunha et al., 2010: 319–330; De Rond, 2005; Mendoca, Sandro, Miguel Pina e Cunha, and Stewart R. Clegg. 2008. *Unsought Innovation: Serendipity in Organizations.* Paper presented at the Entrepreneurship and Innovation—Organizations, Institutions, Systems and Regions Conference, Copenhagen, CBS, June 17–20.

40. De Rond, 2005.

41. Hauser, 2008.

42. Hagel et al., 2010.

43. Cunha et al., 2010: 324.

44. Cunha et al., 2010; Mendoca et al., 2008.

45. Ferguson, as cited in De Rond, 2005: 21.

46. Dew, 2009: 735.

47. De Rond, 2005; Mendoca et al., 2008.

48. Mendoca et al., 2008.

49. Cunha et al., 2010: 327.

50. Danzico, Liz. 2010. "The Design of Serendipity Is Not by Chance," *Interactions,* September + October: 16–18; Mendoca et al., 2008.

51. Cunha et al., 2010: 326.

52. De Rond, 2005: 18.

53. Brown, 2005.

54. Roberts, 1998.

55. Cunha et al., 2010; Delcourt, 2003; Diaz de Chumaceiro, 2004; Williams, Elizabeth Nutt, Elvie Soeprapto, Kathy Like, Pegah Touradji, Shirley Hess, and

Clara E. Hill. 1998. "Perceptions of Serendipity: Career Paths of Prominent Academic Women in Counseling Psychology," *Journal of Counseling Psychology* 45(4): 379–389.

56. Betsworth and Hansen, 1996; Dew, 2009; Hagel et al., 2010; McCay-Peet, Lori and Elaine G. Toms. 2010. "The Process of Serendipity in Knowledge Work," Association for Computing Machinery, Information Interaction in Context Symposium, August; Mendoca et al., 2008.

57. Diaz de Chumaceiro, 2004.

58. Gaglio and Katz, 2001.

59. Kirzner, 1979.

60. Gaglio and Katz, 2001: 97.

61. Smawley, R. B. 1965. "Serendipity: Finding the Unsought," *Journal of Educational Research* 59(5): 177–178.

62. Roberts, 1998.

63. Williams et al., 1998.

64. Van Andel, Pek. 1994. "Anatomy of the Unsought Finding. Serendipity: Origin, History, Domains, Traditions, Appearances, Patterns and Programmability," *British Journal for the Philosophy of Science* 45(2): 631–648.

65. Dew, 2009; Gaglio and Katz, 2001.

66. Brown, 2005: 1232.

67. Brown, 2005; Carter, Bernie. 2006. "'One Expertise among Many'—Working Appreciatively to Make Miracles Instead of Finding Problems: Using Appreciative Inquiry as a Way of Reframing Research," *Journal of Research in Nursing* 11(1), 48–63; Cunha et al., 2010; Dew, 2009; Diaz de Chumaceiro, 2004; Garcia, 2009; Miyazaki, K. 1999. "Building Technology Competencies in Japanese Firms." *Research Technology Management* 42(5): 39–45; Williams et al., 1998.

68. Kirzner, 1979.

69. Cunha et al., 2010: 323.

70. Mendoca et al., 2008.

71. Merton, Robert K. and Elinor Barber. 2004. *The Travels and Adventures of Serendipity: A Study in Sociological Semantics and the Sociology of Science.* Princeton, NJ: Princeton University Press.

72. Busenitz, L. W., 1996. "Research on Entrepreneurial Alertness," *Journal of Small Business Management* 34(4), 35–44.

73. Barber and Fox, 1958; Betsworth and Hansen, 1996; Williams et al., 1998.

74. Betsworth and Hansen, 1996.

75. Gaglio and Katz, 2001.

76. Barber and Fox, 1958.

77. Barber and Fox, 1958.

78. Barber and Fox, 1958: 131.

79. Cunha et al., 2010.

80. Mendoca et al., 2008; Lawley, James and Penny Tompkins. 2008. "Maximising Serendipity: The Art of Recognizing and Fostering Potential—A Systematic Approach to Change," *The Clean Collection,* June, http://www.cleanlanguage.co.uk/articles/articles/224/1/Maximising-Serendipity/Page1.html.

81. Mendoca et al., 2008.

82. Gaglio and Katz, 2001.

83. Cunha et al., 2010; De Rond, 2005; Mendoca et al., 2008.

84. Van Andel and Bourcier, 2002; De Rond, 2005: 3.

85. Gaglio and Katz, 2001; Lawley and Tompkins, 2008.

86. Mendoca et al., 2008.

87. Cunha et al., 2010.

88. Gaglio and Katz, 2001; Lawley and Tompkins, 2008.

89. Lawley and Tompkins, 2008.

90. Gaglio and Katz, 2001.

91. Gaglio and Katz, 2001.

92. Krumboltz, John D. 1998. "Serendipity Is Not Serendipitous," *Journal of Counseling Psychology* 45(4): 390–392.

93. De Rond, 2005; Gaglio and Katz, 2001; Kirzner, 1979.

94. Barber and Fox, 1958; Brown, 2005; Van Andel and Bourcier, 2002.

95. Dew, 2009; Diaz, 2004; Gaglio and Katz, 2001; Kirzner, 1979.

96. Cunha et al., 2010; Danzico, 2010; De Rond, 2005; Hauser, 2008; Mendoca et al., 2008.

97. Gaglio and Katz, 2001.

98. Brown, 2005; Carter, 2006; Cunha et al., 2010, Merton and Barber, 2004.

99. Mendoca et al., 2008.

100. Gaglio and Katz, 2001.

101. Barber and Fox, 1958.

Chapter 9

The Role of Supply Chain Management in Corporate Strategy

James S. Keebler

WHAT IS SUPPLY CHAIN MANAGEMENT?

In a *Harvard Business Review* article published in 1958, Jay Forrester introduced a theory of management that recognized the integrated, interdependent nature of organizational relationships in distribution channels.[1] He pointed out that system dynamics can influence the activities of various business functions and their impact on production and distribution performance. Forrester stated that "there will come general recognition of the advantage enjoyed by the pioneering management who have been the first to improve their understanding of the interrelationships between separate company functions and between the company and its markets, its industry, and the national economy" (p. 52). Thus, the foundation was laid for key strategic management issues and the dynamics of factors associated with what we today call supply chain management (SCM).

In the early 1980s, management attention to the functions of materials management, production, transportation, and warehousing was driven by two significant conditions: opportunities for cost reduction provided by deregulation of transportation, and the oppressively high cost of capital to fund inventories (the prime rate was 20% in 1980). Until the concept of total quality management (TQM) was understood and commonly imbedded in the 1990s, a total systems approach to multiple-company materials, information, and cash flows could not be realized. The commonly used terms of operations management and logistics management began to give way to SCM as a newer, broader perspective for corporate management. The term SCM became a hot topic in the business press and the academic literature by the year 2000. Specific drivers of top management interest in SCM included global sourcing, international markets, growing emphasis on time—and quality—based competition, and a need for stronger, more flexible relationships with key customers and suppliers to mitigate environmental uncertainties. An increasing number of firms began outsourcing noncore activities to improve their return on assets, to give them control, through effective relationships, without the burden of ownership.

In 2001, the *Journal of Business Logistics* published an article "Defining Supply Chain Management."[2] This contribution summarized the existing definitions and supporting constructs of SCM into a framework that produced a robust conceptual model and a unified definition of SCM. Supply chains were defined as the companies involved in the upstream and downstream flows of products, services, finances, and information from initial supplier to ultimate customer. A supply chain orientation (SCO) is the recognition by an organization of the systemic, strategic implications of the activities involved in managing the various flows in a supply chain to satisfy an ultimate customer of that supply chain. This SCO is necessary regardless of the organization's position within the supply chain. SCM is simply the implementation of the SCO, defined as "the systemic, strategic coordination of the traditional business functions within a particular company and across businesses within the supply chain, for the purposes of improving the long-term performance of the individual companies and the supply chain as a whole" (p. 18).

THE INPUT/OUTPUT MODEL
OF THE FIRM, EXPANDED

A simple model of the single firm would require an estimation of its outputs so that the firm can establish the capacities necessary and the inputs required to produce and provide the contemplated outputs. The firm must also add some value in the conversion or transformation process to justify the price paid by its customers, which includes their profit. Figure 9.1 portrays this input/output process.

The fundamental element of a supply chain, then, is the single firm, which both buys from a supplier and sells to a customer. The focal firm's buying activity establishes a linkage to the supplier's selling activity and the focal firm's selling activity links to the customer's buying activity. Thus, the linkages formed by a single firm in a supply chain include at

Figure 9.1
Basic Model of the Firm

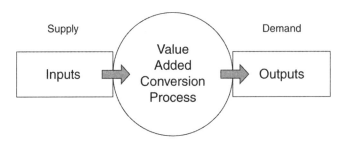

Goal: Balance Demand and Supply,
Manage Flows and Costs

least two other firms. To achieve the proper balance in both supply and demand, or inputs and outputs, each firm in the supply chain must, at a minimum, coordinate the activities of its internal functions and those of the triad it has established. An SCO requires a new unit of analysis—multiple firms in the supply chain, to effectively implement SCM (as is illustrated in Figure 9.2).

Each firm must manage the supply side of its operations, including forecasting, aggregate demand planning, master scheduling, material requirements planning, the bill of materials, production planning,

Figure 9.2
Basic Model of Supply Chain

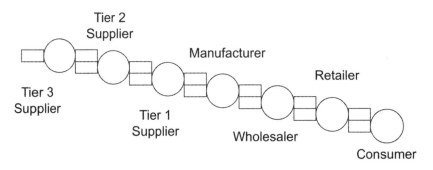

Goal: Consumer Satisfaction,
Profitability for All Firms

purchasing, supplier relationship management, production scheduling, production, and distribution. Each firm must also manage the demand side of its operations, including marketing, development of new products and services, sales, customer service, and customer relationship management. Both supply side and demand side functions must be coordinated to achieve effectiveness and efficiency. Consequently, SCM has two major roles: supply management and demand management. The physical function of a supply chain (supply management) is to convert raw materials into goods, and transport them from one point in the supply chain to the next point and ultimately to the consumer, managing the dimensions of time, cost, quality, and compliance. A market-mediation function (demand management) is to insure that the variety of goods and services reaching the marketplace matches what customers want to buy, how, when, and where they want to acquire them.

KEY FUNCTIONAL ROLES IN SCM

Marketing is the key function for a firm because it answers the following questions: who are, or who should be, our customers; what do they want or need; how, when, and where do they want to acquire those products and services; and why would they want to buy them from us. The firm then has to target whatever market segments they would chose to serve and effectively position their goods and services to create demand for them. The marketing concept is a business philosophy that guides the firm toward customer satisfaction at a profit. It relies on a focus on the customer, and in a supply chain context, on the customer's customer. Profitability can be achieved only by coordinating all marketing activities with the other internal business functions. Marketing is the expectation setter, the promise maker. Other functions are the promise keepers. All functions must be invested in each other's success. All should have a market orientation, which is generating, sharing, and responding to market information. The management of the entire firm depends on the marketing concept and a market orientation to unify a firm's focus, to define the roles of each function, to promote interfunctional coordination, to direct the reengineering of the organizational system, to facilitate interfirm relationships, and to improve business performance.

Sales has traditionally focused on prospecting for, qualifying, approaching, and presenting to new customers, overcoming objections, getting orders, and following-up to insure customer satisfaction. Salespeople are often tasked with objectives to meet short-term forecasts and budget projections, resulting in oscillations in supply chain flows not necessarily supported by actual demand. The sales' role is changing to implement and facilitate cooperative behaviors with customers and internal functions. As a relationship manager with key customers, salespeople are adopting the

roles of customer advocate and consultant. This requires gaining expertise in their firm's internal processes, systems, and capabilities, as well
as those of the customer. The goal for sales is to help the customer better manage and market the customer's business, earning their trust and
loyalty through information sharing, joint planning and decision making,
and focus on the customer's success.

Customer service can be a function or department, a set of order-
processing activities, a strategy, and a business philosophy. In many
firms today, the quality of service experienced by the customer is both
an order qualifier and an order winner. It can be a source of competitive
advantage. Customer service is a set of performance outcomes that deliver customer value. Since not all customers are equal, criteria must be
established to segment customers so that the best service can be delivered to the most valued customers. By identifying unprofitable customers based on cost to serve, their behaviors can be managed to achieve a
profitable relationship, or they can be eliminated, freeing up scarce resources to apply to profitable customers. Since customers buy benefits
and satisfaction, increasing their perceived benefits and/or decreasing
the customer's cost will enhance their value of the relationship with the
firm. Increasingly important is the quality of the customer-perceived interface, which includes product and service availability and convenience,
as well as responsiveness and reliability. A goal for every firm is to make
it easy for their customers to do business with them, to be accessible, responsive, flexible, and reliable.

Research and development (R&D), often referred to as new products'
development, is a critical strategic function of the firm. Inputs include
people, information, ideas, equipment, facilities, funds, and time. Outputs include proposals, research, testing, patents, process technologies,
publications, cost reductions, product improvements, and new products.
These new products might include breakthrough products; "it's new for
us" products; new, improved or next-generation products; line-extension
products; or repackaged, repositioned, or recycled products. The consequences of R&D include survival, risk abatement, capital avoidance,
faster time to market, increased market share, and revenue and profit improvements. Traditionally, R&D has developed and controlled intellectual
properties, "sold" services to internal clients, interfaced with government, explored new markets, integrated TQM in all functions and processes, and managed the timing of new product introductions. The cost
at the new product design stage is usually less than 10 percent of the total
development costs, but the decisions made in the design stage affect between 60 and 80 percent of the total development costs. The new product
development process from idea generation to commercialization must be
coordinated internally with marketing, engineering, manufacturing, purchasing, and logistics to insure that the decisions at the design stage are

compatible with current systems and technologies, both internal to the firm and with customers and suppliers.

Production is a function that creates significant added value. It might involve manufacturing, assembly, creating assortments, or merchandising, depending on the product and the firm's position in the supply chain. The production plan and schedule directs the what, when, where of production. In the last 100 years, U.S. production has evolved from craft production to mass production, to lean production to supply chain production. Craft production occurred in the pre-industrial age. Highly skilled workers using simple and flexible tools made exactly what the customer asked for, one item at a time, and accommodated a high amount of variability in raw materials. It was slow, but it was tailored to unique customer requirements. Mass production occurred in the early 20th century to reduce the time and costs of production. It produced standardized products using inflexible machines and semiskilled labor, processing big batches of work at one time, preproducing large inventories in anticipation of demand. Inventories were also used as buffers between machines, which could not handle variability in inputs or stop processing; therefore, defects were handled at the end of the production process. Lean production started to take hold in the United States in the 1970s to provide flexibility for constantly changing markets. It used multiskilled workers and highly flexible machines and emphasized quality at the source. Defects were caught up front or eliminated entirely by improved supplier processes, facilitating just-in-time production and constant replenishment based on demand. Supply chain production involves dispersed or tiered production, where each tier provides subassemblies to downstream customers, the final tier completing all assemblies in the end product. Utilizing postponement, or delayed differentiation, at the final assembly point, some customization can be included in the final product to tailor the product to unique customer requirements, providing make-to-order capability. This is illustrated in Figure 9.3.

Purchasing has traditionally had a tactical emphasis on cost reductions, shorter lead times, quality improvements, and supply management. The supply chain role for purchasing includes establishing and managing long-term supplier relationships, creating access to product and process technologies, and supplier investments through these more strategic relationships. Purchasing now also coordinates with suppliers the demand management function of the firm by involving suppliers in more strategic, joint planning and decision making, value creation, and engineering activities. Now decisions can be made about which firm does a particular kind of work, where this firm should be placed in the supply chain, and how costs and benefits will be shared. Outsourcing of noncore activities to contract manufacturers and third parties can also be planned and managed, better understanding the "make or buy" decision with

Figure 9.3
Supply Chain Production

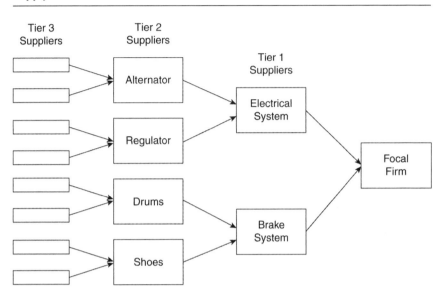

the realization that control does not require ownership. Assets will move to the firms with the lower cost of capital. Collaborative supply chain relationships that are mutual, equal, and perhaps exclusive, are being established.

Logistics is a critical supply chain function focused on planning for and managing the stocks and flows of goods and related information. Major elements include network design, transportation, warehousing, inventory management, order processing, and regulatory compliance. A key decision for any firm is to set the targeted levels of service to be provided and the targeted levels of cost to be incurred by its logistics capabilities for various product/customer segments. Plant and warehouse missions, locations, and capacities are established to service the market demands within acceptable cycle times and costs. Transportation-mode choices are made based on product characteristics, product-demand rates, lead times, and cost. Management of inventory investments in raw materials, work in process, finished goods, and returns has benefitted from the integration of information systems up the supply chain from point-of-sale captured data. Firms are working together to replace inventory with information through more precise scheduling of upstream flows to meet actual demand. Outsourcing of logistics operations requires close coordination with third-party logistics providers and has become a primary cause of increased asset productivity.

STRATEGY ISSUES IN SCM

There are basically three levels of strategy for most firms—corporate strategy, business unit strategy, and product-market segment strategy. As is illustrated in Figure 9.4, the primary corporate strategy is to grow the business, through market penetration, market development, new product/service development, and acquisition or merger. These are the only ways a business can grow.

Sometimes an overly ambitious growth strategy destabilizes the organization when it finds itself doing too much, too quickly, necessitating a change in corporate strategy to stabilize the firm by ceasing the growth and reclaiming control, consolidating its gains as it catches up with itself. Periodically, management recognizes that it has attempted to grow the firm in ways inconsistent with its capability or present desire, and elects then to pursue a corporate strategy of retrenchment, abandoning unsuccessful lines of business or markets. Each of these three corporate strategies—to grow, stabilize, or retrench—has very different ripple impacts on its supply chain.

Larger firms establish various strategic business units (SBUs) under a corporate umbrella. Each of these SBUs serves a unique set of products, a homogeneous set of markets, has a limited number of related technologies

Figure 9.4
Only Four Ways to Grow

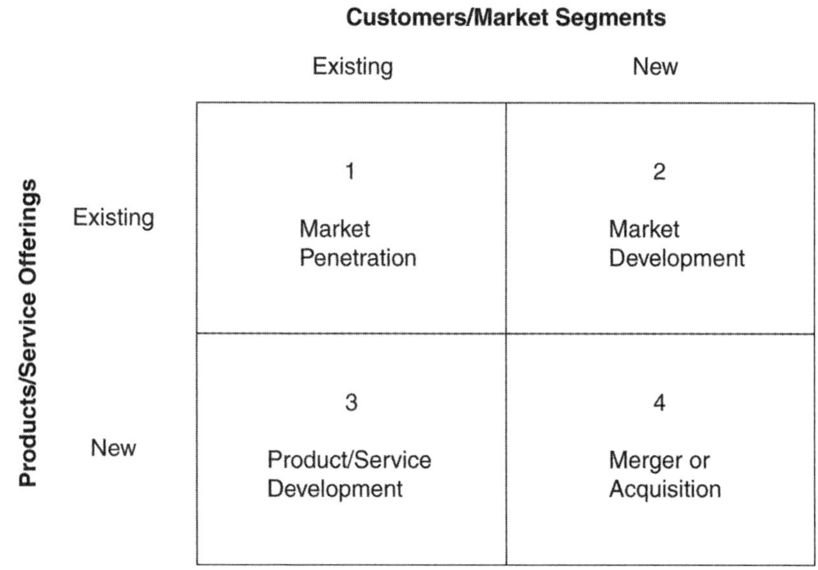

		Customers/Market Segments	
		Existing	New
Products/Service Offerings	Existing	1 Market Penetration	2 Market Development
	New	3 Product/Service Development	4 Merger or Acquisition

with other SBUs, and is responsible for its own profitability. There are basically three kinds of business unit strategies—low cost, differentiated, or focused. Low-cost producers and low-cost providers compete on their ability to be more efficient than existing competitors, and create this barrier to market entry by potential competitors. This works well for standardized products and commodities where consumers cannot discern a distinctive, superior advantage across competitive choices they have. The differentiated strategy is used by firms who compete on the ability to offer something special and unique with their product or service, allowing them the opportunity to avoid competing solely on cost. Highly branded items, trademarked and patented items, and innovative products and services can be successfully marketed as differentiated items. A focused strategy is used by business units that zero in on a specific product-market segment, and is a niche strategy, seeking to dominate, based on a combination of differentiation and cost leadership, a particular market segment. Gerber Baby Food is an example of a focused business unit strategy. Recently, the traditional labels of low cost, differentiated, and focused strategies have been replaced in the literature by the terms operational excellence, product leadership, and customer intimate strategies, respectively, as the "new and improved" terminology.

Product-market segment strategies, found as subsets to the business unit strategies, tend to follow the description of the product life cycles. The four product-market segment strategies are build, hold, harvest, and divest. The build strategy drives and accompanies the introduction and growth period of new product and service introduction. The hold strategy accompanies the maturity stage of the product life cycle, when firms create line extensions and proliferate stock keeping units (SKUs) associated with the product category. The hold strategy might also include actions to repackage or reposition the product. The harvest strategy accompanies the late maturity stage of the product life cycle, with a decision to reduce promotional support and maximize profits while sales volume is still significant. The divest strategy recognizes that the decline stage of the product life cycle has been realized, promoting thoughtful decisions on discontinuing the product at its end of life, or to sell it off while it still has some value.

The focus and consistency of strategy is important. Picking a specific SBU strategy and sticking with it precludes confusion with internal functions and trading partners. Unfortunately, many multiple-SBU corporations rely on centralized logistics functions whose capabilities and culture are asked to support conflicting strategies, such as low cost and differentiated, simultaneously. Not much research has been conducted on strategy conflicts between the sourcing side of the firm and the fulfillment side of the firm, for example, having a low-cost purchasing strategy and a differentiated fulfillment strategy. Since customers select suppliers based on a predominant strategy consistent with their own strategy, it is likely that the consumer or last reseller in the supply chain is best positioned to set the guiding strategy for the supply chain.

Culture plays a critical role in strategy. Cultural norms, core values, and guiding principles must support the chosen strategy. Recognition and reward systems are important in supporting behaviors consistent with the chosen strategy. For example, a recognition and rewards system that does not encourage functional interdependence and collaboration will not support a product leadership or customer intimate strategy. The strategic goals and culture of the organization must be aligned to achieve success.

INTERFUNCTIONAL COORDINATION IS ESSENTIAL

Interfunctional coordination can be defined as the cooperation of the various internal business functions to achieve the overall goals of the firm and insure its responsiveness to environmental changes. To achieve an acceptable degree of interaction and collaboration among the specialized functions of the firm, Mintzberg proposed six basic coordinating functions:[3]

1. Mutual adjustment: the process of informal communication in which people interact with one another to coordinate.
2. Direct supervision: one person coordinates by giving orders to others.
3. Standardization of work processes: direct specification of the content of the work, and the procedures to be followed in order to tightly control different people.
4. Standardization of outputs: specification of what is to be done (i.e., the results of the coordination) so that interfaces between jobs are predetermined.
5. Standardization of skills: loose coordination of people through education on a common body of knowledge and a set of skills that are subsequently applied to work.
6. Standardization of norms: coordination of people through a common set of beliefs.

To these three different dimensions of coordination: (1) cooperative arrangements (mutual adjustment), (2) management controls (direct supervision), and (3) standardization (standardization of work processes, outputs, skills, and norms), other authors would add the additional dimensions of (4) functional expertise and (5) organizational structure.[4]

Interaction and collaboration positively influence a firm's performance as they establish cooperative arrangements and share resources across functions. Management controls can be best achieved when the integrating managers elicit, receive, and strongly consider cross-functional team members' inputs to the decision-making process, which they coordinate. Planning systems and performance control systems are used to standardize outputs, since they predetermine the intended outcomes. Training and education become significant activities in the standardization of skills. Standardization of norms relies on the marketing concept and an SCO, along with the existing culture of the organization. A unified policy, and an aligned recognition and reward system, governing the activities of supply chain participants, which instills a spirit or philosophy of collaboration in the culture becomes the most important factor for success of interfunctional coordination. Although cross-functional coordination is a must, the need for in-depth functional expertise should not be ignored. Decisions made solely in functional silo structures must be avoided. An ideal organizational structure for coordination within a firm must support an internally integrated process for the seamless flows of information, products, services, and finances. The firm's planning and decision making should be organized around key processes, such as planning, sourcing, production, and fulfillment.

INTERFIRM COLLABORATION ON NONCORE COMPETENCY FUNCTIONS (OUTSOURCING)

For every supply chain, there are basic functions that have to be done no matter which firm does them. These supply chain functions include: design, make, brand, price, promote, buy, sell, stock, display, deliver, finance, and manage risk and the relationship with the ultimate customer. Who should perform these functions in any particular supply chain? An important point is that no one company has to manage all these functions. In the early 1900s, Ford Motor Company attempted to perform all the supply chain functions for the purpose of keeping control of all operations. Ford owned the mines that produced the ore that moved on Ford Motor Company ships to Ford steel mills, where Ford steel was used to make Ford automobiles that were sold through Ford dealerships. The huge costs of capital for such vertical integration caused the company to rethink how to balance the need to control operations with the need to manage risk. Today, Ford prefers to integrate based on information sharing, not on asset ownership. Companies are constantly evaluating the questions, What should we do ourselves, and What should we allow someone else to do for us? If the company cannot do something cheaper than someone else, they must ask themselves if the function is a core competency. A core competency is something the firm does well that gives them a competitive advantage in the marketplace. Not everything done well, however, is a core competency. For example, being really good at running the company cafeteria does not give the firm a competitive advantage, and is, therefore, not a core competency. A core competency is something rare, valuable, hard to imitate, and not substitutable. Even though a function might be cheaper to outsource, if it is a core competency, it should not be outsourced.

What is core? This varies for each company in the supply chain. The point is that noncore functions can be shifted to other firms in the supply chain. SCM, then, becomes a great alternative to vertical integration. An example of a firm that recognized its core competency is an American company, who is the number two manufacturer in the world of a particular type of electronics product, yet doesn't make any products. Kodak realized its core competencies were in R&D, estimating demand, and managing the product life cycle of its products. Over a five-year period, it outsourced its production function to five manufacturing subcontractors, its delivery function to three global third-party logistics providers, and its financing function to an outside banking consortium. The results were a significant reduction in per-unit manufacturing costs, significant reduction in its logistics costs, and a substantial savings in financing inventories and operations.

Interfirm collaboration is based on several antecedents: cooperative norms, information sharing, trust, respect, mutuality, conflict-resolution mechanisms, reward sharing, and an interdependence that sustains and enhances the relationship. Consequences include risk reduction, benefits from shared managerial, physical, technological, and financial resources, and improved supply chain competitive advantage. Establishing and maintaining effective supply chain relationships can itself become a core competency. This will become apparent as more and more "virtual" organizations develop.

STAGES OF SUPPLY CHAIN MANAGEMENT

Not all supply chains are equal. Not all companies in a supply chain are equal. Thinking strategically, a supply chain executive might ask: "At what level of competence, or what stage of supply chain maturation, are we? What level or stage should we aspire to achieve?" Firms do have a strategic choice, but they must first understand where they are, and then understand what they must do to transition to a more desirable stage. Figure 9.5 portrays a seven-stage model of SCM based upon the increased degree of complexity a firm manages and the degree of integration it has achieved with trading partners. The first three of these stages are within the capability of a single firm, where autonomy and independence are preferred. The fourth stage, partner driven, begins to require collaboration, integration, and interdependence, which dramatically increase with the last three stages.

Figure 9.5
Supply Chain Stages

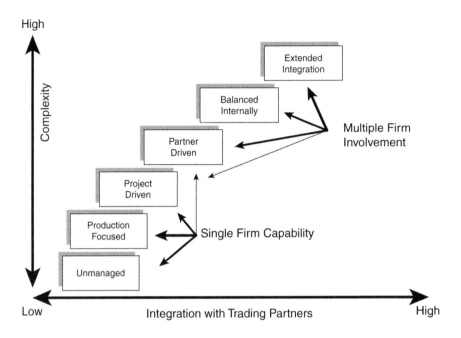

Stage 1: Unmanaged, or Managed by Others

In this stage, functions and firms operate independently. They often lack planning and control activities. Unless they are subcontractors for and are managed by others, these firms often have inefficient and costly operations. The overriding strategy is survival. Management is blind to opportunities and threats. Obviously, firms in this stage are competitively and financially vulnerable.

Stage 2: A Low-Cost Production

Firms in this stage are likely to produce commodity-like consumer products or specialized industrial products; some predictability of demand allows the focus to be on manufacturing excellence. Production-driven synchronization of buying and selling activities prevails. Innovation and customer service are subordinate to standardization and cost control. Logistics activities, inventory management, warehousing and transportation, are suboptimized. Supplier relationships are constantly changing.

Stage 3: Project/Initiative Driven

A series of projects drive incremental internal improvements. Management is primarily results, not process, driven. Alignment and focus are concentrated on achieving short-term goals. An alphabet soup of initiatives may exist simultaneously, such as EDI, TQM, ECR, VMI, MRP, DRP, and ERP. While planning and control systems do exist, the focus is on tactical goals and not on strategic opportunities. Limited coordination with trading partners is found in this stage.

Stage 4: Partner Driven

This stage involves an investment in and responsiveness to meeting key customer, supplier, or third-party logistics requirements. Management sees growth from innovation, services, and speed, in response to customer or supplier requirements. Internal cooperation and a shared focus are driven by the external trading partner. Planning is tied to long-term trading partner needs. Close ties are found with a few key trading partners.

Stage 5: Balanced Internally

Management sees the potential strategic benefits from SCM, and is now focused on market-driven, not production-driven, synchronization. Internal physical and informational flows are integrated. With adequate planning and control systems, significant internal coordination considers the total system of inputs, processes, and outputs. A just-in-time and a make-to-order philosophy is possible due to effective coordination with key immediate customers and suppliers. This stage would be highly desirable for most organizations.

Stage 6: Extended Integration

Management now has a strategic and systemic orientation that drives integration from the customer's customer to the supplier's supplier. The whole organization is actively collaborating with outside trading partners. There is extensive asset and resource sharing between firms. Trust and reciprocity exists with trading partners. Relational, technological, and economic embeddedness provide competitive advantage. More control exists with less ownership. Asset ownership will shift to the firms with the lowest cost of capital. This stage manifests a true SCO in that it is a multifirm system. Multifirm governance structures are established.

Stage 7: Real-Time Connectivity

This stage is mainly aspirational, although the enabling technologies exist today. It is characterized by real-time informational connectivity

Figure 9.6
Characteristics and Strategies of Supply Chain Stages

Supply Chain Stage	Characteristics of Relationships Between Firms within This Stage	Strategies for Firms to Employ to Achieve This Stage
1. Unmanaged or Managed by Others	Subcontractor for another firm. Adherence to requirements. No value engineering.	Opportunistic, temporary relationships. Low cost, or responsive.
2. Production Focused	Internally focused. Optimize manufacturing operations.	Legitimacy, survival. Building correct scale. Efficiency.
3. Project Driven	Change through piecemeal initiatives. Senior functional management sponsor.	Successive suboptimizations of parts of the whole system. Incremental changes.
4. Partner Driven	Responding to important partner. Short-term changes for long-term gains.	Compliance for survival and growth. Shared goals, costs, and benefits.
5. Balanced Internally	Synchronization of inputs and outputs – a process approach. Just-in-time philosophy. Strategic, systemic orientation. Coordination with immediate customers and/or suppliers.	Extensive internal coordination. Elimination of counterproductive behaviors and reward systems. Emphasis on flows, not stocks. Information sharing with trading partners. Make-to-order.
6. Extended Integration	Multifirm trust and cooperation. Shared resources, costs and benefits.	Integration with supply chain flows beyond immediate customers and suppliers.
7. Virtual Network	Information, connectivity and responsiveness. Minimum asset investments.	Real-time, seamless connectivity. Web-based and hollow corporations.

and pipeline visibility for all members of this supply chain. A high level of postponement and customization exists. The focus is on innovation, speed, and flexibility. Enterprise boundaries are blurred. Shared control and success is achieved through connectivity, shared knowledge, and forged capabilities. Both market-driving and market-creation opportunities abound. The supply chain strategies just described are summarized in Figure 9.6.

EIGHT THINGS FIRMS DO THAT DISTINGUISH THEM IN SCM

Firms that aspire to improve their performance through SCM will need to actively focus on these eight initiatives:

1. Manage customer behaviors,
2. Manage product/service offerings,
3. Manage demand, not just the forecast,
4. Manage supply chain flows,

5. Replace assets with information and relationships,
6. Outsource noncore activities (buy versus make),
7. Revamp planning and control systems, and
8. Align recognition and reward systems.

Customers are not all equal. While most firms know who their biggest customers are, they often don't know which customers generate the most profit. They also don't know which ones are unprofitable. Consequently, they can manage customer relationships poorly. The list of active customers should be evaluated annually and segmented based on criteria that differentiate their value to the firm. The segment of highest-value customers should receive the best service. For example, their order lead times could be shorter, their targeted fill rates could be higher, and their deliveries could be made faster than other customer segments. Unfortunately, traditional accounting systems, which rely on period or product costing and cost center allocations, do not provide specific cost information to make evaluations on customer profitability. Activity-based costing (ABC) is needed to be able to associate the cost to serve with the value of service given each customer. ABC involves looking at customer behaviors and the costs associated with serving them. By influencing the customer on what, how much, when, and how they order products and services, the firm can turn unprofitable or marginal customers into profitable ones.

Products and service offerings are not all equal. Just as with customers, the cost to produce and the cost to provide should be evaluated annually using ABC. Most companies will find that a small percentage of its offerings contribute a large share of its profits. Which offerings are unprofitable? Eliminating those or changing the way they are provided to customers to make them profitable will increase overall profitability. As product life cycles and consumer adoption rates dictate strategy changes from build, to hold, to harvest, and to divest, it is important to constantly manage the portfolio of offerings. Most companies learn that by doing less they can earn more, and free up resources to apply to new and more profitable revenue generators.

Forecasting is necessary for most firms, especially those preproducing the independent demand item, or finished good, before orders are received. But forecasting is inexact, and it requires a large investment in buffer inventories. Some firms invest heavily in the forecasting process and the measurement of forecast error, which compares actual demand to forecasted demand. Estimating customer demand to make operating decisions that attempt to balance supply and demand rarely results in zero stock outs and zero safety stocks. However, firms use four methods to attempt to balance supply and demand: (1) change lead times, (2) increase or reduce pricing, (3) build inventory levels, and (4) create production flexibility. If customer demand exceeds current supply, the firm might be able to increase the lead time on that item. The customer can decide to wait, to substitute for something in stock, or search elsewhere. If customer demand is significantly less than current inventory levels for that item, the firm can announce a temporary price reduction, moving future demand forward. It could also announce a temporary price increase, postponing current demand. Building inventory levels, including safety stock, to smooth the effects of both demand and lead-time variability, is a traditional, but expensive method to manage demand and supply imbalances, given production-capacity constraints. Finally, production flexibility, a principle of lean manufacturing, is seen as a solution to demand and supply imbalances. These four methods of managing demand can be used in combination, depending on the level of the firm's interest in utilization of production capacities, safety stock costs, the cost of stock outs, and customer goodwill and loyalty. Managing actual demand is always more important than managing the forecast.

There are numerous flows in the supply chain. These include flows of products, services, cash, and information. Products flow from suppliers through manufacturers, through distributors, through retailers, to final consumers. The flows are triggered by an order from the customer (demand) and flow upstream, or by a previous forecast and flow downstream. These flow in cycles. A retailer will collect product sales' information at the point of sale, or use a reorder point inventory management system, to create orders to send to the distributor. This takes time. The transmission time is very fast if it is electronic, but the time between orders can be days or weeks. The distributor then reviews the orders received, approves them, and assigns them to a shipping location, where the orders are picked, packed, and scheduled to be shipped. This could take hours or days. When the carrier arrives, the order is loaded and transported to the retailer, who receives it into inventory stock or into its retail space. This also takes hours or days. Then the process repeats itself between the distributor and manufacturer, and then again between the manufacturer and its suppliers. When the elapsed times from order to receipt up the tiers of the supply chain are totaled, the overall cycle time is weeks or months. This creates significant, perhaps unnecessary, investments in inventories to cover the lead times and lead-time variability, and also results in out-of-stock and lost sales' opportunities. The entire supply chain flow cycles should be mapped. Process mapping and process reengineering are important tools to reduce cycle times. Sharing information across the supply chain, especially about point of sale, inventory levels, and production schedules, can aid in compressing cycle times significantly, reducing overall cost, and increasing sales and profits.

Assets are expensive. Information is relatively cheap. Significant cost reduction and service improvements can be produced by substituting information for asset investments. The cost of ownership of inventory, plants, equipment, and storage facilities is significant, and to some degree, avoidable. The solution is to use increasingly available and inexpensive information and integrated information technology to reduce investments in expensive assets. Relationships are becoming more important in SCM. Creating and managing relationships with key customers, suppliers, and third-party providers is the very nature of strategic and systemic management of supply chain activities. Governance structures, built through joint planning and decision making and supported by joint investments and shared rewards, are needed for sustainability. Collaboration, connectivity, and integration are essential to improved supply chain performance.

Outsourcing noncore activities is an essential characteristic of SCM. Deciding what is noncore and selecting reliable suppliers to jointly plan the objectives, standards, costs, and shared rewards of successfully outsourced functions is a huge and risky task. It requires committing to a strategic, interdependent relationship. Micro Compact Car AG (MCC), a wholly owned subsidiary of Daimler-Benz, engaged 18 key suppliers in the design and production of the smart car. MCC retains the relationship with the end customer, controls the flow of information, and is able, with little investment, relying on its reliable suppliers, to assemble a customized car in less than five hours, maintaining a two-week lead time from customer order to delivery. This supply chain is based on the proposition of outsourcing noncore activities, and is far superior in performance to any U.S. automotive supply chain. Every firm should examine what functions it could successfully outsource and the implications outsourcing has on its operational and financial performance.

Revamping the planning and control systems to provide alignment and focus throughout the organization will produce significant improvements. It is amazing how little attention the planning function receives in many firms, yet the planning function creates the future of the organization. The last Council of Supply Chain Management Professionals (CSCMP) study on measurement provided the following 10 findings, based on the responses from 355 firms, regarding the overall administration of supply chain measurement:[5]

1. One-quarter of measures captured were considered not accurate;
2. One-fifth of measures captured were not interpreted similarly within the firm;
3. One-third of measures captured were not interpreted similarly between firms;
4. One-fifth of measures captured were not readily understandable to guide actions;
5. Two-fifths of measures captured were not comprehensive;
6. One-fifth of measures captured were not considered cost effective;

7. One-quarter of measures captured were not compatible internally;
8. One-third of measures captured were not compatible between firms;
9. One-quarter of measures captured were not compatible with cash flow measures; and
10. One-quarter of measures captured *encouraged* counterproductive behaviors.

Additionally, the study found there was too much emphasis on efficiency measurement (utilization and productivity) and not enough on effectiveness (performance). Just as every process has a customer, who judges its performance, and should have an "owner," who is responsible for its performance, so, too, do measures have customers and owners. Every measure needs an owner, to care about meeting the needs and expectations of the measure's customer, and *to initiate appropriate improvements in the activities measured.* Any measure lacking either an owner or a customer should be abandoned. Standardized performance reporting should be regularly challenged for need and usefulness, and eliminated where possible. The challenge is not to create more measures, but rather to measure fewer, actionable activities, where customers and owners of the measures can work together to plan the objectives, set the standards for performance, evaluate results, and make improvements. Good administration will eliminate nonproductive measurement activities.

Recognition and reward systems can either motivate or demotivate employees. They should be fair, meaningful, and tied to performance. They can also encourage either appropriate or dysfunctional behaviors. For example, incentivizing customers and rewarding salespeople and for the end-of-quarter, end-of-year sale push that causes spiked workloads and excessive costs in distribution is a practice that is counterproductive. Salespeople, and customers, anticipate the incentives to hold off orders until the end of the period, creating a permanent, unnecessary oscillation in sales that is not directly tied to demand. Experience tells us that people do what gets rewarded. Functional activities should not be rewarded. Instead, cross-functional teams could be rewarded based on the performance of the overall process they manage. Organizations must design and use recognition and reward systems to create alignment and focus on organizational goal and objectives.

NOTES

1. Forester, Jay. W. (1958), "Industrial Dynamics: A Major Breakthrough for Decision Makers," *Harvard Business Review,* Vol. 38 (July/August), pp. 37–66.

2. Mentzer, John T., William DeWitt, James S. Keebler, Soonhong Min, Nancy W. Nix, Carlo D. Smith, and Zach G. Zacharia (2001), "Defining Supply Chain Management," *Journal of Business Logistics,* Vol. 22, No. 2, pp. 1–25.

3. Mintzberg, Henry (1996), "Reading 6.2: The Structuring of Organizations." In H. Mintzberg and J. B. Quinn (Eds.), *The Strategic Process: Concepts, Context, Cases* (3rd Edition), Upper Saddle River, NJ: Prentice Hall.

4. Mentzer, John T. (2004), *Fundamentals of Supply Chain Management, Twelve Drivers of Competitive Advantage*, Thousand Oaks, CA: Sage Publications.

5. Keebler, James S., Karl B. Manrodt, David A. Durtsche, and D. Michael Ledyard (2000), *Keeping Score: Measuring the Value of Logistics in the Supply Chain*, Oak Brook, IL: Council of Supply Chain Management Professionals.

Chapter 10

Employee Engagement and Strategic Management: A Case Study from Palestine

Yara A'sad and
Andrew R. Thomas

Employee engagement as a strategic management tool is the focus of this chapter. In addition to some discussion about the importance employee engagement plays in achieving the strategic goals of the organization—through the creation of a healthy working environment, where everyone can be influential and active in fulfilling bigger objectives—we will discuss a Palestinian firm that recently implemented this approach and succeeded.

This case might fly in the face of recent reports that consistently detail how employees are increasingly disengaged from their jobs. For example, a report by Towers Perrin HR Services titled "Winning Strategies for a Global Workforce" stated that only 14 percent of global workers are highly engaged in their jobs and that managers are mostly at fault for the lack of more significant employee engagement.[1]

We recognize that this level of dissatisfaction may very well be due to the current economic downturn, when companies of all sizes and shapes shed employees in huge numbers after the onset of the global financial and economic crises of late 2008 and early 2009. The employees who remained were often faced with longer hours, more responsibilities, and reduced levels of compensation.

The concept of employee engagement is far more prevalent on the applied side than in the academic literature. The business press and consulting firms have been widely reporting the move across industries that encourage managers to engage their employees beyond the most basic levels of their employment. The belief is simple: more engaged employees are happier, and this translates into greater organizational productivity and a stronger corporate culture. Although this intuitively sounds good, there is not a lot of empirical research to back this up. Nevertheless, as numerous studies consistently report, there is very little doubt that employees around the world are more dissatisfied than satisfied with their current jobs.

"Employee engagement" has emerged in the past decade as a viable strategy for dealing with the unavoidable change and upheaval companies' face. The Gallup Organization's "Q12" survey has become the foundation for seemingly any firm trying to find out the degree of engagement, or lack thereof, that its employees possess.[2] Gallup identified a strong link between levels of employee engagement, leadership effectiveness, and organizational success. An extensive multiyear study involving more than 100,000 employees, in 2,500 functions, and 12 industries revealed a number of specific workplace conditions that provide a direct link to organizational and employee success. Gallup has labeled these factors the "Q12." When present at high levels, these factors are the hallmark of an environment where employees can develop and grow. From this research, Gallup identified the concept of the "engaged workforce." Not surprising, organizations reporting high performance levels also had high levels of employee engagement.

The 12 questions Gallup asks are:

- Do I know what is expected of me at work?
- Do I have the materials and equipment I need to do my work right?
- At work, do I have the opportunity to do what I do best every day?
- In the last seven days, have I received recognition or praise for good work?
- Does my supervisor, or someone at work, seem to care about me as a person?
- Is there someone at work who encourages my development?
- At work, do my opinions seem to count?

- Does the mission/purpose of my organization make me feel like my work is important?
- Are my coworkers committed to doing quality work?
- Do I have a close friend at work?
- In the last six months, have I talked with someone about my progress?
- At work, have I had opportunities to learn and grow?

What is an "engaged worker"? According to Gallup, engaged workers are really the top or "best in class" performers in the organization. They are the employees who contribute, perform, and take a keen interest in doing their best. The impact highly engaged workers can have on an organization is dramatic. Gallup found the following results in organizations with high levels of employee engagement versus those organizations that reported low levels of engagement:

- 50 percent higher levels of employee retention,
- Levels of customer loyalty 56 percent higher than average,
- Reported 38 percent above the average productivity ratings, and
- Returned 27 percent higher profitability than organizations where employees were not highly engaged.[3]

When employees join an organization, they're usually enthusiastic, committed, and ready to be advocates for their new employer. Simply put, they're likely to be highly engaged. But often, that first year on the job is their best. Gallup's research reveals that the longer an employee stays with a company, the less engaged he or she becomes. Yet, although the idea of getting employees to be more engaged is a sound one, the implementation of the notion oftentimes comes up short, as the company's culture is simply not ready.

Evan Smith, vice president and general manager of Hypertherm, a New Hampshire–based designer and manufacturer of advanced metal cutting products, has spoken about how his company keeps employees engaged. Hypertherm is consistently selected as one of the best companies in America to work for. Founded in 1968 in a two-car garage, the company has its roots in building long-term relationships with its 1,000 "associates." Although 32 percent of the firm is employee owned through an ESOP, and profit sharing annually averages 10 to 15 percent, Mr. Smith attributes the strong level of highly engaged employees to a culture that goes beyond compensation. Throughout its four-plus decades, the company has never had a layoff. Although peaks and troughs have inevitably occurred,

Hypertherm has consciously pursued the strategy of reorienting its existing associates to new opportunities. In the spring of 2009, when the company, like so many others, was experiencing a massive slowdown—almost 50 percent from the peak just a year before—Hypertherm ramped up its R&D spending and dedicated substantially more resources to workforce development. In short, Hypertherm has aligned employee engagement with its longstanding corporate culture.[4]

THE TRADITION OF COMMUNITY ORGANIZING IN PALESTINE

Like all other peoples and the places where they live, Palestine is unique. One component that tends to set Palestine apart is the level of community organizing that lies at the core of the culture. The country's chronic political instability that regularly shapes fundamental institutions such as education and human rights, has compelled the Palestinian people to most often turn to the grassroots to solve problems. Unlike in the West, where functioning central governments work to ensure stability and the public good, there has been no such centralized governmental presence throughout most of Palestine's history. Long ago, Palestinians realized that to meet the basic needs of life and beyond, they would depend on their ability to locally organize communities. As Palestine has moved inexorably toward nationhood, the long-missing central government has finally begun to emerge. Dynamic national leaders and, more importantly, national institutions are starting to take hold. Still, community organizing remains at the center of any policy decision and its implementation.

According to the Marin Institute, one leading think tank that focuses on grassroots movements, "Community organizing is a long-term approach where the people affected by an issue are supported in identifying problems and taking action to achieve solutions. The organizer challenges those he or she works with to change the way things are—it is a means of achieving social change through collective action by changing the balance of power. The tactics and strategies employed by the organizer are similar to the processes of leadership including timing the issue, deliberate planning, getting the attention of the populace, framing the issue in terms of the desired solution, and shaping the terms of the decision-making process."[5]

Community organizing brings voices to add collective power and strengthens an issue. It is a key part of an overall strategy to make changes in a community that are widely felt, and that reflects the wishes of the people. This requires the organizer to not only listen and be responsive to the community, but also to help community residents develop the skills necessary to address their own issues in a sustainable manner. At the heart of community organizing are inclusion, ownership, relationship building, and leadership development. Community organizing looks at collective solutions—large numbers of people who engage in solutions that impact even more people. These people usually live in the same neighborhood, town, or block.

Community organizing begins here, with the need to address the local need, through developing the local industry and enhancing the skills of the workforce in order to create firms that are capable of competing locally, growing larger, and entering new markets. In order to grow an industry and develop the capacity of its employees, massive investments are needed. The question remains whether the national economy of Palestine, or the government, which relies on foreign aid to cover its public needs and expenses, will be able to properly fund economic development. Community organizing in Palestine has always been at the forefront of political, economic, and social change. As a centralized government has taken root as a result of the Oslo agreement with the Israelis in 1996, the Palestinian economy became one of the major areas of focus for many community organizers.

ENVIRONMENTAL FACTORS

To better understand the context of community organizing within Palestine, it is necessary to briefly explore environmental factors (economic, political, and social) of the area.

Economic Factors

The Palestinian economy has witnessed many ups and downs, mainly due to the general political situation. GDP growth averaged over 10 percent per year between 1994 and 1999, but slumped following the outbreak of violence in 2000, with the Palestinian economy experiencing one of the worst recessions in modern history. However, GDP has always rebounded when given the chance, increasing by 8.5 percent in 2003 and 6 percent in 2005, reaching the same level as in 1999.[6]

The GDP recorded an increase by about 9 percent during the three quarters of 2010 compared with the same period of 2009. The growth was concentrated in economic activities with the largest share of GDP in agriculture and fishing, construction, wholesale and retail trade, transport, storage and communications, services, and public administration. The construction activity recorded the highest growth rate during that period, by about 36 percent GDP per capita for the Palestinian Territories. This increased by 5 percent during the third quarter of 2010 compared with the same quarter of 2009.[7]

There was a 3 percent increase in the total number of workers during the first three quarters of 2010, compared with same period of 2009. This was due primarily to an increase in the number of workers in the construction industry and services sector in the Palestinian Territories. The unemployment rate during the first three quarters of 2010 reached about 24 percent compared with 25 percent during the same period in 2009. The unemployment rate declined in the West Bank from 17.7 to 17.3 percent and in the Gaza Strip from 38.4 to 37.9 percent. Still, the rate of unemployment is woefully high and a great strain on the Palestinian people.[8]

Regarding trade movement in Palestine (the total exports and imports), there was an increase during 2010 in revenues of the value-added tax related to trade exchange with Israel. In 2010, exports increased by 8 percent compared with 2009, and imports increased by 6 percent compared with 2009.[9]

Prices consumer prices had increased from January to November 2010 by 3.58 percent compared with the same period in 2009 and that resulted in the decline of the purchasing power.[10]

The year 2010 had witnessed additional government reforms in tax collection in line with the reform and development plan that the government has been implementing since 2007. Local revenues (tax and nontax) accounted for about 38 percent of total revenues and that covered part of current expenditures, thus reducing dependence on foreign support to cover the budget.

Government revenues had increased by 17.3 percent during the first three quarters of 2010 compared with the same period in 2009, whereas government expenditures declined by 2.7 percent. In addition, the deficit in the general budget declined by 22.5 percent during the first three quarters of 2010 compared with the same period in 2009.

The industrial sector had witnessed a decline by 6 percent during the first three quarters of 2010 compared with the same period in 2009. The total number of workers in the industrial sector had increased by 2 percent during the first three quarters of 2010 compared with the same period of 2009 (increase by 2.3% in the West Bank and a decrease by 2.4% in the Gaza Strip). Industrial activity constitutes about 13 percent of total GDP.[11]

Political Factors

Due to the political situation in Palestine, local companies face severe export restrictions, not only from the international markets where Palestinian products are viewed as being below standard, but also from Israeli restrictions on borders, which are aimed at weakening the overall Palestinian economy by enforcing harsh restrictions and regulations on the export of Palestinian goods. In addition, many Arab countries include

Palestinian products within the list of Israeli products that all Arab countries boycott.

The combined area of the West Bank and Gaza is small—only 6,020 square kilometers. However, Palestine suffers from various political obstacles caused by Israeli restrictions, including a "separation wall," which is frequently closed, and the difficulty of movement for goods and people within the West Bank and the Gaza Strip.[12] The total population of the Palestinian Territories at mid-2010 was about 4.05 million, 2.51 million in the West Bank and 1.54 million in Gaza Strip. One out of every fifth of participants in the labor force is unemployed in the first quarter of 2010. Most of the population of Palestine is young, with about 57 percent below the age of 20. Declining fertility rates, however, will reduce the relative size of the youngest section of the population, those under 20 years of age.[13]

Social Factors

The Palestinian National Authority was formed after the Gaza-Jericho Agreement, signed in Cairo on May 4, 1994, which created a Palestinian nation that would be governed by the Palestinian National Authority, with restrictions over borders and control of resources.

The Palestinian market is dependent on foreign products. Negative perceptions about the quality of locally manufactured products, accompanied by a lack of awareness about product improvements, led to the weak positioning of local products within the local market.

As a result of this perception there was a call for the improvement of quality and standards of the local production through a monitoring of the manufacturing processes and compliance with international standards. In response, the Palestinian Authority used its legal system to address these issues. Furthermore, and in a call for supporting the local products, the Palestinian Ministry of National Economy initiated a campaign in January, 2010, promoting local products; this was in addition to the boycotting of all Israeli products that are manufactured in settlements established on the Palestinian Territories. This campaign had been adopted to a high degree by all the government departments and by the public as well. The launch of this campaign came in response to the Israeli restrictions imposed on Palestinians.[14]

BIRZEIT PHARMACEUTICAL COMPANY (BPC)

BPC, established in 1974, is Palestine's leading manufacturer of generic medicines, with a working capital of $150,000. Today, its working capital is $50 million. BPC's market is not limited to the Palestinian Territories; the company has a well-established presence in different export markets, mainly, Algeria and East Europe. It continuously invests in its quality, and is able to compete within the national and international market; by the year 2006, BPC was able to establish its first international manufacturing company located in Algeria. BPC seeks continuous development, and is currently in the process of finalizing a new building constructed according to FDA standards, with the goal of producing an oncology product. As of 2010, BPC is the exclusive local Palestinian company that manufactures oncology products.

Factors contributing to the success of BPC include obtaining the latest quality standards certificates such as CGMP (current good manufacturing practices) and the ISO certification for quality systems. In addition, its strong financial position, highly educated and well-trained staff members distributed among the different departments, and a management team with long years of experience and high credibility provide a solid footing for the company.

BPC is one of the major companies that focus on communal and economic development in Palestine. The company invested the capital necessary to establish a financial stock market brokerage company (Lotus Financial Investment Co.), a microfinance bank (Al Rafah Microfinance), an insurance company (Al Takafol Islamic Insurance Co.), a real estate company (Abraj), and several venture capital investments.

BPC's Mission

BPC realizes that the significance of the Palestinian pharmaceutical industry extends far beyond the size of its revenues, and therefore has a vision to be the backbone of the health-care security system in Palestine and the region, through the manufacture of superior-quality products. BPC's efforts and role in supporting the Palestinian community have been diversified; the company views its investment in establishing new companies that can provide work opportunities to the people of Palestine, and that can affect the growth of the national economy, as a communal role.

Since 2005, BPC has shifted its social responsibility vision from the traditional one that focused on supporting health institutes, promoting education by granting scholarships, sponsoring researchers, and supporting cultural events and athletics, into a more directed vision focusing on serving the needs of the community by addressing communal problems that were not touched by the government.

BPC was one of the leading companies initiating unique and innovative corporate social responsibility (CSR) projects, with set focus and a strategic vision, directed through a well-studied plan that focused on spreading awareness about the company, its status, products, investments, growth, and quality. In less than five years the company succeeded in building a solid image within the local market, resulting in increased awareness among Palestinians, numerous requests to visit its facilities, and demand for BPC's products.

Employees

BPC employs 300 people, within its main location in Palestine. However, due to the company's 35 years of growth, BPC decided to enlarge its premises and to bring all employees together under one roof instead of having three branches in one city. This was not welcomed by employees and resulted in dissatisfaction and operational difficulties. As a result, it was difficult to get the company's teams working together, serving the bigger goal of supporting the company's success and mission.

The BPC Employee-Engagement Strategy

One of us (Yara A'sad) was initially approached by BPC to implement a corporate responsibility project, which would serve in building the public image of the company. Once Yara started designing the project, she quickly realized that in order to build an external image, BPC also needed to focus on building its image internally by motivating its employees, getting them to work in teams, and aim toward the bigger goals of the company.

To begin with, she studied the status of BPC's employee culture. Multiple focus group sessions were held across the organization with employees at every level. Further, several one-on-one interviews were conducted, and as a result, she designed a project intended to address the issue.

Since more than 40 percent of the employees reside in rural villages around Ramallah city, we chose the villages that would include groups of more than six people within each village, thereby end up with 10 groups. The goal was to enhance the skills and qualifications of group members by providing around 100 employees with various training sessions, including sessions on the process of working in teams, cooperating and communicating while away from work, communication skills and networking, team building, leadership, proposal writing and budgeting, and time management. The details of the project and its goals were explained to all the teams as follows:

The Company normally spends more than 50,000 dollars annually on communal development projects, and therefore, instead of having BPC PR management design and set the projects of which the company would serve its social responsibility, BPC envisioned acquiring and covering its role in social responsibility by engaging its employees. The company will qualify its personnel, then will request teams to elect a leader, distribute roles of each team member. Team members should meet regularly. Each member should have a role in this project, and after training sessions, the groups should each go to their villages and work on an official proposal to be submitted to a managerial committee, consisting of eight people: three from the top management, three employees that did not participate in the project, and two external people who are not from within the company. The proposals should present a developmental project that groups from each village would like to implement. This should describe the project, its budget, the reason this project is beneficial, and who would benefit from it, of course including the fact of how this project would address the image building of the Company.

A competitive process followed, through which the company awarded $20,000 to the priority project and $10,000 to the second- and third-place finishers. The remaining $20,000 was then distributed among the rest of the seven teams to serve as a motivator and to show gratitude to the people who participated.

The project was implemented over six months, during which all teams were competing, motivated, and challenged. The company realized that by implementing this project, it was enhancing the skills and qualifications of its employees. The next step was to encourage employees to work on developing their home villages, to design and implement development projects that would be announced in their communities, and which would make them proud of their accomplishments. The goal was to unite teams instead of letting them remain distracted by the company's reorganization and to use the new initiatives to promote the company's name throughout the country.

One hundred employees participated in this project, and the rest of the 200 were given the chance to participate in voting for the projects. All employees got the chance to participate in implementing the winning project by attending events and activities in the field and by having each group supervise and implement its own project within its respective village.

After the implementation phase a survey was distributed to the two sets of employees. The first set was for the employees who participated in the project, and the second set targeted the employees who didn't participate. The results reflected on the motivation of the employees, their loyalty and commitment to the company, and the successful achievement of the project's goals.

In addition, awareness about BPC within the community was growing, resulting in a wide coverage for the image of the company all around the country. Market share rose from 18 percent within the local market to 21 percent, mainly due to having consumers request BPC's products by name from their doctors and from the OTC medicines as well.

As a result of the project, employee motivation and productivity were enriched. The employees who participated in the project became more active, more involved in team work, and worked as moderators among those who found it difficult to fit within the newly formed teams in the company. Those who didn't form groups in the first session requested the company to re-implement the same project the following year, thereby allowing new groups to be formed; this encouraged the CEO of the company to announce the sponsorship of the same project for three years. This allowed all employees to participate and be motivated.

As a result of the team-work enhancement, the employees were sharing their thoughts more openly with management, and were more open about their needs; as a result, employees formed a company-sponsored football team as a way for them to promote and build the company's name. The management of BPC, after realizing and acknowledging the effect of the project on its culture, people, and market share, further invested in enhancing its employee engagement by promoting various activities, and enhancing the role of effective monthly meetings for all the members of the company. These meetings encouraged brainstorming and listening sessions, and proved a means through which top management was able to initiate what are known as knowledge management (KM) channels among employees. Finally, the BPC management initiated the establishment of an internal blog that both the employees and the management could use to secure an open communication channel.

LESSONS LEARNED

An employee-engagement approach can help companies to deal with the challenges not only of a business that is running in a regular global environment, but also during a crisis, such as the recent recession, because by establishing trust, the management can unlock more of the knowledge and commitment of individual employees. As Paul Drechsler, CEO of Wates Group, said, "a leader's focus on engagement is even more important during difficult times to motivate, engage and ultimately retain your people." Engagement can enable organizations to retain their employees' support while taking and implementing difficult decisions. Indeed, unlike the experience in previous recessions, many companies have in the past year worked closely and collaboratively with staff to mitigate the effects of scarce credit and collapsing markets on the workforce.

Moreover, despite the effects of the current economic climate, there is an increasing number of young graduates and who have grown up experiencing only good economic conditions. Despite the present recessionary conditions, these young graduates will not be likely to put up with working lives where they are expected to hang their brains and individuality at the door, or buckle down under a command-and-control management style. A less-deferential population is less and less willing to subsume their individuality in any area of their lives. Life is no longer about orders and top-down decisions for the generations that grew up in a world of globalization, openness, creativity, and individual appreciation and spirituality. Therefore, expectations need to be met by the new graduates, who are fresh, enthusiastic, optimistic, and looking forward to work and personal development. In order to get the best out of these graduates, managers need to understand the needs of the new workforce, and to provide them with at least some of those needs in order to absorb more of the talents that can help make the market grow and the economy boom again. As the saying goes, "People join organizations but they leave because of managers."

NOTES

1. John Michael Farrell and Angela Hoon, "What's Your Company's Risk Culture," *Business Week*, May 12, 2009, p. 27.

2. The Gallup Organization introduced the notion of employee engagement in two bestselling books: *First, Break All The Rules: What the World's Greatest Managers Do Differently* (Simon & Schuster, 1999) and *Follow This Path: How the World's Greatest Organizations Drive Growth by Unleashing Human Potential* (Warner Books, 2002).

3. Ibid.

4. Interview with authors, July 13, 2011.

5. Marin Institute Website, http://www.marininstitute.org.

6. Hassouneh, Muhammad and Abu Libdeh, Hasan. "Palestine Investment Conference." Retrieved March 26, 2010, from Presentation Notes Online Website, http://www.scribd.com/doc/25577574/Palestine-Investment-Conference-Bethlehem-28.

7. Palestinian Central Bureau of Statistics: "The Performance of the Palestinian Economy during the year 2010." Retrieved January 22, 2010, from http://www.pcbs.gov.ps/portals/_pcbs/PressRelease/PalEconomic_2010_E.pdf.

8. Ibid.

9. Ibid.

10. Ibid.

11. Ibid.

12. Hassouneh, Muhammad and Abu Libdeh, Hasan. "Palestine Investment Conference." Retrieved March 26, 2010, from Presentation Notes Online Website, http://www.scribd.com/doc/25577574/Palestine-Investment-Conference-Bethlehem-28.

13. Shehadeh, Loay. Palestinian Central Bureau of Statistic: Fertility Is Declining While Unemployment Is on the Rise. 2009. Retrieved April 1, 2010, from http://english.pnn.ps/index.php?option=com_content&task=view&id=6102.

14. Karama. Palestinian Minister of Economy: "Karama" Website Kick Off to Support Palestinian Products. 2010. Retrieved March 18, 2010, from http://www.aknews.com/en/aknews/2/119982/.

Chapter 11

The Soft Stuff Is the Hard Stuff: How Relationships and Communications Can Drive the Execution of Business Strategy

Linda Clark-Santos and
Nancy K. Napier

In this chapter, we take a somewhat contrarian approach and explore the value of "soft" skills—specifically, building strong relationships and communicating effectively—in driving the effective execution of strategy. We divided the chapter into five parts. First, we describe *what* happens with relationships and with communication that might contribute to the failure to execute business strategy. Next, we discuss *why* relationship and communication problems happen—including the power of organizational culture, competition among peers, the rise of cynicism, the isolation of executives, and the impact of organizational design. The third section focuses on what happens as a result of these problems. The fourth section covers the *now what?*—that is, recommendations for different groups on how to contribute to better execution of business strategy, including actions for leaders and individual contributors in large organizations and in start-ups, and for students and professors who teach them. Finally, we close the chapter describing the potential benefits of implementing the recommendations.

In working on the chapter, we decided to use as a main content base the 30-year business experience and expertise of one of the authors. Although she (Linda) has extensive academic experience (as a faculty member and dean), she has spent much of her career in strategic human resource management of several organizations, ranging from Ore-Ida (division of HJ Heinz) in Idaho, to H-E-B Grocery Company in Texas, to Washington Mutual and Starbucks in Washington State. Thus, many of the examples and knowledge come from "doing" not just teaching.

WHAT MIGHT CAUSE A BUSINESS STRATEGY TO FAIL?

Executives typically spend considerable time, effort, and resources in the development of a robust business strategy. However, some firms struggle to translate their strategic intent into crisp execution. Typically, the core business depends on technical expertise to deploy the strategy. The strategic intent of large, publicly held companies is the responsibility of the executive group in consultation with the board of directors. In smaller, more entrepreneurial start-ups, the purpose and strategic intent come from a leadership group generally headed by the founder. Whether the organization is large and well established or is new and fresh, it is critical that those working in the organizations understand the marketplace opportunity the leaders are trying to seize. Once leaders effectively communicate the strategy, individuals and work groups should be able to see how their work contributes to the success of the company.

Though often overlooked, two factors affect the successful execution of business strategy: (1) strong working relationships across the organization, and (2) effective communication about the strategy. We discuss each below.

Relationships

Generally, most companies define working relationships vertically—that is, managers and their direct reports. In large organizations, the reporting relationships may be "matrixed"—which means that reporting relationships are based on multiple intersecting dimensions such as functions, geography, or product. In other words, one person may report to more than one boss depending upon where the individual resides and the nature of his/her work. These intersecting relationships add complexity that can create confusion and thus impede execution.

In smaller, entrepreneurial companies, the roles and reporting relationships may be fluid—evolving and changing as the company continues to define itself and its niche. In such a setting, individuals and managers may also find that their roles and responsibilities evolve. Those close to the founder and his/her top leaders may find themselves in situations that require them to demonstrate leadership or to take on duties not reflected in their original titles or jobs and perhaps beyond their current capability. The ambiguity and fluidity of roles and responsibilities can hinder crisp execution and damage relationships—particularly among newly hired talent and those who have longer tenure.

Communication

Another reason many organizations stumble in executing their strategy may lie in diluted or confused communication. Though the communication is still generally top-down, in a matrixed organization, messages may flow from more than one source—with reinterpretations stemming from the various legitimate, but possibly conflicting, vantage points. In large companies, with many layers of management and several business units, the communication of the strategy can be diluted or reinterpreted as it penetrates the organization. Communication flow of strategy is generally top-down with each layer of management editing or interpreting the message along the way. As a result, the final message might be contorted or confused—rather like a photo reproduced repeatedly from an increasingly fuzzy photo rather than the clear original.

In smaller, more entrepreneurial organizations, the founder and his/her colleagues may communicate informally and haphazardly as the strategy takes shape. In the haste to refine and revise their approach as the opportunity and their offering become more clearly defined, they are likely to send messages "on the fly" rather than craft clear, definitive communication. Furthermore, the sense of urgency and resulting breakneck pace that is common in such organizations may compound the confusion and further overshadow important strategic messages.

The Bottom Line

The result in both larger and smaller organizations may be the same: ineffective communication about the strategic direction of the firm coupled with weak or convoluted relationships can impede the successful execution of the firm's strategy.

WHY DO RELATIONSHIP AND COMMUNICATION PROBLEMS HAPPEN?

In this section, we cover six reasons why communication and organizational relationship problems can occur, illustrating the challenge that leaders face in successfully integrating all the elements that make for effective strategy execution.

The Power of Organizational Culture: Leaders Create Culture and Culture Trumps Strategy

Culture is generally defined as a set of norms that guide behavior within an organization. A more informal definition of culture is "what and how things get done." Corporate culture develops over time through a variety of practices and rituals. According to William Schneider of the Corporate Development Group, the behaviors and practices of leaders shape the culture of their organizations.[1] These include a variety of human resources practices as well as how the organization's members make decisions, deal with conflict, and foster innovation. In addition, the physical environment itself shapes culture.

Many practices come into play in shaping culture—including hiring, rewards and compensation, advancement, and employee development. The ways in which these practices emerge and operate within organizations say much about what the culture is and what types of behaviors and actions leaders value.

Hiring decisions—that is, who is invited to join the organization and in what capacity—signal where the organization is headed and what is likely to be important in the future. The way that new hires are assimilated also indicates how mindful the leaders are about the culture and values of the organization and how committed they are to the success of each individual. Specific considerations include the following: Are people selected for their values fit or is technical expertise all that matters? Who participates in the hiring process? And how are new hires assimilated—is it "sink or swim" or is there a formal onboarding process designed to bring people up to speed and to ensure their success?

Other signals about what the organization values come from how it rewards and recognizes achievement. Examples include the following: Are titles used to recognize and reward achievement of business goals? Is recognition done publicly or privately? Are monetary rewards used to encourage certain kinds of behavior? And finally, who makes the most money and who is promoted will send powerful messages about what it takes to succeed. In particular, employees will notice who succeeds and moves up and who fails and moves out. They will then draw conclusions about what it takes to thrive and prosper in the organization.

Employee-development programs are another indicator of culture. The types of training and development the organization invests in as well as the process it uses signal what the organization leaders consider valuable and how important learning is to the future success of individuals and the firm. The degree to which programs are formal and structured versus informal and unstructured gives clues to the culture. Another indicator is whether employees may sign themselves up or must be sponsored by an executive. Even more telling is whether topics and programs are selected and designed to serve the business strategy and company objectives or offered as a "perk," catering to employee interests, rather than to organizational strategic needs. Finally, do the programs actually prepare people for advancement and help them contribute to the firm's strategic direction?

Other factors that shape culture include:

- Who participates in making decisions and how are decisions communicated?
- Do the leaders encourage feedback?
- Do the leaders avoid conflict?
- Is innovation valued—or seen as a threat to the status quo?
- Is the physical work environment open and informal—or structured and hierarchical?

All of these leadership behaviors and practices implicitly tell others in the organization what is important and how they should behave. These behaviors will "trump" explicit statements regarding strategy, vision, mission, and values. Whether leaders like it or not and whether they are aware of it or not, their behavior sends strong messages and sets the tone for the entire organization.

As Nilofer Merchant, author of *The New How,* writes in her blog, "After working on strategy for 20 years, I can say this: culture will trump strategy, every time. The best strategic idea means nothing in isolation. If the strategy conflicts with how a group of people already believe, behave or make decisions it will fail. Conversely, a culturally robust team can turn a so-so strategy into a winner. The 'how' matters in how we get performance."[2]

All-Stars and "A Players": Competition Undermines Cooperation

A second factor that impedes the crisp execution of strategy is internal competition. Many executive groups include people who are best-in-class functional experts or general managers who possess sufficient political savvy to advance. These "A players" may act like a group of baseball all-stars relying on their individual technical expertise but lacking real teamwork. In an organization with such an all-star culture, A players rise to the top and peers may compete with each other more than they cooperate. At the top of the organization, the competition becomes even more fierce—with higher stakes, bigger egos, and fewer players. Such a competitive attitude at the top sets the tone for peer relationships deeper in the organization. In fact, lateral peer relationships can be among the most challenging to cultivate. Generally, there is no great incentive to develop peer relationships since peers have no formal power over each other. They do not decide on promotions, recognition, or compensation for each other. Even in organizations that use 360-degree feedback tools as part of their feedback loops, there is little one can do to openly influence the career trajectory of a peer. Often, they are rivals in the quest to succeed their boss or to win another coveted role. Indeed, some leaders may in fact encourage peer competition. As one chief executive officer put it, "I like it when people are competing for promotion . . . it keeps their heads in the game." A consequence of such competition is that peers may believe that another's success will come at their own expense, so there is little reason to help that peer succeed. Rather, there is often more reason to undermine a peer's success.

Furthermore, the A players at the top may show little appreciation for the B players deeper in the organization. Some management experts, however, suggest that B players may be the glue that holds organizations together during difficult times.[3] These valuable and steady B players may become disenfranchised over time, though, if the all-stars operate in their own self-interest rather than the good of the organization and if that behavior is rewarded and recognized.

Executive Turnover Breeds Cynicism

As the tenure of executives has declined[4] and turnover has once again spiked, many organizations have suffered jolting changes in direction and strategy. For example, in 2011, the (former) CEO of Hewlett-Packard (HP), Leo Apotheker, announced the sale or spin-off of HP's PC division as a major shift in business strategy. Within months, Apotheker was out and a new CEO, Meg Whitman, reversed the decision. We can only imagine the turbulence and the resulting tug of war these decisions must have wrought inside the organization.

So common was turnover and change in strategic direction at the top in another large organization that the middle managers, in a dark and not-so-private joke, called themselves the "We-Be's"—as in "We be here when you are gone." In another organization, one of us watched five CEOs come and go in a two-year period, each with his own take on what the organization needed for success. The managers and employees became increasingly disenchanted and disengaged as the door at the top revolved. This kind of cynicism undermined teamwork and commitment, evidenced by the exodus of many talented people and the eventual consolidation with another company.

Some organizations, however, have made stability and constancy of purpose critical for success. Apple, over several years, has consistently communicated its direction and executed its strategy. Even people outside the firm can articulate Apple's primary business strategy—to develop cool, well-designed products that customers do not think to ask for but must have once they see them. Further, most fans of U.S. business know how CEO Steve Jobs introduced new products—in his signature black mock turtleneck and jeans standing on a stage with the product in his hand. The image conveys clarity and no confusion whatsoever. The fact that these messages and images (will) live on after Jobs's death is indicative of their sustained power and compelling impact.

Executives Become Insulated and Isolated

A fourth factor that often leads to business-strategy failure is that executives become isolated and as a result lose touch with their organizations. As business organizations increasingly become the result of mergers, consolidations, and acquisitions over organic growth,[5] it becomes increasingly difficult for executives to really know what is going on deep in their organizations. Not only is it lonely at the top, but executives can also become increasingly insulated. Some, like the now infamous CEOs of Lehman Brothers or AIG, may isolate themselves on purpose, but generally it is simply more difficult to stay in touch as an organization grows. Too many layers and too many players not only dilute the messages going out from the senior leadership, but can also filter and distort feedback coming in.

When one of us joined a large publicly held company as a senior vice president (SVP), she experienced firsthand how many layers in an organization can dramatically slow down the work flow. Still new to the organization and just getting to know her team, she received a work assignment that required some specialized computer skills. She inquired and learned that a member of her staff had such skills. She approached the individual whose workstation was just a few steps away and asked for help. The staff member replied that the SVP would need to check with the staff member's supervisor first. And so off the SVP went to the supervisor. She quickly learned that the individual she first approached reported to someone, who reported to someone, who reported to someone, who reported to someone, who reported to someone (sigh) who reported to the SVP. In a team of nine, there were seven layers of management. What should have been a 10-minute conversation turned into an hour. An illuminating hour, to be sure, especially since the SVP would later be charged with streamlining the organization and reducing unnecessary layers. She knew a good place to start.

In addition to the primarily top-down flow of communication, many large organizations have little or no two-way communication—no "listening posts" to identify the concerns and questions of the workforce and mid-level managers. If leaders make an effort to understand the concerns of middle managers and individual contributors, they not only create cohesion deeper in the organization but they also become better equipped to remove barriers to progress. Absent two-way communication with appropriate feedback loops, their leadership is hollow—leadership by exhortation rather than by example, inspiration, or vision.

Moreover, executives may think that more communication is better communication, not realizing that multiple messages and channels can actually reduce effectiveness. In one large organization (60,000 employees with five business units), a new head of internal communication conducted an audit to determine how many communication vehicles existed. His study revealed that over 270 formal communication publications—both print and electronic—were developed and delivered regularly. The cost and confusion of so many messages actually diminished understanding of the business strategy and limited real traction and results.

Isolated Executives Communicate Poorly about the Direction of the Business

In many cases, opportunities for mid-level managers to hear firsthand from the executive team about the strategic direction of the business are limited. Instead, many large organizations invest heavy resources in an annual leadership conference to bring hundreds—even thousands—of managers together. In such settings, executives often miss the opportunity to explain and refresh the business strategy in person, opting instead for a series of speeches. These speeches can range from a straight-from-the-heart but off-the-cuff monologue to a tightly rehearsed but passionless speech designed to inform but not to inspire. In one painful example at a large meeting following a business downturn, a CEO took questions from the audience after his speech. One brave individual asked about the logic of layoffs when executive compensation was on the rise. The CEO chuckled and said that yes, it was true that he was highly paid and that he had every intention of continuing to be so. As the audience gasped, he then called for the next question.

In other cases, firms may choose a more entertaining format. Keynote speakers might be television comedians or other performers. At one such conference, one of us was asked to host a breakout session. She chose to introduce the firm's new leadership competency model that would serve as the foundation for performance reviews and leadership-development programs. As the agenda firmed up, she was dismayed to learn that one session offered concurrently—and thus competing with hers—was a simulation of a television game show, complete with prizes and the celebrity host.

Though designed and delivered with good intentions, such events can fail to truly engage the hearts and minds of the audience in the business. Strategy therefore remains in the hands and the heads of a few at the top.

In smaller, entrepreneurial organizations, the founders and executives may thrive on the chaos and adrenaline of the start-up and value those who can tolerate the same. However, the pace that these entrepreneurs enjoy and the ambiguity they tolerate may take its toll on others. Some employees may be reluctant to seek clarity or wish for greater stability lest they be seen as malcontents not well suited to an uncertain start-up environment. As a result, the entrepreneur may not realize that people are confused or concerned about the direction of the firm.

Many other questions about communication about strategy include:

- What channels are used?
- How frequently are such messages sent?
- Whose voice is used?
- How complicated or simple are the messages?
- How relevant are the messages?
- Are there any feedback loops that invite clarification?

Organization Design Impedes Lateral Relationship Building

In addition to the top-down flow of communication in both formal and informal channels, the organizational design may impede the development of strong lateral relationships. Typically, meetings focus on the vertical organization—managers and their direct reports. The opportunities to meet and get to know peers—those at the same level across the organization—are rare.

As we mentioned earlier, some enlightened organizations try to create *esprit de corps* among their managers by hosting large leadership conferences. However, as we also previously noted, these events may focus more on style than substance. Further, the schedule can be rigidly structured with huge plenary sessions coupled with concurrent breakout sessions that follow. Generally, these breakouts are either designed to entertain or are structured to serve a vertical slice—again managers and their direct reports. In either case, there is little opportunity for networking and cross-functional or cross-unit relationship building. So, the vertical design of the organization defines—and restricts—relationships. Consequently mid-level managers find it difficult to gain a broader, more strategic view of the organization and how their work combines with others for the success of the firm.

Moreover, management retreats that are designed to build teamwork and *esprit de corps* are limited to functional teams with a leader and his/her direct report team. Although there may be value in such events to build internal teamwork, they generally focus inward on the needs of the group rather than on the broader strategy. If "guest" executives are asked to attend to address broader organizational issues, their vantage point is that of the executives rather than peers of the target audience. Once again, there is limited opportunity to develop peer relationships and to learn more broadly about the organization from the perspective of peers.

Conversely, in an unprecedented move, an innovative executive in one large publicly traded company sponsored a customized leadership-development program that was designed and delivered to a horizontal slice of the organization. In the program, one segment was focused on identifying common problems and brainstorming solutions. Each individual was asked to bring a recurring problem and brief the larger group. As the problems were identified and the discussion ensued, participants discovered that others had solved the very problems that they had found so perplexing. One rather quiet participant raised his hand and commented, "You know, I just realized that for most of our problems, the answer is in the room." An inspiring silence fell over the group as people began to nod and smile. That evening over dinner, much of the discussion focused on the fact that though the participants had much in common and in some cases had worked in the same company for many years, they had never had a chance to really get to know each other and explore what they had in common and how they might help each other.

With a matrixed organizational design, the design itself can present challenges. In such a design, an individual might have two or more bosses. In such situations, the competition for attention from those bosses may cause great confusion and stress. Having to juggle priorities, meeting schedules, and performance expectations from more than one boss can breed despair and undermine teamwork. Again, competition is likely to eclipse cooperation when rival loyalties and competing priorities abound.

Interestingly, although matrixed designs might sound effective, working inside such a design is extremely complex. In his book, *Designing Matrix Organizations That Actually Work*,[6] Jay Galbraith, a recognized expert in organizational design, describes companies that may have as many as six matrixed dimensions around which they are organized. Then, he suggests that perhaps the number of dimensions that could be used within an organization is unlimited. However, many who live the matrixed life might disagree, as the complex web of relationships in such organizations cannot help but cloud messages, strain interactions, confound loyalties, and confuse priorities.

In smaller, entrepreneurial organizations, the organizational design may be "flat"—with the founder and a few trusted "lieutenants" running the show. As the organization grows and new talent is hired, the relationships and responsibilities may evolve in the minds of those at the top but can be quite obscure to those just joining. In one such organization, one of the trusted lieutenants was expected to train new hires but was given no formal charge to do so. A new hire, selected for considerable expertise and talent, then resented the guidance of the lieutenant. There was no formal reporting relationship and the leaders had not made clear that the new hire should look to the lieutenant for direction, support, and training. Not wanting to disappoint the founder, the lieutenant struggled for months to make the situation work. By the time expectations were clarified to get everyone back on track, the new hire's relationships within the firm had deteriorated beyond repair and he left the organization.

In sum, talented people can struggle in an organization where roles and expectations are not clear and where relationships are not strong. If the organizational chart has so many arrows and dots that it starts to look like a Ferris wheel, rest assured that there is sufficient role confusion. Such organizations may waste resources and lose needed talent—and results are likely to suffer.

SO WHAT HAPPENS AS A RESULT?

The challenges and problems stemming from weak relationships and poor communication can ultimately undermine the success of an organization. The biggest impact is that people will simply disengage or completely withdraw. Specifically, outcomes may include lack of engagement, short-term focus, silos, lower confidence, and higher confusion and frayed relationships.

The cynicism resulting from frequent changes in leadership and/or strategy results in shallow commitments that reduce the level of engagement. Though they may stay, the disenfranchised mid-level managers and "B players" in large firms are less likely to go the extra mile for the good of the organization. Furthermore, highly talented people who have opportunities elsewhere may leave altogether. In other words, those who stay may disengage and others will simply leave for a better opportunity. In smaller, more entrepreneurial firms, the lack of clear communication about the future direction and strategic intent of the business can cause talented people to curb their enthusiasm and question their commitment. When engagement suffers, business results suffer as well.[7]

To survive the turbulence of constant change of leadership or direction, many employees may concentrate on the short term with no regard for the future. This short-term focus robs the organization of the staying power that will sustain the organization during tough times and propel them forward during better times. Decisions become slow and progress abates as people "hunker down" into a survival mode and simply wait for the next wave of change to hit. In large organizations, poor communication and relationships can lead to the emergence of silos. When that happens, peers across the organization refrain from working together and sharing information. In one such situation, one business unit was working hard to launch a new product line that would compete directly and succeed at the expense of another unit within the same firm. Ultimately both initiatives failed after wasting resources and straining relationships—in some cases beyond repair. Though silos are less likely in smaller but growing organizations, the informal nature of relationships and evolution of responsibilities can ultimately create dysfunction as the firm matures. Because they value the energetic and informal start-up environment and eschew anything that seems too "corporate," many entrepreneurs resist creating a more formal structure as the firm matures. As a result, their success may stall as the need for greater clarity and direction emerges.

Another result from poor communication and relationships is that confidence dissipates and confusion abounds. Employees may lack a clear understanding of strategy and may be confused about their role in execution. Too many messages and too few with real information about the strategy erode understanding and hinder execution. Employees are likely to lose confidence in their leadership, which compounds the lack of commitment.

Finally, relationships fray and focus turns inward. Competing loyalties and priorities place individuals in no-win situations where they simply cannot please everyone. As a result, they may pursue their own self-interest rather than working for the greater good. The causes of the downfall of great civilizations are often internal strife coupled with external threat.[8] Just like great civilizations, great companies can fail as well.

SO WHAT CAN YOU DO?

Given the plethora of what can cause business-strategy execution to go off track, it is amazing organizations ever do it right. So what actions can improve the chances of successful execution of business strategy? In the closing section, we offer suggestions *directly to* different groups—executives, middle managers, and individual contributors of both large and small organizations, as well as for students and professors who teach them. Students need to remember that they will likely one day *be* those executives and managers at small or large firms. So even though the day seems far away, they should keep in mind there are some actions they could take in the future.

Actions for Executives in Large Organizations

Set the Tone

First, recognize that what you do and say sets the tone for the rest of the organization. Remind yourself that culture trumps strategy, and your actions shape the culture. Make a conscious effort to serve as a role model for teamwork and call attention to its importance. Evaluate the teamwork of your executive group and communicate your expectation that they function together for the greater good of the organization. Tell them that, as executives, they should put on the "big company hat" rather than their "small, functional hat." Hold yourself accountable for creating broad-based understanding of the business strategy. Constantly ask yourself what you can do to get everyone moving together into the future. Finally, reward and recognize those who are strong team players.

Streamline and Audit Communication

Focus on a few essential messages about strategy and direction; repeat and reinforce those messages often. Use the communication channels and vehicles that are most appropriate and compelling for your organization. Learn to use technology to add a personal touch to your broad, strategic messages and use those messages in inspiring ways to get results. Help people understand their contribution to the success of the enterprise. Recognize when you are altering your course and communicate accordingly. Avoid assuming that everyone will "get it" if you change direction. Take special care to take your leadership team and your workforce with you as you chart the course into the future.

Use Listening Posts

Third, establish some "listening posts" to enhance two-way communication. Avoid relying entirely on your direct reports to tell you what is going on deeper in the organization. Use all-employee surveys to put your finger on the pulse of your organization. Use the results to make it easier for people to execute and drive the business. Conduct focus groups of high performers to learn what prevents them from doing their jobs well. Attend the focus groups yourself to hear firsthand what people are thinking, and ask a recorder to document the results. Invite horizontal slices (peers from a variety of functional areas and geographies) to lunch or coffee and take the opportunity to discuss your business strategy and answer questions. Again, ask someone to record what you learn and then work to address issues you identify. And make sure that the actions you take do not feel punitive or reflect badly on those who had the courage to speak up about their concerns.

Create Social Capital and Look Widely for Solutions

Cultivate broad-based solutions to vexing problems by offering cross-functional action learning development programs to high performers across the organization. Action learning programs[9] bring together high-performing peers from various areas of the business to solve real business problems under the sponsorship of a key executive. These high performers have an opportunity to develop skills and insights needed by the business and to advance their understanding of the business while they develop strong, enduring peer relationships. When they have completed their action learning experience, equip them with messages that create deeper, broader understanding of strategy and deploy them across the organization. Use them as a cadre of cross-functional peers who can look beyond their areas of purview for holistic solutions to difficult challenges.

Develop Simple Organizational Design

Simplify the organization to eliminate unnecessary confusion and conflict. If you have a matrixed organization, your top management team must provide integrated direction and model integrative behavior.[10] Develop clear charters for lateral and vertical units. Create integrating mechanisms—such as councils (again with clear charters)—that foster collaboration as needed to ensure the right amount of coordination for critical tasks. Figure out how you are going to deal with internal conflicts and how you want your leaders to escalate matters that need resolution. Clarify roles by calling on all managers to eliminate ambiguity and make sure who is accountable for which core processes that might be shared by two or more managers—who gets 51 votes and when? Ask your managers to target their communication and coordinate where needed to avoid confusion. Recognize that working in a matrix is difficult, so limit the number of dimensions to those that are absolutely essential. Do whatever you can to keep things simple. In addition, monitor the number of layers in your organization and resist the temptation to add layers as you grow. If too many layers are impeding your progress and limiting your success, determine what kind organizational design principle will best serve your business—customer focus, product line, geographic, front office-back office, for example.[11]

Develop and Use Peer Relationships

Even senior managers can benefit from peer relationships. Unfortunately, such peers are not likely to reside within your organization. As a result, you may want to look outside not only your firm but also your industry to cultivate new and creative solutions. Seek out others from diverse sectors but from organizations with similar philosophies about performance. An example is a six-year-long group called "the Gang."[12] This group of seven includes organizations ranging from dance to software and advertising, law enforcement to football, theater to health information. Senior leaders meet to compare problems and lessons, and have discovered over the years that they have more in common (despite their divergent industries) than not. As one of the leaders has said, "once best practices in your industry are documented, they become normal practices. Going outside your field is where you get new ideas."

Actions for Entrepreneurs in Start-ups

Entrepreneurs face different facets of the challenges relating to communication, relationships, and design. We suggest those of you starting new organizations to focus on five key actions.

Be Clear about What You Are Doing

First, think through the business opportunity you are striving to seize and articulate your offering. Develop a few crisp messages to communicate your strategy and repeat them often. If your strategy and offering are still in flux, admit it but work hard to clarify and refine your thinking. Engage trusted sources to help you define the opportunity you see and how you plan to seize it. Realize that much of your talent lies in your vision, but your success may be defined by your ability to communicate.

Refresh Your Communication as Your Strategy Evolves

If you are fully engaged in your new start-up, you will know what is happening sooner and faster than most others, including employees. So you avoid assuming that others see what you see. Instead, display your thinking to foster understanding and generate clarity. Make a conscious effort to refine and revise your messages as you grow. Develop your own leader's voice[13] to help you send the right messages the right way. Collect and capture anecdotes that help tell your story and that of your firm.

Reward the Soft Skills

Recognize and reward those who have the "soft" skills of building relationships and communicating effectively—particularly if those are attributes you don't possess. Seek out those who have the skills of persuasion, collaboration, and conflict resolution, and make sure they have a place and a voice on your leadership team.

Have Clear Roles and Responsibilities for All

As your organization evolves, clarify roles and responsibilities of your "lieutenants." Review their responsibilities periodically to make sure you have not given them informal responsibility without formal authority.

Recognize that the high level of ambiguity that you, at the top of the organization, find thrilling may be debilitating to those on your team. Cultivate appropriate listening posts to keep in touch with the needs and concerns of your growing organization and to ensure that valued members of your team are fully engaged.

Consciously Align Your Culture with Your Business

As your organization grows, give thought to what kind of design will best serve your business strategy.[14] Resist the urge to let things grow haphazardly until the point at which things stop working and results suffer. And pay attention to reporting relationships to make sure they are clear and that you can hold people accountable in appropriate ways.

In addition, decide what kind of culture you want to create. Consider what kind of workplace environment is best suited to your business and your workforce and then act accordingly. Remind yourself that culture trumps strategy, and that your actions shape the culture. Be aware that the culture will be created whether you intend it or not and that your actions will be its most powerful influence.[15]

Choose Wisely and Assimilate New Talent Fully

As you need new talent, select carefully—not only for technical expertise but also for cultural fit. Involve key members of your current team in the hiring process to make sure they have a voice. As you welcome new members to your organization, assimilate them thoughtfully and thoroughly. Avoid the temptation to let the new hire sink or swim. Communicate expectations clearly and often. Recognize that the onboarding experience of new hires will likely determine to determine how long they will stay and how successful he/she is likely to be.[16]

Actions for Mid-Level Managers, "Lieutenants," or Individuals

Separate from top managers at large and start-up companies are the managers deeper in an organization who execute strategy. They too face unusual challenges on the soft stuff, and we offer several suggestions.

Understand Strategy

First, make it your business to understand the strategy thoroughly. Make an effort to understand how your work contributes to the success of the business. If you are a manager, explain how the work of your unit fits into the big picture and help people feel that they are part of something larger than themselves.

Adjust When You Need To

Partly because you may not develop the strategy, you need to learn how to understand and read it, especially as changes in direction or strategy are in the works. As you recognize it, you will need to adjust accordingly. Resist the temptation to hunker down and protect the status quo. Have the courage and the wisdom to embrace the change and become an advocate. Inform yourself about the reasons for the change and understand the implications for your work. If you cannot truly commit and remain engaged, consider whether you should pursue a different position elsewhere. Recognize that remaining but resisting could stall your career.

Develop and Nurture Peer Relationships

Rather than seeing them as competitors, find and cultivate your peers in other areas of the business. Assist others when you can and develop a reputation as a strong team player. Know when to lead and when to follow. Support others in their efforts to strengthen lateral relationships. Reach out beyond your area to develop relationships and understand the big picture. Seek and seize opportunities to work with peers across the organization. Ask how you can help others to succeed and how together you can contribute to the success of the organization.

In addition to those within your organization, find a professional buddy outside your organization—someone you can trust and use as a sounding board. Cultivate your ability to consider work challenges from a different vantage point by seeking the perspectives of those outside your immediate area. Expand your thinking by growing your professional network and learning from others who are quite different from you.

Develop the Soft Skill of Great Communication

Finally, in addition to embracing change, understanding the strategy, and building strong relationships both inside and outside your organization, make it a priority to develop strong communication skills. Helping others understand how your work fits with theirs and contributing to the success of the firm is a critical leadership skill. Develop your ability to ask penetrating questions that get to the heart of the matter.

The best leaders and managers know the value of questions and use them for at least four different reasons: to *learn,* to *build relationships* and teams, to *solve* problems, and to *find* or anticipate problems. The best also know how to ask questions; so you too should recognize the difference between questions that challenge (and therefore may intimidate) and questions that genuinely ask for more information to enhance your understanding. And then, of course, take care to listen to the answers others provide. While someone else is speaking, resist the temptation to mentally rehearse your next remark.

Actions for Students and for Professors

As we mentioned at the beginning of this section, whether students believe it or not now, they will likely become one of the managers that we talked about previously, whether in a large or small firm, perhaps even the one at the top. In that role, students can either support the successful execution of their organization's business strategy, or be obstacles to it. We hope they choose to help their organizations succeed.

Actions for Students

So what can students do while they are still at universities to enhance their abilities to succeed later? We offer several suggestions. First, instead of dreading group and team projects, welcome the chance to be part of a team that has a goal. Take advantage of opportunities to work with a team, sort out how to achieve a goal, and build strong peer relationships. Recognize that such opportunities are relatively free of risk—that is, failure will not mean job loss—but the skills you will acquire will be a boon for you—and the organization you join—in the future.

Second, cultivate your own communication skills—particularly asking good questions and listening actively. Ask for feedback from your team members on how well you communicate and ask for tips from those you think are good communicators. Watch and learn from those who do well what you have not yet mastered.

Also, learn how to bring out the best in others. Recognize that even difficult people and stressful situations offer you great opportunities to learn and grow. Working with others—even those you dislike—is a requirement of work life; the stronger your interpersonal skills are, the more successful you are likely to be. Develop people skills to balance your technical skills, and realize that both are essential in the workplace of the 21st century.

Finally, grasp the opportunity to gain experience from internships within organizations in ways you might not have fully tapped to date. Watch how people in the organization build relationships in both formal and informal ways. Ask questions about what kind of skills are needed to be hired and then to succeed in the firm.

Actions for Professors

Students are not in the learning process alone, as we know. Professors also have an opportunity and a responsibility to help students cultivate these skills. We offer a few suggestions. First, create assignments that indeed provide true conditions for students to lead and to work as a team. Recognize that too often assignments allow for social loafing, rather than encourage and force engagement by all. Consider allowing a team to sanction members (even to the point of "firing" a member). Add peer assessment at the close of a project to provide useful feedback to the students. If possible, offer the chance for multiple projects with the same team so that members can rotate the leader responsibility. Encourage students to learn to lead *and* be a team player. Cultivate and reward interpersonal skills as well as technical expertise to help students gain these critical abilities that executives value.

Second, acknowledge that students need to learn how to bring out the best in others—even then they are not in charge and are not required to do so. Call on students to find ways to integrate their ideas with the good ideas from other team members—rather than trying to prevail. Learning to cooperate—rather than compete—is, again, a skill that senior executives look for but often do not find in potential employees. Help students learn to draw others out, instead of passively waiting for others to engage.

As students practice working with peers, encourage them to consciously notice and consider the lessons they gain from the experiences, build on them, and adapt the lessons to new endeavors. Cultivate the ability to reflect, which also helps to build the valuable characteristic (alas) of seeing the "bigger picture." By stepping back to reflect, students are also learning to step back and see a broader situation, which in turn can also help instill the understanding of the benefits of cooperation across silos or different functional areas. Though these soft skills are hard to learn, hard to develop, and hard to use, your classroom offers generally safe conditions for students to practice them.[17]

BENEFITS OF IMPLEMENTING THE SOFT STUFF

If executives, entrepreneurs, managers, individual contributors, and those preparing for (and helping to prepare others for) these roles were to cultivate effective communication and relationship building, the so-called soft stuff, a number of good outcomes can emerge.

First, execution might be faster, better, and simpler if the purpose and strategic direction of an organization is clear up, down, and across the organization. Leaders could get better results if they understand the business strategy and how their teams contribute to its successful execution. Furthermore, as business conditions change, organizations could be more nimble in refreshing their strategy and moving ahead without losing traction.

Second, executives—both in large organizations and small start-ups— would be better informed, be closer to the action, and be more accountable. Their willingness and ability to both lead and listen would set an example for the rest of the organization, keep them in touch with reality, and help them to move their businesses ahead.

Third, employee engagement could remain high despite turbulence in the marketplace. With confidence that their leaders are making and communicating sound decisions, people are more likely to stay the course and focus on how to make the organization succeed. A more engaged workforce performs better and gets better results.[18] Relationships create "stickiness," which increases the likelihood that talented people will stay with the organization. This applies for the future employees who are now at universities as well as those already in the employment market. Given the pace of the business environment, globalization, and the benefits (and dangers) of remote connectedness through social media and the Internet, many leaders know that the soft stuff of relationships and communication will be even more important in the future.

Finally, organizations would be positioned for leadership continuity. A work environment that fosters engagement and develops social capital while getting business results is likely to be more attractive to the next generation of leadership talent, who is likely to be less hierarchical than the current generation of leadership.

THE SOFT STUFF IS INDEED THE HARD STUFF

The workplace of the 21st century is a demanding and complex environment. As organizations globalize, industries grow, companies consolidate, and competition intensifies, success is likely to become increasingly elusive. Though there is no substitute for technical competence and expertise, the true winners of the future may be those who can overcome differences, cultivate agreement, and move with others into the future. That, then, is both the challenge and the opportunity. The future is yours.

NOTES

Many thanks to Bianca Jochimsen for her outstanding assistance with this chapter.

1. Schneider, William E. 1994. *The Reengineering Alternative: A Plan for Making Your Current Culture Work.* New York: McGraw-Hill/Irwin.

2. Merchant, Nilofer. 2011. "Culture Trumps Strategy, Every Time." Harvard Business Review Blog Network, March 22. http://blogs.hbr.org/cs/2011/03/culture_trumps_strategy_every.html.

3. DeLong Thomas J. and Vijayaraghavan, Vineeta. 2003. "Let's Hear It for B Players," *Harvard Business Review* 81(6): 96–102.

4. ChiefExecutive.net. 2011. "13 Percent CEO Turnover, Highest Rate in Six Years," ChiefExecutive.net, September 8.

5. The Investment Blogger. 2011. 2011 "Mid-Year Mergers and Acquisitions Update (Part 1)," The Investment Blog, July 6.

6. Galbraith, Jay R. 2009. *Designing Matrix Organizations That Actually Work: How IBM, Procter & Gamble and Others Design for Success.* San Francisco: Jossey Bass.

7. Kowske, Brenda J., Herman, Anne E. and Wiley, Jack W. 2010. Exploring Leadership and Managerial Effectiveness. Kenexa Research Institute WorkTrends Report.

8. Ferguson, Niall. 2011. "America's 'Oh Sh*t!' Moment," *Newsweek,* November 7 and 14.

9. Dotlich, David L. and Noel, James L. 1998. *Action Learning: How the World's Top Companies Are Re-Creating Their Leaders and Themselves.* San Francisco: Jossey Bass.

10. Galbraith, Jay R. 2009. *Designing Matrix Organizations That Actually Work: How IBM, Procter & Gamble and Others Design for Success.* San Francisco: Jossey Bass.

11. Galbraith, Jay R., Downey, Diane and Kates, Amy. 2002. *Designing Dynamic Organizations: A Hands-On Guide for Leaders at All Levels.* New York: AMACOM.

12. Napier, Nancy K., Raney, Gary, Freeman, Ron, Petersen, Chris, Cooper, Jamie, Kemper, Don, Balkins, Jim, Fee, Charlie, Hofflund, Mark, McIntyre, Trey, Schert, John Michael, and Lokken, Bob. 2011. "Gang Rules: Creativity in Unexpected Places," *People and Strategy* 34(3): 28–33.

13. Crossland, Ron and Clarke, Boyd. 2002. *The Leader's Voice: How Your Communication Can Inspire Action and Get Results!* New York: SelectBooks.

14. Galbraith, Jay R., Downey, Diane, and Kates, Amy. 2002. *Designing Dynamic Organizations: A Hands-On Guide for Leaders at All Levels.* New York: AMACOM.

15. Schneider, William E. 1994. *The Reengineering Alternative: A Plan for Making Your Current Culture Work.* New York: McGraw-Hill/Irwin.

16. Herman, Anne E. 2009. *Onboarding New Employees: An Opportunity to Build Long-Term Productivity and Retention.* Wayne, PA: Kenexa Research Institute.

17. Colvin, Geoff. 2008. *Talent Is Overrated: What Really Separates World-Class Performers from Everybody Else.* New York: Portfolio.

18. Kowske, Brenda J., Herman, Anne E., and Wiley, Jack W. 2010. Exploring Leadership and Managerial Effectiveness. Kenexa Research Institute WorkTrends Report.

Chapter 12

The New Reality for Business Institutions: Societal Strategy

Robert Moussetis

An increasingly complex nonbusiness environment has created a greater need for business institutions to expand their strategic thinking and integrate nonbusiness strategies into their formal strategic planning.[1] Although social strategies are evident among the great majority of firms, it is rather a reactive posture versus a proactive and systematic strategy.[2] Generally, firms react to nonmarket issues and rarely have a clear and methodical strategy to engage the nonmarket environment. Nevertheless, ethical responsibility and legitimacy[3] are critical ingredients of the modern business firm[4] that not only require management but also strategizing. Clearly, the business institutions must generate a satisfactory economic performance in an environment of high ethical integrity[5] and outstanding compliance practices.[6]

The great management philosopher, Peter Drucker, has suggested the enhanced societal nature of modern business institutions.[7] He indicated the distinct possibility that in the new pluralistic society the challenges of an organization will greatly be based on power, and thus, highlighting a shift from resources, entrepreneurship, and technological innovation to a new pragmatism dictating success for the business firm.[8] He indicated that institutions "have become carriers of social purpose,

social values, social effectiveness. Therefore, they have become politi-
cized,"[9] signifying the changing nature of the business institution from
a profit-making center to a social instrument with a broad impact on
society.[10] Consequently, business institutions carry a considerable responsibility not only to shareholders[11] but also to an extensive number
of stakeholders.[12] Inevitably, such responsibility invites the question of
planning, strategy, managerial capability, and effectiveness. In contrast,
there is also the suggestion that business is not to be concerned with any
type of societal activities. It was Milton Friedman who suggested that
businesses have no place in society by saying:

> Few trends could so thoroughly undermine the very foundations
> of our free society as the acceptance by corporate officials of social
> responsibility other than to make as much money for their stock-
> holders as possible. . . . Can self-selected private individuals decide
> what the social interest is?[13]

However, such an approach has led companies to short-term thinking,
maximization of profits, and stockholder satisfaction. Although corporate ethical investment is increasingly concerned with the social responsibilities, it is only a small indication of firms departing from the
profit-only position.[14] The transformation of the business institution
from a purely profit-making societal tool to an institution that provides
societal services to its employees (health care, retirement benefits, flexible schedules, etc.) surely has affected the stockholders earnings. However, it is unlikely that business institutions will function without them.
"Businesses are not profit-making centers, but cost effective centers."[15]
Furthermore, the globalization of the economies creates novel challenges
for corporate managers[16] that fall outside the boundaries of established
competitive thinking.[17] The business institutions need to take a note of
the changing nature of the competition since nonmarket factors (regulations, corporate philanthropy, environment, etc.) might dictate success
or failure.

    This essay will argue that the complexity of societal activity requires
an aggregate approach where the exploration of multiple variables (i.e.,
environment, stakeholder power, performance, strategic behavior, managerial capability) cannot take place independently but holistically. A
conceptual map (Figure 12.1) will provide the domain of the major variables and a contextual discussion will attempt to create the common de-
nominator to facilitate empirical research. Moreover, it will argue that
optimal performance is an outcome of the alignment between external
intensity (i.e., external stakeholder power, environmental turbulence)
and internal intensity (i.e., strategic behavior, managerial capability for
political work).

Figure 12.1
Transitional Model

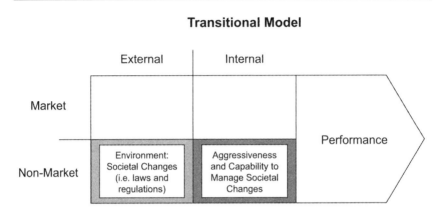

Transitional Model

Performance as an outcome of market/
nonmarket activities and external/internal
managerial capabilities

DESCRIPTION OF THE MODEL

The conceptual model was created to provide the practicing manager with the major variables that a manager would need to consider in developing a societal posture that contributes to the financial success of the firm. Each country presents cultural and political dynamics that are unique; hence, the need for a national posture in each country. In addition, the model was created to facilitate the broader perspective of a potential empirical investigation, to recognize all dimensions critical to the exploratory domain from a multidisciplinary approach, and to facilitate the selection of a research domain(s) while controlling for exogenous variables. Furthermore, it forces a manager to take a multidisciplinary approach by looking at the problem through different scientific optics, such as the cognitive-logical, psycho-sociological, and political perspectives. The sociopolitical environment defines both the market and non-market dynamics. Rule makers will incorporate environmental signals into their decision-making process. Such decisions are subject not only to the general external sociopolitical environment but also to the prevailing national culture and stakeholders. Rule makers establish the canons of the game; hence, the managers receive their information from stakeholders, rule makers, and the firm's internal structure before they render a choice of strategic posture. However, the stakeholders are influenced by the societal strategy performance; therefore, the managerial strategic-posture choice is prompting societal performance as well. In order to put the conceptual model in context, we must explore the basic elements of societal strategy as they relate to societal elements.

ENVIRONMENT AND SOCIETAL STRATEGY

Scholars have explored the gravity of the environment as a determinant of strategy and some have specifically affirmed the societal context of the modern firm (see Table 12.1). Clearly the nonmarket environment (social and political) affects the business activities,[18] pressing the business institution to recognize the strategic implications of the nonmarket activities. Although emerging societal trends induce overall corporate revisions, it is the changes in the social and political environment that trigger corresponding social and political strategies by the business institution.

Although it is postulated that the environment influences strategy, its degree, scope, and extent vary in organizational theory (see Table 12.2). Distinctly, the departure from Weber's theories[19] of treating the firm as a "closed system" triggered research that explored the degree to which a firm depended to the environment.

The environment-organization relationship postulated by the various organizational theories led to the suggestion that firms ought to integrate exogenous political pressures into the comprehensive strategy of the firm. Thus, it is evident that the political pressure exerted on the business firm required the field of strategic management to integrate social policy[20] and societal strategy[21] into the overall corporate strategy and/or strategic posture of the firm. Considering the various environmental conditions (i.e., heavily regulated old industries versus new and novel industries with minimal regulations), it is argued that firms need to investigate the development of an analytical framework to facilitate societal (i.e., political and social) responses by the business firm.[22] There

Table 12.1
Environment, Strategy, and Societal Context of the Business Firm

Issue	Selected Authors
Environment as determinant of strategy	Ansoff, 1965; Thompson and Strickland, 1993; Aguilar, 1967; Hofer and Schendel, 1978; Hofer and Schendel, 1979; Steiner, 1969; Steiner, 1979; Lawrence and Lorsch, 1969; Grand and King, 1982; Burns and Stalker 1961
Societal context of the modern business firm	Scott, 1992; Starling, 1988; Wood, 1990; Ryan, Swanson and Buchholz, 1987; Buchholz, 1995; Steiner and Steiner, 1994; Baron, 1995; Carroll, 1996; Marcus, 1996

Table 12.2
Perspectives on the Environment-Organization Relationship

Theory	Basic Perspectives-Propositions-Modifications	Selected Authors Who Have Written and/or Researched on This Topic
Open systems	Rate of change of organizational systems must correspond to the environmental change	Ashby, 1956; Emery and Trist, 1960 and 1965; Trist, 1981
Resource dependence	Strategic choices to adapt organizations to environmental pressures and uncertainties; thus, to reduce resource dependence	Pfeffer and Salancik, 1978; Ulrich and Barney, 1984
Institutional	Organizations obtain legitimacy from their institutional (political) environment	Jepperson, 1991; Meyer and Rowan, 1977; Scott, 1987; Dimaggio and Powell, 1991
Transaction cost	Organizations seek to economize transaction costs in exchanges with the environment	Williamson, 1981
Stakeholder	Stakeholders seeking influence and/or power constitute the (political) environment.	Freeman, 1984; Wood, 1991
Contingency	Optimal performance is the result of appropriate alignment between the environmental (political) turbulence and managerial behavior and capability	Ansoff, 1979; Ansoff and McDonnell, 1990; Child, 1972; Lawrence and Lorsch, 1967; Mintzeberg, 1973; Ginsberg and Venkatraman, 1985; Fiegenbaum, et. al., 1996
Organizational ecology	Environmental (political) pressure allows only fit organizational forms to survive	Aldrich and Pfeffer 1976; Hannan and Freeman, 1989

are different environmental conditions existing for each business firm, requiring distinct competencies to facilitate a competitive optimization of regulations and public policy.[23] Hence, the development of a measurement of external intensity of the social and political environment offers management a mechanism to assess information to facilitate appropriate responses. The suggestion to adjust organizational systems changes to match the rate of environmental change may have led scholars to coin

Table 12.3
Environmental-Turbulence Descriptions

	Stable Repetitive	Static— Slow Change	Dynamic— Changes Fast but Predictable	Discontinuous but Changes Are Foreseen	Unpredictable Unanticipated
Level of turbulence	1	2	3	4	5

Note: Modified from Igor H. Ansoff and E. McDonnell, *Implanting Strategic Management* (New York: Prentice Hall, 1990).

the term "environmental turbulence"[24] as a measurement of the environmental change.

ENVIRONMENTAL TURBULENCE

The research typology has depicted environments primarily as stable, uncertain, complex, static, dynamic, discontinuous, and turbulent[25] and the variability is known as environmental turbulence. Furthermore, strategy is often determined as a result of environmental turbulence.[26] We have summarized the levels of environmental turbulence based on the literature descriptions and typology of environmental conditions in Table 12.3.

Environmental turbulence was defined as the rate of change of the environment[27] and degree of complexity.[28] However, there is a lack of distinction in the literature of whether environmental-turbulence measurements are for business strategies and/or corporate strategies. Some environmental-turbulence measurement tools are future oriented,[29] whereas others are past oriented,[30] and a third group maintains no clear distinction.[31] Typically, strategic management is associated with future developments and issues that may impact the firm,[32] whereas competitive management[33] is primarily involved with present- and near-future (depending on the industry) strategy. Therefore, a distinction is required when using instruments that measure environmental turbulence. Finally, several theoretical and empirical postulations have suggested that performance is optimized when organizations undertake a careful diagnosis of the environment to assess the levels of turbulence and then decide to respond with the appropriate mode of strategic behavior.[34]

STAKEHOLDER POWER

The nonmarket environment has an impact on managerial decisions; thus, unraveling the complexities and power exerted by diverse stakeholders has led management into an uncharted managerial landscape that requires a holistic conceptualization (at a meta-level) before generating an appropriate strategic approach. It is argued that the strategic behavior and strategic choices displayed by top management are an outcome of stakeholder power and environmental pressure; therefore, political strategy rests on management's capability to demonstrate effectively an understanding of stakeholder power. Society through stakeholders grants legitimacy to the business firm. Legitimacy and survival of an organization depend on the relationship of management with social and political stakeholders;[35] thus, legitimacy grants social and political leverage for a firm when interacting with social and political institutions (i.e., government, NGOs, community-consumer groups, etc.). Therefore, effective and systematic stakeholder management enters the routine managerial domain. Moreover, legitimacy becomes a source of power.[36] The power of various interest groups, through a sociopolitical bargaining process, will determine the firm's success in achieving the preferred sociopolitical strategy.[37] The success of strategic programs depends on the managerial response to stakeholder demands and the relative power of stakeholders for changes in current actions taken by the firm.[38] The relationships between the business institutions, governments, and society generate a corresponding system of stakeholders to whom managers are directly responsible. It is postulated that managerial effectiveness is largely based on the ability to recognize stakeholders, and formulate and implement thoughtful, cohesive strategies.[39] Stakeholders are entities who are likely to be influenced by societal pressures as they relate to corporations, corporate decrees, or have a distinct contractual relationship with the corporation; therefore, they have a stake in the corporation.[40] Managers may be motivated by corporate self-interest, legal or public pressure, or a legitimate desire to benefit the lives of stakeholders.[41] Others have suggested that only those who are directly affected by the actions of the firm can be considered as stakeholders of the corporation.[42] If a stakeholder has either "power" or "legitimacy," stakeholder management is crucial to the firm.[43] Stakeholder management is a strategic tool[44] and since government is the primary stakeholder in the regulatory and legislative process,[45] success in the market place will largely depend on success in the social and political arena first.[46]

STRATEGIC BEHAVIOR AND STRATEGIC CHOICES

Strategic behavior leads to different levels of performance.[47] However, what type of strategic behavior produces optimal performance? The typology developed by Miles and Snow[48] provided a foundation for other scholars of organizational behavior interested in the relationships between strategy, structure, and process. Validity and reliability have

Table 12.4
Managerial Approach to Change

Level of turbulence	1	2	3	4	5
Managerial capability for societal response	Evades changes	Conforms to changes	Pursues familiar changes	Pursues new alternatives	Searches for novel changes

also been affirmed as usable to explore organizations and their strategies.[49] This typology is also consistent with theoretical and empirical studies over the last two decades.[50]

Porter's[51] typology focuses on concentrated industries[52] and represents an excellent tool for an existing industry (therefore addressing the primary premise of low cost, differentiation), but offers neither guidance for industries in highly entrepreneurial, creative, and innovative settings, which are still in a pre-infancy stage, nor strategic direction for political strategy. Table 12.4 summarizes the types of strategic sociopolitical responses employed by an array of researchers and practicing managers. The suggestion is that organizations employ a different organizational response (endogenously driven behavior) depending on the environmental (exogenously driven process) conditions (contingency), which facilitates the goal of this exploratory research to associate environmental turbulence and strategic behavior orientation to performance.

Several authors also have suggested that the aggressiveness of strategic managerial behavior for societal response must match the intensity of the changes in the societal environment.[53]

Strategic choices are an outcome of stakeholder power and environmental pressures.[54] Strategic choices are manifested into goals; however, scholars have long argued the intricacies and interplay of the firm's goals.[55] Although there is a cost associated with failure to manage the political agenda of the firm, the most important is the loss of choice-making discretion.[56] Managers who are involved in developing strategic choices of social goal strategies must realize the opportunities and constraints presented by the political process and legal structures.[57] Moreover, strategic choices are an outcome of a strategic posture, which is developed through assessment of the environment and stakeholder aggressiveness.[58] Once the firm has engaged in environmental analysis, management must make strategic choices about how to best adapt or respond to the results of the environmental scanning. The result of environmental scanning and strategic diagnosis[59] provides the business institution with an array of strategic choices.[60]

MANAGERIAL CAPABILITY FOR
SOCIAL AND POLITICAL RESPONSE

Although researchers have affirmed the need for corporate sociopolitical strategy, there is minimal research on the development of the managerial capability for such work. Managers need to understand diverse ideologies, acquire skills in coalition building, bargaining in the sociopolitical domain, stakeholder power, etc.[61] Moreover, firms must develop managerial skills for political response[62] and define their social and political marketplace with the same intensity as they define their competitive market place. Managers are responsible for the formulation and implementation of strategies regarding corporate sociopolitical activities that produce public-policy outcomes that are favorable to the firm's economic success.[63]

Management should possess capabilities for rethinking traditional beliefs and understanding the political process and skills in political behavior. Moreover, management should develop a political infrastructure capable of recognizing the political market domain of the firm, which will facilitate the necessary sociopolitical networking and relations critical to the profit-making activities.[64] The formulation and implementation of social goals[65] will allow management to increase its capabilities and claim success in the sociopolitical arena *before* stakeholders[66] exert social pressure and/or laws and regulations are implemented to address relevant issues.

SOCIETAL PERFORMANCE

Management is interested to see how the corporate political activity will be justified in the operational context of strategic management. Therefore, they must establish a correlation between societal activities and performance. There is some evidence that companies that perform in a socially responsible way are as profitable.[67] Although top managers have a perceived value of corporate political strategy, there is very little evidence to support the view that corporate political performance improves economic performance. There are some studies that suggested a correlation between corporate political activity and performance.[68]

WHY SOCIETAL STRATEGY?

It is evident that the business institutions will face a competitive arena in which a considerable number of nonmarket activities[69] (politics, social responsibility) will seriously affect economic performance. Nevertheless, it is possible to incorporate both sides by accepting that stockholder profit maximization is obtained through a broader strategy, which goes beyond competitive strategy to include societal strategy. Although there are strong indicators suggesting that business and societal benefits do not mix well, the business institution has no choice but to expand its scope to include a greater strategic angle that will accommodate both economic and noneconomic objectives.

The strategic landscape for the modern business firm has changed. The arsenal of weapons needed to combat the competitive realities is beyond the scope of functional management. Increasingly, corporate social responsibility (CSR) contributes to shaping the contents of management education.[70] The competitive environment has been extended into rather uncharted territories for most firms. For example, Microsoft, a highly entrepreneurial and successful company, encountered a battle that falls out of the technological and competitive boundaries, that is, the societal challenge (legal justification of market aggressiveness). Market dominance had created a different theater of war for Microsoft. Regardless of the opinions surrounding the legal position of Microsoft, it was evident that the political posture of Microsoft failed to foresee the societal implications of market dominance. Nonetheless, corporate managers are not trained to assume such roles. Firms will ultimately rely on hired guns to fight the societal battles of the firm. However, "managers are responsible for both market and nonmarket strategies and nonmarket analysis should be integrated with the analysis of market forces."[71] In speculating about the anticipated explosion of the biotech industry, we can only hypothesize the societal ramifications[72] and issues arising from biotech products (i.e., wealthy individuals cloning themselves for parts, sex selection, etc.). Consequently, the modern business firm must vigorously consider the societal environment[73] and strategize proactively.

This is not an issue only concerning large firms but also the small firm.[74] For example, in most suburban areas of a large city, pizza restaurants will often support little league sports. The question then arises whether they can afford not to participate in such social responsibility activities because a competitor may assume such a role. Therefore, whether it is a deliberate strategy for the restaurant owner or a reaction to the surrounding environment, it is clear that this type of strategy is not concerned with profitability, product innovation, or quality of service, but is about creating an image favorable to the stakeholders of the establishment often at a considerable cost.[75] Furthermore, the same restaurant owner might want to keep an eye on the political scene of her/his community, where issues like zoning, transportation, etc., may have a critical impact on her/his business. Therefore, even the small businessperson must deliberately explore the wider societal ramifications impacting her/his business.

The modern firm's objectives will need to be supplemented with noneconomic objectives and that the "firm transformed from a purely

Figure 12.2
Socioeconomic and Political Environment

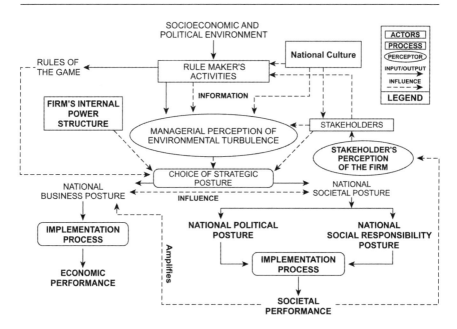

economic institution to a socioeconomic institution of society."[76] It is evident that the modern business institution is faced with a broader scope of strategic challenges. Such strategic challenges are not new and for years firms have employed instruments to counter such issues (public affairs, government affairs, lobbyists, planned giving, etc.). For the most part, these activities became part of a business only upon discovering, for example, a public issue demanding a response by the respective business (reactive). Therefore, the societal strategic posture of the firm has generally been reactive, as opposed to proactive. The mounting pressure from such nonmarket activities begs the question for a reconfiguration of the strategic approach of the modern firm. Societal strategy[77] must become an integral part of the corporate strategy to facilitate the firm's societal role effectively and efficiently. It is also critical to establish the long-term societal implications of the firm's competitive strategy. Competitive strategy employs mechanisms that explore near-future opportunities with near-future performance, although the societal implications of such strategy lie into the far future. According to Peter Drucker, "in the years to come, the most needed and the most effective—indeed perhaps the only truly effective—approach to 'social responsibility' will be the determination of social needs before departing into the creation of financial gains." The interaction between the socio and political environment is illustrated in Figure 12.2.

Therefore, societal strategy is the nonbusiness strategic activities involved with the social responsibility and the legitimacy of the firm. Social responsibility is granted with the task of maintaining an ethical behavior and conduct business in a socially responsible manner. The legitimacy strategy attempts to maintain and/or create rules that are favorable to the firm.[78]

ELEMENTS OF SOCIETAL STRATEGY

If we divide the overall strategy of the business firm into two major categories, market and nonmarket strategies, societal strategy is the nonmarket strategy. Distinctly, business firms must not only function in an environment of outstanding ethical practices (social responsibility) but also must maintain effective management of the rules of the game (legitimacy). The social responsibility strategies and legitimacy strategies[79] constitute the societal strategy of the firm. Both elements are not ingredients of the profit-making activities; however, modern firms cannot function without them.

When attempting to define business legitimacy, we encounter a diversity of opinions. Is legitimacy the institutionalization of an organization, the rightful control of power, the relationship of members and nonmembers, the institution's extent of authority, the institution's acceptance by stakeholders, or simply how the business is being accepted? Since this is a rather evasive concept, we would accept all of them and proceed with a more critical question. What does it mean for a business organization? Hence, the critical element for the business firm would be the utility of legitimacy and therefore *legitimacy strategy*. Moreover, the understanding of legitimacy strategy permits a holistic approach to the concept of business legitimacy. Legitimacy strategy refers to the nonvoluntary activities presented to the firm by the political environment. When the political structure accepts corporate activities, then such activities are attributed as legitimate. Therefore, firms must engage in a process that will generate acceptable behavior by the elected officials. The representation of business firms with offices of government affairs in Washington is an indicator of the deliberate strategy[80] of the business firm to influence legislators in the creation of favorable rules. Firms routinely donate funds[81] to representatives of both parties. Such activity aims almost exclusively to generate favorable rules to the business firm. Success is measured by the legislation of rules that will enhance competitive advantage for the firm.

In contrast, we propose the voluntary constraints on the firm to label them as *social responsibility strategies*. For example, when a pizza restaurant supports the little league games and a large firm maintains a "planned giving division," it is evident that business entities, regardless of their size, voluntarily contribute to the community and society.

Although motives may be different, such voluntary activities involve practices that go over and above the legal requirements of the firm, normally attributed as ethical practices or socially responsible behavior. Hence, we define social responsibility strategy as the strategy that pursues voluntary activities aiming to contribute to society and enhance the image of the corporation.

Ethicists will argue that business firms could provide societal contributions without any motivating factors other than the satisfaction of the recipients. However, when considering the firm's responsibilities to shareholders and/or general financial constraints, I would argue strongly against such an assertion. For example, firms never provide anonymous donations (how would they explain it to stockholders). Regardless the firm's size, ethical considerations and social contributions not only aim to provide societally, but also to enhance the firm's image in aspiration of generating a better market performance. Moreover, the term "planned giving"[82] or "strategic philanthropy"[83] is indicative of the strategic considerations by the firm, including the small business owner. It is also fair to suggest that we have examples of business contributions that follow an emotional path rather than a logical path of "planned giving" activities.

Under those broad definitions, we are incorporating areas such as corporate political strategy, social responsiveness, ethical strategies, environmental strategies, lobbying, grassroots, public affairs strategy, government affairs strategy, stakeholder strategy, coalition-building strategies, testimony strategies, political entrepreneurship, communication and public advocacy, and judicial strategies.

On a microlevel, some subelements of societal strategy are:

1. Social audit strategies: A diagnosis of the firm's social responsibility and social causes it chooses to support, and the development of the modalities to support such causes and socially responsible behavior.
2. Code of ethics strategies: Voluntary constraints that the firm chooses to undertake to respect the internal and external environment of the firm.
3. Socially responsible investment funds: Investments by the firm in socially acceptable funds. Usually, socially responsible investment means not investing in questionable funds associated with industries or companies that may violate standards for the environment, human rights, product safety, and so forth.
4. Corporate philanthropy: Charitable contributions, donation of resources, or involvement with local, national, and international causes.
5. Enlightened self-interest strategies: Efforts by the firm to create a favorable, ethical image.

We often find these strategies under the label of ethical strategies. Ethical strategies are intended to enhance competitiveness, preserve legitimacy, deter white-collar crime, and to promote trust.[84]

LEGITIMACY STRATEGIES

Sociopolitical legitimacy entails authority,[85] approval, or conformity to the legal rules[86] as devised by the respective authorities.

Firm legitimacy is a small part of management often better understood by its absence. An organization lacking legitimacy renders itself incapable of pursuing its goals effectively. Basic firm legitimacy refers to the right to exist and make a profit, while following the rule of law; however, legitimacy is earned as a result of organizational values and norms that are acceptable to society.[87] The global volatility and interdependence of economies have created a novel legitimacy landscape for the corporations today. Increased global competitiveness coupled with unemployment, income inequality, labor, environment, and human rights have brought corporate legitimacy to the forefront of our society. A new societal sentiment is rising against the corporation.[88] Recently, the increased inequality and uncertainty introduced by the global financial crisis, particularly in the West, also established loss of faith in the capitalist system to deliver organizational legitimacy through its:

1. Public relations strategies: Involve communication with the media, investors, brokerage houses, financial institutions, image building, employee communications, etc., with sole purpose of maintaining and improving the company position (e.g., the recent public reassurances by Ford and Firestone about their products).[89]
2. Government-business relationship strategies: Involve monitoring the local, state, national, and international regulatory and legislative bodies, assessing the impact of rules, and taking appropriate action to create favorable rules (i.e., lobbying).[90]
3. Regulatory strategies: These are strategies designed to protect rights, handicap competitors, and/or gain favorable advantage (i.e., preventing a company from bringing their generic product into the market).[91]
4. Political and legal strategies: These are the strategies the firm pursues to influence the rules of the game and enhance its financial performance.[92]

Therefore, nonmarket strategy has become as important as, if not more than, the market strategy. Recent examples of this nonmarket strategy would be the steps undertaken by Firestone—the tire manufacturer—and

Ford: they maneuvered their ethical *and* political posture to diffuse financial impact.

WHO PERFORMS THE SOCIETAL STRATEGY?

Managerial Capability for Societal Response

Managers are responsible for the formulation and implementation of societal strategies that produce public-policy outcomes that are favorable to the firm's economic success.

Society did not have any great expectations from corporate management until the 1940s and management functioned without any interference from society. However, the accommodation period ended and corporate management entered the socialization period, when it began to be influenced by society. The gap between the organization's performance and society's expectations increased. It was apparent that in the sociopolitical environment of the firm, the management needed to devise different responses for different levels of turbulence.

Presently, firms need to develop societal-response capabilities for productive societal response and management should possess capabilities of rethinking traditional beliefs and understanding the political process and skills in political behavior. Moreover, management should develop a political infrastructure capable of recognizing the societal market domain of the firm, which will facilitate necessary social networking and relations critical to the profit-making activities. Management is responsible for the social responsibility strategies and for legitimacy strategies.[93]

Managerial requirements for ethical capabilities are difficult to assess since there is no universal agreement on all moral issues. Considering the responsibility of the management to the firm and its stakeholders, ethical capability is inevitably guided by self-interest. However, we must point out that self-interest and moral concerns are not the same.[94] Management should employ tools that allow the firm to prioritize issues based on their urgency[95] and thus provide the manager with a classification mechanism to identify issues and their potential impact and to proceed with formulating and implementing strategies. Considering the diversity of issues, managers should have the option of considering the views of experts but retain the ultimate responsibility for the course of action.

In contrast, management can claim success in the political arena only before issues become laws and regulations. Managerial capability involves formulating and implementing social goals with a clear understanding of both the legislative process and the power of stakeholders. Managers must not only understand the legal and/or regulatory structure but also the political process, which will help them provide a contributing social strategy to the overall corporate strategy. Since the nonmarket issues are critical to the performance of the firm, managers are responsible for developing, formulating, and implementing societal strategies that accommodate the design of favorable policy and/or image to the firm.

CONCLUSION

The transformation of the business institute into a sociopolitical and economic institution indicates the emerging need for the development of a proactive posture to manage the nonmarket environment effectively. Accelerated globalization and technological development present modern firms with novel issues that require solutions that are very different from current competitive practices. Human rights, environment, technology, and employment conditions are only a few issues—coupled with the capability for instant media exposure around the world—that dictate that the firms should have in place a well-devised strategy to counter potential issues, while preferably preventing them from becoming issues.

In summary, we propose that societal strategy involves the voluntary and nonvoluntary activities of the firm with the aim of enhancing the business (functional-competitive) strategy. By accepting the notion of a broader strategic angle for the business institution to include societal components, business practitioners and academicians recognize, at the very least, the impact of societal [nonmarket] affairs on the competitive [market] activities. Such an approach will facilitate the development of a corporate need to study and manage nonmarket strategies systematically. Business schools and researchers will develop additional tools to assist business practitioners. Practicing managers will develop a higher degree of cognizance of the potential impact, or the lack of it, of nonmarket strategies.

NOTES

1. Baron, David P. 1993. *Business and Its Environment.* Englewood Cliffs, NJ: Prentice Hall.

2. Ansoff, Igor H. and McDonnell, E. 1990. *Implanting Strategic Management.* New York: Prentice Hall.

3. Kernisky, Debra A. 1997. "Proactive Crisis Management and Ethical Discourse: Dow Chemical's Issues Management Bulletins 1979–1990." *Journal of Business Ethics* 16(8): 843–853.

4. Carroll, Archie and Shabana, Kareem S. 2010. "The Business Case for Corporate Social Responsibility: A Review of Concepts, Research and Practice." *International Journal of Management Reviews* 12: 1.

5. Marcy, Richard T., Gentry William A., and McKinnon, Rob. 2008. "Thinking Straight New *Strategies* Are Needed for *Ethical* Leadership." *Leadership in Action* 28(3): 3.

6. Eliason, Michael J. 1999. "Compliance Plus Integrity." *Internal Auditor* 56(6): 30–33.

7. Drucker, Peter F. 1980. *Managing in Turbulent Times.* New York: Harper & Row. See also the work by Brown (2001); Ansoff and McDonnell (1990); and Baron (1993).

8. Drucker, Peter. 1985. *Management: Tasks, Responsibilities, and Practices.* New York: Harper & Row.

9. Drucker, Peter F. 1984. "The New Meaning of Social Responsibility." *California Management Review* 53–63. See also the work by Steiner and Steiner (1994); Buchholz and Rosenthal (1995); Carroll (1996); and Marcus (1993)2.

10. Cho, Charles H., Patten, Dennis M., and Roberts, Robin W. 2006. "Corporate Political Strategy: An Examination of the Relation between Political Expenditures, Environmental Performance, and Environmental Disclosure." *Journal of Business Ethics* 67(2): 139.

11. Wood, Donna J. 1990. *Business and Society.* Glenview, IL: Scott Foresman/ Little, Brown Higher Education.

12. Freeman, R.E. 1984. *Strategic Management: A Stakeholder Approach.* Boston: Pitman.

13. Friedman, Milton. 1982. *Capitalism and Freedom.* Chicago: University of Chicago Press.

14. Williams, Stephen. 1999. "U.K. Ethical Investment: A Coming of Age." *Journal of Investing* 8(2): 58–76.

15. Drucker, Peter F. 1984. "The New Meaning of Social Responsibility." *California Management Review* 26(2): 53–63.

16. Tan, Justin. 2009. "Multinational Corporations and Social Responsibility in Emerging Markets: Opportunities and Challenges for Research and Practice." *Journal of Business Ethics* 86: 151–153.

17. Judge, William. 2009. "The Complexity of International Corporate Governance Research." *Corporate Governance: An International Review* 17(5): 525.

18. Sethi, Prakash S. and Falbe, Cecelia M. ed. 1987. *Business and Society: Dimensions of Conflict and Cooperation.* Lanham, MD: Lexington Books; Carroll, Archie B. and Hoy, Frank. 1984. "Integrating Corporate Social Policy into Strategic Management." *Journal of Business Strategy* 4(3): 48–57.

19. Weber, Max. 1947a. *Theory of Social and Economic Organizations,* Translated by A.M. Anderson and T. Parsons. New York: Oxford University Press.

20. Carroll, Archie B. and Hoy, Frank. 1984. "Integrating Corporate Social Policy into Strategic Management." *Journal of Business Strategy* 4(3): 48–57.

21. Ansoff, Igor H. and McDonnell, E. 1990. *Implanting Strategic Management.* New York: Prentice Hall.

22. Sethi, Prakash S. and Falbe, Cecelia M., ed. 1987. *Business and Society: Dimensions of Conflict and Cooperation.* Lanham, MD: Lexington Books.

23. Wood, Donna J. 1986. *Strategic Uses of Public Policy: Business and Government in the Progressive Era.* Boston: Pitman.

24. Ansoff, Igor H. and McDonnell, E. 1990. *Implanting Strategic Management.* New York: Prentice Hall; Drucker, Peter F. 1980. *Managing in Turbulent Times.* New

York: Harper & Row; and Wood, Donna J. 1990. *Business and Society.* Glenview, IL: Scott Foresman/Little, Brown Higher Education; Peery, Newman S. 1995. *Business, Government, and Society Managing Competitiveness, Ethics, and Social Issues.* Englewood Cliffs, NJ: Prentice Hall.

25. Emery, F. E. and Trist, E. L. 1965. "The Casual Texture of Organizational Environments." *Human Relations* 18: 21–32; Duncan, R. B. 1972. "Characteristics of Organizational Environments and Perceived Environment Uncertainty." *Administrative Science Quarterly* 17: 313–327; Post, James E. 1978. *Corporate Behavior and Social Change.* Reston, VA: Reston Publishing Company.

26. Ansoff, Igor H. and McDonnell, E. 1990. *Implanting Strategic Management.* New York: Prentice Hall; Buchholz, Rogene A., and Rosenthal, Sandra B. 1995. "Theoretical Foundations of Public Policy: A Pragmatic Perspective." *Business & Society* 34(3): 261–279; Drucker, Peter F. 1980. *Managing in Turbulent Times.* New York: Harper & Row; Peery, Newman S. 1995. *Business, Government, and Society Managing Competitiveness, Ethics, and Social Issues.* Englewood Cliffs, NJ: Prentice Hall; Post, James E. 1978. *Corporate Behavior and Social Change.* Reston, VA: Reston Publishing Company; Vernon-Wortzel, Heidy. 1994. *Business and Society: A Managerial Approach.* Burr Ridge, IL: Irwin; Wood, Donna J. 1990. *Business and Society.* Glenview, IL: Scott Foresman/Little, Brown Higher Education.

27. Jurkovitch, Ray. 1974. "A Core Topology of Organization Environment." *Administrative Science Quarterly* 19: 380–394.

28. Thompson, James D. 1967. *Organizations in Action.* New York: McGraw-Hill.

29. Ansoff, Igor H. and Sullivan, Patrick A. 1993. "Optimizing Profitability in Turbulent Environments: A Formula for Strategic Success." *Long Range Planning* 26: 11–23.

30. Tan, Justin J. and Litschert, Robert J. 1994. "Environment—Strategy Relationship and Its Performance Implication: An Empirical Study of the Chinese Electronics Industry." *Strategic Management Journal* 15: 1–20.

31. Naman, John L. and Slevin, Dennis P. 1993. "Entrepreneurship and the Concept of Fit: A Model and Empirical Tests." *Strategic Management Journal* 14: 137–153.

32. Ansoff, Igor H. and McDonnell, E. 1990. *Implanting Strategic Management.* New York: Prentice Hall; Armstrong, Scott J. 1982. "The Value of Formal Planning for Strategic Decisions: Review of Empirical Research." *Strategic Management Journal* 3(3) (July–September): 197–211; Hamel, Gary and Prahalad, C.K. 1994. *Competing for the Future.* Boston: Harvard Business School Press.

33. Porter, Michael E. 1980. *Competitive Strategy.* New York: Free Press.

34. Ansoff, Igor H. and Sullivan, Patrick A. 1993. "Optimizing Profitability in Turbulent Environments: A Formula for Strategic Success." *Long Range Planning* 26: 11–23; Morrison, Allen J. and Kendall, Roth. 1992. "A Taxonomy of Business-Level Strategies in Global Industries." *Strategic Management Journal* 13: 399–417; Post, James E. 1978. *Corporate Behavior and Social Change.* Reston, VA: Reston Publishing Company; Thwaites, Des and Glaister, Keith. 1992. "Strategic Responses to Environmental Turbulence." *International Journal of Bank Marketing* 10(3): 33–40; Vernon-Wortzel, Heidy. 1994. *Business and Society: A Managerial Approach.* Burr Ridge, IL: Irwin.

35. Peery, Newman S. 1995. *Business, Government, and Society Managing Competitiveness, Ethics, and Social Issues.* Englewood Cliffs, NJ: Prentice Hall.

36. Mintzberg, Henry. 1983. *Power In and Around Organizations.* Englewood Cliffs, NJ: Prentice-Hall; Wood, Donna J. 1990. *Business and Society.* Glenview, IL: Scott Foresman/Little, Brown Higher Education.

37. Ansoff, Igor H. and McDonnell, E. 1990. *Implanting Strategic Management.* New York: Prentice Hall.

38. Freeman, R. E. 1984. *Strategic Management: A Stakeholder Approach.* Boston: Pitman.

39. Vernon-Wortzel, Heidy. 1994. *Business and Society. A Managerial Approach.* Burr Ridge, IL: Irwin; Donaldson, Thomas and Preston, Lee E. 1995. "The Stakeholder Theory of the Corporation: Concepts, Evidence, and Implications." *Academy of Management Review* 20(1): 65–91.

40. Brummer, James J. 1991. *Corporate Responsibility and Legitimacy.* New York: Greenwood Press.

41. Ibid.

42. Ackoff, Russell L. 1981. *Creating the Corporate Future.* New York: John Wiley & Sons.

43. Carroll, Archie B. 1993. *Business and Society: Ethics and Stakeholder Management.* Cincinnati: South-Western Publishing.

44. Freeman, R. E. 1984. *Strategic Management: A Stakeholder Approach.* Boston: Pitman.

45. Buchholz, Rogene A. and Rosenthal, Sandra B. 1995. "Theoretical Foundations of Public Policy: A Pragmatic Perspective." *Business & Society* 34(3): 261–279; Wood, Donna J. 1990. *Business and Society.* Glenview, IL: Scott Foresman/Little, Brown Higher Education.

46. Ansoff, Igor H. and McDonnell, E. 1990. *Implanting Strategic Management.* New York: Prentice Hall; Baron, David P. 1993. *Business and Its Environment.* Englewood Cliffs, NJ: Prentice Hall.

47. Morrison, Allen J. and Kendall, Roth. 1992. "A Taxonomy of Business-Level Strategies in Global Industries." *Strategic Management Journal* 13: 399–417.

48. Miles, R. A. and C. C. Snow. 1978. *Organizational Strategy, Structure and Process.* New York: McGraw-Hill.

49. Shortel, S. M. and Zarac, E. 1990. "Perceptual and Archival Measure of Miles and Snow's Strategic Types: A Comprehensive Assessment of Reliability and Validity." *Academy of Management Journal* 33: 817–822.

50. Ansoff, Igor H. and Sullivan, Patrick A., et al. 1993. "Empirical Support for a Paradigmic Theory of Strategic Success Behaviors of Environment Serving Organizations." *International Review of Strategic Management* 4: 173–203; Hambrick, Donald C. 1983. "Some Tests of the Effectiveness and Functional Attributes of Miles and Snow's Strategic Types." *Academy of Management Journal* 26(1): 5–26; McDaniel, Stephen W. and Kolari, James W. 1987. "Marketing Strategy Implications of the Miles and Snow Strategic Typology." *Journal of Marketing* 51(4) 19–30; Ramaswamy, Kannan, Thomas, Anisya S., and Litschert, Robert J. 1994. "Organizational Performance in a Regulated Environment: The Role of Strategic Orientation." *Strategic Management Journal* 15: 63–74.

51. Porter, Michael E. 1980. *Competitive Strategy.* New York: Free Press.

52. Segev, Eli. 1989. "A Systematic Comparative Analysis and Synthesis of Two Business-Level Strategic Typologies." *Strategic Management Journal* 10: 487–505.

53. Frederick, William C., Post, James E., and Davis, Keith. 1992. *Business and Society: Corporate Strategy, Public Policy, Ethics.* New York: McGraw-Hill; Ansoff,

Igor H. and McDonnell, E. 1990. *Implanting Strategic Management.* New York: Prentice Hall.

54. Child, John. 1972. "Organizational Structure, Environment and Performance: The Role of Strategic Choice." *Sociology* 6: 1–22; Mintzberg, Henry. 1983. *Power in and Around Organizations.* Englewood Cliffs, NJ: Prentice-Hall; Murray, E. A. 1978. "Strategic Choice as a Negotiated Outcome." *Management Science* 960–972; Miles, Robert H. and Kimberly S. Cameron. 1982. *Coffin Nails and Corporate Strategies.* Englewood Cliffs, NJ: Prentice Hall.

55. Smith, Adam. 1937. *An Inquiry into the Nature and Causes of the Wealth of Nations.* 1776 Reprint. New York: Modern Library; Cyert, R. M. and March, J. G. 1963. *A Behavioral Theory of the Firm.* Englewood Cliffs, NJ: Prentice Hall;

56. Post, James E. 1978. *Corporate Behavior and Social Change.* Reston, VA: Reston Publishing Company.

57. Vernon-Wortzel, Heidy. 1994. *Business and Society: A Managerial Approach.* Burr Ridge, IL: Irwin.

58. Ansoff, Igor H. and McDonnell, E. 1990. *Implanting Strategic Management.* New York: Prentice Hall.

59. Ansoff, Igor H. and McDonnell, E. 1990. *Implanting Strategic Management.* New York: Prentice Hall; Vernon-Wortzel, Heidy. 1994. *Business and Society. A Managerial Approach.* Burr Ridge, IL: Irwin.

60. Ibid.

61. Ansoff, Igor H. and McDonnell, E. 1990. *Implanting Strategic Management.* New York: Prentice Hall.

62. Post, James E. 1978. *Corporate Behavior and Social Change.* Reston, VA: Reston Publishing Company; Sethi, Prakash. 1982. "Corporate Political Activism." *California Management Review* 24(3): 32–42; Vernon-Wortzel, Heidy. 1994. *Business and Society: A Managerial Approach.* Burr Ridge, IL: Irwin; Greening, Daniel W. and Gray, Barbara. 1994. "Testing a Model of Organizational Response to Social and Political Issues." *Academy of Management Journal* 37: 467.

63. Ansoff, Igor H. and McDonnell E. 1990. *Implanting Strategic Management.* New York: Prentice Hall; Keim, Gerald D., and Baysinger, Barry D. 1988. "The Efficacy of Business Political Activity: Competitive Considerations in a Principal-Agent Context." *Journal of Management* 14(2): 163–180.

64. Ansoff, Igor H. and McDonnell, E. 1990. *Implanting Strategic Management.* New York: Prentice Hall.

65. Vernon-Wortzel, Heidy. 1994. *Business and Society: A Managerial Approach.* Burr Ridge, IL: Irwin.

66. Useem, Michael. 1985. "The Rise of the Political Manager." *Sloan Management Review* (Fall), pp. 15–26.

67. Vogel, David. 2005. *The Market for Virtue.* Washington, DC: Brookings Institution.

68. Sitkin, Sim B. and Bies, Robert J. (eds.) 1994. *The Legalistic Organization.* Thousand Oaks, CA: Sage Publications; Ramaswamy, Kannan, Thomas, Anisya S., and Litschert, Robert J. 1994. "Organizational Performance in a Regulated Environment: The Role of Strategic Orientation." *Strategic Management Journal* 15: 63–74.

69. Campbell, John L. 2007. "Why Would Corporations Behave in Socially Responsible Ways? An Institutional Theory of Corporate Social Responsibility." *Academy of Management Review* 32(3): 946–967.

70. Kletz, Pierre. 2009. "Research in Social Responsibility: A Challenge for Management Education." *Management Education* 47(10): 1582–1594.

71. Baron, David P. 1995. "Integrating Market Strategies and Non-Market Strategies." *California Management Review* 37(2): 47–65.

72. Marks, John. 2008. "Genetic Governance: Health, Risk and Ethics in the Biotech Era." *Theory, Culture and Society* 25(2): 157–160.

73. Lawrence, Ann T. and Weber, James. 2009. *Business and Society.* New York: McGraw-Hill.

74. Bengston, Anna, Pahlberg, Cecilia, and Pourmand, Firouze. 2009. "Small Firms' Interaction with Political Organizations in the European Union." *Industrial Marketing Management* 38(6): 687–697.

75. Quinn, John J. 1997. "Personal Ethics and Business Ethics: The Ethical Attitudes of Owner/Managers of Small Business." *Journal of Business Ethics* 16(2): 119–127.

76. Ansoff, Igor H. and McDonnell, E. 1990. *Implanting Strategic Management.* New York: Prentice Hall.

77. Husted, Bryan W. and Allen, David B. 2007. "Corporate Social Strategy in Multinational Enterprises: Antecedents and Value Creation." *Journal of Business Ethics* 74(4): 345–361.

78. Ibid.

79. Chen, Jennifer C., Patten, Dennis M., and Roberts, Robert W. 2008. "Corporate Charitable Contributions: A Corporate Social Performance or *Legitimacy Strategy?" Journal of Business Ethics* 82(1): 131–144.

80. Vining, Aidan R., Shapiro, Daniel M., and Borges, Bernjard. 2005. "Building the Firm's Political (Lobbying) Strategy." *Journal of Public Affairs* 5(2): 150–175.

81. Gipp, Narissa, Kalafatis, Stravros P., and Ledden, Lesley, 2008. "Perceived Value of Corporate Donations: An Empirical Investigation." *International Journal of Non-profit and Voluntary Sector Marketing* 13(4): 327–346.

82. Bernstein, Phyllis. 2005. "Financial Advisers and Planned Giving: Doing the Right Thing." *CPA Journal* 75(6): 62–63.

83. Campbell, David and Slack, Richard. 2008. "Corporate 'Philanthropy Strategy' and 'Strategic Philanthropy': Some Insights from Voluntary Disclosures in Annual Reports." *Business and Society* 47(2): 187–212.

84. Marcus, Alfred A. 1996. *Business Strategies, Ethics and the Global Economy Society.* Boston: Irwin-McGraw-Hill.

85. Haveman, Heather A., Hayagreeva Rao, and Srikanth Paruchuri. 2007. "The Winds of Change: The Progressive Movement and the Bureaucratization of Thrift." *American Sociological Review* 72: 114–142.

86. Rao, Hayagreeva, Calvin Morrill, and Mayer N. Zald. 2000. "Power Plays: Social Movements, Collective Action, and New Organizational Forms." *Research in Organizational Behavior* 22: 237–282.

87. Matthews, M.R. 1993. *Socially Responsible Accounting.* London: Chapman and Hall.

88. Warren, R., 1999. "Company Legitimacy in the New Millennium." *Business Ethics: A European Review* 8: 214–224.

89. Ibid.

90. Ibid.

91. Baron, David P. 1993. *Business and Its Environment.* Englewood Cliffs, NJ: Prentice Hall.

92. Ansoff, Igor H. and McDonnell, E. 1990. *Implanting Strategic Management.* New York: Prentice Hall.

93. Baron, David P. 1995. "Integrating Market Strategies and NonMarket Strategies." *California Management Review* 37(2): 47–65.

94. Ibid.

95. Ansoff, Igor H. and McDonnell, E. 1990. *Implanting Strategic Management.* New York: Prentice Hall.

Chapter 13

Strategy and Entrepreneurship—A Discussion of Strategic Entrepreneurs

Franco Gandolfi

INTRODUCTION

The term *entrepreneur* is, in many ways, one of the most excessively used and misunderstood modern-day business concepts. "Entrepreneur" is often used to refer to individuals who own their businesses. These people may have launched a business endeavor from scratch, purchased an existing entity, or inherited a business operation. It must be understood, however, that an entrepreneurially minded person is much more than a mere owner and/or operator of a business endeavor. So, what exactly is an entrepreneur?

The term entrepreneur has its origin in the French word *entreprendre*, which literally translates into "undertaking." Over the years, the term has taken on a variety of meanings. On the one extreme, an entrepreneur is a person who is exceptionally talented and skilled and who is seen as a pioneer of revolutionary change, possessing characteristics found only in a small fraction of society. On the other extreme, an entrepreneur is simply a person who pursues a business-type endeavor. In such a capacity, it is probable that he or she is working for himself or herself. Unsurprisingly, many definitions of an entrepreneur have emerged. Some of the definitions are as follows:[1]

- A person who organizes, manages, and assumes the risks of a business or enterprise;
- A person who possesses a new enterprise, venture, or idea and is accountable for the inherent risks of the outcome;
- A person who organizes, operates, and assumes the risk for a business venture;
- An owner or manager of a business enterprise who, by taking risks and initiative, attempts to make profits; and
- An individual with a vision who orchestrates the time, talent, money, and resources of other people to make the vision real.[2]

The last definition of an entrepreneur is interesting from a number of viewpoints: First, there is no reference to the assumption of *risk* in that the entrepreneur has passed the risk element onto investors. Second, there is no reference to a *new venture*; an entrepreneur can orchestrate a vision of existing businesses into a more efficient and effective organization of business entities. Third, there is no reference to *profitability* in that some of the greatest, manifested visions have been in the world of not-for-profit endeavors. Fourth, there is no reference to *the operation of a business*, since many forms of businesses, including licensing and franchising, have emerged to enable others to operate businesses. Last, the reference to *vision* suggests that the actual vision may not be owned by the entrepreneur; he or she may have borrowed or even stolen somebody else's vision.

THE ENTREPRENEUR AND THE NOTION OF VISION

Consistent with this definition, an entrepreneur is alleged to have the innate ability to conceive, conceptualize, and cast a vision. History books are filled with examples of visionary entrepreneurial leaders. Some notable ones are the following:

- *Thomas Edison:* His vision was to provide relief from human drudgery and the elevation of the human spirit through science;
- *Henry Ford:* His vision was to bring mobility to the masses, specifically to bring the cost of a car down to where the worker who built it could afford to buy it;
- *Sam Walton:* His vision was for people to save money so they could live better;
- *Bill Gates:* His vision was to see a personal computer on every desk and in every home; then to empower people through great software;

- *Steve Jobs:* His vision was to have an Apple computer on every desk (not realized yet) and for people to have an Apple device in every hand (currently being realized);
- *Richard Branson:* He has several visions, from being able to provide affordable records for everyone to affordable travel to destinations in outer space (not realized yet); and
- *Walt Disney:* He also had multiple visions; one of them was to create the happiest place on earth.[3]

The one characteristic that all these visionary entrepreneurial leaders had or have in common was or is the aspect of a distinctive vision. These leaders envisioned things that did not yet exist and created and transformed the visions into reality. Of course, although there is high probability that these distinguished leaders experienced many great obstacles and challenges, they nonetheless mastered the ability to orchestrate other people's resources in order to breathe life into their visions.

SOME HISTORY OF ECONOMIC THEORIES UNDERLYING ENTREPRENEURSHIP

At its most basic, the notion of economic theory is concerned with two major societal questions. First, how does a society utilize scarce resources to create and build wealth? Second, how does that society distribute the created wealth among its members? Wealth creation and wealth distribution present fundamental and, at times, even controversial questions pertaining to the development and progress of any society. It has long been established that entrepreneurship, human creativity, and the innovation of scientific ideas are major mechanisms and catalysts for the creation and distribution of societal wealth. The notion of entrepreneurship is not new. In fact, some authors have reported that entrepreneurship has been around for quite some time and, as a direct result, a number of different schools of thought have emerged, including the classical capitalist economic theory, the neoclassical theory, and the Schumpeterian school of thought.

Classical Capitalist Economic Theory

Back in 1776, Adam Smith, a Scottish social philosopher and economist, described a capitalist as an owner-manager who organized, synthesized, and combined resources into an industrial enterprise. It was during this time that the French term *"entrepreneur"* was introduced in order to identify the owner-manager, or entrepreneur, of an industrial enterprise.[4]

Neoclassical Theory

The classical capitalist economic theory espoused the view that "self-interest," also referred to as "the invisible hand," would guide participating individuals toward entrepreneurial behavior. However, by the end of the 19th century, economic theorists argued that the market comprised many buyers and sellers who interacted in a way that ensures that supply equals demand. The market was seen at equilibrium (i.e., balanced) and, thus, perfect. This would be achieved, it was argued, by fluctuations in prices and supply levels. Therefore, it was posited that wealth would be created and distributed due to the nature of the perfect market. Within this school of thought, there is little place for the traditional manager-owner, the entrepreneur. The neoclassical theory is widely regarded and taught as the mainstream view of economics. Also, within this framework, a perfect market is defined as having (1) many buyers and sellers, with neither group wielding a decisive influence on the market prices, (2) prices set by the markets themselves, (3) products and services that are equivalent in substance but differ in price, and (4) buyers and sellers that have access to complete knowledge of the market and the transactions that occur.[5]

Schumpeterian Vision

In the early 20th century, Austrian economist and political scientist Joseph Schumpeter rejected neoclassical economic thinking. He took a decisive pro-entrepreneurship stance and argued that innovation capability was the key driving force for new goods and services. Schumpeter posited that the market was chaotic rather than perfect due to entrepreneurs continually providing the markets with creative ideas and innovative solutions. In fact, the concept of "creative destruction" rescinds the neoclassical theorists' notion of a perfect market. New ideas, products, and services create a dynamic market mechanism, producing demand that leads to perpetual wealth creation and wealth distribution.[6]

Evolving Views of Entrepreneurship

Simply put, an entrepreneur is an individual involved in an entrepreneurial activity. As pointed out, a multitude of definitions on the notions of entrepreneur and entrepreneurship have emerged. Various professionals view these elements through the lenses of their respective disciplines. For instance, the economist views the entrepreneur as a factor of production, alongside land, labor, and capital. The sociologist asserts that certain cultures promote or impede the developing forces of entrepreneurship. In India, for example, the Gujaratis and Sindhis are known for their sense of entrepreneurship. To a psychologist, an entrepreneur is a person driven by certain intrinsic forces, such as the need to attain something, to experiment, to accomplish, or perhaps to escape the authority of others. To a businessman, an entrepreneur may be a threat or an aggressive competitor, whereas to another businessman the same entrepreneur may be an ally, a source of supply, a customer, or someone who creates wealth for others, as well as someone who finds better ways to utilize resources, reduce waste, and generate jobs that others are glad to assume.[7]

Various influential contributors have understood entrepreneurs in different lights over time. Some of the more notable views on entrepreneurs include the following:

Richard Cantillon (1725): An entrepreneur is a person who pays a certain price for a product to resell it at an uncertain price, thereby making decisions about obtaining and using the resources although consequently admitting the risk of enterprise.

J. B. Say (1803): An entrepreneur is an economic agent who unites all means of production—land, labor, and capital—in order to produce a product. By selling the product in the market he pays rent of land, wages to laborers, and interest on capital. The difference is his profit. He shifts economic resources out of an area of lower and into an area of higher productivity and greater yield.

Joseph Schumpeter (1934): Entrepreneurs are innovators who use a process of challenging the status quo of existing products and services and setting up new ones.

David McClelland (1961): An entrepreneur is a person with a high need for achievement. He is energetic and a moderate-high risk taker.

Peter Drucker (1964): An entrepreneur continually seeks change, responds to it, and exploits opportunities. Innovation is a specific tool enabling the effective entrepreneur to convert a source into a resource.

Peter Kilby (1971): Emphasizes the role of the imitator—entrepreneur who does not innovate per se but imitates technologies innovated by others.

Albert Shapero (1975): Entrepreneurs take initiative, accept the risk of failure, and have an internal locus of control.

Gifford Pinchot (1983): Introduced the concept of the *intrapreneur* as an entrepreneur within an already established organizational entity.

Although many definitions and understandings of entrepreneurship exist, all stress four basic aspects of being an entrepreneur regardless of the field. First, entrepreneurship inherently involves the creation process. Something new is created, possessing value both to the entrepreneur and to the audience for which it is designed and developed. Such an audience may be the market of buyers for business innovation, the hospital's administration for a new admissions procedure, prospective students for a new college program, or the constituency for a new service provided by a not-for-profit organization. Second, entrepreneurship requires the full devotion of the necessary *time and effort*. Only those going through the entrepreneurial process appreciate the significant amount of time and effort it takes to create something new and to make it operational. Third, assuming *risks* is yet another aspect of entrepreneurship. Depending upon the field of effort of the entrepreneur, these risks take a variety of forms, but usually center around financial, psychological, and social areas. The fourth and final part of the definition involves the *rewards* of being an entrepreneur. The most important of these rewards include independence and personal satisfaction. Money is viewed less as a reward and more an indicator of the degree of success for profit-seeking entrepreneurs.

TYPES OF ENTREPRENEURS: A CATEGORIZATION

Unsurprisingly, a number of different types of entrepreneurs have been identified over the years.[8] Some of them include:

1. *Nascent* entrepreneur (i.e., an individual considering pursuing entrepreneurship);
2. *Novice* entrepreneur (i.e., an individual moving into entrepreneurship for the first time);
3. *Serial* entrepreneur (i.e., an individual has launched several entrepreneurial endeavors in a sequential fashion);
4. *Lifestyle* entrepreneur (i.e., an individual who, valuing passion before profit when launching a business, combines personal interests and talent with the ability to earn a living long term);
5. *Habitual* entrepreneur (i.e., an individual has launched or is currently launching several entrepreneurial endeavors in a parallel fashion); and
6. *Entrepreneurial* manager (i.e., an individual has the characteristics of an entrepreneur but is in an employment relationship with an employer; also called an *intrapreneur*).

Although the distinction of the types of entrepreneurs has at least some academic value, the more significant issue is the question of what exactly constitutes a *successful* entrepreneur. To state it differently, what are some key characteristics, attributes, attitudes, and behaviors that successful entrepreneurs have shown to possess and display?

CHARACTERISTICS OF SUCCESSFUL ENTREPRENEURS

Stevenson's Six Dimensions

Howard Stevenson studied successful entrepreneurs in both start-up and established business situations and developed a preliminary description of entrepreneurial behaviors based on six critical dimensions of business practice.[9] At one end of each dimension, there is the individual entrepreneur who feels confident enough to be able to seize an opportunity irrespective of the resource requirement. At the other end of the dimension, there is the individual manager who attempts to employ and fully utilize the disposable resources as efficiently as possible. Table 13.1 depicts the six dimensions and their extremes graphically.

Stevenson's work highlights six personal traits that successful entrepreneurs possess: tolerance for ambiguity, the ability to create an illusion of stability, risk management, attention to detail, endurance, and a long-term perspective. Stevenson remarked that entrepreneurs have the tendency to identify opportunities, harness and pull together the required resources, execute and implement an action plan, and harvest the rewards in a timely and flexible way.

The Mind of an Entrepreneur—Timmons's Work

Jeffrey Timmons studied the mind of various successful entrepreneurial individuals and found that entrepreneurs share a common set of

Table 13.1
Six Dimensions of Entrepreneurship

Key Business Dimension	Entrepreneur	Traditional Manager
Strategic orientation	Opportunity driven	Resource driven
Commitment to opportunity	Quick and short	Long and slow
Commitment to resources	Minimal with many stages	Complete in a single stage
Concept of control	Use or rent	Own or employ
Management structure	Networks with little hierarchy	Formalized hierarchy
Compensation and rewards	Value-based and team-based	Individual and hierarchical

Source: Adapted from H. Stevenson, "A Perspective on Entrepreneurship, in *The Entrepreneurial Venture*, eds. W. Sahlman et al., 2nd ed., pp. 7–22 (Cambridge, MA: Harvard Business School Press, 1983).

attitudes and behaviors.[10] Accordingly, Timmons posits that successful entrepreneurs:

1. Work very hard;
2. Are driven by a deep sense of commitment and perseverance;
3. Have an optimistic outlook;
4. Strive for integrity;
5. Have a competitive desire to excel and win;
6. Are dissatisfied with the status quo;
7. Seek opportunities and improvements constantly;
8. Use failure as a tool for learning, development, and growth;
9. Shun perfection in favor of effectiveness; and
10. Hold a strong belief that they can personally make a difference.

Moreover, Timmons suggested that successful entrepreneurially minded individuals possessed solid general management skills and business know-how and were found to be endowed with creative and innovative capabilities.

In a similar vein, the Entrepreneurship Forum of New England suggests the following six qualities of a successful entrepreneur:[11]

Dreamer: Imagines how something can be better and different.

Innovator: Demonstrates how the idea applied outperforms current practice.

Passionate: Expresses so the idea creates energy and resonance with others.

Risk taker: Pursues a dream without all the resources lined up at the start and distributes the risk.

Dogged committer: Stays with executing the innovation and to make it work.

Continuous learner: Explores constantly and evolves to do best practice.

Characteristics of Entrepreneurs—Bygrave's Work

William Bygrave studied the characteristics of entrepreneurs and presented a list of 10 salient characteristics in the form of 10 "Ds" that were found in successful entrepreneurial individuals.[12] These key characteristics and their description are depicted in Table 13.2.

Having reviewed some of the key characteristics of successful entrepreneurs, what does the actual process of entrepreneurship entail?

THE PROCESS OF ENTREPRENEURSHIP

A number of scholars have conceptualized, analyzed, and formalized the process of entrepreneurship. The process of entrepreneurship, at its

Table 13.2
Key Characteristics of Successful Entrepreneurs

Characteristics	Description
Decisiveness	Entrepreneurs make decisions swiftly and decisively.
Dedication	Entrepreneurs are completely dedicated and work tirelessly.
Destiny	Entrepreneurs wish to be in charge of their own destiny.
Details	Entrepreneurs are obsessed with the critical details.
Determination	Entrepreneurs implement entrepreneurial ventures with great determination and commitment.
Devotion	Entrepreneurs are deeply devoted and absolutely love what they do.
Distribute	Entrepreneurs distribute ownership with key employees.
Doer	Entrepreneurs act upon their decisions resolutely.
Dollars	Entrepreneurs view the bottom line as the measure of success rather than as a motivational driving force.
Dream	Entrepreneurs are visionaries and possess the ability and drive to materialize their own dreams.

Source: Adapted from W. Bygrave, *The Portable MBA in Entrepreneurship*, 2nd ed. (Hoboken, NJ: Wiley, 1997).

most basic, is a three-stage process comprising opportunity discovery, venture creation, and exploitation.[13] Accordingly, this three-phase process comprises the following distinct stages:

- *The innovation phase:* It is in this phase that the entrepreneur conceives, generates, and selects ideas for new products and services.
- *The implementation phase:* This process is generally triggered by a decision to pursue an idea and encompasses the acquisition of viable resources, including, among others, capital, labor, and technology.
- *The growth phase:* It is in this phase that the new entrepreneurial venture first shows signs of progress, growth, and commercial success. As such, the entrepreneur needs to secure new resources, especially managerial capacity, in order to support and sustain the viable growth of the entrepreneurial initiative.

Of course, each phase is affected by a variety of external factors, such as personal characteristics of the entrepreneur, the environment, and the characteristics of the actual innovation.[14]

At the heart of an entrepreneurial process is an opportunity. The recognition and assessment of opportunities is critical to the viability and success of entrepreneurial endeavors. A good business opportunity rests on an underlying demand for the product or service. Such products and services should possess value-adding properties that generate profits (for-profit endeavors) or create self-sufficiency (not-for-profit endeavors). Next, resources need to be harnessed and utilized judiciously. More specifically, in the early stages of an entrepreneurial activity, the entrepreneur needs to minimize and tightly control all resources; in later stages he or she will seek to maximize and own the resources. The understanding and appointment of team members is crucial for success since the team requires persistence, tolerance, ambiguity, creativity, leadership, communication, and adaptability. Ultimately, the tool that integrates these three elements together—opportunity, resources, and team—is the business plan.[15]

INFLUENCING THE ENTREPRENEURIAL ENGAGEMENT—A MOTIVATIONAL ASPECT

Why do people take personal, financial, and social risks pertaining to entrepreneurial activities? It has been reported that individuals decide to pursue elements of entrepreneurship for a number of reasons. One distinction that has been made in the literature is the aspect of positive or *pull* factors versus negative or *push* factors of entrepreneurship.[16] Examples of so-called pull strategies include the need for achievement, a desire to be independent, and social-development possibilities. In contrast, "push" factors may include dissatisfaction with the present professional and/or financial situation, family pressures, involuntary exit from employment, and the risk of unemployment. Within the context of global entrepreneurship, the distinction between opportunity-based and necessity-driven entrepreneurship is of great significance.[17]

Although there are a variety of discussions contrasting opportunity-driven versus necessity-driven entrepreneurship, there appears to be some agreement that necessity entrepreneurs are driven mainly by push motivations, although pull factors predominate for opportunity-based entrepreneurs.[18] Opportunity entrepreneurship reflects many start-up ventures seeking to take advantage of arising business opportunities, whereas necessity entrepreneurship exists due to a lack of better professional choices. Opportunity entrepreneurs frequently pursue business opportunities for personal interest and while still employed.[19] Individuals pursuing entrepreneurial activities out of necessity may see these opportunities as their best current choice, although not necessarily the preferred occupation. Still, a necessity-based activity may evolve into an attractive alternative over time.[20]

Empirical research shows that the distinction between opportunity-based and necessity-driven entrepreneurship is an important one in both theoretical and practical terms. First, it has been reported that opportunity and necessity entrepreneurs differ in terms of level of education, socioeconomic characteristics, and age.[21] Second, a start-up situation has consequences in the way the operation is managed as well as for its ensuing business performance. For instance, individuals who launch their own businesses due to financial incentives tend to behave differently from individuals who desire to create an entrepreneurial venture in order to pursue work-life choices.[22] Necessity-driven entrepreneurs tend to be less satisfied than their opportunity-motivated peers. At the micro level, the outcomes have revealed aspects of inferior performance on the part of necessity entrepreneurs, whereas at the macro level, opportunity and necessity entrepreneurs have shown to have a different impact on job creation and economic growth.[23] Third, the study of the interplay between business activity and entrepreneurial cycles has shown that opportunity entrepreneurship leads the business cycle by two years, although necessity entrepreneurship leads the business cycle by only one year.[24] Last, it has been observed that the determinants of nascent opportunity and necessity entrepreneurship differ, yielding important consequences for policy makers. Measures to stimulate necessity-driven entrepreneurship do not necessarily benefit opportunity-driven entrepreneurship, and vice versa.[25]

ENTREPRENEURSHIP VERSUS INTRAPRENEURSHIP

In many ways, the successful entrepreneur embodies the popular vision and manifestation of business success in today's world. The entrepreneurially savvy individual starts a new venture from scratch, secures the required resources, and builds it into a sustainable business venture. Of course, this takes a tremendous amount of vision, innovation, and dedication. It has been well documented in both the literature and popular press that the process of entrepreneurship is ridden with peril and tangible risk. Sadly, many entrepreneurial start-ups end up in commercial demise. Unsurprisingly, not everyone aspires to become an entrepreneur. Moreover, although there are probably tens of millions of potential entrepreneurs in the United States alone, most people simply are not in a position to pursue their entrepreneurial dreams and ideas for a variety of reasons, including financial constraints, family concerns, and others.[26]

The values and aspirations of the ambitious entrepreneur are not confined to new start-ups. The goals and rewards of the entrepreneurially minded person are in fact realizable within the confines of existing organizations. The *intrapreneur*, also known as the internal entrepreneur or corporate entrepreneur, has become increasingly recognized for his or her capacity to act as a catalyst to build and add value to the organization's overall performance and success.[27]

The term intrapreneur first appeared in a research paper by U.S. management consultants and authors Gifford and Elisabeth Pinchot in 1978 and entered into the *American Heritage Dictionary* in 1992. An intrapreneur has been defined as:

> A person within a large corporation who takes direct responsibility for turning an idea into a profitable finished product through assertive risk-taking and innovation.[28]

The advent, definition, and conceptualization of the concept of intrapreneurship were products of commercial developments of the late 20th century. This era was dominated by large corporations bloated with extraneous employees, heavy on hierarchy and hierarchical layers, burdened by slow communication systems, and stifled by a rigid interface between the organizations and their many stakeholders. Indeed, it was in the late 20th century and the early days of the 21st century, where revolutions in technology and communication unfolded, which in turn have affected markets and entire societies. As a direct consequence, organizations have become fluid, actions instantaneous, and change discontinuous and unrelenting.

In the midst of all these unveiling changes, firms rely heavily on their ongoing innovative capabilities for vitality and success. Clearly, it is now widely understood that information is ubiquitous, ideas are pervasive, and most resources are readily available. This combination, presenting both challenges and opportunities for firms and employees, may in fact constitute the beginning of a new age of entrepreneurship: the rise of the intrapreneur.

Intrapreneurship mobilizes individuals within organizations to put their passion, creativity, innovative capacity, and talents into play in order to maximize their creative potential and achievements. Firms are forced to foster an environment where an intrapreneurial mindset among employees can develop and thrive. It has been reported that such attempts yield increased levels of employee motivation, engagement, and retention, as well as heightened innovation ultimately leading to the development of a competitive edge. Although there are legitimate concerns for both employers and employees, including the fear of unrelenting change and the risk of losing valuable resources, yet in this day and age, developing and empowering intrapreneurially minded people is critical to the ongoing success, relevance, and triumph of any organization.

So, how can a culture of intrapreneurship within firms be attained? First and foremost, the intrapreneur does not need an assigned intrapreneurial role by the firm. The intrapreneur needs to empower himself or herself to create his or her own "enriched" role for the betterment and sake of the organization. Second, intrapreneurship can be found in any organization; for-profit and not-for-profit, small and large, local and global, mainstream and niche, private and public, as well as in all industries and government-owned agencies. Third, intrapreneurship is not confined to the development of new processes, products, and services. Intrapreneurial behavior on the part of an employee permeates all organizational facets and includes improving efficiencies, developing new markets, and taking existing products and services to new heights.

Examples of Intrapreneurial Activities

A number of firms have reaped deep admiration, fame, and prominence for cultivating internal intrapreneurial cultures that promote individual and organization innovation. A well-cited example of the power of intrapreneurial innovation is the well-known *Skunk Works* group at Lockheed Martin. This group, originally named after a reference in a cartoon, was first assembled in 1943 in order to build the P-80 fighter jet. The project was secretive and internally protected since it was to become part of the United States' war efforts.[29]

At 3M, formerly known as the Minnesota Mining and Manufacturing Company, employees are allowed to spend up to 15 percent of their working time on projects for the advancement of the firm. Based on the initial success of this practice, 3M has since introduced a $3 million in-house intrapreneurial program to fund projects that may not necessarily attract funding through ordinary channels. These so-called "Genesis" grants offer up to $85,000 to selected innovators to carry forward their projects.[30]

A number of technology firms have a strong culture of innovation and in-house development. Prominent examples include Hewlett-Packard (HP), Microsoft, Intel, Oracle, and Google. The last-named has been recognized frequently for permitting its employees to spend up to 20 percent of their time pursuing in-house innovation and intrapreneurial activities.[31]

A classic example of intrapreneurially minded individuals and their subsequent successes is found in the ascent of John Warnock and Charles Geschke, formerly employees at Xerox. Frustrated with the rigidity of the Xerox culture and disenchanted with the lack of support for their innovative ideas, Warnock and Geschke both resigned from Xerox as employees and launched Adobe Systems, which is now an S&P 500 firm with revenues close to $4 billion.[32]

STRATEGIC ENTREPRENEURSHIP

The 21st-century business landscape has been characterized by revolutionary, unpredictable change, increased levels of risk, fluid firm and industry boundaries, new managerial mindsets, and innovative business models. In fact, this new atmosphere can be described in terms of four distinct driving forces: change, complexity, chaos, and contradiction.[33] The ability to navigate through this challenging environment has become a focal point of scholars in the disciplines of economics, strategic management, and entrepreneurship. "Strategic entrepreneurship" is a relatively new term that has arisen in the business literature representing the intersection of strategy and entrepreneurship. To date, the exact nature of strategic entrepreneurship has remained somewhat elusive and abstract.[34]

Strategic entrepreneurship has been discussed mainly within the realm of corporate entrepreneurship. Strategic entrepreneurship refers to a broader array of entrepreneurial phenomena. Although they may or may not result in new business entities being added to the firm, they all involve organizationally consequential innovative activities that are adopted in the pursuit of sustainable competitive advantages. It has been reported that strategic entrepreneurship involves opportunity-seeking (i.e., entrepreneurship) and advantage-seeking (i.e., strategic management) behaviors simultaneously.[35] These innovations are the foci of strategic entrepreneurship initiatives and represent the means through which opportunity is created and exploited. As such, innovation can occur anywhere and indeed everywhere within the firm.

An emphasis on an opportunity-driven mindset enables management to obtain a competitively advantageous position for the firm. Such innovations may constitute fundamental changes from the organization's *past* strategies, products, services, markets, structures, capabilities, or business models, or, alternatively, the innovations may represent fundamental bases that differentiate the firm from its industry competition. Thus, there are two salient aspects that ought to be considered when a firm showcases strategic entrepreneurship. They are:

1. To what degree is the firm transforming itself relative to where it was in the past?
2. To what degree is the firm transforming itself relative to industry benchmarks and standards?[36]

As noted previously, some organizations are known to exhibit very high levels of innovation consistently; they are known as entrepreneurially minded firms whose operations are deeply rooted in entrepreneurial corporate cultures. However, innovation is not confined to the culture but may be embedded in the actual industry in which the firm operates. For instance, technology-based and fashion-related industries have a tendency to demonstrate continuous entrepreneurial behaviors. Therefore, innovation per se may not prove to be the basis on which firms are differentiated from their industry rivals. Rather, it may be the products, services, and processes that result from innovation that determine how well they are differentiated from the industry rivals.

Literature shows that strategic entrepreneurship can take on five distinct forms, namely, strategic renewal, sustained regeneration, domain redefinition, organizational rejuvenation, and business model reconstruction.[37]

In *strategic renewal,* the organization redefines its relationships with its competitors by altering its competitive strategies and practices. As such, new strategies constitute strategic renewal when they represent a fundamental repositioning of the organization within its competitive landscape. Strategic renewal has also been labeled strategic innovation or value innovation.

Second, *sustained regeneration* refers to an entrepreneurial practice whereby the organization introduces new products and services or enters new markets on a regular basis. Within this strategic framework, the firm is in constant pursuit of entrepreneurial opportunities. Sustained regeneration serves as a basis for pursing competitive advantages where short product-life cycles, rapidly changing technological standards, and segmenting product categories and market arenas are common practice. Sustained regeneration cannot be represented by a one-off event but exists when a corporation demonstrates a pattern of recurrent new product innovations and market entries. Therefore, firms that pursue sustained regeneration practices enjoy a reputation of innovation powerhouses.

Third, *domain redefinition* refers to an entrepreneurial strategy whereby the organization creates a new product-market arena that others have not yet recognized or explored. Within this framework, firms move into unchartered waters or "blue oceans."[38] Technically speaking, these pioneering elements are product-market arenas in which new categories are represented. Domain redefinition can lead to the redefinition of boundaries of existing industries or provide a landscape for the emergence of new industries. There is an underlying expectation that first-mover status will provide a basis for sustainable competitive advantage for the firm.

Fourth, *organizational rejuvenation* refers to an entrepreneurial strategy where the organization purports to improve or sustain its competitive position by modifying existing internal processes, capabilities, or structures.[39] Within this framework, the emphasis of the innovation is to focus on a set of core attributes linked with the firm's internal operations. As such, the main effort is to create a powerful organizational vehicle through with the firm's strategy can be implemented. Organizational rejuvenation has the capacity for the firm to attain a sustainable competitive advantage without changing its business strategy, product offerings, or served markets. In fact, there are times when organizational rejuvenation entails a fundamental redesign of the entire firm, such as a business process reengineering (BPR) endeavor, which purports to reconfigure an organization's value-chain elements. Organizational rejuvenation can also involve single innovations that have deep implications for the organizational entity, such as a strategic restructuring effort, or multiple smaller innovations that collectively contribute to increased levels of effectiveness or efficiency at strategy implementation. However, in true organizational rejuvenation, the innovative endeavors cannot simply imitate initiatives that are commonplace to the industry but must, at least temporarily, differentiate themselves from existing industry practices.

Fifth, *business model reconstruction* refers to an entrepreneurial strategy where the organization recalibrates its business model to improve operational efficiencies. Popular activities within the business model reconstruction model include strategic elements, such as outsourcing, which rely upon external contractors for activities previously provided internally, and vertical integration, which combines supplier or distributor functions within the ownership or control of the firm.

STRATEGIC ENTREPRENEURSHIP— CONCEPTUAL FRAMEWORKS

Simply put, strategic entrepreneurship can be considered as the intersection of two distinct bodies of literature: strategy and entrepreneurship. This entity comprises the integration of both concepts and constitutes a combination of "exploration" and "exploitation" aspects. More specifically, strategic entrepreneurship, defined as *exploration* for future sources of competitive advantage, combined with *exploitation* of current sources of competitive advantage, has been proposed as a way for decision makers to manage uncertainty.[40]

A number of conceptual frameworks have appeared in the business literature. The foundational conceptual framework of strategic entrepreneurship, which was published in 2001, comprised six key domains.[41] It has been posited that activity in these six areas can be jointly classified as entrepreneurial and strategic. These domains are as follows:

1. Innovation (i.e., creating and implementing ideas);
2. Networks (i.e., providing access to resources);
3. Internationalization (i.e., adapting swiftly and expanding);
4. Organizational learning (i.e., transferring knowledge and developing resources);
5. Growth (i.e., stimulating success and change); and
6. Top management teams and governance (i.e., selection and implementation of strategies).

Management scholars originally commented that there was an overly strong emphasis on strategy, overlooking the themes central to entrepreneurship. As a consequence, a revised framework emerged a few years later, which included external networks and alliances, resources and organizational learning, and innovation and internationalization.[42] Although the models have similarities, the latter framework with its emphasis on resources, competencies, and capabilities has a strengthened view on both strategy and entrepreneurship. In 2003, the original authors of the 2001 framework introduced a modified framework having revised the dimensions pertinent to entrepreneurship. They included the aspects of entrepreneurial mindset, entrepreneurial leadership, entrepreneurial culture, the strategic management of resources, and the application of creativity to develop innovations. The full integration of these dimensions is believed to result in wealth creation.[43] It has been reported that the modified model reflects a substantial change in the direction of the literature. Thus, there are four key dimensions that are commonly associated with the notion of strategic entrepreneurship:

1. An entrepreneurial mindset consisting of insight, alertness, and flexibility to use appropriate resources;
2. Entrepreneurial culture and leadership where innovation and creativity are fostered;
3. The strategic management of resources which includes human, social, and financial capital; and
4. The application of creativity to foster both incremental and radical innovation.

Later in the first decade of this new millennium, it was underscored that strategic entrepreneurship should strike a balance between opportunity-seeking (i.e., exploration) and advantage-seeking (i.e., exploitation) behaviors, thereby highlighting the importance of and need for continuous innovation.[44] Additional models and frameworks have since been established and published. However, the strategic entrepreneurship emphasis has to some extent remained theoretical with little guidance and practical support.

INTEGRATING ENTREPRENEURSHIP WITH STRATEGY

Reviewing the bodies of literature of entrepreneurship and strategic management suggests strongly that both disciplines are concerned with firm performance. Although entrepreneurship promotes the pursuit of sustainable competitive advantages by means of market, process, and product innovations, it is strategic management that presents the tools for firms to establish and exploit sustainable competitive advantages within a confined environmental context.

In order to integrate entrepreneurship with strategy, it is important to discuss the concepts of dominant logic and dynamic dominant logic. The former, *dominant logic,* refers to the way in which executives understand and conceptualize a business operation and make critical decisions regarding the allocation of resources. Dominant logic has been defined as the lens through which managers see emerging opportunities and options for the firm.[45] Put differently, dominant logic relates to the main means and methods that a firm utilizes in order to pursue profits—that is, how a firm has succeeded or continues to succeed in its operations. Interestingly, although the dominant logic of a firm attempts to capture prevailing mindsets, it also filters and interprets information obtained from the environment, which, ultimately, guides the strategies, systems, processes, and displayed behaviors within an organizational entity. As such, managers have been found to consider only information that is perceived to be relevant to the entity's dominant logic.

The latter concept, *a dynamic dominant logic,* is an extension of the original concept of dominant logic whereby entrepreneurship acts as the basis on which the firm is to be conceptualized and resources are to be allocated.[46] As a dynamic dominant logic, entrepreneurship has the capacity to promote strategic agility, flexibility, creativity, and continuous improvement throughout the organization.[47]

It has been posited that entrepreneurship is more than a preselected course of action; it is certainly more than a managerial mindset. Entrepreneurship has the ability to provide a theme or direction for a firm's entire business operation. Strategically speaking, entrepreneurship must be an integral part of an organization's business strategy. Although strategy determines the direction of a firm, it is the integration of entrepreneurship into strategy at the organization level that has the capacity to greatly enhance the strategic possibilities of the firm.[48]

Finally, the purposeful integration of entrepreneurship into strategy has two key aspects: entrepreneurial strategy and a strategy for entrepreneurship. Entrepreneurial strategy encompasses discussions and issues regarding the application of creativity and entrepreneurial thinking to the development of a core strategy for an organization. Strategy for entrepreneurship, in contrast, is concerned with the need to develop a strategy to guide entrepreneurial activities taking place within the organization.[49] This, however, is based upon the understanding that firms that embrace entrepreneurship outperform firms that fail to focus on entrepreneurship in the long run.[50]

ENTREPRENEURSHIP EXTENDS ITS INFLUENCE—
THE RISE OF THE SOCIAL ENTREPRENEUR

The notion of social entrepreneurship is an emerging academic discipline challenged by competing and conflicting definitions, conceptual frameworks, and limited empirical evidence. It is clear that the process of entrepreneurship can be applied to the creation of economic as well as social goals. Indeed, the late Peter Drucker suggested that the entrepreneur always looks for change, responds to change elements, and exploits change as opportunities.[51] This is regardless of whether the opportunity has commercial or social motivations. Traditionally, the focus of institutional entrepreneurship has been on for-profit entities, whereas the term social entrepreneurship has been used to describe activities with social purposes. However, in recent years, social entrepreneurs increasingly have been seen as individuals pursuing entrepreneurial (i.e., for-profit) activities with embedded social purposes.

Over the past decade, the discussion on social entrepreneurship, especially in the popular media and in the business press, has focused on the successes of high-profile business entrepreneurs. In 2006, for instance, Bill Drayton, founder of Ashoka, a not-for-profit organization dedicated to promoting and supporting social entrepreneurs, publicly proclaimed that social entrepreneurship has the capacity to spark a worldwide productivity miracle. Drayton's ideas have since enticed influential business individuals including eBay founder Jeff Skoll, who launched the Skoll Foundation with its focus on promoting social entrepreneurship.

So what exactly motivates social entrepreneurs? The Skoll Foundation describes these social entrepreneurs as individuals who are motivated by altruism and a profound desire to promote the development and growth of equitable civil societies who pioneer innovative, effective, and sustainable approaches to meet the needs of the marginalized, the disadvantaged, and the disenfranchised. As such, social entrepreneurs are the wellspring of a better future.[52]

The response from the academic community on the emergence of this new phenomenon has been less enthusiastic. Although scholars have examined and conceptualized social entrepreneurship, the field has remained immature and lacks depth, richness, and prescription.[53]

How can a social entrepreneur be defined? A social entrepreneur is an individual, group, network, organization, or alliance of organizations that seeks sustainable, large-scale change through pattern-breaking ideas in what or how governments, nonprofits, and businesses do to address significant social problems.[54] More pragmatically, a social entrepreneur is an individual who recognizes a social problem and uses entrepreneurial principles to create a business venture in order to generate social change. Although a traditional business entrepreneur typically measures the success of his or her efforts in terms of profitability and return on investment (ROI), the social entrepreneur is interested in furthering social and environmental goals.

A debate over the exact definition of social entrepreneurship persists, reinforcing the need for a more constrained definition.[55] It appears that the current literature lacks empirical evidence of the successes, scalability, and sustainability of social improvements. It has even been reported that the proliferation of new social entrepreneurial activities may actually create competition and inefficiencies in an already highly fragmented social sector.[56]

Social entrepreneurship has been studied and analyzed from three distinct approaches. The first approach views not-for-profit organizational entities as social entrepreneurships. The second approach, in contrast, focuses on how social entrepreneurship can be successful through profit mechanisms, and a third approach emphasizes and focuses on the social-change aspects of social entrepreneurship.[57] Unambiguously, the latter view is comparable with a Schumpeterian perspective in that entrepreneurs are essentially agents of change.

Social Entrepreneurs—Past and Present

Interestingly, although the formal study of social entrepreneurship is relatively new, it must be clear that the notion of the social entrepreneur has existed throughout human history. Indeed, socially minded, entrepreneurially driven individuals whose tireless work typifies the concept of social entrepreneurship have literally changed the world. Some of them include the following:

- *Vinoba Bhave*—Founder of India's land-gift movement;
- *Akhtar Hameed Khan*—Pakistani founder of the grassroots movement for rural communities (i.e., Comilla model) and the low-cost sanitation program for squatter settlements (i.e., Orangi pilot project);
- *Maria Montessori*—Italian founder and developer of the Montessori approach to early childhood education;
- *Florence Nightingale*—English founder of the first nursing school and creator of modern-day nursing practices;
- *Robert Owen*—Welsh founder of the worldwide cooperative movement; and
- *Friedrich Wilhelm Raiffeisen*—German principal founder of the credit union and cooperative bank sectors now forming a major segment of the European banking system.

The endeavors of some (if not all) of these individuals have brought about deep societal impact and lasting change on a global scale. Equally important, the list of contemporary social entrepreneurs shows a rich diversity of individuals who have aspired and continue to tackle society's most pressing problems using creative and innovative entrepreneurial solutions.

The following snapshot is a small, incomplete overview:

- *Ibrahim Abouleish*—Egyptian founder of *SEKEM,* a biodynamic agricultural firm, alternative medicine, and educational center based in Cairo.
- *Ela Bhatt*—Indian founder of *SEWA* (self-employed women's association) and *SEWA Bank.*
- *Bill Drayton*—American founder of *Shoka, Youth Venture,* and *Get America Working!*
- *Marian Wright Edelman*—American founder and president of the *Children's Defense Fund* (CDF) and strong advocate for disadvantaged American children.
- *Jamie Oliver*—English TV chef who campaigns to improve children's diet at schools. He also trains young people to become chefs. He founded a social enterprise, *Fifteen,* which employs newly trained youngsters.
- *Muhammad Yunus*—Bangladeshi founder of the *Grameen Bank* and inventor of the microcredit, which earned him the 2006 Nobel Peace Prize.
- *Willie Smits*—Indonesian founder of the *Borneo Orangutan Survival Foundation* and founder and chairperson of the *Masarang Foundation.*

There are various debates over who does and who does not count as a social entrepreneur. For instance, some have advocated restricting the term to founders of organizations that rely upon earned income generated directly from paying customers. This is in contrast to others who have extended this by including incomes earned by contracting with public authorities, and yet others include receiving grants and donations as part of the social entrepreneurship model. Most fundamentally, discussions continue regarding the delineation between business entrepreneurship, with its focus on wealth creation and economic development, and social entrepreneurship with its emphasis on generating social capital and "making the world a better place."[58]

CONCLUDING THOUGHTS

This chapter has established that strategic entrepreneurship is the utilization and stimulation of entrepreneurial activity in order to attain strategically defined goals, including but not limited to differentiation, diversification, integration, and the pursuit of sustainable competitive advantages. Entrepreneurial activities present significant potential to achieve such ambitious goals and are thus deemed effective tools for the strategically minded executive. The research has also established that strategic entrepreneurship is comparable with the notions of corporate entrepreneurship at the strategic and corporate levels and intrapreneurship at the more tactical, operational, and individual levels. Like entrepreneurship in a broad sense, strategic entrepreneurship is a business phenomenon that has antecedents and outcomes at various levels of analysis. This field of management will benefit from further conceptual and empirical study.

Finally, at the individual level, strategic entrepreneurial activities entail the systematic pursuits and exploitation of opportunities that align with a person's existing knowledge and available resources, even where the creation of wealth may not be the final goal. On a more corporate, regional, or national level, strategic entrepreneurship embodies the design and development of a framework that fosters entrepreneurial endeavors by individuals, agencies, and firms pursuing organizational, regional, and national goals. These goals are not confined to financial development and economic growth; they also include the sustainable use of natural resources, as well as the pursuit of improved levels of individuals' well-being and overall quality of life.

NOTES

1. http://www.merriam-webster.com/dictionary/entrepreneur.

2. http://bizarfinancing.com/secure/what-is-an-entrepreneur-do-you-qualify-as-one.

3. http://bizarfinancing.com/secure/what-is-an-entrepreneur-do-you-qualify-as-one.

4. Kirchoff, B.A. (1997) Entrepreneurship economics, In *The Portable MBA in Entrepreneurship*, W. Bygrave (ed.) (pp. 444–474), Hoboken, NJ: Wiley.

5. Ibrahim, G., and Vyakarnam, S. (2003) Defining the role of the entrepreneur in economic thought: Limitations of mainstream economics, http://www.mendeley.com/research/defining-role-entrepreneur-economic-thought-limitations-mainstream-economics/.

6. Schumpeter, J.A. (1934) *The Theory of Economic Development*, Cambridge, MA: Harvard University Press.

7. Hisrich, R.D., Peters, M.P., and Shepherd, D.A. (2005) *Entrepreneurship*, 6th Edition, New York: McGraw-Hill Irwin.

8. Vyakarnam, S., and Hartman, N. (2011) *Unlocking the Entrepreneur Inside!* Singapore: World Scientific Publishing.

9. Stevenson, H. (1983) A perspective on entrepreneurship, In *The Entrepreneurial Venture*, W. Sahlman, et al. (eds.), 2nd edition., pp. 7–22, 1999, Cambridge, MA: Harvard Business School Press.

10. Timmons, J. (1999) *New Venture Creation: Entrepreneurship for the 21st Century*, 5th edition, New York: McGraw-Hill.

11. http://www.vitae.ac.uk/researchers/1312/Entrepreneurship—intrapreneurship.html.

12. Bygrave, W. (1997) *The Portable MBA in Entrepreneurship*, 2nd edition, Hoboken, NJ: Wiley.

13. Shane, S., and Venkataraman, S. (2000) The promise of entrepreneurship as a field of research, *Academy of Management Review,* 25 (1), 217–226.

14. Moore, F. (1986) Understanding entrepreneurial behavior: A definition and model, *Academy of Management Proceedings,* pp. 66–70.

15. Timmons, J. (1999) *New Venture Creation: Entrepreneurship for the 21st Century,* 5th edition, New York: McGraw-Hill.

16. Gilad, B., and Levine, P. (1986) A behavioral model of entrepreneurial supply, *Journal of Small Business Management,* 4, 45–53.

17. Reynolds, P. D., Bygrave, W. D., Autio, E., Cox, L. W., and Hay, M. (2002) *Global Entrepreneurship Monitor, 2002 Executive Report.*

18. Block, J. H., and Wagner, M. (2007) Opportunity recognition and exploitation by necessity and opportunity entrepreneurs: Empirical evidence from earnings equations, In Solomon, George T. (ed.), *Proceedings of the Sixty-Sixth Annual Meeting of the Academy of Management,* ISSN 1543–8643.

19. Reynolds, P. D., Camp, S. M., Bygrave, W. D., Autio, E., and Hay, M. (2001) *Global Entrepreneurship Monitor, 2001 Executive Report.*

20. Kautonen, T. and Palmroos, J. (2009) The impact of a necessity-based start-up on subsequent entrepreneurial satisfaction, *International Entrepreneurship and Management Journal,* DOI: 10.1007/s11365–008–0104–1.

21. Block, J. H., and Wagner, M. (2007) Opportunity recognition and exploitation by necessity and opportunity entrepreneurs: Empirical evidence from earnings equations, In Solomon, George T. (ed.), *Proceedings of the Sixty-Sixth Annual Meeting of the Academy of Management,* ISSN 1543–8643.

22. Hessels, J., Gelderen, M., and Thurik, R. (2008) Entrepreneurial motivations, aspirations and their drivers, *Small Business Economics,* 31 (3), 323–339.

23. Wong, P. K., Ho, Y. P., and Autio, E. (2005) Entrepreneurship, innovation and economic growth: Evidence from GEM data, *Small Business Economics,* 24, 335–350.

24. Koellinger, P. D., and Thurik, A. R. (2009) Entrepreneurship in the business cycle, *Tinbergen Institute Discussion Paper,* TI09–032/3, http://www.tinbergen.nl/discussionpapers/09032.pdf.

25. Bergmann, H., and Sternberg, R. (2007) The changing face of entrepreneurship in Germany, *Small Business Economics,* 28, 205–221.

26. http://in2marketing.wordpress.com/2011/02/07/reinventing-the-intrapreneur-for-the-21st-century/.

27. http://www.investopedia.com/terms/i/intrapreneur.asp#axzz1XMbSINeo.

28. http://www.intrapreneur.com/MainPages/History/Dictionary.html.

29. http://www.skunkworks.net/.

30. http://www.ey.com/GL/en/Services/Strategic-Growth-Markets/Igniting-innovation--how-hot-companies-fuel-growth-from-within---Set-up-a-formal-structure-for-intrapreneurship

31. http://www.pcmag.com/article2/0,2817,2340546,00.asp.

32. http://knowledge.wharton.upenn.edu/article.cfm?articleid=2038.

33. Hitt, M. A., and Reed, T. S. (2000) Entrepreneurship in the new competitive landscape, In G. D. Meyer and K. A. Heppard (eds.), *Entrepreneurship as Strategy* (pp. 23–47), Thousand Oaks, CA: Sage Publications.

34. Kuratko, D. F., and Audretsch, D. B. (2009) Strategic entrepreneurship: Exploring different perspectives on an emerging concept, *Entrepreneurship Theory and Practice,* 33 (1), 1–17.

35. Ireland, R. D., Hitt, M. A., and Sirmon, D. G. (2003) A model of strategic entrepreneurship: The construct and its dimensions, *Journal of Management,* 29 (6), 963–989.

36. Kuratko, D. F., and Audretsch, D. B. (2009) Strategic entrepreneurship: Exploring different perspectives.on an emerging concept, *Entrepreneurship Theory and Practice,* 33 (1), 1–17.

37. Covin, J. G., and Miles, M. P. (1999) Corporate entrepreneurship and the pursuit of competitive advantage, *Entrepreneurship Theory and Practice,* 23 (3), 47–63.

38. Kim, W. C. and Mauborgne, R. (2005) Blue ocean strategy: From theory to practice, *California Management Review,* 47 (3), 105–121.

39. Kuratko, D. F. and Audretsch, D. B. (2009) Strategic entrepreneurship: Exploring different perspectives, *Entrepreneurship Theory and Practice,* 33 (1), 1–17.

40. Ireland, R. D., Hitt, M. A., Camp, S. M., and Sexton, D. L. (2001) Integrating entrepreneurship and strategic management actions to create firm wealth, *Academy of Management Executive,* 15 (1), 49–63.

41. Luke, B., Verreynee, M. L., and Kearins, K. (2010) Innovative and entrepreneurial activity in the public sector: The changing face of public sector institutions, *Innovation: Management, Policy and Practice,* 12 (2), 138–153.

42. Hitt, M. A., Ireland, R. D., Camp, S. M., and Sexton, D. L. (2001) Guest editors' introduction to the special issue strategic entrepreneurship: Entrepreneurial strategies for wealth creation, *Strategic Management Journal,* 22 (6–7), pp. 479–491.

43. Ireland, R. D., Hitt, M. A., and Sirmon, D. G. (2003) A model of strategic entrepreneurship: The construct and its dimensions, *Journal of Management,* 29 (6), 963–989.

44. Ireland, R. D. and Webb, J. (2007) A multi-theoretic perspective on trust and power in strategic supply chains, *Journal of Operations Management,* 25: 482–497.

45. Prahalad, C. K. (2004) The blinders of dominant logic, *Long Range Planning,* 37: 171–179.

46. Morris, M. H., Kuratko, D. F., and Covin, J. G. (2008) *Corporate Entrepreneurship and Innovation,* Mason, OH: Thomson/South-Western Publishers.

47. Kuratko, D. F., and Audretsch, D. B. (2009) Strategic entrepreneurship: Exploring different perspectives on an emerging concept, *Entrepreneurship Theory and Practice,* 33 (1), 1–17.

48. Kuratko, D. F., Ireland, R. D., and Hornsby, J. S. (2001) Improving firm performance through entrepreneurial actions: Acordia's corporate entrepreneurship strategy, *Academy of Management Executive,* 15 (4), 60–71.

49. Kuratko, D. F. and Audretsch, D. B. (2009) Strategic entrepreneurship: Exploring different perspectives on an emerging concept, *Entrepreneurship Theory and Practice,* 33 (1), 1–17.

50. Morris, M. H., Kuratko, D. F., and Covin, J. G. (2008) *Corporate Entrepreneurship and Innovation,* Mason, OH: Thomson/South-Western Publishers.

51. Drucker, P. (1985) *Innovation and Entrepreneurship,* New York: Harper & Row.

52. http://bricksandmortar.wordpress.com/social-entrepreneurship/.

53. Dees, J.G., and Anderson, B.B. (2006) Framing a theory of social entrepreneurship: Building on two schools of practice and thought, In R. Mosher-Williams (ed.), *Research on Social Entrepreneurship: Understanding and Contributing to an Emerging Field.* ARNOVA Occasional Paper Series, 1 (3), 39–66.

54. Light, P.C. (2006) Reshaping social entrepreneurship, *Stanford Social Innovation Review,* 4 (3), 46–51.

55. Center for the Advancement of Social Entrepreneurship (CASE) (2008) Advancing the field of social entrepreneurship, Durham, NC: Center for the Advancement of Social Entrepreneurship, Fuqua School of Business, Duke University, http://www.caseatduke.org/.

56. Nicholls, A. (2006) Playing the field: A new approach to the meaning of social entrepreneurship, *Social Enterprise Journal,* 2 (1), 1–5.

57. Mair, J., and Marti, I. (2006) Social entrepreneurship research: A source of explanation, prediction and delight, *Journal of World Business,* 41: 36–44.

58. http://usasbe.org/knowledge/proceedings/proceedingsDocs/2009/PaperID187.pdf.

Index